A·N·N·U·A·L E·D·I·T·I·O·N·S

Human Sexuality 01/02

Twenty-Sixth Edition

EDITOR

Susan J. Bunting
Lincoln College

Susan Bunting is the coordinator of curriculum and instruction at Chestnut Health Systems, a therapist for Employment Development Associates, and an instructor in sociology and psychology at Lincoln College in Illinois. Dr. Bunting received her B.S. and M.S. in sociology and her Ed.D. in curriculum and instruction from Illinois State University. She has taught, counseled, trained, and developed curriculum in human sexuality, sexual abuse, substance abuse, self-esteem, child and human development, learning disabilities, marriage, family, and intimate relationships. Dr. Bunting publishes pamphlets, instructional materials, articles, and books in these areas.

1, 8, 12, 13, 20, 22, 23, 45.

McGraw-Hill/Dushkin
530 Old Whitfield Street, Guilford, Connecticut 06437

Visit us on the Internet
http://www.dushkin.com

Credits

1. Sexuality and Society
Unit photo—Courtesy of Kimberly Cox.
2. Sexual Biology, Behavior, and Orientation
Unit photo—AP/Wide World Photo by Darcy Padilla.
3. Interpersonal Relationships
Unit photo—United Nations photo by Bedrich Grunzweig.
4. Reproduction
Unit photo—Courtesy of the North Carolina Coalition on Adolescent Pregnancy.
5. Sexuality Through the Life Cycle
Unit photo—© 2000 by Cleo Freelance Photography.
6. Old/New Sexual Concerns
Unit photo—© 2000 by Sweet By & By/Cindy Brown.

Copyright

Cataloging in Publication Data
Main entry under title: Annual Editions: Human Sexuality. 2001/2002.
    1. Sexual behavior—Periodicals. 2. Sexual hygiene—Periodicals. 3. Sex education—Periodicals.
4. Human relations—Periodicals. I. Bunting, Susan J., comp. II. Title: Human sexuality.
ISBN 0-07-243334-5   155.3'05   75-20756   ISSN 1091-9961
© 2001 by McGraw-Hill/Dushkin, Guilford, CT 06437, A Division of The McGraw-Hill Companies.

Twenty-Sixth Edition

Cover image © 2001 by PhotoDisc, Inc.

Printed in the United States of America   1234567890BAHBAH54321   Printed on Recycled Paper

To the Reader

In publishing ANNUAL EDITIONS we recognize the enormous role played by the magazines, newspapers, and journals of the public press in providing current, first-rate educational information in a broad spectrum of interest areas. Many of these articles are appropriate for students, researchers, and professionals seeking accurate, current material to help bridge the gap between principles and theories and the real world. These articles, however, become more useful for study when those of lasting value are carefully collected, organized, indexed, and reproduced in a low-cost format, which provides easy and permanent access when the material is needed. That is the role played by ANNUAL EDITIONS.

We all need to learn about sex. The healthy management of sex is essential to successful living and sex-happiness is a part of our total happiness.[1]

Sex lies at the root of life, and we can never learn to reverence life until we know how to understand sex.[2]

We must eradicate sexual illiteracy.[3]

All sane people ought to know about sex nature and sex functioning.[4]

We believe that sexual knowledge can lead to reasoned, responsible interpersonal sexual behavior and can help people make important personal decisions about sex. In short, learning about sexuality is an invaluable preparation for living.[5]

You have just read the words of several prominent sexologists. What they have to say quite forcefully and dramatically about the subject and study of sex seems pretty similar, doesn't it? Well, they were written in 1891, 1919, 1967, 1982, and 1995. Can you guess which is which?

As readers of the twenty-sixth edition of *Annual Editions: Human Sexuality,* and as you embark on this twenty-first century study of sexuality, it is important for you to get a broader perspective on the issues by trying a few more "guess the era" questions. This time, however, we'll make it a little easier. Which advice was given by a clergyperson in 1968 and which in 1998?

We need more sex, not less, but we need sex with soul.[6]

It's smart to know what you need to know (about sex).[7]

How about these three looks at "today's" challenge of society and sexuality—written in 1933, 1950, and 1969?

Today, the American people are trying to break out of this vicious circle of unhappy marriages, maladjusted children, desperate, bitter, frustrating lives; they are tired of evasions and ignorance. There is a strong desire to learn the truth about sex and its place in our lives.[8]

The atmosphere in which sex teaching takes place has gradually become more open, more accepting, less fearful and less likely to produce opposition.[9]

Sexual psychology, normal and abnormal, as well as sexual hygiene, nowadays attracts a general interest and attention heretofore undreamed of.[10]

And finally, a quote many of you can show your parents because it was written about them, not you:

In today's most technologically advanced societies, members of the younger generation are making it clear—in dress and music, deeds and words—just how unequivocally they reject their elders' sexual world.[11]

So readers, as you begin your examination of human sexuality at the dawn of this new century, try to remember that some things have changed, some things will change, and many things are likely to stay much the same. Maybe that's why it's important to emphasize the human in human sexuality.

Annual Editions: Human Sexuality 01/02 is organized into six sections. *Sexuality and Society* notes historical and cross-cultural views and analyzes our constantly changing society and sexuality. *Sexual Biology, Behavior, and Orientation* explains the functioning and responses of the human body and contains expanded sections on sexual hygiene, diseases, and conditions affecting sexuality and functioning, and guides to preventive and ongoing sexual health care. *Interpersonal Relationships* provides suggestions for establishing and maintaining intimate, responsible, quality relationships. *Reproduction* discusses some recent trends related to pregnancy and childbearing and deals with reproductive topics, including conception, contraception, and abortion. *Sexuality Through the Life Cycle* looks at what happens sexually throughout one's lifetime—from childhood to the later years. Finally, *Old/New Sexual Concerns* deals with such topics as sexual abuse, rape, sexual harassment, and legal and ethical issues regarding sexual behavior. It closes with a focus on the future of sex and questions whether the first decade of the twenty-first century will see movement toward a middle ground on four heretofore sexual dichotomies.

Also, in this edition of *Annual Editions: Human Sexuality 01/02* are selected *World Wide Web* sites that can be used to further explore the topics. These sites will be cross-referenced by number in the *topic guide.*

The articles in this anthology have been carefully reviewed and selected for their quality, readability, currency, and interest. They present a variety of viewpoints. Some you will agree with, some you will not, but we hope you will learn from all of them.

Appreciation and thanks go to Loree Adams for her suggestions and expertise; to Michael Fatten, Mychele Kenney, Sue LeSeure, and Sarah Oberst for their willingness to act as two-way sounding boards; to Mary Roy for her organization and assistance, to Ollie Pocs for inspiration, and to those who have submitted articles and reviewed previous editions. We feel that *Annual Editions: Human Sexuality 01/02* is one of the most useful and up-to-date books available. Please return the postage-paid article rating form on the last page of this book with your suggestions and comments. Any book can be improved. This one will continue to be—annually.

Susan J. Bunting
Editor

1. F. Caprio, 1967 2. H. Ellis, 1891 3. R. Westheimer, 1995 4. H. Long, 1919 5. Masters, Johnson & Kolodny, 1982 6. T. Moore, 1998 7. C. Shedd, 1968 8. Lewin & Gilmore, 1950 9. Broderick & Bernard, 1969 10. H. Ellis, 1933 11. McLuhan & Leonard, 1967.

Contents

UNIT 1

Sexuality and Society

Ten selections consider sexuality from historical and cross-cultural perspectives and examine today's changing attitudes toward human sexual interaction.

The concepts in bold italics are developed in the article. For further expansion please refer to the Topic Guide, the Glossary, and the Index.

UNIT 3

Interpersonal Relationships

Six selections examine the dynamics of establishing sexual relationships and the need to make these relationships responsible and effective.

The concepts in bold italics are developed in the article. For further expansion please refer to the Topic Guide, the Glossary, and the Index.

UNIT 4

Reproduction

Four articles discuss the roles of both males and females in pregnancy and childbirth and consider the influences of the latest birth control methods and practices on individuals and society as a whole.

The concepts in bold italics are developed in the article. For further expansion please refer to the Topic Guide, the Glossary, and the Index.

UNIT 5

Sexuality Through the Life Cycle

Five articles consider human sexuality as an important element throughout the life cycle. Topics include responsible adolescent sexuality, sex in and out of marriage, and sex in old age.

The concepts in bold italics are developed in the article. For further expansion please refer to the Topic Guide, the Glossary, and the Index.

ix

UNIT 6

Old/New Sexual Concerns

Thirteen selections discuss ongoing concerns of sexual abuse, violence, and harassment, gender roles and issues, and sex in the media.

The concepts in bold italics are developed in the article. For further expansion please refer to the Topic Guide, the Glossary, and the Index.

The concepts in bold italics are developed in the article. For further expansion please refer to the Topic Guide, the Glossary, and the Index.

Topic Guide

This topic guide suggests how the selections in this book relate to the subjects covered in your course.

The Web icon (⊙) under the topic articles easily identifies the relevant Web sites, which are numbered and annotated on the next two pages. By linking the articles and the Web sites by topic, this ANNUAL EDITIONS reader becomes a powerful learning and research tool.

TOPIC AREA	TREATED IN	TOPIC AREA	TREATED IN
Abortion	40. Hidden Health Threat ⊙ **1, 9, 16, 20, 21, 26**		45. Gender Blur 46. Can You Love God and Sex? 47. Satori in the Bedroom ⊙ **4, 5, 9, 10, 14, 16, 17, 28, 32**
Abuse/Rape/ Sexual Harassment	1. Another Planet 16. Too Much of a Good Thing 33. Teaching Schools a Lesson 35. Christy's Crusade 36. When Preachers Prey 37. Of Professors and Pedophiles 41. Criminal Injustice ⊙ **29, 30**	**Homosexuality/ Bisexuality**	1. Another Planet 5. Amsterdamned 17. What Made Troy Gay? 18. Out of the Fold? 19. Five Sexes, Revisited 21. New Flirting Game 31. Sex in School? It's Required! 32. Sex Ed: How Do We Score? 33. Teaching Schools a Lesson 45. Gender Blur ⊙ **2, 7, 8, 9, 10, 16, 17, 24, 25, 28, 32**
Aging	6. World Made Flesh 9. "Uniform for Today Is Belly Buttons" 10. Second Sexual Revolution 12. Male Sexual Circuitry 13. Science of Women & Sex 15. Prostate Dilemmas ⊙ **22, 23, 25**	**Legal/ Ethical Issues**	1. Another Planet 3. Little Hope, Less Help 4. Breaking the Silence 5. Amsterdamned 14. America: Awash in STDs 18. Out of the Fold? 27. How Old Is Too Old to Have a Baby? 32. Sex Ed: How Do We Score? 33. Teaching Schools a Lesson 35. Christy's Crusade 36. When Preachers Prey 37. Of Professors and Pedophiles 38. Legislating Morality 39. Pregnant? You're Fired! 40. Hidden Health Threat 41. Criminal Injustice 42. Porn.con? ⊙ **1, 2, 20, 26**
Birth Control/ Contraception	1. Another Planet 26. Protecting Against Unintended Pregnancy 31. Sex in School? It's Required! 32. Sex Ed: How Do We Score? 40. Hidden Health Treat 45. Gender Blur ⊙ **1, 9, 16, 18, 19, 20, 21, 27**		
Female Sexuality	1. Another Planet 2. Rwandan Sorrow 6. World Made Flesh 13. Science of Women & Sex 19. Five Sexes, Revisited 20. Why We Fall in Love 21. New Flirting Game 28. What Mother Nature Teaches Us About Motherhood 35. Christy's Crusade 36. When Preachers Prey 39. Pregnant? You're Fired! 40. Hidden Health Threat 41. Criminal Injustice 45. Gender Blur 46. Can You Love God and Sex? 47. Satori in the Bedroom ⊙ **3, 4, 5, 7, 8, 9, 10, 14, 16, 17, 32**	**Male Sexuality**	1. Another Planet 6. World Made Flesh 7. Male Box 8. Never Too Buff 11. Are You Man Enough? 12. Male Sexual Circuitry 15. Prostate Dilemmas 16. Too Much of a Good Thing 17. What Made Troy Gay? 19. Five Sexes, Revisited 21. New Flirting Game 29. Pregnant Pleasures 36. When Preachers Prey 37. Of Professors and Pedophiles 45. Gender Blur 47. Satori in the Bedroom ⊙ **7, 8, 9, 10, 13, 14, 15, 16, 17, 28**
Gender/ Gender Roles	6. World Made Flesh 7. Male Box 8. Never Too Buff 11. Are You Man Enough? 13. Science of Women & Sex 17. What Made Troy Gay? 19. Five Sexes, Revisited 20. Why We Fall in Love 21. New Flirting Game 28. What Mother Nature Teaches Us About Motherhood 30. Sexuality and Young Children 36. When Preachers Prey	**Media**	5. Amsterdamned 6. World Made Flesh 8. Never Too Buff 14. America: Awash in STDs 18. Out of the Fold? 22. What's Your Love Story?

⊙ AE: Human Sexuality

The following World Wide Web sites have been carefully researched and selected to support the articles found in this reader. The sites are cross-referenced by number and the Web icon (⊙) in the topic guide. In addition, it is possible to link directly to these Web sites through our DUSHKIN ONLINE support site at *http://www.dushkin.com/online/*.

The following sites were available at the time of publication. Visit our Web site—we update DUSHKIN ONLINE regularly to reflect any changes.

General Sources

1. National Institutes of Health (NIH)
http://www.nih.gov
Consult this site for links to extensive health information and scientific resources. The NIH is one of eight health agencies of the Public Health Service, which, in turn, is part of the U.S. Department of Health and Human Services.

2. SIECUS
http://www.siecus.org
Visit the Sexuality Information and Education Council of the United States (SIECUS) home page to learn about the organization, to find news of its educational programs and activities, and to access links to resources in sexuality education.

Sexuality and Society

3. Human Rights Practices for 1998 Report: India
http://www.usis.usemb.se/human/human1998/india.html
Read this U.S. Department of State USIS (U.S. Information Service) report on India's human rights practices for an understanding of the issues that affect women's mental and physical health and well-being in different parts of the world.

4. Q Web Sweden: A Women's Empowerment Base
http://www.qweb.kvinnoforum.se/index.htm
This site will lead you to a number of pages addressing women's health issues and discussing societal issues related to sex. It provides interesting cross-cultural perspectives.

5. SocioSite: Feminism and Women's Issues
http://www.pscw.uva.nl/sociosite/TOPICS/Women.html
Open this University of Amsterdam Sociology Department's site to gain insights into a number of issues that affect both men and women. It provides biographies of women in history, an international network for women in the workplace, and links to family and children's issues, and more.

6. Women's Human Rights Resources
http://www.law-lib.utoronto.ca/Diana/
This list of international women's human rights Web sites provides interesting resources on marriage and the family; rights of girls; sexual orientation; slavery, trafficking, and prostitution; and violence against women.

Sexual Biology, Behavior, and Orientation

7. Bibliography: HIV/AIDS and College Students
http://www.sph.emory.edu/bshe/AIDS/college.html
This Emory University site contains an in-print bibliography of articles dealing with HIV/AIDS and college students. Some 75 articles addressing sexual behaviors and behaviors related to HIV/AIDS, primarily from academic and professional journals, are listed.

8. The Body: A Multimedia AIDS and HIV Information Resource
http://www.thebody.com/cgi-bin/body.cgi
On this site you can find the basics about AIDS/HIV, learn about treatments, exchange information in forums, and gain insight from experts.

9. Healthy Way
http://www.ab.sympatico.ca/Contents/health/
This Canadian site, which is directed toward consumers, will lead you to many links related to sexual orientation. It also addresses aspects of human sexuality over the life span, general health, and reproductive health.

10. Hispanic Sexual Behavior and Gender Roles
http://www.caps.ucsf.edu/hispnews.html
This research report from the University of California at San Francisco Center for AIDS Prevention Studies describes and analyzes Hispanic sexual behavior and gender roles, particularly as regards prevention of STDs and HIV/AIDS. It discusses gender and cultural differences in sexual behavior and expectations and other topics of interest.

11. James Kohl
http://www.pheromones.com
Keeping in mind that this is a commercial site with the goal of selling a book, look here to find topics of interest to non-scientists about pheromones. Links to related material of a more academic nature are included. Check out the diagram of "Mammalian Olfactory-Genetic-Neuronal-Hormonal-Behavioral Reciprocity and Human Sexuality" for a sense of the myriad biological influences that play a part in sexual behavior.

12. Johan's Guide to Aphrodisiacs
http://www.santesson.com/aphrodis/aphrhome.htm
"The Aphrodisiac Home Page" provides links to information about a multitude of substances that some believe arouse or increase sexual response or cause or increase sexual desire. Skepticism about aphrodisiacs is also discussed.

Interpersonal Relationships

13. American Psychological Association
http://www.apa.org/psychnet/
By exploring the APA's "PsychNET," you will be able to find links to an abundance of articles and other resources related to interpersonal relationships throughout the life span.

14. Bonobos Sex and Society
http://songweaver.com/info/bonobos.html
This site, accessed through Carnegie Mellon University, includes an article explaining how a primate's behavior challenges traditional assumptions about male supremacy in human evolution.

15. The Celibate FAQ
http://mail.bris.ac.uk/~plmlp/celibate.html
Martin Poulter's definitions, thoughts, and suggested resources on celibacy, created, he says, "in response to the lack of celibate stuff (outside of religious contexts) on the Internet," and his perception of the Net's bias against celibacy can be found on this site.

16. Go Ask Alice

http://www.goaskalice.columbia.edu
This interactive site provided by Healthwise, a division of Columbia University Health Services, includes discussion and insight into a number of personal issues of interest to college-age people—and those younger and older. Many questions about physical and emotional health and well-being in the modern world are answered.

17. Sex and Gender

http://www.bioanth.cam.ac.uk/pip4amod3.html
Use the syllabus, lecture titles, and readings noted in this site to explore sexual differentiation in human cultures, the genetics of sexual differentiation, and the biology of sex roles in nonhumans.

Reproduction

18. Ask NOAH About Pregnancy: Fertility & Infertility

http://www.noah.cuny.edu/pregnancy/fertility.html
New York Online Access to Health (NOAH) seeks to provide relevant, timely, and unbiased health information for consumers. At this site, the organization presents extensive links to a variety of resources about infertility treatments and issues.

19. Childbirth.Org

http://www.childbirth.org
This interactive site about childbirth options is from an organization that aims to educate consumers to know their options and provide themselves with the best possible care to ensure healthy pregnancies and deliveries. The site and its links address a myriad of topics, from episiotomy to water birth.

20. Medically Induced Abortion

http://www.nejm.org/content/1995/0333/0009/ 0537.asp
Read physician Richard Hausknecht's *New England Journal of Medicine* article about medical abortion using methotrexate and misoprostol.

21. Planned Parenthood

http://www.plannedparenthood.org
Visit this well-known organization's home page for links to information on the various kinds of contraceptives (including outercourse and abstinence) and to discussions of other topics related to sexual and reproductive health.

Sexuality Through the Life Cycle

22. American Association of Retired Persons (AARP)

http://www.aarp.org
The AARP, a major advocacy group for older people, includes among its many resources suggested readings and Internet links to organizations that deal with the health and social issues that may affect one's sexuality as one ages.

23. National Institute on Aging (NIA)

http://www.nih.gov/nia/
The NIA, one of the institutes of the National Institutes of Health, presents this home page to lead you to a variety of resources on health and lifestyle issues that are of interest to people as they grow older.

24. Teacher Talk

http://education.indiana.edu/cas/tt/tthmpg.html
This home page of the publication *Teacher Talk* from the Indiana University School of Education Center for Adolescent

Studies will lead you to many interesting teacher comments, suggestions, and ideas regarding sexuality education and how to deal with sex issues in the classroom.

25. World Association for Sexology

http://www.tc.umn.edu/nlhome/m201/colem001/ was/wasindex.htm
The World Association for Sexology works to further the understanding and development of sexology throughout the world. Access this site to explore a number of issues and links related to sexuality throughout life.

Old/New Sexual Concerns

26. Abortion Law Homepage

http://members.aol.com/_ht_a/abtrbng/index.htm
This page explains the background and state of abortion law in the United States. *Roe v. Wade, Planned Parenthood v. Casey*, feticide cases, and statutes are among the important subects discussed.

27. Infertility Resources

http://www.ihr.com/infertility/index.html
This site includes links to the Oregon Health Sciences University Fertility Program and the Center for Reproductive Growth in Nashville, Tennessee. Ethical, legal, financial, psychological, and social issues are discussed.

28. Men's Health Resource Guide

http://www.menshealth.com/new/guide/index.html
This resource guide from *Men's Health* presents many links to topics in men's health, from AIDS/STDs, to back pain, to impotence and infertility, to vasectomy. It also includes discussions of relationship and family issues.

29. Other Sexual Violence Resources on the Web

http://www.witserv.com/org/ocrcc/resource/resource.htm
Open this useful site for Links to Other Sexual Violence Pages. For example, it has a link to "Men Against Rape," a site maintained by the D.C. Men Against Rape organization, providing men's perspectives on sexual violence.

30. Sexual Assault Information Page

http://www.cs.utk.edu/~bartley/saInfoPage.html
This invaluable site provides dozens of links to information and resources on a variety of sexual assault–related topics: child sexual abuse, date rape, incest, secondary victims, and offenders.

31. Third Age: Love and Sex

http://www.thirdage.com/romance/
This interactive site explores a current topic: relationships forged on the Internet. Browse here to hear various viewpoints on the issue. Advice columnists and psychologists add their perspectives.

32. Women's Studies Resources

http://www.inform.umd.edu/EdRes/Topic/WomensStudies/
This site from the University of Maryland provides a wealth of resources related to women's studies. You can find links to such topics as body image, comfort (or discomfort) with sexuality, personal relationships, pornography, and more.

We highly recommend that you review our Web site for expandedinformation and our other product lines. We are continually updatingand adding links to our Web site in order to offer you the most usableand useful information that will support and expand the value of yourAnnual Editions. You can reach us at:
http://www.dushkin. com/annualeditions/.

Unit Selections

1. **Another Planet,** Anouk Ride
2. **Rwandan Sorrow,** Karl Taro Greenfeld
3. **Little Hope, Less Help,** Michael D. Lemonick
4. **Breaking the Silence,** Tom Masland
5. **Amsterdamned,** Anita Dubey
6. **The World Made Flesh,** Vanessa Baird
7. **The Male Box,** Gloria Jacobs
8. **Never Too Buff,** John Cloud
9. **"The Uniform for Today Is Belly Buttons,"** Gigi Guerra
10. **The Second Sexual Revolution,** Jack Hitt

Key Points to Consider

❖ Have you ever spoken to a young person from another culture/country about sexuality-related ideas, norms, education, or behavior? If so, what surprised you? What did you think about their perspective or ways?

❖ Do you fee the American culture is too permissive or too rigid with respect to sexual norms, expectations, and laws? Why? What changes would you recommend?

❖ Do you support comprehensive sex education and condom distribution on the street as ways to address increased teenage sexual activity? Why or why not?

❖ What do you think can and should be done about HIV/AIDS in developing countries?

❖ What do you make of the increased popularity of body-piercing, tattooing, and other body adornments for both genders and wider age groups?

❖ Would you ever consider visiting a nude recreation resort or beach? Why or why not? If your answer was that you would consider such a visit, when would you do so, i.e., 20s, . . . 30s, . . . 50s . . . ?

 **Links** **www.dushkin.com/online/**

3. **Human Rights Practices for 1998 Report: India**
   http://www.usis.usemb.se/human/human1998/india.html
4. **Q Web Sweden: A Women's Empowerment Base**
   http://www.qweb.kvinnoforum.se/index.htm
5. **SocioSite: Feminism and Women's Issues**
   http://www.pscw.uva.nl/sociosite/TOPICS/Women.html
6. **Women's Human Rights Resources**
   http://www.law-lib.utoronto.ca/Diana/

These sites are annotated on pages 4 and 5.

People of different civilizations in different historical periods have engaged in a variety of modes of sexual expression and behavior. Despite this cultural and historical diversity, it is clear that human sexuality is a dynamic and complex force that involves psychological and sociocultural as well as physiological facets. Our sexuality includes our whole body and personality while we learn what it means to be sexual and to behave sexually within the structure and parameters of our era through our family, social group, and society. By studying varying cultures and eras we see more clearly the interplay between the biological, psychological, and sociocultural, as well as between the person, generation, and society.

For several centuries, Western civilization, especially Western European and, in turn, American cultures, have been characterized by an "antisex ethic." This belief system includes a variety of negative views and norms about sex and sexuality, including denial, fear, restriction, and the detachment of sexual feelings and behavior from the wholeness of personhood or humanity. Indeed, it has only been in the last 50 years that the antisex proscriptions against knowing or learning about sex have lost their stranglehold so that people can find accurate information about their sexual health, sexual functioning, and birth control without fear of stigma or even incarceration.

One generalization on which sociologists and others who study human behavior anywhere in the world can agree is that social change in beliefs, norms, or behavior—sexual or otherwise—is not easily accomplished. When it does occur, it is linked to significant changes in the social environment and usually happens as a result of interest groups that move society to confront and question existing beliefs, norms, and behavior. Changes in the social environment that have been most often linked to changes in sexuality and its expression include the invention of the car, the liberation of women from the kitchen, changes in the legality and availability of birth control, the reconsideration of democratic values of individual freedom and the pursuit of happiness, the growth of mass media, and the coming of the computer age. The social groups that have been involved in the process of this sexual/social change have also been far-reaching. In the United States they include the earliest feminists, the suffragettes; Margaret Sanger, the mother of the birth control movement; mainstream religious groups that insist that "sexuality is a good gift from God"; publishers of sex education curricula for youth; pioneering researchers like Alfred Kinsey, Havelock Ellis, William Masters, Virginia Johnson, and others; and a panorama of interest groups who have advocated changes, demanded rights, or both. Many events, people, and perspectives have played a role in sexuality beliefs and behaviors today.

Still it is clear that many things have changed with respect to sexuality and society. One of the most dramatic is from the "don't-talk-about-it" to an "everyone's-talking-about-it" communication norm. Current examples range from baby-boomer women and menopause, to prominent politicians or athletes and oral sex, adultery, prostate cancer, or impotency.

However, it is also clear that some things have not changed as much as we might expect, given the increased talk, information, and availability of birth control and other sexual health products and services. It is not characteristic for the majority of people of any age to feel comfortable with and communicate about sexual feelings, fears, needs, and desires. Negotiating, even understanding, consent and responsibility seems even harder today than when we were not talking. The incidence of unplanned, unwed, and teenage pregnancies, sexually transmitted diseases (some life-threatening), molestation, incest, rape, and sexual harassment continue to be troubling. At the same time, despite more knowledge than ever before and the efforts of many in the educational, medical, and political spheres, the dream of healthy, positive, and fulfilling sexuality still eludes individuals and society as a whole.

This unit overviews historical, cross-cultural, and current issues and trends in order to illustrate the connectedness of our values, practices, and experiences of sexuality. In so doing it is meant to challenge readers to adopt a very broad perspective through which their examination of today's sexuality, and their experience of it, can be more meaningful. Only in so doing can we hope to avoid a fear-based return to the "antisex ethic" of the past while striving to evaluate the impact and value of the social changes that have so profoundly affected sexuality at the dawn of the twenty-first century.

The articles in the first subsection, *Historical and Cross-Cultural Perspectives*, reveal some surprising contradictions and paradoxes in sexuality and society. The opening article focuses on youth from a variety of cultures and illustrates the international nature of the mixed messages that adults give teenagers about sex, as well as the universality of the older generation fearing the sexual openness and appetites of the younger generation. The middle three articles address sexual health-related tragedies in developing and underdeveloped countries. The final article explores the 30-year "experiment" of legalized prostitution and personal drug use in Amsterdam, the Netherlands.

The five articles that make up the second subsection, *Changing Society/Changing Sexuality*, address pivotal issues of sexuality today. Each attempts to place these changes within a historic perspective while discussing the conflicting assessments and uncertain future of these changes. The opening article, "The World Made Flesh" exposes the range of cultural meanings attached to bodies and beauty. The next two articles address masculinity or the personal and cultural meanings and roles associated with being a male and ring some warning bells about the current and future direction that gender roles, identities, and relationships seem to be taking. Next we get to take an informative peek at nudism without shedding our clothes. The closing article addresses a "revolutionary" topic, the increased medicalization of sexual function and dysfunction that exploded nationally and internationally just before the turn of the twenty-first century. According to many, this societal and cultural change fits the definition of "The Second Sexual Revolution."

Another **planet**

Anouk Ride reports on the mixed messages that teenagers are being given about sex and argues that young people have rights too.

YOU can't feel me up when I'm ten, then come back when I'm nineteen and tell me not to have sex with my boyfriend, Maria shouts loudly down the phone over the street noise of Baguio City, the Philippines.[1] She is not alone in decrying the contradictory and condescending views that adults hold about young people and sex.

According to global surveys young people everywhere feel they are ruled by adults who tell them how to behave—but then refuse to give them control over their own bodies and their own sexuality.[2] Nor do they protect them from exploitation. While the media, religious leaders and governments decry the fact that kids are having sex and 'family values' are breaking down, they have failed to protect young people from the dangers of unwanted and unsafe sexual relations.

This is universal. In the Majority World early and forced marriages, female genital mutilation and prostitution deny young men and women their own sexuality. In Africa, two million girls between seven and twelve are genitally mutilated and worldwide two million girls are introduced to the sex market each year.[3]

In Western countries kids are sent mixed messages by the media. They're told that early sexual initiation is bad, but are bombarded with images of teenagers as sexual toys. Who is cool in the fashion world? Models that are young and childlike. Fashion designer Calvin Klein recently popularized this image with ads depicting young women (such as British super-model Kate Moss) in provocative poses. Critics said this was an example of 1990s fashion excess—but Klein and most designers have used half-dressed, pouting teenagers to sell their clothes for years. Society sexualizes children—and then tells them sex is bad.

In many Western countries sexual abuse of children is rife. In the US victims below the age of ten account for 29 per cent of rape cases and 62 per cent of cases involve victims fifteen years old or less. And these are reported cases only.[4] The overwhelming majority of abuse is by someone known to the victim. Often the very adults who are in positions of trust with young people—relatives, neighbours, parents—are those who destroy their self-esteem and disturb their sexual development.

Adults think young people need to be controlled. And society generally has the same view towards the poor, the uneducated and 'minorities' such as ethnic groups and homosexuals. So young people from these backgrounds have even more societal pressures on their sexual behaviour. In the West the highest rates of teenage pregnancy are found among girls living in poverty with low education levels or job prospects. In Britain, in a poor district of East London, one in ten teenage girls gets pregnant while in the wealthier boroughs of Kingston and Richmond the rate is less than half that.[5] One in every ten births worldwide is to a teenage

---

Sex, drugs—and rights for all! A charter for young people's sexual rights.

Cheer up

Sexuality is part of normal teenage development, not a monster to be locked away and starved. Young people need a chance to grow into their bodies, understand their reproductive systems and be responsible in their sexual relations. Sex is about relationships, personal discovery—and fun.

Get real

Methods for contraception and prevention against STDs should be explained and discussed fully and in terms kids can understand by people they can relate to. Knowledge is not enough—they need support not judgement.

Boys *too*

Sex-education programs and services are not just for girls. Young men want to know sexual techniques, what to do to avoid pregnancy and information about STDs.

Right laws

Young people are entitled to contraception which is safe, legal, affordable and available. They have a right to be protected from disease.

Sex ed

Education of young people will only work if adults too learn about sex and young people's rights.

Parts Are Private

Parents should not overrule youth rights. Abuse of young people must be condemned. Privacy and confidentiality of services is essential.

7—letter word

Respect. If older people respect teenagers, the feeling will be mutual.

 From *New Internationalist*, July 1998, pp. 28-30. © 1998 by New Internationalist Publications, Ltd. Reprinted by permission.

mother. Sometimes getting pregnant is the only way a teenager can boost her self-esteem and add a sense of purpose to her life.

Society perpetuates the powerlessness of girls through poverty, class or caste and lack of education. Hari from Nepal describes a girl from her village: 'Mona was pregnant with her seventh child, having married a 17-year-old boy at the age of 14. Being of a low caste, with no education, she didn't have any control over her own life. If she had been given the opportunity of education to make her own money and an awareness of her body, she would not have become the slave of tradition and society.'[2]

Many girls marry for money or protection: 'I got married because of a super-painful childhood, because my father was always hitting me,' said one Chilean girl.[5] Early marriage means that girls have little power within the relationship so cannot control if and when they have children.

And having babies before their bodies are fully formed puts them at risk of a range of life-threatening illnesses—the most common cause of death in teenage girls around the world.[3] Fistulae (a rupture between the bladder, rectum and vagina often caused by giving birth too young) is one horrific example. Girls are left infertile and incontinent and

become social outcasts. Inadequate access to safe contraceptives means that in places like São Paulo, Brazil, the number of young girls admitted to hospitals due to complications from unsafe abortions is greater than the number of births.

Even societies classified as democratic and liberal are far from accepting young people's sexuality, particularly when it is seen as not 'normal'. In Australia, where one of the best-selling, locally produced movies was *Priscilla, Queen of the Desert* and where Sydney's Gay and Lesbian Mardi Gras is the nation's biggest street party, research indicates that around a third of young

ACTION/READING

Women's Health Movement

The Asian-Pacific Resource and Research Centre for Women (ARROW), 2nd Floor, Block F, Anjung Felda, Jalan Maktab, 54000 Kuala Lumpur, Malaysia. Tel: +603 292 9913; e-mail: women@arrow.po.my An information and resource centre focusing on women and development. Reproductive rights is one of its main areas. **Committee on Women, Population and the Environment** (CWPE), c/o Population and Development Program, Hampshire College, Amherst, MA 01002, US. Tel: +1 413 582 5506; e-mail: cwpe@igc.apc.org Provides alternative analyses of the relationships between population poverty and environmental degradation and challenges both population control and anti-abortion forces. **International Reproductive Rights Research Action Group** (IRRRAG), c/o Women's Studies, Hunter College, CUNY, 695 Park Avenue, New York, NY 10021, US. Tel: +1 212 772 5682; e-mail: IRRRAG@igc.apc.org A grassroots research project on reproductive issues and women's rights, based in seven countries. The results are being published in *Negotiating Reproductive Rights: Women's Perspectives Across Countries and Cultures*, edited by Rosalind Petchesky and Karen Judd (Zed Books 1998). **International Women's Health Coalition** (IWHC), 24 East 21st St, New York, NY 10010, USA. Tel: +1 212 979 8500; e-mail: iwhc@igc.apc.org Supports projects and aid agencies aiming to promote high-quality women's reproductive health. **Women's Global Network for Reproductive Rights**, NZ Voorburgwal 32, 1012 RZ Amsterdam, The Netherlands,

Tel: +31 20 620 9672; e-mail: wgnrr@antenna.nl An autonomous international network campaigning for the right of women to decide whether, when and with whom to have children.

Family planning/United Nations

United Nations. Fund for Population Activities (UNFPA), 220 East 42nd St, New York, NY 10017, US. Fax: +1 212 557 6416. Website: http://www.unfpa.org The main UN organization dealing with fertility issues. Publishes The State of World Population report each year. **World Health Organization** (WHO), 1211 Geneva 27, Switzerland. Fax: +41 22 791 4870. Website: http://www.who.ch Produces the annual *World Health Report*. **International Planned Parent Federation** (IPPF), Regent's College, Inner Circle, Regent's Park, London NW1 4NS, England. Tel: +44 171 487 7900; e-mail: ippfinfo@ippf.attmail.com The largest non-governmental family-planning organization.

Worth reading . . .

Abortion: Between Freedom and Necessity, Janet Hadley (Virago 1996). A well-argued case for abortion which also acknowledges the difficulties and dilemmas. 'Population and reproductive rights'. Focus on Gender, Vol. 2, No. 2, June 1994 (Oxfam). A range of perspectives on reproduction in a Majority World context. *Our Bodies, Ourselves*, the Boston Women's Health Book Collective (Penguin 1996). A classic, recently updated. Pandora's Clock: *Understanding our Fertility*, Maureen

Freely and Celia Pyper (Heinemann 1993). A humorous look at the ambiguities and emotions surrounding pregnancy and birth. *Private Decisions, Public Debates: Women, Reproduction and Population* (Panos Institute 1994) has a range of articles by journalists from the Majority World. Panos (Tel: +44 171 278 1111; e-mail: panoslondon@gn.apc.org) also produces briefing papers on reproductive rights. *Population and Reproductive Rights: Feminist Perspectives from the South*, Sonia Corrêa and Rebecca Reichmann, (Zed Books/Kali for Women/DAWN 1994). A critical Southern view of the debates around population, reproduction and development. *Reproductive Health Matters* is a quarterly journal with in-depth analysis and up-to-date news on women's health and rights. (29-35 Farringdon Rd, London EC1M 3JB, England. Tel: +44 171 242 8686; e-mail: 100663.3504@compuserve.com) *Reproductive Rights and Wrongs: The Global Politics of Population Control*, Betsy Hartmann (South End Press 1995). A detailed and searing analysis of the politics and history of population control which argues for a more woman-based perspective. *Where Women have no Doctor: A health guide for women*, A. August Burns, Ronnie Lovich, Jane Maxwell, Katharine Shapiro (Hesperian Foundation 1997). A practical guide, useful for its down-to-earth explanations. *Women, Population and Global Crisis*, Asoka Bandarage (Zed Books, 1997). Places the population debate in a broad historical and social justice-oriented perspective. *The Legacy of Malthus* (forthcoming), Eric Ross (Zed Press 1998). A political economy critique of Malthusian theory and its applications in Europe and the South.

lesbians and gays have attempted suicide. The main cause of their depression was a common feeling that they lacked adult support.[6]

This is not surprising when some 'experts' are clearly living on another planet. One academic seriously proposed forced permanent contraception for ten- to seventeen-year-old girls worldwide. Meanwhile, Phyllis Schlafly, an anti-feminist campaigner in the US, says: 'It's very healthy for a young girl to be deterred from promiscuity by fear of contracting a painful, incurable disease or cervical cancer or sterility or the likelihood of giving birth to a dead, blind or brain-damaged baby.'[7]

People often believe that if young people are taught about sex this will promote immorality and recklessness. But sexual-abstinence programs, popular in the US, have never been effective in delaying the onset of intercourse. Research indicates that increased information about sex encourages a later start to sexual relations, higher use of contraceptives and fewer sexual partners.[2]

Kids are having sex despite adult disapproval. 'Heavy-handedness, brainwashing and moralizing will not stop the young from engaging in sexual activity,' says Elmira from Kazakhstan.[2] In fact, improvements in nutrition have led to girls worldwide becoming fertile more than two years earlier than previous generations. So most young people have a longer period of sexual relations before marriage than their parents. In sub-Saharan Africa eight out of ten people below the age of twenty are sexually experienced as are seven out of ten teenagers in many developed countries and at least half of all teens in Latin America.

Although they are sexually active, young people are ill-equipped to deal with the consequences of sex. Without access to information, contraception and equal rights they have high rates of sexually transmitted diseases (STDs) and unwanted pregnancies. Half of all new HIV infections are among the 15 to 24 age group—predominantly in South-East Asia and sub-Saharan Africa. And one out of every twenty adolescents contracts an STD each year.

Almost all young people say that they need more information on all aspects of their sexual and reproductive health. More than three-quarters in a global youth survey were aware of the risks of STDs including HIV/AIDS. But a significant number of young people, particularly in Arab states and some parts of the Far East, believed STDs and AIDS were not a personal concern.

'STDs are only a problem for homosexuals, sex workers and drug addicts—it is scientifically proven,' said a young respondent reciting common knowledge in Yemen.[2] In India a study found most young people encountered sex earlier than in previous decades, but still thirty-six per cent of those interviewed had no idea what led to conception and only five per cent of them were using contraceptives.[8] Up to 60 per cent of adolescent births throughout the world are unplanned.

Many youth workers say that teenagers, due to the lack of sex education and an inability to talk with parents, rely on the media and friends for advice. Most young people feel awkward talking to their elders about sex. In a recent survey of youth in 54 countries more than half said they felt too embarrassed to discuss sex with adults.[2] 'Adults have got this ideology that young people are being rude if they express their thoughts, so sometimes I just feel like a stray, an alien' says Sarah from Botswana.[1]

But knowledge alone is not enough—young people, especially girls, need to feel empowered when it comes to sex.

One girl from Trinidad and Tobago says adamantly: 'If he does not have a condom, the woman should say: "If you don't have you can't get."'[1] But in practice it is difficult—in Canada one survey found although 85 per cent of youth claimed to be very knowledgeable about contraception, only 11 per cent of female university students and 19 per cent of male students always used condoms, which were seen as 'uncool'.[9] Girls and young women said they lacked the power to negotiate condom use and were subject to strongly held views about traditional male and female roles in sexual relationships.

Kids also need the law on their side. But often sex is illegal, with 15 or 16 being the average minimum age of consent. Shantal, a youth worker in Barbados, explains the dilemmas this can create: 'A mother wanted to have the partner of her 13-year-old daughter arrested for statutory rape. . . . The young girl said that she had not been raped and had willingly consented to sex. The young man, who was 21, was her boyfriend and she would never forgive her mother if she had him arrested. The case was eventually dropped because the girl refused to testify. Young people see themselves as sexual beings.'[1]

Young people are always going to have sex (or have it forced upon them). It is a denial of their rights to refuse them contraception and protection against STDs. What is needed when a 13-year-old goes to a clinic or to a doctor for contraception is clear information, support and counselling to ensure that the teenager is able to choose sexual relations and is confident of their control over the situation. It is a basic human right to have control over your own body. In fact, it may even be the one thing anyone can truly 'own'—so why deny this to people just because they are young?

Young people have identified their needs in order to ensure they are informed, safe and empowered in their sexual relations. Before heading off to meet her friends in Baguio City, Maria offers a final opinion. 'I am tired of being told what to do. I would like older people to listen to my experiences and my questions,' she says confidently. 'But change will be impossible if adults do not learn from us.'[1]

1. Interviews by Anouk Ride and International Planned Parenthood Foundation. Some of the names of people in this article have been changed.
2. *Generation 97* (International Planned Parenthood Federation 1997).
3. *Rights of women in relation to sexuality and reproductive health* (Swedish Association for Sex Education 1997).
4. *Reproductive Health Matters*, November 1996.
5. *Reproductive Health Matters*, May 1995.
6. *Sexuality and Youth Suicide,* (Sexuality and Youth Suicide Project, Australia, 1997).
7. Janet Hadley, *Abortion: Between Freedom and Necessity* (Virago 1996).
8. *The Sex Files* (Family Planning Association of India/Sex Education, Counselling and Training 1996).
9. *Sex and Reproductive Health Rights in Canada* (website by Katherine McDonald <http://www.hcsc.gc.ca/canusa/papers/canada/english/reprod.html>)

RWANDAN SORROW

For the nation's expectant mothers, pregnancy is often a death sentence. Newborns fare little better. Across the land, heartbreak replaces joy

By **KARL TARO GREENFELD**/KIBUNGO

THE MUSUHURA REFUGEE CAMP was literally a purgatory, a place of suffering and expiation, where 40,000 Rwandan Hutu like Joseph Havamungo, 29, and Nereciana Mushank-wano, 20, wandered amid the huts strung together of relief-agency donated blue plastic sheeting, trash-can fires and hastily dug pit latrines and sought to scavenge the one thing that could sustain life in this place: hope. They were between countries. Host Tanzania didn't want them, and if they returned to Rwanda, they feared Tutsi would seek revenge for the genocide perpetrated by Hutu extremists just two years before. The landscape around the camp symbolized the prospects for the internees in it, scrubby hills that had been denuded of arboreal life, every twig and branch gathered for cooking-fire fuel. Yet Joseph still roamed the hills most days, seeking wood to sell for Tanzanian shillings that he could trade for precious food.

The sameness of his days, however, ended when he met Nereciana. They were from adjacent districts in Kibungo prefecture, Rwanda. She had a round, happy face, full cheeks, short, curly hair and good, straight teeth. She wore silver bangles, which jingled as she and Joseph walked together around the road that marked the perimeter of the camp, talking about home, about the avocado and eucalyptus trees, the rolling, verdant hills and the cooler air of Kibungo. Nereciana had sharp, slightly downcast, eager, probing eyes. When she spoke, Joseph detected a confidence in her tone; she knew what she was saying when she told of her desire to have a family. And

when she talked about God, Joseph became very quiet, for he was Catholic but not so devout as she.

1 IN 9 WOMEN WILL DIE DURING CHILDBIRTH

In Rwandan tradition, if a boy meets a girl and decides he loves her, he finds her father, and negotiations begin. It is called an *inkwano*—the price a prospective bridegroom must pay the bride's family. Since this was a refugee camp, though, and personal survival, never mind personal wealth, was hard to come by, the bridal price was below market: one cow, payable in some distant future when Rwandan Hutu would have cows and land to graze them on. A Catholic priest presided over the ceremony, attended by the other refugees from Havamungo's Rwankogoto village and sealed in the eyes of the community by the *Bourgemeister,* who wished them bountiful loins and strong children.

For Joseph and Nereciana, their relationship was a reprieve, a warm place in the heart of this darkness. And even when Tanzanian troops surrounded the camp, launched tear gas into the compound and ordered the refugees onto the roads back to

Rwanda, Joseph and Nereciana, holding hands as two links in a 40-mile chain of humanity, could go with hope, believing—despite rumors that Tutsi were waiting at the other end of the Rusumo bridge over the Kageva River to castrate returning Hutu males—that God would watch over them and return them to safety. There were some positive signs: the Red Cross had set up biscuit and water stations to feed the procession of 400,000, some of whom had wrapped plastic bags around their bloody feet. "The camp was so terrible, and the trip back was so terrible—nothing that was waiting for us could have been worse," Joseph says of the return to Rwanda.

The country to which they returned was a wasteland. Rwanda, a landlocked nation squeezed between Tanzania and the Republic of the Congo, has always been among the most crowded countries on earth—6.7 million people packed into a country the size of Vermont, not a good thing for an agrarian society whose primary economic unit is the family farm. The overpopulation is among the first things a visitor notices—and it has been cited as a sociological cause for the genocide. Rwanda is one of those countries, like India, where you are almost never out of sight of another human being. The entire country has been stripped of its jungle, savannah and bush to make way for handkerchief-size plots of manioc or peanuts or the prize cash crop, coffee.

Yet, all those factors aside, Rwanda today can be understood only through the harsh prism of the genocide that ravaged it in 1994. That bloodbath, fueled by an incendiary combination of misguided Belgian colonial policy, divisive domestic politics, ethnic stereotyping and tragic French foreign policy, took the lives of 800,000 of the minority Tutsi. The genocide, and the concurrent civil war during which the Tutsi minority took control of the country, devastated the infrastructure and exterminated the professional class. There were fewer than a dozen doctors within Rwanda's borders in 1997, and no more than 100 nurses. Hospitals were destroyed by retreating Hutu forces, as were power plants, factories and government buildings. The country that had once been a bastion of orderly if somewhat squalid agrarian capitalism was reduced to Stone Age living standards. In 1993, before the genocide, 53% of households were below the poverty line; by 1997, that figure had risen to more than 70%. Women's life expectancy was down to about age 43. "We needed to start from the beginning again," says Antoinette Uwimana, subprefect for the Kibungo region. "We had no infrastructure, no education, no water, no roads. All needed to be rebuilt, and we didn't even have an executive class. Agriculture was our only resource."

RETURNING REFUGEES SUCH as Joseph and Nereciana found the fields lying fallow, the last few harvests still rotting on the stem. This wave of humanity could have precipitated a disaster had not the new Tutsi government headed by Paul Kagame secured international aid and, even more miraculously, somehow managed to bridge the bloody tribal divide. There were Tutsi reprisals against Hutu, but for the most part the reintegration of Hutu refugees into Rwandan society went smoothly.

Joseph and Nereciana reinhabited a familial plot in Rwankogoto and began the process of building their dirt-floor, four-room hut from bamboo, reeds and mud. The house, perched on a hillside overlooking a fertile valley, catches morning sun and stores the warmth all day within its thick stucco walls. They built a thatched-roof outhouse, a rabbit hutch and a chicken coop. They cleared four acres of farmland and sowed their first crop: manioc, beans, peanuts, pineapples and sweet potatoes. Her sisters lent Nereciana pots and empty jerricans that she filled with bananas, yeast and hops to ferment banana beer.

"A new beginning was happening," Joseph says. "We built this house together with our bare hands." In the mornings Nereciana would don her black-and-white *igitenge* (a sort of floral skirt) and rubber flip-flops and head out with Joseph to work the fields. Nereciana, a talkative woman, loved recounting the tales of Bakame, a mythical rabbit who is always playing tricks on humans and other animals. And for Joseph, hunched over, listening to his wife, it seemed that even though life was hard, "this was, for us, a time of great hope."

How to Help
Online: An $8 Miracle

IT DOESN'T TAKE MUCH to help Rwanda's expectant mothers—about three minutes on your PC. But even that can make a tremendous difference. For a variety of reasons—mostly related to simple hygiene and poor access to medical care—Rwanda remains the most dangerous place on the planet to get pregnant. The lifetime risk of death from pregnancy there is about 400 times greater than in the developed world. For Rwanda's mothers, what should be a joyful experience is painful, frightening and risky.

While birthing conditions in Rwanda may not improve for years, it is possible to offer meaningful help. The International Rescue Committee has developed special birthing kits that you can purchase and that will be distributed to Rwandan mothers and rural midwives. The kits—which include clean cloths for the mother and baby, umbilical sutures, razor blades, soap and other necessities—can be purchased for $8 at *www.netaid.com/survivalproject*. The site also makes it possible to purchase obstetrical-delivery kits for doctors and basic health-emergency kits for isolated areas. All the money will go right to aid; none will be used to pay overhead for the organizations involved.

IRC

SIMPLE AID: Birthing kits, which cost $8 at *netaid.com*, help with a cleaner birth—key to reducing the deaths of mothers and babies

In the spring, Nereciana walked up the hill to visit an *ababyaza* (traditional midwife) for a consultation. The woman felt Nereciana's stomach and pelvis, asked her questions about her menstrual cycle and then deduced what the couple had begun to suspect: Nereciana was pregnant.

One of the ironies of suffering a national tragedy on the scale of Rwanda's is that once the crisis is off the front pages of the world's newspapers, the emergency-relief money stops flowing—precisely when the country needs ever larger foreign contributions to restart a moribund society. Particularly hard hit has been Rwanda's medical establishment, which is grappling with some of the most pressing public-health issues on the planet. At least 11% of the population is HIV positive. Malaria, cholera and other diseases are rampant and periodically spike to epidemic levels. Malnutrition is a chronic problem here as in much of Africa, with 10% of the children afflicted. And infant mortality rates at 125 deaths per 1,000 births are at double the world average. For such doctors as Emmanuel d'Harcourt, 34, a program manager for the International Rescue Committee, that means having to build a health-care system in the midst of a full-blown health crisis, improvising with scarce foreign aid and an overburdened Ministry of Health. "There is so little room for error," he says. "The resources are so scarce. It's like parking a car in a space with a millimeter of clearance on each side."

The issue of maternal mortality—mothers dying in childbirth—is particularly perplexing to D'Harcourt. In Rwanda becoming pregnant is tantamount to a death sentence. The lifetime risk of death from labor complications in this part of Africa is 1 in 9. The risk in the U.S. is 1 in 4,000. Numerous factors including nonexistent prenatal care, malnourishment and unsanitary delivery conditions jeopardize the health of mothers and babies. "It's impossible to predict complications," says D'Harcourt. "That's the difficulty with maternal mortality. You can't predict what will go wrong. Certainly, quality of care and treatment play a huge role here." What that means is that even when complications ensue, with the right medical care, lives can be saved. But in Rwanda, where the causes of infection run the gamut from dirty swaddling cloth to unclean razors used to cut umbilical cords, lack of even the most rudimentary measures means that such commonplace complications as pre-eclampsia or sepsis can turn fatal. "Our resources are so limited, we can't put in an IV just in case there is hemorrhaging," says Silas Ruberandinda, director of the Mutenderi Health Center. "We can't even spare the catheters."

More than 90% of the deliveries in Rwanda are facilitated by traditional midwives. These women often learn their trade from their mothers, by watching other village women give birth and by giving birth themselves. "I had no formal training," says

Modesta, a traditional midwife. "I'm only learning now how to recognize risk factors and to decrease the risk of infection." Their equipment often consists of little more than cloth, an old blade and a string to tie off the umbilical cord. While the Rwandan government hopes eventually to have most women deliver in hospitals, that is wishful thinking in a country with only a few thousand hospital beds. The best chance of lowering maternal and infant mortality is equipping midwives with a few simple tools: razor blades, cloth, swaddling, disinfectant, soap and rubber gloves, plus training in hygienic techniques. The cost of the kit is $8.

When a baby is born in Rwanda, a traditional ceremony takes place on the eighth day of the child's life. Banana beer is served, and the community gathers as the newborn is brought out and held up to the sky. The infant is scrutinized, and names are suggested by family, friends and neighbors until the father hears one that sounds right.

NERECIANA HAD BEEN LOOKing forward to this ceremony. It is considered bad luck in Rwanda to think up names for a baby before birth; too many don't make it out of the womb alive. But as Nereciana grew heavy with child and finally could no longer waddle out to work in the fields, she imagined the ceremony, the party, the happy times ahead. Joseph was laying in a supply of banana beer. Ripe pineapples, Nereciana's favorite fruit, were abundant. The birth and the naming ceremony would be, after the camp and the long march back, a new beginning.

On a bright evening in early spring, the villagers of Rwankogoto gathered in and around the couple's tiny hut, sipping banana beer, speaking quietly among themselves. Joseph entered the dirt-floor living room. He looked dazed. He had been weeping.

He hadn't been expecting a funeral.

A few hours after her contractions began, Nereciana was racked by spasms and began complaining of violent abdominal pain. At first Joseph and neighbor Beatrice Nyirahabimana thought the severe contractions of first labor caused her pain. But after eight hours, it was clear that some vital force was leaving Nereciana. Joseph went to seek help. "I'm too weak," Nereciana said to Beatrice. "I'm dying, aren't I?"

The fetus' heart may already have stopped beating when Nereciana died. The cause of her death remains unknown: pre-eclampsia may have brought on seizures, or her uterus may have ruptured. But a larger cause is blisteringly clear: Rwanda is a nation so poor in goods and so weak in spirit that it cannot even give birth to a future. Nereciana's death, a tragedy that still lives in Joseph's sad eyes, was part of the slow genocide of hope, a sin that can be undone only by the miracle of an outside world that cares.

Little Hope, Less Help

The epidemic has hit with devastating force—and things will get much worse before they get better

By MICHAEL D. LEMONICK

AS A METAPHOR FOR HOPELESSNESS, it's hard to equal the AIDS crisis in sub-Saharan Africa. Twenty-four million of the area's people are HIV-positive—70% of the world's infected population. Thirteen million Africans have already died of AIDS, and 10 million more are expected to die within five years. In South Africa, 1 in 5 adults is infected; in Botswana the rate of infection is 1 in 3; in Zimbabwe it is 1 in 4. According to the U.S. Census Bureau, by 2003, AIDS-related deaths will slow population growth in some of these nations to zero, and the population in Botswana, Zimbabwe and South Africa will actually start to decline. Life expectancy by the end of the decade would normally have been about 70 in this part of Africa; as a result of AIDS it will plummet to 30. Said the Census Bureau's Karen Stanecki at last week's 13th International AIDS Conference in Durban, South Africa: "It is hard to comprehend the mortality we will see in these countries."

But terrible as these numbers are, they're bound to get worse. While some of the talk in Durban focused on modest advances in AIDS treatment—and on South African President Thabo Mbeki's flirtation with discredited ideas about what causes AIDS—the central dilemma of the conference was how to fight this voracious plague under the conditions that made the continent so vulnerable in the first place.

One reason AIDS has hit sub-Saharan Africa so hard is that the public health system in many countries is inadequate to deal with even "conventional" disease, let alone a grinding juggernaut like AIDS. According to the World Bank, the region averages $34 per

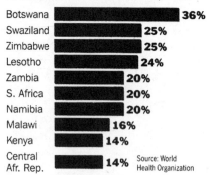

INFECTED Percent ages 15-49 with HIV/AIDS, 1999

Botswana	36%
Swaziland	25%
Zimbabwe	25%
Lesotho	24%
Zambia	20%
S. Africa	20%
Namibia	20%
Malawi	16%
Kenya	14%
Central Afr. Rep.	14%

Source: World Health Organization

person annually in health-care spending—and far less in places like Nigeria and Kenya—compared with an average of $2,485 in developed countries like the U.S. Less than half the people in the area have access to clean water, and just over half of all children are vaccinated against diphtheria, polio and tetanus. The notion that African countries can somehow buy and distribute the expensive drugs that can prolong life for those infected with HIV—even at the drastically subsidized rates that some companies have promised—is farfetched. Beyond that, the illness and death of so many workers is draining what little strength these already weak economies have.

Another problem is that while AIDS is almost completely preventable, prevention methods must be taught to potential victims. Yet sex education of any sort is rare in Africa, and many people lack even the most basic understanding of how the disease is

spread. Upon hearing that AIDS in Africa was mostly a heterosexually transmitted disease, for example, prostitutes in western Kenya started offering clients unprotected anal sex. Since they considered this form of sex "homosexual," they figured they'd be safe.

Even getting Africans to talk about sexually transmitted disease is difficult, says Susan Muguro of the Kenya branch of Standard Chartered Bank, which has begun its own AIDS-awareness programs. The bank's trainers get staff members used to talking about AIDS, safe sex and condoms by making them call out the names of body parts such as penis and vagina. "At first," says Muguro, "people were giggling and blushing. Typhoid wastes us; malaria wastes us; but this disease touches the core of humanity—our sexuality."

Strong leadership from public officials may help, but most African governments have been slow even in admitting they have a problem. It is only in the past 18 months that President Daniel arap Moi of Kenya and President Robert Mugabe of Zimbabwe have used the word disaster in relation to AIDS.

Yet amid the despair, at least two countries have managed to address these problems. Led by President Yoweri Museveni, Uganda started a public AIDS-education program in 1990 that has driven the rate of new infections down dramatically in some places. And Senegal, with its own awareness program, has also cut taxes on condoms and got religious leaders to participate in AIDS education. As a result, Senegal's infection rate is a mere 1 in 50 adults, one of the lowest in Africa.

The notion that developed countries could do more to subsidize the cost of drugs was given impetus by a study reported in Durban last week. Such aid has been dismissed in part on the grounds that patients on these medicines need more monitoring than local health officials can possibly provide. But pilot projects in Ivory Coast, Senegal and Uganda have proved that even poor patients can stick reasonably well to a regimen without constant supervision.

If that's true, then drug companies and Western governments have lost a major excuse for inaction. When the G-8 economic summit convenes this week in Okinawa, AIDS will be a major item on the agenda. And while the African crisis may worsen, it's at least possible that last week's consciousness-raising meeting in Durban could mark a change in attitude—and perhaps even a tiny glimmer of hope.

—*Reported by Peter Hawthorne/*
Cape Town and
Simon Robinson/Nairobi

THE POLITICS OF AIDS

When the President Is a Dissident

Thabo Mbeki has one of the hardest jobs in world politics: following Nelson Mandela as President of South Africa. He has to make good on the promise of liberation, even as many of the country's postapartheid hopes are collapsing amid low economic growth, soaring unemployment and a crime wave that is tearing at the social order. As the leader of Africa's economic and military powerhouse, Mbeki is also expected to play regional statesman and peacemaker, and to lead an aggressive campaign against the AIDS epidemic ravaging the continent.

It is in this fight that he has most disappointed his backers. Mbeki has resolutely proved to be his own man, most notably by endorsing the views of scientists who believe that HIV and AIDS may not be related. That kind of thinking generally gets researchers laughed off as flat-earthers, but the stakes are much higher for Mbeki, who is the leader of a country engaged in a fierce campaign against one of the world's fastest rates of infection. Never mind that the Clinton Administration once championed him as one of the key architects of an African renaissance. "South Africa," enthused Vice President Al Gore last year, "is blessed with a leader in Thabo Mbeki who has been speaking out forcefully, boldly and often [on AIDS]."

Hence Washington's consternation when Mbeki's forceful, bold voice began speaking out often against the scientific assumptions of current AIDS therapies, refused to supply AZT to pregnant women to prevent transmission of HIV in the womb and then invited "AIDS dissident" scientists to sit on a prestigious national advisory panel. Disquiet deepened last week when Mbeki, opening the international AIDS conference, maintained that "we [can] not blame everything on a single virus" and stressed poverty as the most important factor. Almost everyone—including some of his most loyal political allies—has been stunned by Mbeki's HIV skepticism. But there's no question that Africa's dire poverty turbo-boosts HIV's spread and, worse, renders it a death sentence in most cases. Of the 5 million people with AIDS in Africa today, only 20,000 are receiving treatment, because governments can't afford the necessary drugs and infrastructure.

Mbeki is believed to have encountered "dissident" thinking last year during a late-night Web-browsing session, and it's hardly surprising that he may have been searching for an intellectual escape route from the implications of his country's nightmare. Over the next decade, AIDS is expected to devour up to 20% of South Africa's national wealth. Half its population of 15-year-olds is expected to die of the disease. Far from a renaissance, sub-Saharan Africa is in the throes of a plague of medieval proportions. Even at 80% discounts, treatment therapies are simply beyond the means of the continent's governments, leaving them to worry about simply containing the spread of the disease—a tricky enough problem in its own right.

There's certainly something to be said for Mbeki's vigorous intellectual independence. He won't be told what to do by anyone. But even Mbeki's supporters fear that his stubbornness on AIDS may be increasing the risks to his countrymen. Pressure is growing for him to re-evaluate his contrarian stance on HIV and—at the very least—to allow AZT treatment for pregnant women. That demand in particular was endorsed last Friday by a man Mbeki can't easily refuse: Nelson Mandela.

—*By Tony Karon.*
With reporting by Peter Hawthorne/
Cape Town and Karen Tumulty/

Breaking the Silence

AIDS experts are convening in South Africa, one of the nations suffering most from the plague. Task one: get kids to wise up to what's killing them. The story of a crisis within a crisis.

BY TOM MASLAND

LIKE TEENAGERS EVERYWHERE, THE girls of Khayelitsha Site B understand that breaking up with a boyfriend can be painful. But in this dirt-poor squatter camp on the outskirts of Cape Town, teen love gone sour carries special risks. A jilted boy—or one who suspects his girlfriend is playing the field—will sometimes retaliate by subjecting the girl to group sex with his friends. "They ask you to go somewhere, and the others are all there," says Asanda Sizani, 16, as her friends abandon skipping rope in a dusty field to cluster around a visitor. "Seven or eight boys in a room. They discuss about you, decide among themselves and they line up. They call it *ifoli*." (*Foli* means "line.") Another girl chimes in. "If you don't want him, he is going to do it," says Hosipho Jentile, 17. "This is a rape. But only the strongest report it." Adds Sizani: "Most of the girls here get pregnant or they get AIDS."

Ifoli may be extreme behavior, practiced by a minority. But the casual manner in which South African teens discuss coercive relationships and unprotected sex is staggering, and reflects a crisis within a crisis. Adolescents everywhere are occasionally oblivious to their own mortality, and the youth of southern Africa are no exception. But what is abhorrent or risky behavior elsewhere can be suicidal—or homicidal—here. Sub-Saharan Africa faces the worst AIDS plague on the planet, and South Africa is one of the worst-hit countries. Some 4.2 million South Africans are living with AIDS, and the overall HIV-infection rate has jumped to nearly 20 percent, from 13 percent in 1998.

Appalling new statistics on the AIDS crisis will be a special focus of this week's 13th Annual International AIDS Conference in Durban, South Africa. The theme is "Break the Silence." UNICEF will make news by announcing results of a recent study on the spread of HIV among young people. Those figures will underscore mortality projections announced two weeks ago by UNAIDS, the Geneva-based umbrella organization. Among the findings: HIV infection rates are far higher among African teenage girls than among boys, in part because of physiology and also because the girls often have sex with older men; and about half of all 15-year-olds in the worst-hit countries will die of the disease. AIDS already has left more than 12 million orphans. Other studies are equally alarming. In Luanshya, Zambia, missionary Robert Bona recently tested 200 teenage schoolgirls for HIV. All but four were HIV-positive.

That makes 196 more teenage girls among millions of walking dead. There is no vaccine for AIDS, and severe poverty and grossly inadequate health services put the most effective treatments for prolonging the lives of people with HIV beyond reach for the overwhelming majority of Africans. In the absence of a cure, prevention is far and away the best way to combat the disease. And prevention can mean only one thing: changing sexual behavior and attitudes.

That's a battle many African governments have been hesitant to wage. In South Africa, politicians have been slow to treat AIDS with the urgency it deserves—and President Thabo Mbeki has recently come under fire for flirting with controversial theories about the causes of AIDS. But leaders have publicized the dangers of unsafe sex. In the early 1990s the new black-led government was preoccupied with making a peaceful transition from white-minority rule. Nonetheless it put a nationwide AIDS-awareness program in place. Information was delivered via "life skills" classes in public high schools. Posters went up that mimicked liberation slogans:

VIVA CONDOMS! Nearly every public official in South Africa, from Mbeki down, has worn a red AIDS ribbon.

Yet those and other efforts to break through to teenagers about the dangers the young face—and about the right of a woman to refuse sex—have so far proved no match for custom, cultural confusion and peer pressure. "They say, 'We are going to die anyway, so what's the use of using a condom'," says Sheila Mathemba, 20, of the Viros, a township rap group. "They say, 'Unless it's flesh on flesh, it's not real sex.' They don't want to take responsibility." The group's latest song declares: "AIDS is going to kill you—you vibe [party] and vibe all these weekends, but you don't care about yourself."

Why has the safe-sex effort failed so abjectly? The best answer may be that changing the way people act during their most private moments isn't easy under the best of circumstances. "I don't think we know about what influences behavior and how to change behavior," says Dr. Dave Pinchuck, a psychologist who heads a clinic serving schools in the impoverished Cape Flats. "There is so much coercion. For a lot of girls there is no choice."

Deeply ingrained customs and modern upheavals have both fed the crisis. In many precolonial African societies, it was common for successful men to take multiple brides, sometimes by paying a dowry—usually cows—to members of the bride's family. In some cultures, widows were expected to become the wives of a brother-in-law or other relative. Many such practices now survive alongside imported beliefs, which can also be controversial: Roman Catholicism, for instance, forbids the use of condoms. The problem of reaching South African teenagers, in particular, may be exacerbated because of the recent political past. The

A Plague on the Young

Throughout sub-Saharan Africa—the zone most devastated by AIDS—young people are becoming increasingly vulnerable to the epidemic. A look at the tragically youthful face of AIDS:

SUFFER THE CHILDREN

African children represent the vast majority of kids around the world affected by AIDS, many of them inheriting HIV at birth.

CHILDREN UNDER 15 YEARS	SUB-SAHARAN AFRICA	REST OF THE WORLD
Living with HIV/AIDS, end of 1999	1.0 million	0.3 million
Newly infected during 1999	515,000	105,000
Deaths during 1999	430,000	50,000
Deaths from beginning of epidemic to end of 1999	3.3 million	0.5 million
Orphaned by AIDS at end of 1999	12.1 million	1.1 million

THE UNPROTECTED

Percentage of young people 15–19 who say they do not know of any way to protect themselves against HIV/AIDS

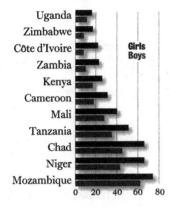

Girls
Boys

Uganda
Zimbabwe
Côte d'Ivoire
Zambia
Kenya
Cameroon
Mali
Tanzania
Chad
Niger
Mozambique

0 20 40 60 80

DEVASTATED YOUTH

Women of all ages are more likely than men to become infected with HIV. But young girls are particularly vulnerable to the virus. Percentage of 15–25-year-olds living with HIV/AIDS:

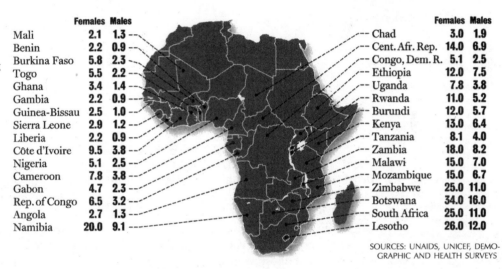

	Females	Males
Mali	2.1	1.3
Benin	2.2	0.9
Burkina Faso	5.8	2.3
Togo	5.5	2.2
Ghana	3.4	1.4
Gambia	2.2	0.9
Guinea-Bissau	2.5	1.0
Sierra Leone	2.9	1.2
Liberia	2.2	0.9
Côte d'Ivoire	9.5	3.8
Nigeria	5.1	2.5
Cameroon	7.8	3.8
Gabon	4.7	2.3
Rep. of Congo	6.5	3.2
Angola	2.7	1.3
Namibia	20.0	9.1

	Females	Males
Chad	3.0	1.9
Cent. Afr. Rep.	14.0	6.9
Congo, Dem. R.	5.1	2.5
Ethiopia	12.0	7.5
Uganda	7.8	3.8
Rwanda	11.0	5.2
Burundi	12.0	5.7
Kenya	13.0	6.4
Tanzania	8.1	4.0
Zambia	18.0	8.2
Malawi	15.0	7.0
Mozambique	15.0	6.7
Zimbabwe	25.0	11.0
Botswana	34.0	16.0
South Africa	25.0	11.0
Lesotho	26.0	12.0

SOURCES: UNAIDS, UNICEF, DEMO-GRAPHIC AND HEALTH SURVEYS

country suffered what Mbeki has called a "moral collapse" during the apartheid years, when the government institutionalized racism. Black children were encouraged to reject authority, and adults have had a hard time restoring control.

Violence against women has become all too common—and accepted—by young people of both sexes. According to a three-year study released last month by Johannesburg's Southern Metropolitan Local Council, eight out of 10 young men think women are responsible or partly responsible for causing sexual violence. Twelve percent of young women believe they have no right to avoid sexual abuse, and more than half of the young people interviewed—both male and female—believe that forcing sex with someone you know does not constitute sexual violence. There is often a double standard at work: men are frequently proud to have mistresses, yet they also consider it shameful to a fam-

ily when a person dies of AIDS. For that reason physicians often falsify death certificates of their patients, obliquely marking the cause as "heart failure" or "stopped breathing." The teenagers most at risk think they don't know anyone who has died of AIDS. "People choose not to look into the face of the monster," says Roland Jethro, a history teacher at Guguletu Comprehensive High School near Cape Town.

Frank talk with students at Guguletu Comprehensive is eye-opening. Many boys want to have a "bestie"—No. 1 girlfriend—and secondary girlfriends, known as the "bread." Girls want one boyfriend for love, one to "stun"—or look good with—and others for backup in case their boyfriends leave them. Girls complain that their boyfriends won't use condoms, especially if they've been partying. "Sex with a condom," says one young man, "is like eating a sweet with the wrapper on." A new national survey of people 15 to 30 found only half said they had used protec-

tion the last time they had sex—a figure that may be high.

South African officials insist they're finally seizing the nettle of sex education. The new strategy focuses on talking the kids' language, and using deejays and others with credibility among teenagers to spread the word. Straight talk—and street talk—may not be enough, however. South Africa's best-known singer, Miriam Makeba, plans to invite pop stars to an AIDS-awareness concert this fall in Pretoria, where the singers will also tape public-service announcements to be aired around the continent. But what teenagers really need, Makeba says, is to be terrified. "We have to have people see someone who is about to die from AIDS, and that person must tell the story," she told NEWSWEEK. "We have to shake them and show them that this thing exists and it kills, by showing them someone talking . . . from their deathbed." In the best-case scenario, South African kids will eventually think it's cool to look the monster square in the face, and live to tell the tale.

AMSTERDAMNED

Has Holland's decriminalization of prostitution and recreational drugs created a beacon of social tolerance or, as its critics contend, transformed a majestic city into a cesspool of depravity?

By Anita Dubey

Like the toreador's cape to the tantalized bull, Amsterdam's famous red-light district casts a magnetic spell over the thousands of university students who descend upon the city each summer. The Van Gogh Museum, the tulip fields, the tranquil canals and quays of the "Venice of the North" are must-sees, but most young travelers come to Amsterdam with two items foremost on their itineraries: to get high and to get laid.

Just five minutes away from Amsterdam's Central Station, the red-light district offers two commodities you can't legally purchase in virtually any other Western nation: pot and sex. On busy evenings, the area is like an adults-only carnival, with sightseers, clients and drug dealers all prowling the sex shops and red-lit window brothels. The prostitutes, preening or looking bored in their lingerie, charge about $25 for 20 minutes. For first-timers, it can be a monstrous display of sleaze.

Designated debauchery may be the best way to term the Dutch method. Rather than penalizing vice, they monitor it. Rather than trying to jail appetite, they localize it. It's an approach that keeps order and rakes in taxes in the process. And it's kinder to everyone involved. "The core of how the Dutch think is the same as everyone," says Pascale Geerts of The Red Thread (De Rode Draad), a prostitutes' advocacy organization. "They just try to solve problems in different ways." And the solution they have decided upon is not to criminalize pot and prostitution but to control and confine them. Clearly drawn red-light districts and streetwalking zones keep the naughtiness away from residential neighborhoods and shopping areas. Coffee shops selling marijuana and hash can't sell alcohol and are limited on how much dope they can stock and sell.

Tolerance has been part of the Dutch character for centuries. German Jews and Chinese sailors were among those seeking refuge in Amsterdam in the 20th century, while in earlier centuries it was French Hugonots and other European Jews. But permitting drugs and prostitution tests the reaches of tolerance. "[Holland] is a humanistic place that lets everyone do what they want, as long as they don't bother anyone else," says Corrie Louwerier, owner of the coffee shop Homegrown Fantasy, echoing what could pass for a national slogan.

She says her name is Kelly. Twenty years old, attractive, energetic and chatty in a way that makes you feel you've known her for a while, she leads me to the window brothel she rents in Amsterdam's Red Light District, in an alley beside the Old

 From *Ego*, Premiere Issue, pp. 33-39. © 2000 by Ego Magazine. Reprinted by permission.

Church. One tequila has her loosened up. Without it, she explains, "I feel shy to stand in the window at first." She'll have more later, to get her through the night.

We step into her window to enter a small, clean room with a single bed and sink, which rents at $85 a night. "I love sex. I love S&M," she says as she sets out potpourri, candles and incense. "I charge 100 guilders for a fuck 'n' suck." Kelly lays down her own rules. She doesn't have a pimp, unlike many girls. "It is not possible to touch my titties. Extra activities like that cost more."

She changes from jeans into chunky black high heels, a black camisole and panties with the word "fuck" written all over in all sizes. She steps back to show off her body piercings. There's one through each nipple, one in her belly button and one through her shaved genitals. As she places a stuffed cow with a watch on its neck near the bed, she tells me the cow was a gift from a girlfriend, and the watch, a fake Gucci, from an ex-boyfriend. Kelly says her mom kicked her out when she got pregnant at the age of 15. She stayed with a friend and had an abortion. Then one night, some girls took her out to work and she made $250. There was no looking back. Now, each night, six times a week, she gets at least 10 customers and makes $1,000. "Every day I get money and I spend money," Kelly says. "The sex and money are the best part."

Of course, some of the Dutch are bothered, but there isn't any serious talk of forbidding cannabis use or suppressing prostitution. They had their chance. In the 1960s, hippies and students were lighting up joints in public for the first time, in droves. Initially, they were arrested, but soon the Dutch set up two government commissions to determine a policy. Both commissions looked at drugs based on their risks and the context in which they were used. Their final reports warned that stigmatizing users could be more

HOW TO RUN A COFFEE SHOP

First, you'll need a license from the city. It costs about $400 for two years. Next, you need product. Here's where it gets tricky. You can sell up to five grams to customers as long as they're 18. But it's actually illegal for suppliers to sell to you. So you have to have some underground connections. Once things are up and running, make sure you never stock more than 500 grams. Be careful; they're pretty serious about confiscating pot around here. In fact, in the last decade, the Dutch regularly seized more each year than any European Union country, except Spain. The police may drop by three or four times a year to weigh your inventory and check customers' IDs. Screw up, you could lose your permit. Keep in mind, too, it's not the most reputable venture. "My two kids couldn't say their mom had a coffee shop," says Louwerier. You'll need a euphemism. "Convenience store" works.

damaging than the drugs themselves and separated "soft" drugs like cannabis from "hard" drugs like heroin and cocaine. "If you distinguish the risks, it's possible to enter a more rational discussion than if you dismiss all drugs with a grand sweep," says Peter Cohen, an associate professor and director of the Center for Drug Research at the University of Amsterdam.

This distinction eventually became part of the country's Opium Act in 1976, which essentially decriminalized the possession of cannabis for personal use. The Netherlands couldn't violate the international Single Convention on Narcotic Drugs it had signed in 1961, so, technically, it is illegal to possess cannabis. But the government did choose to prosecute selectively so that people who bought for personal use wouldn't be arrested. For serious drug users, treatment, not

prison, was considered the preferred penalty. The first coffee shops opened in the late 1970s. Today there are more than 1,000 outlets selling cannabis products across the country, as well as smart shops offering magic mushrooms.

Louwerier, a former nurse, opened Homegrown Fantasy in central Amsterdam 11 years ago. She stocks 17 kinds of Dutch-grown pot. Her store is a cozy place where, she says, "people can smoke a joint, socialize, play games, be creative." She has customers of all ages, including seniors who buy bonbons and cakes for medical problems. "[Pot] is kind of like a tranquilizer. People take it to be quiet. There's no harm done. The government earns money while people [become] docile." She says her only problems have been with customers who'd been drinking elsewhere, after she refused to sell to them.

It would figure that with legalization, the majority would give cannabis a try, but that hasn't happened. Overall, about 16 percent of the Dutch say they've smoked pot, according to a 1997 national study. Compare that number to Germany, which has a slightly lower rate at 14 percent, or to the United Kingdom, where 22 percent have used, according to figures from the European Monitoring Centre for Drugs and Drug Addiction. "It has shown that making access to drugs easier does not make people use them," says Cohen. The United States, meanwhile, has double the rate of marijuana use as the Netherlands. Americans risk being thrown in jail, but 33 percent of them said they've tried the drug at some point in their lives.

Where the Dutch system falters is in underage sales. Among those aged 12 to 17 who brought cannabis, 40 percent said they got it from a coffee shop, which is illegal. But the policy has separated the markets, as intended. When asked where they bought cocaine, amphetamines or Ecstasy, about three-quarters of Dutch adults mentioned family, friends, acquaintances or home dealers. Just two percent mentioned coffee shops.

"There isn't any hard drug use here," says Louwerier. "It's a very good way to regulate people."

Finding a way to govern prostitution has been a more recent exercise. With the explosion of the sex industry in the '70s and '80s, Amsterdam, a city of 700,000, had about 400 window brothels and 50 sex clubs. Things were clearly getting out of hand.

As with cannabis, official policy eventually changed to reflect practice and to regulate it. Last year, the Dutch government approved the regulation of voluntary prostitution. When the law goes into effect in October, cities will have powerful new opportunities to manage the industry through local licensing of brothels. To many, the law is also a step forward in acknowledging prostitution as a profession. "We see it as a good development," says Geerts. "Doors will be opened. It's a new step in the recognition that prostitutes exist."

To get and keep a license, a brothel must fulfill criteria related to its location (away from schools or churches), building conditions (ensuring safety and hygiene) and management (no forced drinking, unsafe sex or illegal workers). City officials can enter brothels to inspect them. City bylaws can be used to close down offenders, which is easier then using courts to prosecute for pimping, according to the Institute for Prostitution Issues in Amsterdam.

From a consumer's point of view, the downside is that while licensing has sanitized the profession, it has also sterilized it. "When you enter a brothel now, it's like going to a butcher's place," says Geerts. "Tiles have replaced carpets. It's become a clean thing, where it used to be furry and red. All the mystery of the atmosphere is disappearing."

There are side effects to all this broad-mindedness, those who don't participate in the sex-and-drug trade still have to live with it—and near it. Anton Bruning, an athletic 27-year-old Amsterdam resident, for more than three years lived near the Leidseplein, a square packed with bars, coffee shops and restaurants. "Sometimes you see totally stoned or very drunk tourists throwing up in front of your house, and you wonder if the system works so well," Bruning says.

Plus, the grander attractions of Amsterdam, the canals and museums, get obscured. Bruning says he once went sightseeing with a Japanese visitor who told him the Red Light District was the best thing he'd ever seen after the Great Wall of China. Still, Bruning points out that most people who live in central Amsterdam choose to do so and accept the nuisance. He wouldn't raise a family in the city—not to avoid the sex and drugs, but because it's crowded and kids have no place to play.

Most Dutch tolerate legal prostitution, which is not the same thing as accepting it. "The attitude is, 'you can be a prostitute, but please not on my street,'" says Mariska Majoor, the 31-year-old founder of the Prostitute Information Center. In the late '70s, prostitutes began prowling outside the red-light districts and disturbing residents. City bylaws ban streetwalking, so police responded with arrests. "When you put pressure on one area, you get a problem somewhere else," says Piet Valkenburg, an officer with Utrecht Police Department.

One solution was to set aside designated areas for streetwalking, called tolerance zones. It was not a popular idea at first. "There's something dirty and really weird about it," says Bruning. "But I think it works." But when the first zones open in the '80s, they were met with protests and vandalism. On the opening night of Amsterdam's tolerance zone, neighboring residents blocked the roads and set tires on fire. "Everybody says it's good we have these streetwalking zones," says Marieke van Doorninck, a policy consultant, "but nobody wants a streetwalking zone in their neighborhood."

Out of this mess the Dutch did eventually create successful tolerance zones in eight cities. The zone in Utrecht, a city of 210,000, is considered a model example. Opened in 1986, it is accessible to the city center by public transportation. A police presence several nights a week helps keep order and ensures that all prostitutes working there are registered. Between 7 p.m. and 2 a.m. each night, sex workers are allowed to walk along a designated area as cars cruise by. The transaction takes place in a parking area, complete with dividers for privacy, called a "finishing-off zone."

PROSTITUTE POWER

The Red Thread has been protecting prostitutes' concerns since 1984. But it hasn't become a true union as originally envisioned. "The stigma is too great to become a member," says spokesperson Pascale Geerts. With the new law governing the sex industry going on the books in October, things may change. The Red Thread is hoping to unionize, but Geerts doesn't know how it will play out. "The word 'prostitution' has a subconscious, archetypal meaning for all people. Even psychologists project their traumas on you," says Geerts, a feisty, articulate 30-year-old who joined an escort service to help cover costs when she was studying psychology at the University of Amsterdam.

Part of the effort to get prostitution legitimized is obtaining group health care. So far it's been denied, though a deal with an insurance company once came close. "At the last minute, the company refused," says Marieke van Doorninck of the Institute for Prostitution Issues. "They said they had Christian clients who wouldn't like it. The prostitutes replied that they had Christian clients, too."

Streetwalking, meanwhile, has vanished from the city center. "I think the concept of a tolerance zone works with certain conditions," says Mariska van Keulen, manager of the Association of Living Room Projects. "You need cooperation with the police and trust from the women. The zone must be close to the center of the city and have a finishing-off area it's also important to involve residents at an early stage."

Prostitutes are fined $120 for working outside the zone, with increasing penalties for each offense. But fines aren't the biggest incentive to follow the rules. Last summer, a prostitute went outside the zone with a customer, says van Keulen. She was beaten up and died two days later.

Even if it appears more orderly, the sex industry is harsher than it was 20 years ago. The growth in sex clubs and influx of migrant prostitutes after the fall of Communism drove prices down. Prostitutes now do more for less money. "When I was working, anal sex was outrageous," says Geerts. "Now, it's common." There are also more competing outlets. "There's the porno industry, sex telephone lines and the Internet. There's also Dutch TV. Zap it on, and you see silicone tits everywhere.

"Tell the Americans," Geerts jokes, "if they want to get rid of prostitution, they should legalize it."

To survive, she says, prostitutes will have to specialize in techniques that only a live body can provide. Last week, a man wanted Kelly to pee in his mouth for $250. She thought it was sick, but she did it. Once a guy wanted her to walk all over his body and face in high heels, but she couldn't do it and sent him off to a friend.

She wouldn't work as a streetwalker or with an escort service, where she'd be forced to do things she didn't want. Working without a pimp, she's in control, and she's happy for now. "It's just like a normal job," she says. If a guy gives her trouble, she can call out to the girls next door, or push a button and the cops will be there in five minutes.

The future? She says it can wait. She's had offers to fly to the U.S. to work in the porn industry, where she was told she could make $20,000 a day. But she doesn't want to give up her window—the summer tourist season is around the corner.

The **world** made
flesh

Bodies. Human bodies.
We love them.
We need them. But
examine the body,
and you will see a lot
more besides, argues
Vanessa Baird.

Along the white corridors are garish, coloured illustrations showing parts of the body I hardly knew existed, let alone cared about.

They take on particular significance now, some organs and their functions especially so.

We make our way, down one floor, to the operating theatre. Above its twin doors are strict instructions not to enter. A few yards away, opposite the doors, are a couple of tables with blue covered chairs. Here we sit and wait.

Not for the first time am I aware of a horrible congruence. I was in the early stages of putting together this issue of the **NI** on the theme of 'the body' and had just finished commissioning the main articles, when there was a phone-call saying that a close relative has been taken quite unexpectedly, seriously, ill.

He is now behind those swing doors, fighting for his life.

Strangely, during these hours, while his actual body is undergoing a massive medical assault, it's not his body that fills my consciousness. Maybe because it doesn't bear thinking about. But I don't think this is the only reason.

As I gaze out of the window, up to the dark, ragged fringes of fir trees on the snow-clad mountains, I think not of his body but of his love for snow. And as I watch the birds darting and weaving between the eves, their lives and gestures so vital yet vulnerable, it's his vitality, his spirit that fills my mind.

After ten hours in the operating theatre the surgeon comes out. The operation was very tricky, but it's worked. The patient has age and strength on his side.

The next day we visit him. The first thing he does, in between all the tubes, and without a moment's hesitation, is to beckon and kiss us each in turn.

And it's perfect. The simplest, most direct way of expressing all the love, fear, relief, hope, gratitude. Bodily communicating what desperately needs to be said, but would take volumes to say in words.

Body politics

Returning to Oxford I find, on my desk, the piles of books I'd started reading on 'the body'. It's a trendy, 'hip' area of study these days. Much of the work is being done not by biologists but by philosophers, psychoanalysts and feminist theorists, drawing inspiration from French thinkers such as Hélène Cixous, Jacques Lacan, Michel Foucault, Jacques Derrida or Luce Irigaray. Debates on the 'materiality' versus the 'discursivity' of the body abound. And a lot of it is frankly impenetrable to the general reader.

I flick open one of the less jargon-bound collections and read: 'The body of woman is the site where culture manufactures the blockade of woman.' My mind quietly boggles at the prospect. Another text offers: 'Poststructuralist discourse analysis engages with the extra discursive of social reality (social practices, institutions etc) and of *corporeal* bodies (their physical beings) . . .' Well, there you are.

I find it hard to relate these writings either to the feelings aroused by the personal experience of the body of a loved one at risk or to the subjects that lie at the heart of the *New Internationalist's* concerns. Issues like the right to the basic, vital things your body needs to survive: food, water, shelter, access to healthcare. The right not to have your body violated by others, be they oppressive regimes, employers or those with most clout within your family or community.

But there is a connection. These texts may not dwell on what bodies need, but they do examine what bodies 'mean'. And what bodies 'mean' in a particular culture or society actually plays a crucial role in determining who can have what they need in their lives and who can't.

More explicitly, inequalities in the world are established and maintained by the 'meaning' that we give different bodies.

It's often extremely crude. For example, in many parts of the world, if you are born with a female body you are automatically denied control over your own life. You are the possession of your father or your brothers or your uncles until you become that of your husband and later your sons. Inferiority is 'read' into your body at birth. Your very chances of survival may be affected. In Bangladesh girls have a 70-percent higher mortality rate than boys for the simple reasons that they are fed less and are less likely than their brothers to be taken to a health clinic if ill.[1]

Gender is not the only issue. Not so long ago—before 1994 to be precise—if you were one of the 30 million South Africans with a black-skinned body you had to live in designated areas and were not even allowed to vote in elections in your own country.

The stamping of inequality on our bodies occurs in an infinite variety of ways. If you are disabled you generally do not have the same rights to a job or to mainstream education as an able-bodied person. In many countries—Romania springs to mind—you

From *New Internationalist,* April 1998, pp. 7-10. © 1998 by New Internationalist Publications, Ltd. Reprinted by permission.

are likely to be incarcerated in an institution at birth.

Body prejudice also comes in more subtle guises. It may be focused on what you actually do with your body. If you come from a class background in which it is usual to sell your bodily or manual skills rather than your cerebral abilities then the chances are you will receive lower wages and be less valued for the work you do. Unless, that is, you happen to enjoy the elevated status of a sports celebrity or supermodel.

Finally, your chances in life can be determined by whether your body conforms to your society's ideals of beauty. This has been particularly true for women. Without political or economic power, a woman is entirely dependent on male patronage and thus male ideas of how she should behave and appear. Typically, this is internalized by women and becomes an obsessive concern with physical appearance. It's not just a case of 'you are your body', but 'you are what your body looks like'. If you have any doubts about the continued power and prevalence of this, consult any magazine rack.

If we look at the body, we can see the world. If we look at how different bodies— black, white, male, female, rich, poor—are viewed, and what kind of privileges or privations that accrue to them, then we see a picture of the world of human, social and economic relationships. In this sense the body is 'the world made flesh'.

Skinny things and nipple rings

And look at bodies we do. For we are fascinated by them. Although most major religions in the world maintain that our temporal bodies are not the most important thing in life and it's our eternal souls that really count, body-consciousness rules supreme.

It makes sense in a way. Our bodies are our prime source of pleasure and pain, our first point of contact with the world. What would our lives in the world be without our bodies? They are a source of delight. Cultures and religions that have tried to deny the flesh have almost always lapsed into hypocrisy. Such regimes—be they Catholic or Puritan—become obsessed with the flesh, especially female flesh. The women in Tehran or Kabul trying to navigate kerbs and potholes via the tiny permissible slits in their veils, are at the sharp end of such denials.

The joys of physicality may be simple, like feeling the air on your face as you step out on a Spring morning. The cold smoothness of a stone. The rugged bark of a tree. The exhilaration of water. The comfort of the bodies of loved ones. The intimacy of loving eroticism. The magic of sex.

The body is also an amazingly powerful medium for transmitting information and emotions between living creatures. Even when people are speaking to each other face-

to-face, two-thirds of their communication is non-verbal body-language.[2]

But our fascination with the body far exceeds these simple functions and pleasures. It can also be a very potent zone of self expression, giving scope to tremendous creativity on the one hand, dreary uniformity on the other. It has lead to extraordinary feats of dance and athletics, and dazzling displays of imagination when it comes to adornment.

The young and trendy wear Billabong, be they in Brisbane or Bogotá

International and popular culture bombards us non-stop with body consciousness. Beautiful bodies are used to sell almost anything. And there's a lot of money to be made in the products and services of the body business, be they the provision of fashionable 'energy' drinks or cosmetic surgery. As Jeremy Seabrook says in his article *Of human bondage* (see "New Internationalist," April 1998) human bodies are the world's biggest cash crop. The body is both the means of industrial production and the market for its products.

What the body business most profitably taps into is our use of our bodies to identify ourselves. This need is fundamental and universal. Tribal markings are everywhere to be seen: in the etched cheeks of a Yoruba villager in Southern Nigeria and the pierced nipple of a gay teenager in a Liverpool night-club; in the pure-silk sari of the Bombay socialite and the designer tie of the Wall Street financier.

With the globalization of the world economy, and the aggressive marketing of 'cool' body images, the definitions of desirability and available identities seem to become increasingly narrow. The young and trendy wear Billabong cult clothing, be they in Brisbane or Bogotá. And traditional aesthetics are rapidly being replaced by a Westernized, globalized image.

Nowhere is this more painfully expressed than in the hyper-slender model for women, the 'Barbie-doll' look that has swept the world. Recently there have been reports of anorexia—previously thought to affect only white middle-class teenagers—among young black women in Southern Africa. 'In African culture beauty is traditionally associated with round bodies but as Western culture creeps into this society, so anorexia is affecting more and more Africans,' quotes Tsitso Rampuku, reporting from Lesotho, where there has been a spate of recent cases.

Across the border, in South Africa, it's a similar story. Malinda Motaung, a nurse

working in Bloemfontein, says she has noticed a big increase in an illness that was unknown in her clinic five years ago. Mampho Mokhethe, mother of a 17-year-old anorectic, blames this on the way young urban women are bombarded with images of beautiful and successful women. 'And almost without fail, they are thin,' she says. 'The subtle message is: if you want to get ahead, you had better look like supermodel Naomi Campbell.'[3]

Anorexia has to do with more than fashion. It has to do with power. Although a few males are affected, it's mainly a female problem. For many young women, eating is the area in which they feel they can have real control. US academic Susan Bordo quotes Aimee Liu, an ex-anorectic recreating her mindset at the time of her illness: 'Energy, discipline, my own power will keep me going. I need nothing and no-one else . . . I will be master of my own body, if nothing else, I vow.'

Like the flesh-denying ascetic, the anorectic's ability to live with minimal food makes her feel powerful and worthy of admiration in a world from which, at the most profound level, she feels excluded and unvalued.[4]

The terrible irony is that it is so self-defeating. As Bordo points out, the symptoms of anorexia isolate, weaken and undermine its sufferer, as she turns the life of the body into an all-absorbing fetish. In effect she capitulates to patriarchy's traditional demand that women limit themselves and live in a shrunken world.

Ultimately others—principally medical professionals—intervene, and take control.

The body in parts

Few encounters require that we willingly submit our bodies to a group of strangers, to examine, prod, poke, inject and even cut open. But that, in theory, is what we do when we cross the threshold into a doctor's surgery or a hospital. If you are in pain or in danger it's only natural to want someone to make you better, to magic the trouble away. You may feel so grateful to that person that you don't question too closely the magic they are using, or its premise. The power we hand over to our chosen healers is really quite astounding when you stop to think about it.

Until the 1970s the authority of orthodox Western medicine went virtually unchallenged. Although it borrows much of its terminology from the Classical Greeks, it does not use the same premise that mind, spirit and body are interconnected. Rather it uses the Cartesian notion that mind and body are quite separate entities and the body is but a kind of biological machine.

This mechanistic view has given birth to the stereotype of the consultant zooming in on an organ or a condition, ignoring the person it belongs to and then talking to colleagues about it in technical language the patient doesn't understand. This is not just the hackneyed stuff of comic movies. Although slowly changing, it's still the experience of many people around the world when they come into contact with the medical profession.

Medical anthropologist Nancy Scheper-Hughes reports that poor people in Brazil fear that health professionals will 'steal their organs' for transplant. This fear is in a sense realistic, but it can also be seen as a symbolic response to a medical approach that has scant regard for the integrity of the human being.

In the rich world, too, there is growing disenchantment with Western medical system that treats people as though their bodies were machines, with parts that may go wrong and need discrete and specific treatment.

This has fed the growth of 'holistic' approaches and alternative therapies. Most popular are acupuncture, homeopathy and osteopathy. More than one in three people in Britain has consulted an alternative health practitioner, and similar figures apply in Australia, Canada and the US. Even the World Health Organization has criticized doctors for failing to accept acupuncture as a useful complementary medical technique.

Many argue that the boom in alternative medicine is giving patients choice and more power over their own bodies. This is debatable, as some alternative practitioners can be even more interventionist and paternalistic than orthodox doctors.[5]

But the idea that mind, body and spirit are interconnected, and that they have their own self-healing mechanisms, is gaining currency even in the most unexpected quarters.

I recall the surgeon who operated on my relative. He had said prior to the operation that during it he would be doing half the work, the patient would be doing the other half. And as I watched the birds and thought of the flow of his mind, body and spirit, this felt absolutely right.

One body, one world

We tend to think of the body as an entity with firm contours. In fact it is mainly fluid: two-thirds of it is water. If we thought of our bodies more in this way, I wonder what difference it would make. Would our thinking about our bodies be less hard and possessive? Would we think in terms of sharing an economy of vitality? Would we think differently about inner and outer, about self and other, about the boundary between your body and my body?

The word 'body' is not always personal and individualistic. It can also be used to describe a collection of people. It's long been recognized by ethicists that belonging to a 'social body' makes it possible to equate one's own good with that of another and thus to refrain from mutual injury, violence and exploitation. Why shouldn't the terms of reference be expanded to include the universal body, the international body of humanity?

Let's conclude with a little holistic exercise. The world is a body, your body. The top half of your body, the Northern part, say, gets all the goodness it needs to survive and more. In some parts it's actually quite bloated.

The bottom half, the Southern part, say, is in a state of perpetual struggle to get what it needs to survive. It has plenty of vitality, is capable of joy, but somehow it never gets quite enough goodness or nourishment in relation to the energy it expends just to stay alive.

In between the two, somewhere below your belly, is a belt. A very tight belt. It has to be that way, you are told, because your Northern body and your Southern body are different.

Not a very healthy state of affairs. Might it not be a good idea to loosen the belt a bit, let some of the goodness and nourishment flow around the whole body? Wouldn't Northern and Southern body benefit from this?

Your toes would probably agree.

1 United Nations, *Women: Challenges to the Year 2000,* New York, 1991. 2 Alan Pease, *Body Language,* Sheldon Press, 1997. 3 Tsitso Rampuku, 'Health fears as slimming mania hits Africans', Gemini News Service, London, 1997. 4 Susan Bordo, *Unbearable Weight: Feminism, Western Culture and the Body,* University of California Press, 1993. 5 Dr Vernon Coleman, *Spiritpower,* European Medical Journal, Barnstaple, 1997.

THE MALE BOX

Could it be a trend? Two books in the last few months that take a feminist look at men. Susan Faludi's *Stiffed* (which raised the hackles of just about every man who reviewed it) explores modern men adrift in a world with no satisfactory definition of masculinity. Suzanne Braun Levine's *Father Courage* (out in April) takes a look at the gentler side of guydom. It's a given that we can't make our feminist revolution without one half of the world's population. So we asked Faludi and Levine to talk about the things they discovered while on the trail of the new man.

Interview by Gloria Jacobs

Gloria Jacobs: What made you both want to look at men now? Men are part of the feminist revolution, and yet for a long time it felt that the way to achieve our goals was to see men as the enemy. What's different now?

Suzanne Braun Levine: There's a generation of women whose expectations are greatly expanded. The guys that I spoke to—who were mainly middle-class—had no idea about patriarchy, or feminism even, but they had grown up in households where women were effective; they'd gone to school where girls played soccer; they'd gone to college and shared dormitories and bathrooms with women; they expected to work for a woman at some point in their lives; they thought they'd get married to women who would have professional lives; and when they had children, they would continue an equal kind of setup. The big surprise came with children, when suddenly everybody flipped back to the old modes. Women found themselves almost reflexively taking on the classic mother roles, maybe to compensate for their independence. The men fell into the "helpful" role. We're bereft of role models for fatherhood and for equal marriage. We can't look to our parents, ourselves, or our literature. So we fall back on clichés. That's the struggle now: how to sort out the details of making a family work.

Susan Faludi: It struck me, Suzanne, that none of the men you talked to wanted to be like their fathers. It's what I heard, too. There is no desire to emulate the previous generation. At the same time, there's been a breakdown in all the other traditional ways of being a man, whether it is public service, being honored for loyalty, for any kind of sacrifice for the larger good—all that has been swept away by the commercial culture that admires only the guy who is Number One. You pointed out that there is an urgent longing for fatherhood now. That may be the result of not having a role that involves virtue and cooperation and the traditional realms of working and soldiering on.

It's as much about the breakdown of one world as it is about the desire for a new way of being. The upside is that it has caused men, perhaps in desperation, to finally wake up to the world in their own homes. Some of this comes out of the women's movement: we've encouraged ideals of manhood that include being caring fathers, being tender and equal partners. But the rest of the culture is arrayed against that. As much as men are gratified by their domestic experience, you showed that they feel they need to hide it at work, sneak out the back door to go home early. There's no culture outside the home celebrating men for committing themselves to fatherhood.

Levine: I think that's why they were able to talk to you and me. They trusted us.

Jacobs: But that's been a major criticism of Susan's book: why is a woman writing about men? Do we want men to analyze our lives for us?

Faludi: The men who complained about me writing the book were privileged, affluent journalists. I'm still sorting out what their real beef is—there was such hysterical overreaction. Part of it is that some of them deemed the men I wrote about losers because they didn't cash in on the new economy. A lot of these journalists are part of the new ornamental occupations, where it's about display and celebrity mongering. They were uncomfortable looking at men who had been mowed over by

From *Ms.* Magazine, April/May 2000, pp. 63-69. © 2000 by *Ms.* Magazine. Reprinted by permission.

the culture, because it forced them to look at their own complicity in that culture.

I've also noticed that because of the pressure on men to appear armored and invulnerable to other men, they seem to feel more comfortable revealing themselves to a woman. It feels safer. Women journalists may get a more honest self-examination from a man because he doesn't feel he's going to be hung out to dry for showing his vulnerability. He might even be appreciated.

Levine: Over and over again, the men I interviewed turned to their wives to discuss problems, not to other men. One guy I interviewed had two very close male friends, but not one of them would tell the others if he was in emotional trouble. Instead, one guy's wife would call the other two and say "some TLC is in order." Once this revolution is over, a woman won't need to write a book, but at this point men don't have the vocabulary. Men have to figure out ways to learn from each other, the way women have. Now men are learning from women how to discuss their personal lives. But that's like a left-handed person learning from a right-handed person.

Because I was talking about parenting and children, men were especially eager to talk. They were anxious to get credit and to have a pat on the head, because they have so many moments of feeling inadequate—as any parent does, but men aren't used to feeling inadequate. They're out where they know they ought to be, but not getting any of the perks that explorers usually get.

They have to explain what they're doing. There was one guy I loved: his job was cooking dinner, and he had to go away on a business trip so he loaded up the refrigerator. His comment was, "It's just part of the same tradition. We used to go out and shoot woolly mammoths, now we freeze a few casseroles." That's what men have to do: find new ways of feeling engaged in and part of the larger human experience. They're going to have to find and pass on to their children examples of how this works; it's just a big blank now. So I think they were glad to talk about specific things they had done.

Faludi: I think they also wanted credit because the women in their lives often pay lip service to wanting men to bear half the load, but don't really want to give up authority and power in the domestic sphere. So, as you pointed out, there was all this eye-rolling and condescension. Perhaps the men were gratified to talk to a woman who wasn't going to say, "You're not putting that diaper on right."

Levine: If they only saw me at home! As I began to look at my own behavior, it was a revelation in how many ways, large and small, I wanted everything done my way. Partly because of this sense that terrible things would happen if the children were left alone with my husband—he wouldn't look and they'd get burned.

Faludi: And somehow it would be more your fault.

Levine: Right, it would be negligence on my part. There were so many occasions when I came down hard on him for doing it his way, which I still think is wrong, but not deadly, not so seriously different that it wasn't worth a try. That's the challenge for women now: to ask ourselves, is it possible that there is a way to do this that works even half as well as our way and that lets us off the hook a bit?

Faludi: Do you think the problem is that outside of family life there are so few outlets for feeling like you are contributing in a meaningful way, so both men and women are struggling over who is going to be in charge? The domestic sphere is increasingly the only place where you feel you are doing something that gives a sense of meaning to your life. What struck me with so many of the men you talked to was that their work wasn't anything they could take pride in. How many voice-mails did I return today? Am I on the fast track? I'm thinking, well, even if you are, what does that mean at the end of the day? And what values do you transmit to your kids?

Levine: I know what you are describing. But I found much more of a concern with how to get a grip on the moral development of children. The real urgency is to play a part in your children's lives, especially if they're teenagers, and not let the culture dominate their values and their personalities.

Jacobs: Many people would argue that we already have a generation of kids who are lost in the consumer culture and don't have a sense of an alternative. In your last chapter, Susan, you talk about the disappearance of the civic community. That's central to both your books.

Faludi: It's like we put the kids out to sea in little rafts. That whole generation of move to the suburbs, buy the split-level ranch, buy your kids a lot of video games—something was not transmitted in the way of a moral vision from one generation to the other. What was transmitted was buy, buy, buy. And struggle in this Darwinian consumer ocean to pop up momentarily and have your 15 minutes of fame.

Levine: It seems to me that ordinary families are embattled in this society, and it's a chicken and egg question as to whether they tuned out because they are embattled or they are embattled because they tuned out. But if you're an ordinary family trying to get through the day, the school system isn't responsive; you have to take the day off to go to a school conference. The community isn't there anymore; community services are frittering away. The national political debate has no relevance. The workplace is running on a time-clock that is Martian. You have to expend so much energy just getting the basic things done, and if you talk about family, only the right-wing creeps jump up and say that they know what the family should be.

My fantasy is that all these guys who are learning to be good fathers are going to get the confidence to speak up and make some political noise. That hasn't come yet, which makes me crazy. Recently there was a proposal that unemployment be allocated for paid parental leave, and people freaked out. If that policy were in place, it would say we support the right to pay attention to your family as much as we support the right to earn a living.

Faludi: But what form would the family policy take? Would it just be about having the right to take time off from work?

Levine: The idea was that you would apply for parental-leave insurance in the same way you now apply for unemployment insurance. But it's more than policy. It's about a mind-set, and until there is more willingness to explore some of these questions, all the policy in the world won't make much difference.

Jacobs: If you're saying families have become the most likely leading edge for change, where does that leave the increasing numbers of people who don't want to be parents? Can a concern for families translate into something larger?

Faludi: At the heart of the crisis for the men I talked to was the feeling that there were no honorable things for them to do in the larger world. I would caution against the desire to retreat to the private world of family. You know, "Let's hunker down into our circle and the rest of the world be damned." We need nurturance in the public realm also. There has to be a maternal masculinity that is expressed through civic service and community building, for women and men both.

Levine: "Maternal masculinity" is a great phrase.

Faludi: What was really gratifying to men who felt secure and confident in their manhood was the sacrifice, the dedication, the quiet shouldering of the burden. All those things are really maternal, but are thought of or codified as masculine.

Levine: Certainly many women who haven't had children have played a role in civic life and have made connections between that life and the personal. So far, that's not as attractive an option for men: the caring public life. Also, family isn't only your children, it's also your parents. Caring for elderly parents is where men who aren't involved with children can still experience some of the intimate domestic responses and responsibilities, so you can make the connection between the personal and political without children.

Jacobs: Can we discuss class? Suzanne, you mainly talked to middle-class men, and Susan, you talked to men who had, to a large extent, been left out of the new economy. I'm wondering if working-class men tend to be more involved with their kids simply because their families can't afford most child care?

Faludi: I don't know that the unavailability of child care makes men better fathers. Being frustrated and harried and burdened doesn't usually make for a good parent. If there were quality child care available these guys would probably be in a position to be thinking more consciously about what kind of parents they want to be, as opposed to just trying to hold it together.

Jacobs: But if you are talking about having to give up power in order to create change, these are men who don't have the power to give up. Do they come at this new world differently because of where they are on the economic ladder?

Faludi: The men I interviewed didn't talk about their children much. I think partly because they were exploring their own feelings about being men and what went wrong. That tended to lead to a discussion about their fathers rather than about their children. So many of these men don't feel they have anything to pass on to their children in the way of a real vision of what it means to be a man.

The Promise Keepers were the only men I interviewed who talked about how to be better fathers, but that led them right back to a consumer world: "I'm going to take more time to go shopping with my kids, and we're going to go to Disney, and we're going to play video games together," and I'm thinking, this is not going to change your children's lives one bit. At the same time they were frustrated; it seemed to be the only way of connecting with their children. They would talk about having religious enlightenment to pass on to their children, but the truth is they hadn't really reached enlightenment. A lot of male journalists I know do talk about the one gratifying thing in their lives being their involvement with their children. These guys are able to work part-time at home, their lives are more fluid and manageable, and they have a sense of control. But the men who don't feel any sense of control think, "My damn father abandoned me in this world where I have no social role."

Levine: Part of the problem is that they don't have ways of imagining themselves taking other paths. I don't think men have begun to try to seize their choices. Look at the way they dress. In the downtown of a big city like New York, most men still wear neckties. It speaks to such a limited array of ways to express yourself. There are so many alternatives that haven't come on the radar screen for men yet, that things look bleaker than they might really be.

Faludi: But there isn't a place where people can talk about envisioning a new way. Even in the '60s there were public spaces where people could meet and talk that were protected, temporarily anyway, from commercial invasion. Now, even if you come out of an impoverished ghetto experience and write a song about it or do a video, either you are totally ignored and end up bankrupt, or you are recognized and immediately coopted by the commercial culture. Whether you are outside the new economy or inside, you are within this ever-present commercial camera eye, which is very damaging to creating real social change. Even the women's movement faces that. How do you break out of it?

Levine: A lot of troublemaking came out of women in the playground, because no one was paying attention. They sat around talking about their lives and began to dream of change. Maybe that's part of the appeal of family life, that no one is spying on you, and so it is a secret place where you can foment change. The problem is that everybody is so busy. People don't even go to the playground anymore, and everybody's on the Internet. Maybe the most revolutionary thing to do is to set up shop in a mall to get people's attention.

Faludi: Or pray that some visionary comes along.

Levine: I keep thinking about some guys who were described to me. They're middle-class guys, and they've got power if they would use it. They're on a teleconference on a Sunday afternoon with their kids in the background, trying to keep the kids at bay while they do business. They get together the next day and say, "Oh, were your kids there? Mine were too. Gee, we're all in the same boat." They're in a better position than we ever were to go into the office and say, "What is wrong with this boat? A Sunday telephone conference is not acceptable. Let's make sure it happens when we can really concentrate." Instead they all laugh and say, "This is some tough game we're in."

Faludi: That's because the values of the business culture utterly conflict with the values that would strengthen home life. We're talking about balance, but can you really balance two things when one is about care and nurturance and the other is about cutting someone's throat? Shouldn't we be challenging this kill-everybody-in-your-path, individualistic culture that is spread by the business world?

Levine: It's not really about balancing family and work; it's about finding a reasonable balance between caring, intimate, and vulnerable qualities versus money-making. You don't have to have children to want to nurture the one, and you shouldn't have to be a shark in order to succeed at the other.

Jacobs: What was most surprising about the dreams or desires of the men you met?

Faludi: Men were talking about things that were parallel in many ways to what women were talking about in the '60s and '70s—feeling they were ornamental and there was pressure to display themselves, not just physically, but in terms of image and status. There was a hollowed-out feeling that they had lost any public utility, which is a familiar tune to so many women who ultimately rebelled against being valued for appearance instead of service, creativity, and public responsibility.

I thought, this is encouraging. Look what happened to women—we gave birth to this profound social transformation. But the men weren't challenging it the way women did in the late '60s. They are beginning to sense that something is wrong, yet they feel they can't talk about it without discrediting their manhood. It goes back to the earlier question of why men open up more to women. In the private sphere manhood is not so contingent on public displays of prowess and accomplishment. They're freer to change themselves and embrace an open, gentle, caring role.

Levine: What struck me was how humble the men I met were before this undertaking they had committed to: "I hope I'm doing it right," "I screwed up here," "I'm not measuring up there," all said with a tenacity and courage I hadn't expected. I began to understand how scary it looks to them to go there. I was more touched than I expected to be. I began to realize how much ground there is between the sense that something needs to be done and the ability to do it. That wasn't as hard for women. We spent a lot of time naming things and being vulnerable with each other. Just naming it is hard for them. The big danger is for us to impose our pattern on this second half of the revolution. If it's going to happen, it's not going to happen in the same sequence or with the same kind of drama as ours did.

Faludi: Probably a lot of the anxiety men feel comes from a fear of losing face. To question the way manhood is set up is to disempower yourself. These guys who are struggling to carve out five minutes with their kids, for them to say out loud, "There are no reins in my hand," is a great humiliation.

Jacobs: Is this naming of the problem something they have to do themselves, or can men and women work together?

Faludi: Maybe women's role is just getting out of the way. Suzanne described the eye-rolling and snide remarks from women. I heard a lot of that when I was traveling around: "Oh, who cares about men's pain, let's get back to ours." I was taken aback by that. Don't you want men to be able to change, if for no other reason than that it will make your life better? Men and women should care about it equally. But how to get men to grapple openly so they can bring this out as a serious political issue, that's the hard part.

Levine: The community most likely to make it possible is the workplace. This can't remain a secret for very long, these things men told us. I can't believe it isn't seeping into conversations and decisions in the workplace. And there are women who are carving out alternative work patterns that may be acceptable to men.

Jacobs: But over the last few decades as women have pushed for more flextime and more help to balance work and family, we've ended up working longer and harder than ever. Flextime and family leave haven't made a dent, because other pressures keep overpowering them.

Levine: It's not a question of how you work, it's how you think. That's why it worries me if more people start working at home and communicating electronically, because you will have no place where the tinderbox can take fire. People stand around the watercooler and in the ladies' room and the men's room—those are places where you can make trouble. Everyone says the Internet is so revolutionary. But a generation that sees its community as people in cyberspace is not going to join together to perform the functions that the physical community needs—including voting. They're not going to school meetings, not meeting their neighbors. And when they're home, they're still working.

Faludi: But the workplaces are so infected with this success-at-all-costs mentality that I'm not sure how much water-cooler discussion there is anymore. Women and men have their heads in front of their computer screens and barely talk to other people at work, which is why they've started working at home. The technology has allowed us to outpace our human clock and our human need for interaction, which takes place on a slower, more plodding level. That level is where political ideas start to foment, where collective action takes place.

Jacobs: As feminists, we always thought that women had the least maneuverability, and I think what you are both saying is that in many ways the pressure on men to conform may be as great or greater than what women have faced.

Faludi: For all the idea that men are these armored, free-standing, can't-be-affected-by-the-world-outside-them people, they seem much more vulnerable toward public opinion, or even individual opinion about their manhood, than women. Masculinity seems to be a very insecure suit of clothes that can be ripped away at any moment. Women and men in the U.S. have suffered millions of layoffs in the last decade and a half, and for both it's a terrible thing. But nobody questions the womanhood of a woman who loses her job, whereas men who were laid off, over and over again said to me, "You can't feel like a man." Everything seems to revolve around whether you are man enough; that's a paralyzing experience.

Levine: But men really are changing. Look around and you see it. Men alone with their children doing errands. Choosing

different life plans. I met medical students who are making choices about their specialties based on flexibility. Jim Levine, who works with fathers, describes being called in by companies that want to convince their employees they're family-friendly. They give him a teeny-weeny room for a fathers' meeting, and then announce it. Within hours, 10 and 20 times the number of men the room will hold sign up. And every time, the company is amazed and the men are flabbergasted to see that there are so many of them. Every time!

I'm seeing solid commitments to a different lifestyle that are being made under the radar by individual men who have no idea yet that they are part of a movement. But the truth is, as feminists, I think we have so much ambivalence about helping men make these changes. We resent the privilege they are starting from. At the same time it's natural for us to work together. The real challenge to feminists is to be able to talk about men in a way that is feminist and constructive and political—I don't think we've gotten there yet.

Faludi: There is the understandable desire to hold on to the notion that all men are the oppressors. The irony is that we're operating under a male blueprint, which is "define the enemy and defeat them." For men to free themselves, they can't use the patriarchal model of good guys/bad guys because they are the patriarchy. They are going to have to come up with a more complicated paradigm of social change that doesn't have at its center a personal enemy. They're going to have to come up with a new way of social confrontation, and that will be very important to the advancement of the women's movement also—or any of the twentieth century's great social movements—because we've also neared the end of using the good guys/bad guys model. By struggling to find that new model, men will be freeing themselves but also helping to free up feminism.

Gloria Jacobs is the editor of "Ms."

NEVER TOO BUFF

A new book reveals a troubling obsession: How male self-worth is increasingly tied to body image

By **JOHN CLOUD** Boston

POP QUIZ. WHO ARE MORE LIKELY TO BE dissatisfied with the appearance of their chests, men or women? Who is more likely to be concerned about acne, your teenage son or his sister? And who is more likely to binge eat, your nephew or your niece?

If you chose the women and girls in your life, you are right only for the last question—and even then, not by the margin you might expect. About 40% of Americans who go on compulsive-eating sprees are men. Thirty-eight percent of men want bigger pecs, while only 34% of women want bigger breasts. And more boys have fretted about zits than girls, going all the way back to a 1972 study.

A groundbreaking new book declares that these numbers, along with hundreds of other statistics and interviews the authors have compiled, mean something awful has happened to American men over the past few decades. They have become obsessed with their bodies. Authors Harrison Pope and Katharine Phillips, professors of psychiatry at Harvard and Brown, respectively, and Roberto Olivardia, a clinical psychologist at McLean Hospital in Belmont, Mass., have a catchy name to describe this obsession—a term that will soon be doing many reps on chat shows: the Adonis Complex.

The name, which refers to the gorgeous half man, half god of mythology, may be a little too ready for *Oprah,* but the theory behind it will start a wonderful debate. Based on original research involving more than 1,000 men over the past 15 years, the book argues that many men desperately want to look like Adonis because they constantly see the "ideal," steroid-boosted bodies of actors and models and because their muscles are all they have over women today. In an age when women fly combat missions, the authors ask, "What can a modern boy or man do to distinguish himself as being 'masculine'?"

For years, of course, some men—ice skaters, body builders, George Hamilton—have fretted over aspects of their appearance. But the numbers suggest that body-image concerns have gone mainstream: nearly half of men don't like their overall appearance, in contrast to just 1 in 6 in 1972. True, men typically are fatter now, but another study found that 46% of men of normal weight think about their appearance "all the time" or "frequently." And some men—probably hundreds of thousands, if you extrapolate from small surveys—say they have passed up job and even romantic opportunities because they refuse to disrupt workouts or dine on restaurant food. In other words, an increasing number of men would rather look brawny for their girlfriends than have sex with them.

Consider what they're spending. Last year American men forked over $2 billion for gym memberships—and another $2 billion for home exercise equipment. *Men's Health* ("Rock-hard abs in six weeks!" it screams every other issue) had 250,000 subscribers in 1990; now it has 1.6 million. In 1996 alone, men underwent some 700,000 cosmetic procedures.

At least those profits are legal. Anabolic steroids—the common name for synthetic testosterone—have led to the most dramatic changes in the male form in modern history, and more and more average men want those changes for themselves. Since steroids became widely available on the black market in the 1960s, perhaps 3 million American men have swallowed or injected them—mostly in the past 15 years. A 1993 survey found that 1 Georgia high school boy in every 15 admitted having used steroids without a prescription. And the Drug Enforcement Administration reports that the percentage of all high school students who have used steroids has increased 50% in the past four years, from 1.8% to 2.8%. The abuse of steroids has so alarmed the National Institute on Drug Abuse that on Friday it launched a campaign in gyms, malls, bookstores, clubs and on the Internet to warn teenagers about the dangers. Meanwhile, teenagers in even larger numbers are buying legal but lightly regulated food supplements, some with dangerous side effects, that purport to make you bigger or leaner or stronger.

As they infiltrated the body-building world in the '70s and Hollywood a decade later, steroids created bodies for mass consumption that the world had literally never seen before. Pope likes to chart the changes by looking at Mr. America winners, which he called up on the Internet in his office last week. "Look at this guy," Pope exclaims when he clicks on the 1943 winner, Jules Bacon. "He couldn't even win a county body-building contest today." Indeed, there are 16-year-olds working out at your gym who are as big as Bacon. Does that neces-

BODY BOOSTERS Here are some of the substances some men use to bulk up:

PROTEINS

Protein is the building block of muscle growth. It repairs muscle tissue broken down while training. It's sold in powders and bars under names like MET-Rx and Myoplex. These are acceptable sources of protein, but there is little evidence that they are superior to ordinary foods like skim milk or lean meat. Long-term use of very high doses of protein may cause kidney and liver damage.

FAT BURNERS

Include the drug ephedrine, which comes from the plant Ephedra. Ephedrine is a powerful stimulant used in diet pills, herbal ecstasy and energy-booster products. It promotes fat loss, but weight is quickly retained when use stops. It has caused seizures and strokes, especially among those with high blood pressure and diabetes. The FDA says it has been associated with at least 58 deaths since 1994.

CREATINE

A nutrient found in red meat, it produces energy and helps restore muscle tissue after strenuous exercise. Several studies show it increases lean body mass, though some of this gain is probably water. Long-term use of high doses of creatine hasn't been studied, though there are no known short-term dangers. It comes in many forms: powder, liquid, gum.

ADRENAL HORMONES

Naturally produced in humans and animals, these hormones are partly metabolized into testosterone in the body, and thus are claimed to promote muscle growth. Mark McGwire said he had used them to get a more efficient workout and a faster recovery from weight lifting. (He says he no longer uses them.) It may increase levels of cholesterol and help develop female breast tissue. Long-term dangers are unknown.

DUBIOUS DRUGS

Anabolic steriods classified as controlled substances, are synthetic testosterone that is injected into muscle tissue or taken orally to promote muscle growth and enhance athletic performance. Serious side effects include liver damage, cancer and heart disease. Other prescription products are growth hormones like GHB, which is thought to stimulate natural hormone secretion but is also used as an alternative to ecstasy.

sarily mean that today's body builders—including those 16-year-olds—are 'roided? Pope is careful. "The possibility exists that rare or exceptional people, those with an unusual genetic makeup or a hormonal imbalance," could achieve the muscularity and leanness of today's big body builders, he says.

But it's not likely. And Pope isn't lobbing dumbbells from an ivory tower: the professor lifts weights six days a week, from 11 a.m. to 1 p.m. (He can even mark historical occasions by his workouts: "I remember when the *Challenger* went down; I was doing a set of squats.") "We are being assaulted by images virtually impossible to attain without the use of drugs," says Pope. "So what happens when you change a million-year-old equilibrium of nature?"

A historical loop forms: steroids beget pro wrestlers—Hulk Hogan, for one, has admitted taking steroids—who inspire boys to be just like them. Steroids have changed even boys' toys. Feminists have long derided Barbie for her tiny waist and big bosom. The authors of *The Adonis Complex* see a similar problem for boys in the growth of G.I. Joe. The grunt of 1982 looks scrawny compared

with G.I. Joe Extreme, introduced in the mid-'90s. The latter would have a 55-in. chest and 22-in. biceps if he were real, which simply can't be replicated in nature. Pope also points out a stunning little feature of the three-year-old video game Duke Nukem: Total Meltdown, developed by GT Interactive Software. When Duke gets tired, he can find a bottle of steroids to get him going. "Steroids give Duke a super adrenaline rush," the game manual notes.

To bolster their argument, the *Adonis* authors developed a computerized test that allows subjects to "add" muscle to a typical male body. They estimate their own size and then pick the size they would like to be and the size they think women want. Pope and his colleagues gave the test to college students and found that on average, the men wanted 28 lbs. more muscle—and thought women wanted them to have 30 lbs. more. In fact, the women who took the test picked an ideal man only slightly more muscular than average. Which goes a long way toward explaining why Leonardo DiCaprio can be a megastar in a nation that also idealizes "Stone Cold" Steve Austin.

But when younger boys took Pope's test, they revealed an even deeper sense of inadequacy about their bodies. More than half of boys ages 11 to 17 chose as their physical ideal an image possible to attain only by using steroids. So they do. Boys are a big part of the clientele at Muscle Mania (not its real name), a weight-lifting store that TIME visited last week at a strip mall in a Boston suburb. A couple of teenagers came in to ask about tribulus, one of the many over-the-counter drugs and body-building supplements the store sells, all legally.

"A FRIEND OF MINE," ONE BOY BEGINS, fooling no one, "just came off a cycle of juice, and he heard that tribulus can help you produce testosterone naturally." Patrick, 28, who runs the store and who stopped using steroids four years ago because of chest pain, tells the kid, "The s___ shuts off your nuts," meaning steroids can reduce sperm production, shrink the testicles and cause impotence. Tribulus, Patrick says, can help restart natural testosterone production. The teen hands over $12 for 100 Tribulus Fuel pills. (Every day, Muscle Mania does $4,000 in sales of such products, with protein supplements and so-called fat burners leading the pack.)

Patrick says many of his teen customers, because they're short on cash, won't pay for a gym membership "until they've saved up for a cycle [of steroids]. They don't see the point without them." The saddest customers, he says, are the little boys, 12 and 13, brought in by young fathers. "The dad will say, 'How do we put some weight on this kid?' with the boy just staring at the floor. Dad is going to turn him into Hulk Hogan, even if it's against his will."

What would motivate someone to take steroids? Pope, Phillips and Olivardia say the Adonis Complex works in different ways for different men. "Michael," 32, one of their research subjects, told TIME he had always been a short kid who got picked on. He started working out at about 14, and he bought muscle magazines for advice. The pictures taunted him: he sweated, but he wasn't getting as big as the men in the pictures. Other men in his gym also

made him feel bad. When he found out they were on steroids, he did two cycles himself, even though he knew they could be dangerous.

But not all men with body-image problems take steroids. Jim Davis, 29, a human-services manager, told TIME he never took them, even when training for body-building competitions. But Davis says he developed a form of obsessive-compulsive disorder around his workouts. He lifted weights six days a week for at least six years. He worked out even when injured. He adhered to a rigid regimen for every session, and if he changed it, he felt anxious all day. He began to be worried about clothes, and eventually could wear only three shirts, ones that made him look big. He still felt small. "I would sit in class at college with a coat on," he says. You may have heard this condition called bigorexia—thinking your muscles are puny when they aren't. Pope and his colleagues call it muscle dysmorphia and estimate that hundreds of thousands of men suffer from it.

Even though most boys and men never approach the compulsion of Davis or Michael (both eventually conquered it), they undoubtedly face more pressure now than in the past to conform to an impossible ideal. Ripped male bodies are used today to advertise everything that shapely female bodies advertise: not just fitness products but also dessert liqueurs, microwave ovens and luxury hotels. The authors of *The Adonis Complex* want guys to rebel against those images, or at least see them for what they are: a goal unattainable without drug use.

Feminists raised these issues for women years ago, and more recent books such as *The Beauty Myth* were part of a backlash against the hourglass ideal. Now, says Phillips, "I actually think it may be harder for men than women to talk about these problems because it's not considered masculine to worry about such things." But maybe there is a masculine alternative: Next time WWF comes on, guys, throw the TV out the window. And order a large pizza.

VIEWPOINT ■ Joel Stein

I BLED FOR THIS COLUMN

ICANNOT WAIT TO LATHER UP MY NAKED, HAIRY BODY IN AN INflatable pool full of testosterone gel. I have felt testosterone deficient since I was five, when, surrounded by female friends, I spent my days compiling my sticker collection, listening to the *Annie* sound track, baking in my Easy-Bake Oven and arranging my glass-animal collection. Peggy Fleming had a more masculine childhood than I did.

But I needed to know precisely how unmanly I am, so I went to my doctor to get my T count checked. Unfortunately, my doctor could not administer the test via saliva; he would need a blood sample. That made me consider canceling my appointment, which in and of itself delivered the result I needed. But I made the appointment anyway. In 48 hours I would know how much man was in me.

For a long time, I've overcompensated for my lack of manliness through sportswriting, porn watching and stock buying, but deep down I know I'm a little shy on T. I cannot yell at other drivers, raise my voice, pick up women in a bar or grow a full beard. All whiskey, no matter how expensive, just tastes like burning. Yet deep inside I long to sleep around, to kick some ass, to release my first rap album. As I saw it, I had little choice but to score some of that testosterone gel when it comes out this summer. I could keep it in my jacket pocket for emergency situations, next to my lip balm and antibacterial hand gel. I'm thinking about marketing this as a first-aid kit for wusses.

Waiting for my results, feeling especially insecure, I called my masculinity mentor, Adam Carolla, the host of Comedy Central's *The Man Show*. "I'm guessing you're a little light," Carolla said. He suggested that I sign up for the AndroGel now. "A little extra

aggression, a couple of extra inches on the biceps, a little body hair could help you," he said. When I mentioned my concern about taking unprescribed medication, Carolla suggested that I just eat a lot of beef jerky. "I believe there is a lot of testosterone in jerky. That would be the most logical food to put it in, anyway," I suggested I might enjoy it more as a pasta with a light tomato-basil sauce, which I could market as "testosteroni." Carolla said he had to go.

Still anxious about my results, I called a former girlfriend, figuring she'd make me feel better. "I bet it's freakishly low," she said. "You're afraid of dogs; you once owned an Easy-Bake Oven; and you've never been much for fighting." Now I remembered there were good reasons our relationship didn't work out (one of them being that I told her about the Easy-Bake Oven).

After two neurosis-filled days, my doctor called and told me my testosterone level was totally normal. When I pressed him for a number, he said it was within the normal range of 260 to 1,000. When I really pressed him for a number, he told me it was 302. When I started to freak out about being in the bottom 10%, he again reassured me that it was completely normal. Yeah, normal in that I don't have breasts.

One of my female friends tried to comfort me, saying that women may have hot, wild flings with high-testosterone men, but they settle down with hormonally balanced guys. This did not make me feel better. You'd have to have a T count of 20 for this to make you feel any better. All I could think about was that now I have one less excuse for having an affair. Unless, of course, I'm all hopped up on man gel.

"THE UNIFORM FOR TODAY IS BELLY BUTTONS"

The number of nudist women our age has doubled over the past six years. Gigi Guerra strips down to uncover the scoop.

I **don't** get excited about being naked in group situations. Sure, I've skinny-dipped, played strip poker, streaked, and gone on my fair share of gyno visits—but it's not as if these things helped define who I am as a person. I did what I had to do and then put my pants back on. Simply put, I love wearing clothes. I love buying clothes even more. Strip me of the joy of shopping and you've removed half the woman.

So now I hear that nudism is trendy. Not for old hippies, but for people our age. The American Association of Nude Recreation says the number of their 18- to 34-year-old members has increased by 50 percent since 1994. According to Nicky Hoffman, the administrative director of the Naturist Society (another organization for nudists), almost a third of their members are in their 20s and 30s. And though there are still more guys than girls, Nicky says she wouldn't be surprised if women soon start to outnumber men. To see what the big deal is, I flew to suburban Sacramento, Calif., site of Laguna del Sol, one of the biggest nudist resorts in the country. Needless to say, packing was a breeze.

"I never want to buy a swimsuit again."

"Most people come here for the first time out of curiosity," explains 36-year-old Patty Sailors, a perky, intelligent brunette who, along with her husband, manages Laguna. "The relaxing atmosphere keeps them here." I'm standing with her in the carpeted main office. We're both clothed, defying the hand-painted sign on the wall announcing: THE UNIFORM FOR TODAY IS BELLY BUTTONS. People around us are forking over four bucks a night for campsites, $12 for RV hookups and 90 bills for modern, air-conditioned rooms. Patty says she expects a crowd of at least 500 this weekend.

Tie-dye T-shirts hang on a rack in the back of the room. They're promoting Nudestock, a yearly Laguna blowout that brings hot dogs, a cover band, and vast expanses of uncovered genitals together under the sun. Nudists seem to like theme events. There's even a Truman Capote-esque Black-and-White Ball in April. I ask Patty how a nudist can properly "dress" for such an event. "Oh, people use lots of body paint," she laughs. "Some guys even draw their tuxes on." Is that with or without the cummerbund?

Patty gives me a tour of the grounds in a silver golf cart that looks like a mini Rolls-Royce. As we putt along, she explains that all guests are taken on tours like this—not just as a courtesy, but also to weed out freaks. "We make sure this is not a sexual environment," says Patty. Laguna bills itself as a family resort, and everything here whiffs of kids, couples and young singles keeping their hands to themselves. But about one in 70 people is turned away because they're married and try to come without their spouse. Occasionally, Patty says, others are denied entry because they gawk too much, make crude jokes, or give off weird vibes.

"Most have their first taste of nudism by getting N.I.F.C.," says Patty, as we cruise by a row of mobile homes. I see my first naked person and giggle to myself. "That means Nude In Front of the Computer," she continues, reining in my amusement. "Or, they'll walk around the house nude." We pass a volleyball game. One guy—clad only in a cropped T-shirt—jumps up to spike the ball. His penis follows. I'm simultaneously mesmerized and horrified. Does it hurt?

Patty's first taste of nudism came when she stopped wearing pj's in high school. "Then I started skinny-dipping," she explains. "The main reason I became a nudist is because I don't ever want to have to buy a swimsuit again." She's serious: Bathing attire is

From *Jane,* August 2000, pp. 144-147. © 2000 by Fairchild Publications. Reprinted by permission.

one of the biggest taboos in the world of nudism. Resort-wear designers, take note.

"Clothing hides who you are."

I stay in one of the motel-like rooms. It's spacious and clean, with a huge bed, generic art and a switch-on fireplace. There's even an indoor pool down the hall. It feels like I'm at the Marriott—except for the naked people who keep walking by my door. A water volleyball game is in full swing. (No, not that kind of swing. Get your mind out of the gutter.) I realize that this is the perfect time to get naked—I can run and hide in the pool; everyone will be too busy to notice.

I strip, grab my towel and leave the room. Within seconds, I have a panic attack. I've never had issues with my body, but now I start to obsess: My butt feels too bony, and suddenly a Brazilian bikini wax doesn't seem like such a bad idea. I pray nobody looks at me.

But as soon as I enter the pool area, I'm relieved. Two women on lounge chairs have 10 times the pubic hair I do. A college-aged girl sitting by the hot tub has cellulite. Droopy breasts abound. The variety of penis sizes and shapes is astounding. I'm buck-naked in a room full of imperfections, and strangely, it feels sort of comforting.

Late Friday evening, a DJ kicks off a dance in the clubhouse. I'm perched by the bar, clad only in a gauzy cotton top (it's a little chilly). Though it's strange to socialize with my pubes showing, it's also refreshing to be around broads who aren't constantly in the rest room inspecting their asses in the mirror. Emily, a curly-haired accountant in her early 30s, couldn't care less about pathetic preening. She's been dancing all night with only a sky-blue butterfly clip in her hair, a big diamond ring on her finger and the determination to have a good time. She's here with her daughters, her brother and her fiancé, whom she met through a dating game on the radio. Emily tells me that one of her girls, who has a surgery scar on her chest, likes coming to Laguna because nobody is freaked out by her body. "I don't think [women] should be ashamed to be naked," she shouts over the pounding beat. "Here, it doesn't matter what your body looks like. Clothing is a way for people to hide who they really are."

Back in my room, I stare at my pajamas. I put them on and feel like I'm committing some kind of terrible crime.

"We're naked, not nuts."

It's Saturday. The temperature is supposed to top 100 degrees. Outside there's a sea of flesh that's 50 times more tan than mine. Thank God for SPF 45—I slather it on every square inch of my pasty white body. *Every square inch.*

On my way to Laguna's restaurant for breakfast, I feel beyond exposed. This is my first time fully naked in the light of day. Strangers wave and say hi, but nobody stares. By the time I arrive, I'm feeling unusually relaxed. I spread a towel down on a vinyl booth (nudist etiquette) and eat my melon, cottage cheese and muffin platter.

Post-dining, I walk to the main lawn. There's a volleyball match going on. The organizers are Neil, a tall, tanned engineer, and his 34-year-old wife, Gigi (hey, nice name!), s shy costume designer with long blond hair. Between games, Gigi tells me that nudism helped her become comfortable with her body. Back when she was 20, she and some friends came across a nude beach. Her friends joined in but Gigi thought she was "too fat" to participate. So she sat on a towel all day, sulking. "By the afternoon, I gave in and took all my clothes off," she explains.

Today, she and Neil participate in some form of nude recreation every summer weekend. Gigi has, at last count, windsurfed, square-danced, hiked, biked, and Jet Skied in the buff. Oh, and played volleyball. The couple has a Web site, *www.nakedvolleyball.com,* dedicated to the sport. "People e-mail us and say we need more pornography on the site," Gigi says, rolling her eyes. "They don't understand that nudism is not a sexual thing. We're naked, but not nuts."

Even though I suck at volleyball, I decide to give it a try. Gigi has inspired me. I forget that I'm naked as I jump around, run and punch. It's actually kind of liberating to feel the wind whistle through new places. Then I dive to catch a low ball. I end up sliding across the grass on my butt. A spiky burr wedges itself into one cheek. No more volleyball.

I head off court and run into Lisa. She's 23 years old and about to graduate from college with a degree in business management. She's stunning—sort of a Natalie Wood/Katie Holmes hybrid. But surprisingly, she hasn't been getting unwanted attention from any of the guys. Lisa says her real problem is dealing with the judgments of clothed people. For example, her roommate: "She saw my ass [one day]," says Lisa, "and asked me why I don't have any tan lines." Lisa doesn't think she'll tell her she's a nudist. "People can be really immature about it when they find out," she sighs.

Nudist myths: Guys walk around with erections. I did not see a single one. *All nudists like volleyball.* A survey of nudists found that they most favor swimming, walking and hiking. *Nudists are white trash.* Almost a quarter have a masters or Ph.D. and nearly half make upwards of $50K a year.

"This whole place is a dressing room!"

Late in the afternoon, I stop by the boutique, which is run by Lois, a spirited redhead. As I sift through racks of chiffon floral wraps and try on a Nipple Necklace—a tiny spray of colorful beads that dangles from your dockyard rivets—Lois makes small talk. "Some women ask where the dressing room is," she says, taking a sip of her Koozie-housed Diet Coke. "I tell them that this whole place is a dressing room!"

Next, I head to the river. The trail is gorgeous—fields of tall grass spread in one direction, willow trees dot the landscape in the other. In the distance I see a sign tacked to a fence. It's a warning: YOU ARE LEAVING LAGUNA DEL SOL. CLOTHING REQUIRED BEYOND THIS POINT. I later hear that farm workers on the other side of the fence snoop on the nudie people.

I jump into the cool water of the river. It feels great to swim naked. I climb up on some rocks, and think about how I'm actually starting to enjoy being nude. It now feels liberating. But then yelling interrupts my meditative moment. It's the photographer. I can't hear her over the rushing water. She points at my leg in desperation. I see a big bug crawling up my inner thigh, inches from my genitals. The insects here seem more sexed than the people do.

"I had a nude bridal shower."

"The good thing about being nude," says India, a bubbly 24-year-old with chunky highlighted hair, "is that when [my baby] spits up on me, I just hop in the shower." We're sitting outside the mobile home that she lives in year-round with her 30-year-old husband, Bobby, and their cute son. It's the end of the day and everything is moving slowly. Cows loll about in a nearby field. A big American flag flaps lazily from a pole in their immaculately groomed yard.

Bobby is Laguna's groundskeeper, and India works in town as a hairdresser. They met a few years ago when she gave him a cut. He soon brought her to Laguna for a weekend with his parents. "I grew up strictly religious," she says. "I wouldn't even wear a spaghetti-strap tank top in public." But she appreciated the nudists' nonjudgmental attitude. By Sunday, India was naked. "At first it was weird being naked around my boyfriend's parents, though," she notes.

Bobby proposed to India, nude, at Laguna. "I even had a nude bridal shower," she adds, smiling. India wants to stay here for a long time. She likes the "gated community" feel. "And each weekend, we meet a new young couple," she says excitedly. "I see more people our age here. It doesn't matter who you are or what you do."

I'm buck-naked in a room full of imperfection, and strangely, it feels comforting.

Nudist truths: Tampons are acceptable attire. "But we advise women to tuck the cord," explains Patty. *Nudists are clean.* One woman told me that she showers up to five times a day. *Nudity is more accepted in Europe.* In France, there's a summer community of 40,000. Everything is done in the buff, from banking to grocery shopping.

"Attitudes are changing."

I think about what India says. I haven't heard one person start a conversation with: "Where do you work?" Instead, people chat about simple things like, "How are you today?" or "What SPF you got on?" It's nice to be at a place where your career (or lack thereof) doesn't dictate who you are—housewives and CEOs are on equal footing here. But perhaps the main reason why we women are drawn to nudism is because it makes us feel good about out bodies. Emily, Gigi, Lisa and India all told me as much. And pop culture might actually be helping the call.

"Attitudes are changing," says Nicky. "Larger-sized models and actresses are out there. Nudist organizations are popping up on campuses. At U Penn, there's a Naturalist Student Association. Wesleyan University has a clothing-optional dorm. I even saw an ad for salad dressing that showed a young naked couple on the beach. What does nudity have to do with salad dressing? I have no idea, but it sends a message that naked bodies are okay."

By late Sunday, I've forgotten that I'm naked. At first, I thought nudism was freaky. Now I realize that it's just a way for people to get comfy with themselves. And if you ask me, that's a way better way to go about it than dieting or getting plastic surgery.

Nudists also seem to have found a safe way to escape the pressures of daily life. For me, that's an appealing concept. I'm simultaneously trying to make it on my own, establish my career, pay off debt, and figure out what the hell it is I'm headed for—just like anyone my age. It's weird, but when you take away your clothes, it's like you take a vacation from a lot of your worries. Too bad I'm still addicted to shopping.

The Second Sexual Revolution

Viagra was just the beginning. Soon we will all be medicated and wired for high-performance romance.

By Jack Hitt

It was only two years ago that Bob Dole went on "The Larry King Show" to discuss his prostate-cancer operation. During a commercial break, so the story goes, King leaned over to ask his old friend, confidentially, how he was dealing with the operation's grimmest side effect, impotence. Dole cheerfully informed the talk-show host that there was a new drug, Viagra, and miraculously, it had cured the problem. King asked Dole if he would discuss it on the air, and Dole said sure, why not?

The world was about to become a very different place. Viagra would cycle through the expected paces of pop-culture acceptance with stunning speed. Leno and Letterman got an entire summer's worth of monologues off the subject. For a while the papers regularly pumped out clowning (and possibly true) stories about the drug—there was Frank Bernardo, 70, who left his wife, declaring, "It's time for me to be a stud again"; there was also Gen. Sani Abacha of Nigeria, who died in the midst of a Viagra-fueled encounter with two women in his magisterial bed.

But the jokes are over. Viagra's sales topped $1 billion in the first year, and Pfizer is now the second-largest drug company in the world. The drug's use has leveled off, but consider the level: nearly 200,000 prescriptions are filled each week, and 17 million Americans have used the drug. Viagra has been embraced by the well off (4 percent of the total population of Palm Beach County has a prescription), but not only by the well off. Not long ago, Wal-Mart and Kmart had a Viagra war that drove the per-pill price down from $10 to $7.80.

And so, no one talks about it anymore.

Welcome to the lull. It's as if a freak 20-foot swell crashed on the beach, leaving a few new gullies. It's over. Go back inside. Everything is back to normal. Everything except that tsunami on the horizon.

At this moment, there are at least a dozen new Viagra-like medicines and devices currently in clinical trials. Many of these drugs are for men, but this time around, there are just as many for women—specifically, for a new phylum of illness, female sexual dysfunction, which will soon cycle through the same paces as "erectile dysfunction," setting the word "frigidity" alongside impotence in our dictionary of merry old archaisms. "Our knowledge of sexual health is in revolutionary mode," says Dr. Irwin Goldstein, a Boston University urologist and pioneer in the field.

> **Though most of us are taught to believe that the totality of sex is unknowable, the mechanics of it aren't lofty. Compared to a kidney, our genital rig is the corporeal equivalent of a 1968 VW Beetle engine.**

With $1 billion in sales for Viagra, the research pressure is intense, yielding paper titles like "The Ejaculatory Behavior in Sexually Sluggish Male Rats. . . ." Scientists, doctors and pharmaceutical companies are racing to discover newer and better drugs. Who doubts they will improve the lives of those who suffer from the newly discovered sexual disorders now showing up in the medical journals? But these drugs will also have, some say, an "enhancing" effect on normally functioning people. More important, the temptation for anyone to obtain these drugs will be

Sexual Healing

Soon, a variety of remedies for sexual dysfunction—and ways to enhance sexual performance—will become available to men and women.

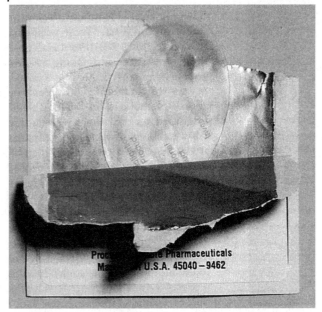

Testosterone patch This device, made by Proctor & Gamble, delivers testosterone to the pelvic region. But it's not for men only. Several companies are working on a version for women whose testosterone production and sex drive have decreased after hysterectomies or other sex-organ surgery.

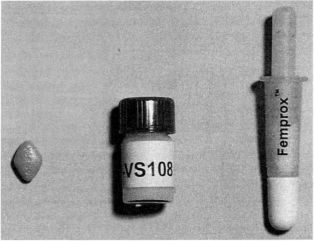

Clitoral device Beyond pills or hormonal creams, one company is taking a nonpharmacological approach to treating women with sexual dysfunction. UroMetrics is developing the Eros Clitoral Therapy Device, a small pump with a cup, about the size of a thimble, that fits over the clitoris. It is designed to stimulate blood flow to the organ, thereby enhancing sensation and lubrication and enabling its user to achieve orgasm more easily.

Viagra The granddaddy of pharmaceutical sex medicine, the little blue pill was introduced to the market in 1998. Its popularity has helped to make its producer, Pfizer, the second-largest drug company in the world.

Prostaglandin E-1 cream To stimulate blood flow to the genital area, Vivus is developing a topical cream for women that contains this ingredient. It is intended to alleviate arousal and orgasm dysfunction and enhance vaginal lubrication.

Alprostadil cream NexMed is working on its own topical cream for women, similar to prostaglandin E-1. It is also developing a topical therapy for male impotence.

more easily satisfied than ever before, since the family of pharmaceuticals inspired by Viagra is entering the market at a time when medicine is decentralizing, slipping the reins long held by doctors. There is already telling evidence that these new sex drugs may well do for medicine what porn did for the Internet—constitute the killer ap that reshapes the industry in an age of patient choice and turboconsumerism.

THOUGH MOST OF US ARE INCULCATED WITH THE belief that the totality of sex is unknowable, maybe even divine, once you've spent some time with the new sex researchers, you learn that the actual mechanics of it all aren't that lofty. Compared to a kidney or a lung, our genital rig is basic stuff, the corporeal equivalent of a 1968 VW Beetle engine. Ensure that the "hormonal milieu" is properly gauged and that there is enough blood flow, and the engineering work is pretty much done—for men and women alike. (Then there needs to be passion, romance and love perhaps, but urologists continue to leave these areas of research to poets and musicians. So far.)

"Not to discount psychological aspects," said Goldstein, who was a member of the team that treated Bob Dole, "but at a certain point all sex is mechanical. The man needs a sufficient axial rigidity so his penis can penetrate through labia, and he has to sustain that in order to have sex. This is a mechanical structure, and mechanical structures follow scientific principles." Goldstein, seated in his office at Boston University Hospital's Sexual Health Clinic, poked his forefinger into the palm of his hand and explained that the "typical resistance" posed by the average vagina is a measurable two pounds. The key is to create an erection that doesn't "deform" or collapse when engaging that resistance.

"I am an engineer," noted Goldstein, who in fact collaborated with Boston University's department of aerospace engineering in formulating his theories. "And I can apply the principles of hydraulics to these problems. I can utilize medical strategies to assess, diagnose and manipulate things that are not so straightforward in psychiatry."

That's something new. For most of the 20th century, any sexual complaint was treated on the couch, not in the lab. Only comparatively recently has impotence been understood to be an organic disease—potentially identifiable and treatable with medicine.

The change is part of a cultural shift that dates back to the birth control pill, when mostly young people were liberated to experiment with sex fearlessly outside of marriage. Many moral conservatives continue to condemn the era for unleashing the Pandoran epidemics of teenage pregnancy, sexually transmitted disease and moral decline. But this telling of the story ignores a more subtle and significant shift. Average folks—young and old, liberal and conservative—began to accept that sex was not a biblical imperative whose sole aim is procreation, but a lively part of good health—something to be enjoyed, like great food

and laughter, well into old age. This is the revolution that Bob Dole has joined at the barricades.

The distinction is not just medical; it's metaphysical. Psychological problems carry with them the full freight of personal responsibility. But a physical problem seems more like a cosmic error, something unrelated to a person's actions. It's no flaw in your manhood or womanhood if your sexual organs don't work. It's a "disorder"—and by being labeled as one, it becomes something detached from your own true self and easier for a patient to emotionally confront and for a doctor to treat.

Breaking through the wall of the patient's superego, though, was only half the challenge for researchers like Goldstein. Medical approaches to sexual problems have been thwarted by another obstacle: there wasn't anything medicine could do about them. "Unless you have a treatment, you don't have a condition," Goldstein said. "If there is nothing for me to say except, 'See a psychiatrist,' then what is the rush to accurately describe and research your condition?"

For the longest time the only treatments were for men, and they were practically medieval. Outside the opaque world of aphrodisiacs, medicine had come up with only one solution for male impotence: the penile implant, a surgical procedure developed by urologists in 1973.

"I can remember," Goldstein said of the slow progress. "It was 1983, when a doctor named Giles Brindley came up with the first drug-induced erection. At a urology meeting, he was wearing sweat pants. He excused himself for a minute and went to the men's room and injected himself. When he came back, he lowered his pants to show us a stunning and natural erection. He walked down the aisle and let us touch it. People couldn't believe it wasn't an implant."

Goldstein noticed a look of considerable distress on my face, and added something that he thought might comfort me: "It was a bunch of urologists."

Not long after Dr. Brindley's performance, a company based in California, Vivus, perfected an erectile suppository called MUSE (medicated urethral system for erection). Although it is effective, it requires that the suppository be inserted in the tip of the penis. Pfizer's truly great breakthrough with Viagra was inventing an erectile treatment that didn't make the average person double over in horror.

As the cures have become more user-friendly, the discourse among the general population has become more comfortable, too. The morning I was meeting with Goldstein, a patient showed up and allowed me to join his consultation on the condition that I would not publish his name.

The patient, a Dominican-born social worker in his 30's, was accidentally kicked in the groin years ago. The damage was severe. A beefy, rounded man, he sits on the examination table sidesaddle, his ankles crossed coyly. Both he and his Rubenesque wife curl their shoulders inward and keep their heads bowed, as if in shame. It's clear that the ripple effect of this simple injury has affected every part of their lives and marriage.

When Goldstein asks the patient what happens when he makes love to his wife, he says, "I don't know." He looks at me with the same tepid smile and pinched eyes that Bob Dole has in that magazine ad. "I don't know," he repeats. It's fascinating to watch Goldstein work this tiny room, this miniature stage, trying to determine just what mix of clinical authority and just-us-guys informality will make this doctor-patient interview work. He has the uncanny ability to radiate locker-room crassness and professional etiquette almost in the same sentence. He's dressed in a crisp gray pinstriped suit, but he possesses a soft casual voice that lopes amiably around his words, like Donald Sutherland's. One wall of his office is covered with half a dozen sheepskins, proving his professional bona fides to anyone who needs that. Over his door is a walrus penis bone, two feet long —a conversation starter for a certain kind of person. The wall plate of his light switch is a cartoon of a doctor and the switch itself doubles as the doctor's . . . well, funny stuff for an altogether different kind of person.

The formal "make love" query isn't working, so Goldstein tries again: "When you lie down naked to fool around with your wife, describe what happens." The social worker's eyes pinch harder. I involuntarily curl my shoulders—as if to acknowledge our common genomic humanity. (I feel certain my face resembles, at this time, the Greek mask of tragedy.)

"It takes a long time, a long time to get ready, you know," he says quickly, as if he fears Goldstein might become even more "street" in his queries. Again, he looks at me. "A long time, you know." I nod furiously and make a noise similar to a kitten coming upon a saucer of milk.

Goldstein says: "Here's what's happening. Normally when you get an erection, the blood flows like this." He walks to a sink and turns the spigot on full blast. "Now what's happening is this." He slows the flow to a trickle. "Everything works. It's just taking too long. One of your arteries to your penis is blocked. The good news is we can fix that with a penis bypass operation." He punches in a video showing a highly magnified surgery, the screen all liquidy pinks. We watch as doctors take a redundant piece of artery from the stomach and then use it to bypass the damaged artery in the penis. "I've done 600 of these operations. You have a highly significant chance for a full recovery."

The patient laughs involuntarily—the kind of irrepressibly giddy laughter that accompanies extremely good fortune on par with winning $100 million or being selected by NASA to fly to the moon. The wife laughs. It's absolutely infectious. I start laughing. It is a small celebration of unadulterated laughter. This news puts everyone in the peppiest mood. We all shake hands, awkward but well meaning, like passing the peace in church.

"I am going to prescribe Viagra for him," Goldstein told me back in his office. "Not for sex. But as a sleeping pill."

Goldstein explained that the average male gets five erections per night in his sleep. "Our belief is that the night erection is the battery recharging time. Your penis is guaranteed to have one and a half to three hours of erection time every night. You know how doctors now recommend taking a single aspirin a day to prevent heart attack? I predict one day there will be evidence to support a medication—something like Viagra—that enhances erections. Call it erectogenic."

HYPOTHESES AND FRESH IDEAS SEEM COMMONPLACE in this new field now that Bob Dole has made the world safe for sexual-health research. Some of them are simple. For instance, Goldstein has made it a minicrusade to banish the standard bicycle seat, which crushes the main nerve cluster leading to the genitalia and, Goldstein believes, accounts for the relatively high incidence of sexual dysfunction among bikers. But a great deal of the cutting-edge discoveries are occurring for women. Last year, the Journal of the American Medical Association published a study reporting that 43 percent of women experience some kind of sexual dysfunction. Just a few weeks ago, the Network for Excellence in Women's Sexual Health was organized to help doctors and health care professionals who want to enter this emerging field.

A lot of the revelations about women stem directly from studies on men. Women also have four or five nightly clitoral "erections," Goldstein said, which are crucial for the maintenance of their sexual health. Yet even among these researchers, the presumption still persists that men's sexuality is mere hydraulics and that women's sexuality is more complex. "We're being forced to realize that men aren't so simple either," Goldstein said, "because of what we've learned about women."

Take, for example, the case of a Boston professor who participated last year in a clinical trial to measure Viagra's efficacy on women and spoke to me only on the condition of anonymity.

"Female sexual dysfunction is a very real problem for some people," the 55-year-old told me, recalling the day in 1994 when she learned she had breast cancer. She endured a lumpectomy, an oophorectomy (removal of ovaries) and finally a hysterectomy. When it was over, she said, "it was as though my mind was capable of being sexual but it was disconnected from my body. There was no there there. I felt like I had been neutered."

Admitting to a "a strong libido," she went to her doctor to find out what she could do. He told her "more or less, women at your age don't care about sex anymore." So she read up, asked around and soon heard about the Boston University clinic run by Goldstein and his two partners, Jennifer Berman, a urologist; and her sister Laura Berman, a sex therapist.

The doctors selected the professor for the early trials, in part because her problem is complex. Viagra achieves its effect by increasing blood flow to the genitals, but that would not be enough. According to the Bermans, the pathways connecting the professor's desire (she felt it cerebrally) with her physical arousal (she felt nothing genitally) had been interrupted. Such communications are facilitated by hormones, specifically the right levels of estrogen and testosterone. She began testosterone cream applications accompanied by an estrogen ring inserted in the vagina like a diaphragm for slow release of the hormone. While this adjustment helped reconnect the brain with the genitals, there still wasn't enough blood flow during stimulation to regularly effect an orgasm. So Viagra, too, was tested.

"The combination was so successful," she said. "With Viagra I have orgasms, much more intense orgasms."

This case reveals just how detailed sexual disorder studies have become in a fairly short time. In fact, in the October 1999 issue of the journal Urology, the three partners at the Boston clinic broke down the four basic kinds of female sexual dysfunction that either are or will soon be treatable. The professor's basic condition is known as Sexual Arousal Disorder. (It even has an Oprah-ready acronym.) Sexual thoughts occur, but they aren't communicated to the genitals.

'When we operated on the female pelvis,' says one doctor, 'we just cut everything out. And I would ask, "Where are the nerves?" And you know what? No one even knew.'

The other ailments are Orgasmic Disorder which includes inorgasmia (inability to have orgasm) and the unnamed condition of "muffled" orgasms. The third new subdisease is Sexual Pain Disorder, which includes vaginismus (involuntary muscle spasms) and dyspareunia (general genital pain). The final one is Hypoactive Sexual Desire Disorder, more or less the opposite of the professor's condition, in which the genitals may or may not work but it hardly matters because the patient lacks libido and the usual sexual thoughts or fantasies that precede a sexual encounter.

Many of these conditions overlap and are often accompanied (or caused) by emotional problems like depression. "It's more of an algorithm," Berman said. But in the overwhelming majority of her patients' cases, she added— and there's a furious debate embedded in the rest of this sentence—the organic disorder precedes the emotional ones.

This is not to say psychological sex problems don't exist. "There is no drug," Laura Berman said, "that will restore a satisfactory sex life to a woman who hates her husband." But she estimated that only about 20 percent of her patients have purely psychogenic problems; for the other patients, there is a raft of new procedures to measure their sexual health.

In many clinics, a typical female patient would first submit to a photoplethysmography. According to James Yeager, chief research scientist with the drug company NexMed, the device is a "black box with wires coming out of it with a kind of penlight that is inserted in the vagina." The woman then stimulates herself while a photo cell in the penlight measures the change in redness of the vaginal tissue and then calibrates blood flow. There are drawbacks to this procedure, which are obvious, and if they're not, send me a postcard and I'll drop you a line. I'm moving on.

At the Boston University Hospital clinic, genital blood flow is measured with a "high-frequency laser duplex Doppler," Laura Berman said, "which is like a sonogram." Then the clinicians also measure vaginal pH (using a digital pH probe), the structural architecture of the organ or "vaginal compliance" (using a Schuster balloon) and finally, clitoral and labial vibratory threshold (using a biothesiometer). "We record these measurements at baseline and after sexual stimulation with a standardized 15-minute erotic video and vibrator," the authors write in their Urology article.

With men, the entire process is quite similar. In the old days, men were outfitted with a "penis cuff"—a wraparound device like a petite blood-pressure gauge. Today, a sonogram is more accurate and yields a photograph mapping out the geographies of blood flow. Once the doctors examine the differentials in these measurements, a diagnosis follows and, when appropriate, medical treatment.

DISCOVERING THOSE TREATMENTS IS THE PROVINCE of researchers, and one of the most pre-eminent of them is Goldstein's colleague and Laura Berman's sister, Dr. Jennifer Berman, one of the nation's few female urologists. Berman agreed to see me under extraordinary circumstances. Only three days before, she had given birth to her son, and the birth was difficult. Still, amazingly trim in her slacks and sailor's peacoat, Dr. Berman said she was happy to come to her office since she also wanted to check on the status of a new grant application for a major research program, which she was eager to explain.

"When I was trained in urology," she said, walking briskly down the street to her lab, "I was struck at the lengths surgeons went to, when operating on men, to preserve the nerves and blood vessels that are connected to the penis. But when we operated on the female pelvis, we just cut everything out. And I would ask, 'Where are the nerves?' And you know what? No one even knew.' She said this, strangely, not with anger but with an explorer's excitement. "So we need fresh cadavers. They're about $3,000 each. You know, if you look in any anatomical text, there are 20 pages on male sexual anatomy and 2 pages on the female. And there are conflicting reports as to how one should describe the female anatomy. We know there is a major plexus of nerves along the cervix but how they connect to the clitoris and vagina is not understood at all. In men, we know that there is a cluster of nerves along the lateral side of the prostate. That's why there's a special operation."

I didn't say anything for a while. It wasn't the usual male-feminist discomfort, although it's never easy being the sole representative of the sex when one of those grotesque inequities pops into view. No, rather, it was an acknowledgment of the air of frontier desperation that characterizes so much of this research: so many obvious things to do, so many cultural obstacles. I imagine there was a similar feeling surrounding anatomy in Dickensian England, when early surgeons robbed graves to find corpses to practice on. Or in the early days of organ transplantation (in the 60's), when doctors would occasionally get caught slipping really nice kidneys from the nearly dead. These dissonances occur in medicine when doctors have sneaked ahead of the culture in redefining something holy—the sanctity of the dead, respect for the living and now: the mystery of sex.

Berman led me into a modern brick building, where we passed through a number of security checks. We stepped into a recovery room, where two surgeons were working on one of Dr. Berman's projects. Five white New Zealand rabbits had just undergone oophorectomies to surgically induce menopause. A sixth was feeling the anesthesia take effect. Her head was flopped forward, now too heavy to lift. Her eyes had gone slack.

Afterward, Berman will test a new treatment. A lot of Sexual Pain Disorder is caused by "inadequate secretion in the vaginal canal," Berman said. So she will administer an agent that will naturally switch on the body's mucosal membranes to start producing lubrication.

In another wing of the lab, she opened a refrigerator and pulled out a tray holding a few dozen capped test tubes.

"These are rabbit cervixes that were removed after the drug test," she said. "They'll be tested to see if there's been an increase in mucosal activity."

She then showed me an "organ chamber." In outsize tubes are clips that hold stretched segments of the smooth muscle from the clitorises, vaginas and penises removed from animal specimens or discarded human tissue after surgery.

"I can do any kind of smooth muscle test," Berman said. "The tissues are placed in these chambers and you look at how they respond to drugs. I can show you how tissue contracts or relaxes. I can stimulate it electronically and look at the reactions in the presence or absence of different drugs. And it's all recorded here." She pointed to a needle scratching across an unscrolling cylinder of paper, like a seismograph.

These tests represent the experiments now being conducted in university labs and corporate R-and-D facilities all over the country. The cumulative lesson of much of this research is leading to two categories of treatments—hormone therapy, which restores desire, and various drugs, which amplify the sensation of arousal. Many companies are researching hormone medicines. Solvay already markets one called Estratest. Organon is in trials with a treatment called tibolone, which is believed to increase desire. Dr. Glenn Braunstein, an endocrinologist at Cedars-Sinai Medical Center in Los Angeles, is working on a "testosterone patch" under grants from the marketing giant Procter & Gamble.

But the real gold rush is occurring in the other field of research—creating a drug to increase blood flow to the genitals. And just as Viagra as a pill was a kind of psychological breakthrough, the researchers looking for other blood-flow solutions want something simple—a tablet or perhaps even better, a quick-acting cream that is stabilized at room temperature so that women can carry it in a purse like lipstick or men can just toss it into a shaving kit. The competition is furious among small firms, each with a blood-flow drug—some for men, some for women—that are anywhere from one to five years from getting to market. Herewith a sampling, complete with active ingredients:

- Vivus: prostaglandin E-1 cream.
- MacroChem: a gel, using a version of prostaglandin E-1 called Topiglan.
- NexMed: alprostadil, a variant of prostaglandin cream.
- Tap Pharmaceuticals: an apomorphine treatment formulated into a small tablet placed under the tongue.
- Pentech Pharmaceutical: ditto.
- Zonagen: phentolamine, in tablets and suppositories.
- Pfizer: Viagra for women (sildenafil).
- Palatin Technologies: a peptide molecule derivative called PT-14; in the earliest test stages.
- ICOS Corporation: a tablet code-named IC351. (That's all they would reveal.) Bill Gates, who may be telling us something, owns almost 13 percent of the company.

I WANTED TO COMPILE A COMPLETE LIST OF EACH and every sex drug currently in trials. But it became an endless pursuit, the research being so frenetic, and the line between legitimate and illegitimate being so confusing. Obviously, once hard science ratified the actual existence of a drug like Viagra, the very reality of it was a wake-up call to America's snake-oil salesmen.

Infomercials have shifted from vegetable slicers and wrinkle tonics to "natural" aphrodisiacs. There is scarcely a tree left standing in the rain forest whose bark hasn't been stripped and tested for the alternative-health industry. The Internet is teeming with unsolicited ads for products with vaguely homonymic names, though none of them come close to Pfizer's allegedly unintended melding of "vital" and "Niagara" to generate the best product name since Coke. Some long-touted aphrodisiacs are now being tested, too. A derivative of chili peppers is in legitimate trials. Does this count as a drug?

NitroMed, a company based in Massachusetts, is working on a mixture of an old passion powder called yohimbe (stripped from the inner bark of the Corynanthe yohimbe tree in tropical West Africa) combined with an amino acid called L-Arginine to see if the two can work effectively as a vasodilator— that is, a chemical that increases blood flow. Then there are the nondrug inventions. A company called UroMetrics is working on a vacuum device, fitted with a small cup the size of a thimble, and intended to draw blood directly to the clitoris. It might be easy to dismiss this as a sex toy, except that it's also in trials for Food and Drug Administration approval, and UroMetrics intends to distribute it only as a medical device via prescription.

With the enraged pace of daily life, who doubts that a drug-enhanced four-minute sexual encounter among harried day traders could become the norm?

While cruising the Patent Office's Web site (www. uspto.gov), I discovered that Vivus's claim to prostaglandin E-1 cream has been challenged by a Tennessee doctor named Michael Wysor. According to his patent attorney, Michael Ebert in New York, Wysor may have filed his invention after the original patent was granted to Vivus, but he believes there are technical challenges that support his claim.

Wysor, who ran two sexual-health clinics, in Knoxville and Johnson City, that have since gone bankrupt, has just finished a book proposal on erectile dysfunction. He has tried his cream on women informally, but refused to elaborate on his methods. That's just how crowded the field has become. Garage inventors are in on it.

The pace of change inside this small research world also means that almost no one is stopping to reflect on the implications of the drugs that are marching—and there really is no stopping them now—toward the marketplace. When I spoke to Leland Wilson, the C.E.O. of Vivus, about his company's new prostaglandin cream, he happily suggested that most women would be able to experience orgasm after just a few minutes of vaginal intercourse. Such a development seemed fraught with truly significant implications—both good and bad—but obviously fraught. When I pressed him to imagine some of the implications, he sputtered through several change-of-subject tactics.

"That is beyond the realm of medicine," he said. There was a quality to the conversation reminiscent of Werner von Braun, who supposedly once said, "I send the rockets up; where they come down is not my business."

IT WOULD BE NICE IF ALL MEDICAL BREAKTHROUGHS were just for the medical complaints outlined by the doctors. But that's not how the world works. With couples holding down two jobs and the enraged pace of modern

life, who doubts that a drug-enhanced four-minute sexual encounter among harried day traders could become the norm? The very idea of a long slow evening probably won't completely disappear. It'll just go the way of sitting on the porch, the 3 o'clock dinner and the literary novel—something experienced over the holidays or on vacation.

"I find it simply incredible this whole thing is happening," said Leonore Tiefer, a psychologist at the New York University School of Medicine and pretty much the only critic of all this research I could find.

"There is no such thing as 'female sexual dysfunction,' " she added. "It's a social construction invented to benefit the drug companies." Tiefer believes that a kind of "magical thinking" infects the way most of us imagine our sexuality. That it can always be better, and that we resist the natural changes that define the arc of a well-lived life: "That's where this disorder comes in and says, 'If there is a change'—and invariably there is a change in life—'then change is bad.' Ah, a problem! So we invent a universal model, a normative view of sex. If you don't get wet for X period of seconds from Y pressure of stimulation, then you have a problem."

Tiefer was evasive when I asked her about the existence of real medical conditions being cured by these new drugs. "What about the placebo effect?" she asked, when I offered up the Boston professor's case as an example. Tiefer believes the medicalization of sex gives people an out—a way to avoid the root cause of their sexual problems. "I don't see many women depressed about the blood flow to the genitalia. They are depressed about many other things about sex, but not that. This research should be done, of course, but with a few dollars, by a few people, in a few places. But it should not be this Boeing of sex research."

Not surprisingly, many researchers dismiss Tiefer's ideas as rear-guard propaganda to protect the sex concession that therapists have held for so long. Fears that the medical establishment will big-foot the psychologists' business is not an imaginary concern these days. The central theme of Peter Kramer's "Listening to Prozac" is the observation that, in the treatment of depression, drug therapy has driven talk therapy right out of business.

"Every disease pharmacology has attacked in the last 50 years," Vivus's Wilson said bluntly, "has at some point been treated by psychologists, and as soon as pharmacology discovers the real organic reason for the disease and a method for treating it, then psychologists moved on to treat something else. That's exactly what's happening here." Precisely because "psychologists have never successfully treated sexual dysfunction in anybody," Wilson said, "business" was the real source of much of the current professional "squabbling." But not all of Tiefer's critics dismiss her apprehensions.

"There is a fear that Viagra might be used like Prozac," Laura Berman said, "as a sort of Band-Aid approach to therapy. And it's a risk, especially in men, that you might be treating the symptoms, not the problem."

But Tiefer also believes that the medical model of research is just too reductive: "They don't look at sex in a robust way. It's the narrowest possible view: does it twitch once or twice? O.K., then, twice is statistically more significant than once. Good girl."

"Viagra does make sex into a very goal-oriented act," Berman conceded. "The question is, What is sex in general? Is the goal to have an orgasm? Or is it to make yourself vulnerable to someone, communicate with them, share yourself with someone? Sex is often the mirror of the larger relationship. So now we have the possibility of the four-minute encounter. What does that do to intimacy?" She paused for a moment, and it was possible to see her concern metamorphose into a new argument: "Maybe a couple would be better off if they combined four-minute sex with a two-hour conversation over wine." This research, she concluded, suddenly finding her voice, will ultimately allow for different choices. "You will also be able to have hours of sex with multiple orgasms," she added, offering up a future of "quickies and slowies, and a whole range of options."

CHOICE. YOU WONDER, WHAT TOOK SO LONG? THE language of the marketplace that has conquered every other domain in contemporary life has at last found a vehicle to enter the bedroom. "This work," Berman said, "is putting something mysterious and uncontrollable under our control. It can be a liberating and exciting shift, or a confining one, depending."

And that's where Viagra and its progeny are truly revolutionary. They enable us to control our own sexual health, pushing the idea of sexuality far beyond the lab or the couch. The Tiefer debate presumes that these medical inventions will stay under the strict control of doctors, that the old rules of the medical-industrial complex still apply.

But the Golden Age of the A.M.A. is over. The appearance of Viagra has taken place at a time when medicine itself is in the process of decentralizing and allowing market forces to guide many decisions. Increasingly, patients are told to take charge of their own health care; politicians debate a "patient's bill of rights." H.M.O.'s themselves are built on the idea that individuals will decide the general direction of their care. Doctors are increasingly called health care "providers" as drugs are now marketed directly to patients. Viagra was one of the first new drugs introduced to the world alongside the slogan: "Ask your doctor about. . . ."

In this loosey-goosey environment, Viagra has already slipped into the recreational underground—far beyond the reach of both psychologists and doctors. Club kids in the big cities use it as a party drug. The practice of poly-pharmacy, taking a couple of different rave drugs, say, Ecstasy or Special K, kills the sex drive. For heavy partiers, Viagra solves the problem; it allows a night of Dionysian dancing to end the way it used to.

Viagra has also found its way into gay subculture. "You have to realize that a lot of men come out of the closet when they are 30 or even 40, and then go nuts," said Eston Dunn, the health education coordinator for the Gay and Lesbian Community Center in Fort Lauderdale, Fla. "If you're heterosexual, you discover your sexuality at 15, and then you go nuts. That's why a lot of older gay men behave like 15-year-olds. In many ways, they really are 15, and a lot of them turn to Viagra to keep up with their own newfound enthusiasm." In the gay party scene, Dunn said, "you used to hear that cocaine lines were put out with straws. Now it's Viagra, like jelly beans in little candy dishes."

The third group using Viagra on the sly is nonimpotent heterosexuals. I found out about this niche accidentally one night at my own dinner table. An old acquaintance stopped over for the night. He's an ambitious man, in his late 30's, the chairman of a well-regarded department of a prestigious university. On about our third glass of wine, he leaned over and asked, "So have you tried Viagra?"

I bolted back. "No, no," he said. "I mean for fun." But I was confused. Pfizer's official pronouncements state clearly that Viagra doesn't really "work" on potent men. My friend, who would not allow his name to be used, said he wasn't talking about the stated effect of Viagra. Although he did in fact get what he thought were unflagging erections, there is another side effect of Viagra. Beside maximizing blood flow, for the three to five hours that the drug is in the body, it also blocks the enzyme that stymies erections just after orgasm.

"My girlfriend always knows when I use it," explained my friend, who has tried the drug roughly 15 times in the last year. "Instead of this carefully choreographed single episode, suddenly I'm a nuclear reactor of love. Definitely. Multiple orgasms in one night." (So female drugs eliminate foreplay, shortening sex, and male drugs lengthen intercourse, extending sex. Once again, men and women pass like ships in the night.)

Pfizer makes it plain that the company does not agree with this kind of cavalier use of Viagra. But Pfizer is being somewhat disingenuous. Just look at the ads for Viagra. The originals in 1998 and 1999 featured what were clearly old men. One image was a barrel-chested fellow with whitening hair wearing a big winter sweater stretched across the healthy bulk of a well-lived life. He is standing in a meadow, hugging his wife, a women in her 60's looking quite good in a pair of jeans. The slogan reads, "Let the Dance Begin."

The new ad, which I clipped in January from a national magazine, has a trim fellow who could be a character on "Friends." He has a mop of brown hair above a smooth forehead. He's embracing a young woman in a white blouse, tossing her mane of pretty red hair. He might be 35, maybe. The slogan reads, "Take the First Step." More elaborate versions speak of a new disease: "If you're not satisfied with your sex life due to poor erections during recent months, talk to your doctor. You may be suffering from mild E.D.—and Viagra can help."

"Not satisfied with your sex life"—now there's a market segment. And what is "mild" E.D.? It's not really defined and could encompass just about any complaint imaginable. Perhaps it's what my friend was describing. He wanted his "maximum" erections to last for as long as he wanted to spend in bed with his lover. Viagra, he said, "lets me do this for hours without ever having to even think about it." And how did he get his prescription? He told his doctor that since he practices safe sex, he'd have less "trouble keeping a condom on" if his penis maintained a maximum blood-flow erection. His "provider" wrote the prescription.

The appeal Viagra has for some of these subgroups has meant that the blue pill is showing up in the underground drug economy. There have been numerous drug busts reported in which Viagra was found individually packaged among cocaine, Ecstasy and pot—ready for dealers to market. In England, according to several published reports, the drug goes by the street name "poke."

I'm skeptical of the "poke" lingo, in part because the street is probably the most inaccessible place to get Viagra. Why go to some dingy corner in a bad part of town when the Internet is filled with sites that sell it easily and cheaply. Of course, the authorities have tried to crack down on the practice of selling pharmaceuticals online. A family-practice doctor in Ohio named Daniel L. Thompson was charged in July with 64 felonies, including 17 counts of drug trafficking for providing Viagra and other prescriptions over the Internet. And in December, President Clinton called on the F.D.A. to take measures to stop the practice. But controlling the Web is futile, as I discovered one day last winter when I typed "Viagra and aphrodisiac" into a search engine and was offered hundreds of choices. The Web sites sound like jokes: drugman.com and mywebdr.com and viagraguys.com. I opted to get my fix from a Web site called kwikmed.com.

After I signed on—I waited while this message scrolled by: "Brought to you by Tide Detergent"—I was instructed to fill out an online medical interview. I was asked obvious questions, like "Are you taking any heart medication?" I told the truth and said no. I was asked only a couple of private questions, but I admitted to no dysfunction whatsoever. Only one question was devoted to ascertaining my "problem." So I wrote: "Life is not as good as it should be"—a philosophical statement I have pretty much always lived by. When I clicked the box marked Send, I instantaneously received a message back saying my doctor had "approved me for Viagra," unless of course my credit card didn't clear. The next morning, at the crack of the workday, barely 12 hours after I had clicked the send button, the FedEx guy appeared with an envelope that rattled when he handed it to me. In a brown bottle were 10 of the famous blue diamond-shaped pills. The crooked label looked as if it had been produced on an Officemax printer. My doctor was someone named "A. Guzman."

As we permit more and more market forces to take command of the health care industry, it shouldn't surprise anyone that the new drug dealer will not be found in the shadows, offering sinsemilla under his breath. He's already sitting right on our desks, his cursor winking at us. As I started to cruise the Internet looking for this underground world, it quickly became clear that, like the culture at large, Viagra had almost instantaneously colonized this frontier, too. One or two hyperlinks from Viagra, and I came upon a book called "Better Sex Through Chemistry."

"The idea of exotic herbal aphrodisiacs has been around forever," said the book's co-author, John Morgenthaler, when I reached him on the telephone. "But people thought they were akin to eating raw oysters. A neat idea, but really just the placebo effect." Viagra, in his mind, changed all that. Morgenthaler's book, and a 1999 sequel, "The Smart Guide to Better Sex From Andro to Zinc," chronicles the new levels of proof that hard science is bringing to the reputations of some of the old folklore remedies. This is evidence-based medicine at its simplest, separating the wheat from the chaff with double-blind placebo-controlled tests. Many of the old remedies hold no interest to researchers—like camel hump fat or jackal bile or dong chong xia cao, a Chinese fungus that grows on dormant worms. (One day, naturalists may credit Viagra for saving the rhinoceros, now on the cusp of extinction due to the popularity of its supposedly aphrodisiacal horn.)

Other traditional remedies, like yohimbe, are being seriously considered. But the rethinking of sex caused by Viagra, according to Morgenthaler, merely signals a much bigger change that the drug is effecting.

"Viagra has opened the subject and legitimized the idea of enhancement drugs," Morgenthaler said. "This is the way it works with Western medicine: first there is this idea that if you have a 'disease' then you need a medicine to treat it. Then some forward-thinking doctor says, 'Why wait for the disease to start?' So we get to talking about 'prevention.' The third step is, 'Why be disease-oriented at all?' Let's just enhance ourselves beyond normal and average." This new era will be brought about by the consumerization of medicine, Morgenthaler noted. By allowing patients to have more of a say in what "medicine" means, we are redefining its purposes.

"What is cosmetic surgery?" Morgenthaler asked. "Isn't it just medicine bent entirely toward enhancement? The other breakthrough area is sports medicine. It's almost entirely about enhancement." Two years ago, Mark McGwire of the St. Louis Cardinals revealed that he was a regular user of an enhancing drug called androstenedione. Many critics weighed in to denounce the corrosive effect of a role model proclaiming the virtues of a drug. Morgenthaler, however, sees McGwire as a brave pioneer, like Dole—someone who has come out of the closet to speak honestly about the brave new worlds these medicines hail.

"There really is an obvious parallel here," said Rachel Maines, author of the highly regarded book "The Technology of Orgasm." Her sober account of the industrial history of the electric vibrator shows how it was invented by a doctor, Joseph Mortimer Granville, in the 1880's and was used exclusively by doctors as a sexual-medical device to better cure hysteria in women by effecting a "hysterical paroxysm." The machine had the added benefit of moving patients more quickly through the office by shortening the old manual method of inducing a paroxysm to an industrial-age 10 minutes. The earliest vibrators easily stayed within the bounds of medicine since "they were steam-powered and you had to keep shoveling coal into the engine," Maines said. But eventual refinements in the machinery meant the vibrator "was democratized—it started with doctors and then slowly became available to everyone."

When I raised with Goldstein the possibility of these new drugs spilling over into the general population, he was outraged. He hardly believed me when I told him I had Viagra in my hands less than a day after going online to find it. When I insisted that it was that easy to obtain, he simply asserted that the government should do something about it. When I told him that I had talked to people who were enjoying Viagra recreationally and that the drug had another life below the surface of medicine's officialdom, he shrugged and said, "It's not right."

Instead he gave me a lecture, outlining the future as he saw it: "When you go to medical school, you can go into ob/gyn, urology, general surgery, endocrinology, cardiology, gastroenterology—but can you find a department of sexual medicine? No. But sexual medicine will find its place in medical schools. There will be a sexual medical specialty with multidisciplinary inputs from many fields. Why? Because all human beings have only several things in common. When they get thirsty, they drink. When they get hungry, they eat." He paused for a minute. "And all are very interested sexual beings. This is the principle upon which I am dedicating my academic career."

No doubt sexual medicine will one day be taught at medical schools. But in permitting that to happen we have defined a certain kind of pleasure as a branch of health (although perhaps not as radically as, say, the Netherlands, where government-financed prostitutes are made available to people with disabilities). Still, the pressure is on to improve something that was once understood to be a lucky side effect to procreation.

The generation that will first sample all these drugs and creams and pills as they come off the R.-and-D. conveyor belts in the next few years is the same one that, in the pop history of America, broke ground by smoking pot in the 1960's and 70's for enlightenment and set off the sexual revolution. It is the same generation whose interest in long-term health gave us jogging and workout spas; the same generation that is perpetually accused of being permanent adolescents; the same generation that has accelerated this economy into overdrive. Does anyone believe that regulation will prevent this same generation from employing drugs, in the words of Leonore Tiefer, "to maintain a 20-year-old vagina to go with their husband's 20-year-old penis"? The underground markets of John Morgenthaler and the Main Street clinics of Irwin Goldstein are not two choices. They are flip sides of the same coin—an inevitable result of the impulse to bring the wonderful world of chemistry into the bedroom.

My bottle of Viagra sits on the second shelf of my medicine cabinet, unopened—a totem of the future. But what's in it? Medicine? Preventive therapy? Enhancement pills? Recreational drugs? The marketplace will let us know soon enough. I look at the little brown bottle every morning and see the name of my new provider, A. Guzman—a genie of turboconsumerism heralding the conquest of choice over the last redoubt of privacy.

Jack Hitt is a contributing writer for the magazine.

Unit Selections

11. **Are You Man Enough?** Richard Lacayo
12. **Male Sexual Circuitry,** Irwin Goldstein
13. **The Science of Women & Sex,** John Leland
14. **America: Awash in STDs,** Gracie S. Hsu
15. **Prostate Dilemmas,** Susan Brink
16. **Too Much of a Good Thing,** Thomas Beller
17. **What Made Troy Gay?** Deborah Blum
18. **Out of the Fold?** David Van Biema
19. **The Five Sexes, Revisited,** Anne Fausto-Sterling

Key Points to Consider

❖ How do you rate yourself with respect to knowing how your body works sexually on a scale from one (very uninformed, not even sure of correct names for parts and processes) to six (well-informed and can troubleshoot sexual health conditions and figure out how to improve sexual response)? What has held your score down or increased it?

❖ How have (or would) you react if a friend confided in you that he or she was having sexual functioning problems, for example, erections or painful intercourse problems? What if the person confiding in you was a coworker? A stranger? Your mother or your grandfather? Who would you talk to if it were you with the problem and what response would you want from the other person?

❖ Rate the following six personal problems from least to most serious for yourself at this time in your life: (a) financial problems, (b) job dissatisfaction, (c) serious illness of a family member, (d) lack of communication with an immediate family member, (e) serious doubt about your religious or spiritual beliefs and (f) sexual dysfunction. Would your rating be likely to change in 5 years? 10 years? 35 years?

❖ What is your opinion about the following statement?

"There is no such thing as sexual addiction. Those people are just making excuses for being irresponsible."

❖ It is rare for people to wonder why someone is heterosexual in the same ways as we wonder why someone is homosexual or bisexual. What do you think contributes to a person's sexual orientation? Do you think it is possible for people not to feel threatened by sexual orientations different from their own? Why or why not?

 **Links**

www.dushkin.com/online/

7. **Bibliography: HIV/AIDS and College Students**
   http://www.sph.emory.edu/bshe/AIDS/college.html
8. **The Body: A Multimedia AIDS and HIV Information Resource**
   http://www.thebody.com/cgi-bin/body.cgi
9. **Healthy Way**
   http://www.ab.sympatico.ca/Contents/health/
10. **Hispanic Sexual Behavior and Gender Roles**
    http://www.caps.ucsf.edu/hispnews.html
11. **James Kohl**
    http://www.pheromones.com
12. **Johan's Guide to Aphrodisiacs**
    http://www.santesson.com/aphrodis/aphrhome.htm

These sites are annotated on pages 4 and 5.

Human bodies are miraculous things. Most of us, however, have less than a complete understanding of how they work. This is especially true of our bodily responses and functioning during sexual activity. Efforts to develop a healthy sexual awareness are severely hindered by misconceptions and lack of quality information about physiology. The first portion of this unit directs attention to the development of a clearer understanding and appreciation of the workings of the human body.

Over the past decade and a half, the general public's awareness of, and interest and involvement in, their own health care has dramatically increased. We want to stay healthy and live longer, and we know that to do so, we must know more about our bodies, including how to prevent problems, recognize danger signs, and find the most effective treatments. By the same token, if we want to stay sexually fit—from robust youth through a healthy, happy, sexy old age—we must be knowledgeable about sexual health care.

As you read through the articles in this section, you will be able to see more clearly that matters of sexual biology and behavior are not merely physiological in origin. The articles included clearly demonstrate the psychological, social, and cultural origins of sexual behavior as well.

Why we humans feel, react, respond, and behave sexually can be quite complex. This is especially true regarding the issue of sexual orientation. Perhaps no other area of sexual behavior is as misunderstood as this one. Although experts do not agree about what causes our sexual orientation—homosexual, heterosexual, or bisexual—growing evidence suggests a complex interaction of biological or genetic determination, environmental or sociocultural influence, and free choice. In the early 1900s sexologist Alfred Kinsey introduced his seven-point continuum of sexual orientation. It placed exclusive heterosexual orientation at one end, exclusive homosexual orientation at the other, and identified the middle range as where most people would fall if society and culture were unprejudiced. Since Kinsey, many others have added their research findings and theories to what is known about sexual orientation. John Money, a Johns Hopkins University researcher, who for the last 30 years has done research and writing on what he calls the sexology of erotic orientation, and Anne Fausto-Sterling, a professor of biology and women's studies at Brown University, who for the last 10 years has been an advocate for intersexuals (people not clearly male or female by anatomy or behavior), recommend that we consider sexuality and sexual orientation as even more multidimensional than Kinsey's continuum. They stand with others who suggest that we pluralize our terms in this area: human sexualities and orientations.

That the previous paragraph may have been upsetting, even distasteful, to some readers emphasizes the connectedness of psychological, social, and cultural issues with those of sexuality.

Human sexuality is biology, behavior, and much, much more. Our sexual beliefs, behaviors, choices, even feelings and comfort levels, are profoundly affected by what our culture prescribes and proscribes, which has been transmitted to us by the full range of social institutions and processes. This section begins our attempt to address these interrelationships and their impact on human sexuality.

The subsection *The Body and Its Responses* contains three informative and thought-provoking articles that illuminate the interplay of biological, psychological, cultural, and interpersonal factors that affect sexual functioning. The first two articles, "Are You Man Enough?" and "Male Sexual Circuitry" focus on male bodies and functioning. The third, "The Science of Women & Sex" focuses on female bodies and functioning. All can be viewed as owner's manuals for each sex. However, we believe all readers should read all three and will undoubtedly learn a great deal of interesting and practical information about sexual health and functioning.

The subsection *Hygiene and Sexual Health Care* addresses three current and important sexuality issues. "America: Awash in STDs" provides both up-to-date factual information on a range of STDs and a thought-provoking examination of the social and political issues involved in, and perhaps hindering, efforts at containing this health crisis. Next, "Prostate Dilemmas" explains both good and bad news about prostate cancer, the most common of the male sexual cancers: early detection means lives saved, but current treatment options may still significantly impair sexual and/or urinary functioning. Finally, the subsection concludes with a tour of the Meadows, a treatment center for sexual addicts, and the stories of people for whom sexual desire and behavior have led to dire consequences.

The *Human Sexualities and Orientations* subsection contains three articles that dramatically demonstrate the changes that have occurred during the last decade with respect to sexual orientation. In the past few years, growing numbers of scientific findings have identified biological, genetic, and hormonal differences between heterosexual and homosexual people. However, these findings have not significantly weakened an American culture often called fundamentally homophobic (or homosexual-fearing). At the same time, more gay, lesbian, bisexual, and transgendered people have publicly acknowledged their orientation, and have become more visible in the public eye via popular magazine stories, television, and movies. They are asserting their desires to be understood and accepted. In this subsection readers will meet some of these people, as well as some of their families, supporters, and critics. At the end, readers can make their own predictions about whether the first decade of the new century will bring a greater understanding and acceptance of the wide range of human sexualities, further entrenchment of homophobia, or an increased polarization of both.

Sexual Biology, Behavior, and Orientation

ARE YOU MAN ENOUGH?

Testosterone can make a difference in bed and at the gym. And soon you'll be able to get it as a gel. But it's a risky substance. And is it really what makes men men?

By RICHARD LACAYO

WHATEVER ELSE YOU MAY THINK about testosterone, you can tell it's a hot topic. Every time you mention that you happen to be writing about it, the first thing people ask is "Can you get me some?" (Everybody, even the women.) Maybe that's not so surprising. If there is such a thing as a bodily substance more fabled than blood, it's testosterone, the hormone that we understand and misunderstand as the essence of manhood. Testosterone has been offered as the symbolic (and sometimes literal) explanation for all the glories and infamies of men, for why they start street fights and civil wars, for why they channel surf, explore, prevail, sleep around, drive too fast, plunder, bellow, joust, plot corporate takeovers and paint their bare torsos blue during the Final Four. Hey, what's not to like?

Until now, it was easy to talk about testosterone but hard to do much about it. About 4 million men in the U.S. whose bodies don't produce enough take a doctor-prescribed synthetic version, mostly by self-injection, every one to three weeks. But the shots cannot begin to mimic the body's own minute-by-minute micromanagement of testosterone levels. So they can produce a roller coaster of emotional and physical effects, from a burst of energy, snappishness and libido in the first days to fatigue and depression later. The main alternative, a testosterone patch, works best when applied daily to the scrotum, an inconvenient spot, to put it mildly. Some doctors recommend that you warm that little spot with a blow dryer, which may or may not be fun.

All of that will change this summer when an easy to apply testosterone ointment, AndroGel, becomes generally available for the first time by prescription. The company that developed it, Illinois-based Unimed Pharmaceuticals, promises that because AndroGel is administered once or more a day, it will produce a more even plateau of testosterone, avoiding the ups and downs of the shots. Though the body's own production of this hormone trails off gradually in men after the age of 30 or so, not many men now seek testosterone-replacement therapy (not that they necessarily need to) or even get their T levels tested. But replace the needles and patches with a gel, something you just rub into the skin like coconut oil during spring break at Daytona Beach, and suddenly the whole idea seems plausible.

Testosterone, after all, can boost muscle mass and sexual drive. (It can also cause liver damage and accelerate prostate cancer, but more on that later.) That makes it central to two of this culture's rising preoccupations: perfecting the male body and sustaining the male libido, even when the rest of the male has gone into retirement. So will testosterone become the next estrogen, a hormone that causes men to bang down their doctor's doors, demanding to be turned into Mr. T? Do not underestimate the appeal of any substance promising to restore the voluptuous powers of youth to the scuffed and dented flesh of middle age. If you happen to be a man, the very idea is bound to appeal to your inner hood ornament, to that image of yourself as all wind-sheared edges and sunlit chrome. And besides, there's the name: testosterone! Who can say no to something that sounds like an Italian dessert named after a Greek god?

But testosterone is at issue in larger debates about behavioral differences between men and women and which differences are biologically determined. A few Sundays ago, the New York *Times* Magazine ran a long piece by Andrew Sullivan, 36, the former editor of the *New Republic,* in which he reported his own experience with testosterone therapy. In two years he has gained 20 lbs. of muscle. And in the days right after his once-every-two-weeks shot, he reports feeling lustier, more energetic, more confident and more quarrelsome—more potent, in all senses of the word.

Looking over the scientific research on testosterone, Sullivan speculated on the extent to which such traits as aggression, competitiveness and risk taking, things we still think of as male behavior, are linked to the fact that men's bodies produce far more testosterone than women's bodies. His answer—a lot—was offered more as an intuition than a conclusion, but it produced a

> **And besides, there's the name: testosterone! Who can say no to something that sounds like an Italian dessert named after a Greek god?**

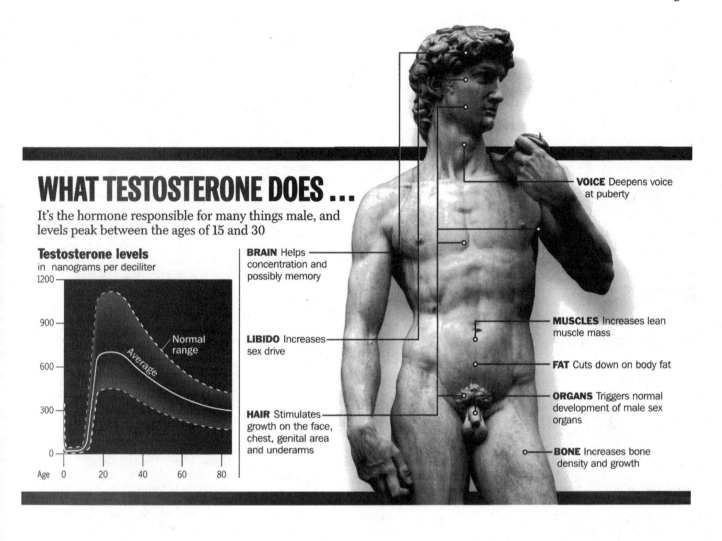

WHAT TESTOSTERONE DOES ...

It's the hormone responsible for many things male, and levels peak between the ages of 15 and 30

Testosterone levels
in nanograms per deciliter

VOICE Deepens voice at puberty

BRAIN Helps concentration and possibly memory

LIBIDO Increases sex drive

HAIR Stimulates growth on the face, chest, genital area and underarms

MUSCLES Increases lean muscle mass

FAT Cuts down on body fat

ORGANS Triggers normal development of male sex organs

BONE Increases bone density and growth

... AND HOW IT IS ADMINISTERED

Taking the hormone in steady, small doses is safest, but not always convenient. A gel form, due in pharmacies this summer, may become the method of choice for boosting testosterone counts.

Injection
HOW OFTEN Every 7 to 30 days
DOSE 100 mg to 350 mg
WHERE Muscle
BENEFITS High doses of testosterone
PROBLEMS Testosterone levels are not steady; high in first few days after injection, they fall back down at the end of a cycle
RISKS Surge of testosterone carries risk of liver problems, blood thickening, acne and breast development and may accelerate growth of existing prostate tumors

Patches
HOW OFTEN Daily
DOSE 4 mg to 6 mg
WHERE Scrotal tissue, back, abdomen or thighs
BENEFITS Controlled, steady delivery of testosterone that mimics natural cycles
PROBLEMS Best absorbed when applied to scrotal skin with a hair dryer. But scrotal skin contains enzymes that break down testosterone too quickly. Possibility of allergic reactions to patch
RISKS May spur growth of existing prostate tumors

Gel
HOW OFTEN Once to several times a day
DOSE 10 mg to 40 mg
WHERE Hairless skin
BENEFITS Controlled, steady delivery of testosterone that mimics natural cycles
PROBLEMS Variable effects. Not long-lasting
RISKS May cause faster growth of existing prostate tumors

Pill
HOW OFTEN 2 to 4 times a day
DOSE 40 mg to 80 mg
WHERE Mouth
BENEFITS Steady levels mimic natural cycles of testosterone
PROBLEMS Liver breaks down most testosterone before it can work. Not commercially available in U.S.
RISKS May increase bad cholesterol and decrease good cholesterol levels. Risk of liver damage

spate of fang baring among some higher primates in the media and scientific world, since it implies that gender differences owe more to biology than many people would like to believe. Three researchers wrote the *Times* to complain that Sullivan had overstated their thinking. In the online magazine *Slate,* columnist Judith Shulevitz attacked Sullivan for favoring nature over environment in a debate in which nobody knows yet which is which. In the days that followed, Sullivan fired back at Shulevitz in *Slate,* she attacked again, and other writers joined in. If testosterone use becomes a true cultural phenomenon, expect the conversations about its role in gender differences to become even more, well, aggressive.

So just what does testosterone actually do for you? And to you? And how does it figure among the physical and environmental pressures that account for head-banging aggression, or even just the trading pit on Wall Street? One reason testosterone enjoys a near mythical status is that myth is what takes over when conclusive data are scarce. Though testosterone was first isolated in 1935, hormone-replacement therapy is one of the few areas of medicine where research on men lags behind that on women.

What we do know is that testosterone is an androgen, as the family of male sex hormones are called, and these hormones, in turn, are made up of the fat known as steroids. Both men and women produce testosterone in their bodies, men in the testes and adrenal glands, women in the adrenal glands and ovaries. But men produce much more—the average healthy male has 260 to 1,000 nanograms of testosterone per deciliter of blood plasma. For women the range is 15 to 70. But because men differ on how effectively their bodies process the substance—for instance, some have more receptors around their body that absorb it—a man on the low end of the normal range can still have all the testosterone he needs for normal sex drive and other benefits. In healthy men, levels also vary during the day, peaking around 8 a.m., which is why men commonly awaken in a state of sexual arousal, and dropping as much as half before bedtime.

Testosterone is the substance that literally turns boys into boys in the womb. In the first weeks after conception, all embryos are technically sexless. Around the sixth week of gestation, the presence of the Y chromosome in males triggers a complex set of signals that cause a surge in testosterone. Among other things, that sets in motion the formation of the penis and testes. In adolescence, boys undergo another eruption that deepens their voices, causes hair to form on their bodies and allows their muscles to enlarge. Testosterone in the blood of teenage boys can jump to as high as 2,000 nanograms, which helps explain teenage boys.

One possible danger of easy-to-use testosterone is that it might become a tempta-tion to younger males looking to bulk up at the gym. Not many of them would be able to demonstrate the diminished T counts that would allow them to get it legally from their doctors, but the potential for a black market in AndroGel is not hard to imagine among teens and guys in their 20s—and older—who hear stories about a new substance stronger than the supplements available over the counter and easier to use than anabolic steroids that are injected. For teens in particular, the dangers of testosterone overload are not just acne and breast development but a shutting down of bone growth—though they may be at an age that makes them almost deaf to the risks. For older men, studies indicate that high levels of T do not necessarily cause prostate cancer but do fuel the growth of tumors once they occur, which is why chemical castration is one means of treating the disease in the advanced stages.

Gay men may have been one of the first populations to talk up testosterone replacement, which is often part of the treatment regimen for HIV-positive men like Sullivan, author of the New York *Times* Magazine piece. They produced a buzz about increased sex drive and better results at the gym, things that happen to be of interest to a lot of straight men too, especially middle-age baby boomers looking to put themselves back in the driver's seat as far as their sex drive is concerned. "These men already come in asking for [testosterone]," says Dr. Louann Brizendine, co-director of the program in sexual health at the University of California, San Francisco. "This generation came out of the sexual revolution. They really identify themselves as sexual beings. And they don't want to give that up."

At 66, Gene Teasley, who operates a family business that makes banners in Dallas, is a decade older than the baby boomers, but he gets the idea. About nine years ago, he went to his doctor complaining of less interest in sex. Since then, he has been getting testosterone shots once every two weeks. "I've enjoyed the results not just in the sexual way but also in a broader way of feeling healthier. I have more of a desire to work out, be outdoors and do more athletic things," he says. "Everybody wants to feel like they felt in their 20s and 30s."

Some researchers are taking seriously the still controversial notion of "male menopause," a constellation of physical changes, including fatigue, depression and drooping libido, that they believe can be traced to the decline of hormones, including testosterone, in men over 50. Others are not so sure. "One thing we have to recognize is that the decline in testosterone is also intertwined with changes, such as decrease in blood flow, and psychological and social changes too," says Dr. Kenneth Goldberg, medical director of the Men's Health Center in Dallas. "Simply expecting to take men who are androgen de-ficient and expecting testosterone to fix it all—it just can't be."

Yet even the passage of time doesn't guarantee that a particular man's testosterone will decline to a level that much affects how he feels, at least not by middle age. Middle-age men who preserve the body weight they had in their 20s may have no falloff at all, while overweight adult men of any age tend to have lower testosterone levels. This means that a couple of the *goombahs* on *The Sopranos* are probably deficient, though maybe I should let you be the one to tell them that.

Once you get past the proven links between testosterone, libido and muscle mass, the benefits of having higher levels of testosterone become harder to prove, though no less interesting to hear about. Just how much of a role does this play in producing behaviors such as aggression, competitiveness and belligerence? Men who take testosterone by injection routinely report that in the first days after the shot, when their T counts are especially high, they feel increased confidence, well-being and feistiness—what you might call swagger. They also describe feeling snappish and fidgety.

Jim—not his real name—is a family therapist who was 40 when he started taking the shots because of fatigue and a so-so interest in sex, which had led him to get his T levels tested. The first day or two after the shot, he says, he's on pins and needles. "My fiancé knows to steer clear. I tend to be short-tempered, more critical, and I go around the house looking for problems. I live out in the country, so right after I get the shot I get out the weed whacker and the chain saw, and I just go crazy."

Gee. Even putting aside for a moment the much increased danger of prostate cancer, do we really want men to turn later life into a hormonal keg party? The thought could be mildly exasperating to women, who might be forgiven for greeting the news with the same feelings china shop-keepers have for bulls. But this is the point at which the discussion of testosterone veers into the metaphysical.

Outside the bedroom and the gym, just what does testosterone do for you? Studies in animals have repeatedly shown that testosterone and aggression go hand in hand. Castrate species after species, and you get a pussycat. Boost the testosterone with injections and the castrated animal acts more like a tiger. In one study of men, when the testosterone levels were suppressed (in this case by researchers using medications) libido and dominant behaviors dropped. But when a mere 20% of the testosterone was added back, libido and domination climbed to the levels where they had started. Which suggests that men do not need much of the stuff to go on doing whatever it is they have already learned to do.

Other studies have shown that men with naturally higher testosterone levels are more aggressive and take-charge than men with slightly lower levels. When two sports teams meet, both teams will show an increase in testosterone during the game. "In the face of competition, levels of testosterone will rise," says Alan Booth, a sociologist at Penn State University. "This prepares the competitor and may help increase the chances for a win. It could be that the rise in testosterone has physical benefits, such as visual acuity and increased strength. But only the winning team continues to show high testosterone after the game."

For this exercise, you don't even have to picture the Packers vs. the Vikings. The T boost also happens during nonphysical competitions, like chess games and trivia contests. Whatever the game, in evolutionary terms this makes sense. Among the primates from whom we are descended, the victorious male in any encounter may have needed to maintain high testosterone levels in the expectation that his position in the pecking order would be challenged by the next guy coming up.

But here it gets complicated. Does higher testosterone produce more aggressive behavior? Or does the more aggressive male—whose aggression was learned, say, at home or in school or in the neighborhood or on the team or in the culture at large—call for a release of testosterone from within himself for assistance? And if testosterone really does determine male behaviors like aggres-sion, then what are we to make of the fact that although testosterone levels are pretty equal in prepubescent children, boys and girls already demonstrate different behaviors?

What we know for certain is this: aggressive behavior and testosterone appear in the same place. And aggressive behavior seems to require some testosterone in your system. But researchers have yet to show conclusively that adding a little more in males who already have a normal range of the stuff does much to make them more aggressive or confrontational. In one study, Dr. Christina Wang of UCLA found that men with low testosterone were actually more likely to be angry, irritable and aggressive than men who had normal to high-normal levels of testosterone. When their testosterone was increased during hormone-replacement therapy, their anger diminished and their sense of well-being increased. "Testosterone is probably a vastly overrated hormone," says Robert Sapolsky, a Stanford University biologist and author of *The Trouble with Testosterone.*

All the same, there are social implications connected to the one area in which we know for a fact that testosterone matters—sex drive. Married men tend to have lower testosterone. It's evolution's way of encouraging the wandering mate to stay home. (In newly divorced men, T levels rise again, as the men prepare to re-enter the competition for a mate.) If aging men start to rou-tinely boost their testosterone levels, and their sexual appetite, to earlier levels, will they further upset the foundations of that ever endangered social arrangement called the family? "What happens when men have higher levels than normal?" asks James M. Dabbs, a psychology professor at Georgia State University. "They are just unmanageable."

Dabbs, the author of *Heroes, Rogues and Lovers,* a book about the importance of the male hormone, is another researcher who believes that T counts for a lot in any number of male moods and behaviors. "It contributes to a boldness and a sense of focus," he insists. It's possible for the scientific community to come to such disparate conclusions on the stuff, not just because the research is slim but because the complexities of human behavior are deep. If we're verging on a moment when testosterone will be treated as one more renewable resource, we may soon all get to focus more clearly on just what it does. But if men, in a culture where the meaning of manhood is up for grabs, look to testosterone for answers to the largest questions about themselves, they are likely to be disappointed. One thing we can be sure of is that the essence of manhood will always be something more complicated than any mere substance in the blood.

—Reported by Lisa McLaughlin and Alice Park/New York

Male Sexual Circuitry

by Irwin Goldstein
and the Working Group for the Study of Central Mechanisms in Erectile Dysfunction

Five hundred years ago Leonardo da Vinci made an observation about the penis that rings true even today for many men and their partners. The Renaissance scientist, inventor and artist—one in a long line of investigators who have attempted to solve the riddle of penile rigidity—observed that this seemingly wayward organ has a will of its own. "The penis does not obey the order of its master, who tries to erect or shrink it at will, whereas instead the penis erects freely while its master is asleep. The penis must be said to have its own mind, by any stretch of the imagination," he wrote.

Da Vinci, who dissected cadaverous penises from men who had been executed by hanging, was the first scientist to recognize that during an erection, the penis fills with blood. In his perception that the penis acts of its own free will, however, this multitalented scholar was wrong.

Far from having a mind of its own, the penis is now known to be under the complete control of the central nervous system—the brain and spinal cord. As William D. Steers, chair of the department of urology at the University of Virginia, has noted, any disturbance in the network of nerve pathways that connects the penis and the central nervous system can lead to erection problems.

In the past few decades the study of erections has been redefined. Thanks to advances in molecular biology, we now have a better understanding of the processes within the penis that lead to erection and detu-

mescence, the return of the penis to a flaccid state. Armed with this knowledge, we have begun to explore how the brain and spinal cord control erections and other sexual functions. The field is still young, but we are optimistic that these efforts will lead to new therapies for the millions of men who suffer from sexual dysfunction—and we expect that some of these findings will also inform treatments for women. Although research on women has lagged far behind that on men, we are beginning to elucidate the striking similarities—as well as differences—between the sexes in regard to sexual function.

An erection is a carefully orchestrated series of events, with the central nervous system in the role of conductor. Even when the penis is at rest, the nervous system is at work. When a man is not sexually aroused, parts of the sympathetic nervous system actively limit blood flow to the penis, keeping it limp. The sympathetic nervous system is one of two branches of the autonomic nervous system—the part of the central nervous system that controls largely "automatic" internal responses, such as blood pressure and heart rate.

Dynamic Balance

Within the penis, and throughout the nervous system, a man's sexual response reflects a dynamic balance between excitatory and inhibitory forces. Whereas the sympathetic nervous system tends to inhibit erections, the parasympa-

thetic system—the other branch of the autonomic nervous system—is one of several important excitatory pathways. During arousal, excitatory signals can originate in the brain, triggered perhaps by a smell or by the sight or thought of an alluring partner, or by physical stimulation of the genitals.

Regardless of where the signals come from, the excitatory nerves in the penis respond by releasing so-called proerectile neurotransmitters, including nitric oxide and acetylcholine. These chemical messengers signal the muscles of the penile arteries to relax, causing more blood to flow into the organ. Spongy chambers inside the penis fill up with blood. As these expand, they compress the veins that normally drain blood from the penis. This pressure squeezes the veins until they are nearly closed, trapping blood within the chambers and producing an erection. (Viagra—also known as sildenafil—works by slowing the breakdown of one of the chemicals that keeps the muscles relaxed, thereby holding blood in the penis.)

During an erection, the penis not only receives nerve signals but also sends them to the spinal cord and brain. The penis has an unusually high density of specialized tactile receptors; when these receptors are stimulated, their signals course to the spinal cord and brain, where they influence nerve pathways from these higher centers. So although the penis does not "think" for itself, it keeps the brain and spinal cord well

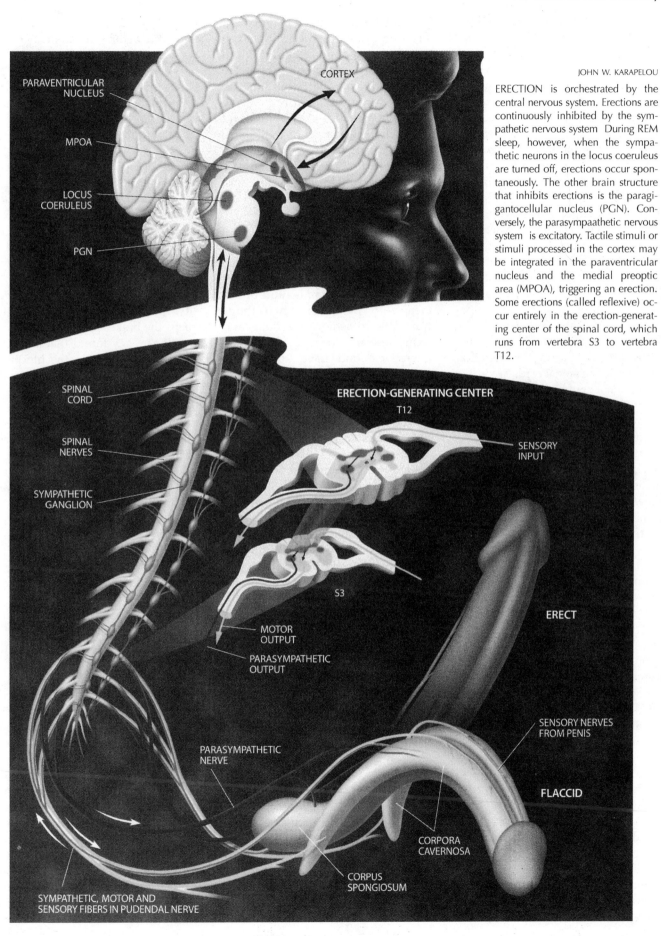

JOHN W. KARAPELOU

ERECTION is orchestrated by the central nervous system. Erections are continuously inhibited by the sympathetic nervous system During REM sleep, however, when the sympathetic neurons in the locus coeruleus are turned off, erections occur spontaneously. The other brain structure that inhibits erections is the paragigantocellular nucleus (PGN). Conversely, the parasympaathetic nervous system is excitatory. Tactile stimuli or stimuli processed in the cortex may be integrated in the paraventricular nucleus and the medial preoptic area (MPOA), triggering an erection. Some erections (called reflexive) occur entirely in the erection-generating center of the spinal cord, which runs from vertebra S3 to vertebra T12.

apprised of its feelings. After a man climaxes or the arousal has diminished, the erection quickly subsides. The sympathetic nervous system again limits blood flow into the penis, which returns to its soft state.

Circumstances that increase the activity of the sympathetic nervous system—such as stress or exposure to cold—can temporarily shrink the penis by making it more flaccid. Conversely, switching off the activity of the sympathetic nervous system enhances erections. Nocturnal erections are a good example of this phenomenon. These occur primarily during rapid eye movement (REM) sleep, the stage in which dreaming occurs. During REM sleep, sympathetic neurons are turned off in the locus coeruleus, a specific area of the brain stem, the part of the brain that connects to the spinal cord. According to one theory, when this sympathetic brain center is quiet, proerectile pathways predominate, allowing nocturnal erections to occur. We often refer to such erections as "battery-recharging mechanisms" for the penis, because they increase blood flow, bringing in fresh oxygen to reenergize the organ. (Episodes of nocturnal arousal also occur in women. Four or five times a night—that is, during each episode of REM— women experience labial, vaginal and clitoral engorgement.)

Some erections, called reflexive erections, are generated entirely in the spinal cord. Much like touching a finger to a hot burner triggers a rapid withdrawal of the hand, physical stimulation of the penis can set off a spinal erection reflex in some situations. So crucial is reproduction to our perpetuation as a species that it appears that the capacity to create an erection has been wired into nerve circuits near the base of a man's spine.

In humans, most of the evidence for this finding has come from observations of soldiers with spinal cord injuries, particularly veterans wounded in World War II. Before then, the general belief was that men with spinal cord injuries were per-

manently and completely impotent and sterile. Although we now know that this view is mistaken, it is understandable. The spinal cord is the information superhighway for the nervous system, shuttling nerve stimuli to and from the brain and the peripheral nerves of the rest of the body. If the spinal cord is damaged, this flow of nerve impulses can be interrupted in myriad ways, depending on where the injury occurs and how extensive it is.

Yet, as physician Herbert Talbot reported in a classic study in 1949, men with severe or complete spinal cord injuries often continue to have erections. In his examination of 200 men with paraplegia, two thirds were able to achieve erections, and some were able to engage in vaginal intercourse and have an orgasm. Even though devastating war injuries left these men paralyzed and unable to control many basic bodily functions, the ability to have erections was often preserved.

These observations—and information from studies in laboratory animals as far back as the 1890s—led to the discovery that an "erection-generating center" is located in the sacral segments of the spinal cord (that is, just above the tail end of the spine, between the S3 and T12 vertebrae). Physical stimulation of the penis sends sensory signals via the pudendal nerve to this erection center. The incoming signals activate connector nerve cells called interneurons, which then stimulate nearby parasympathetic neurons. These neurons send erection-inducing signals from the sacral spine to the penile blood vessels. As long as this reflex arc remains intact, an erection is possible.

The Brain's Brakes

Observations of men and laboratory animals with spinal cord damage have led to another intriguing finding: when the brain is disconnected from the erection-generating center in the spinal cord, erections typically occur more frequently and

with less tactile stimulation than they did before the injury. For instance, Benjamin D. Sachs, an experimental psychologist at the University of Connecticut, found in 1979 that spinal transaction in rats caused an increase of more than 1,000 percent in the number of erections and a 94 percent reduction in the time it took for the animals to become erect.

It seemed as if, in the disconnection of the brain from the body, some inhibitory control over erections was removed. This proved to be the case. In 1990 physiologists Kevin E. McKenna and Lesley Marson, then at Northwestern University, identified the brain center that keeps the brakes on spinal-mediated erections. They found that a specific cluster of neurons in the hindbrain (an evolutionarily ancient part of the brain that controls such basic functions as blood pressure and heart rate) is in charge of this central inhibition. When McKenna and Marson destroyed this group of neurons— called the paragigantocellular nucleus, or PGN—in a male rat's brain, the inhibition disappeared, causing more frequent and intense erections.

These researchers then made another significant discovery about the brain's role in suppressing erections. They found that the PGN neurons send most of their axons down to the erection-generating neurons in the lower spinal cord. There the PGN nerve endings release the neurotransmitter serotonin—a chemical messenger that inhibits erections by opposing the effects of proerectile neurotransmitters.

This discovery may have important implications for the millions of men and women who take serotonin-enhancing drugs to treat depression and other mental health problems. Drugs such as Prozac and Paxil, which belong to the widely used class of drugs called selective serotonin reuptake inhibitors (SSRIs), work in part by increasing brain levels of serotonin. These drugs often cause sexual dysfunction as an unwanted side effect, most commonly delayed or blocked ejaculation in men and, in women, reduced sexual desire and difficulty reaching orgasm.

The work of McKenna and his colleagues provides an explanation for how this side effect may occur. By increasing serotonin in the central nervous system, SSRIs may tighten the brain's built-in brakes on erection, ejaculation and other sexual functions in some people.

As often happens in medicine, however, one person's side effect can be another's therapy. The inhibitory properties of SSRIs have been shown to be helpful for men with premature ejaculation, a condition in which a man climaxes too quickly, typically before vaginal penetration or a few seconds thereafter. SSRIs are effective in delaying orgasm in these men, most likely because they increase central inhibition. Although more research is needed, SSRIs may also hold promise in treating sexual disorders that are associated with excessive or inappropriate sexual urges, such as paraphilias—for example, pedophilia, a sexual interest in children.

Considering that sex makes the world go 'round, or at least keeps us on the planet, it is not clear why these elaborate inhibitory controls have evolved. Although no one knows for sure, some intriguing theories have been advanced. John Bancroft of Indiana University believes that for most men this central inhibition is adaptive, keeping them out of trouble that might arise from excessive or risky pursuit of sexual enjoyment. These internal brakes also may help prevent a man from having repeated ejaculations during sexual encounters, which could lower his sperm store and reduce fertility.

Also, as with many pleasures in life, an erection can become too much of a good thing if it lasts too long. An erection that persists longer than four hours—a phenomenon that may occur in men with sickle cell anemia and in those who use certain drugs—is considered a medical emergency. Called priapism, this condition traps blood within the erect penis, leading to permanent damage if not treated promptly: if freshly oxygenated blood is not brought in, tissue starvation can occur.

Despite the benefits of central inhibition for most men, Bancroft believes it can cause problems for others if it is too strong or too weak. If a man has too much central inhibitory control—if, say, his brain serotonin levels are too high—he may develop sexual dysfunction. Conversely, if his central inhibition is too low, he may be more inclined to engage in high-risk sexual behaviors, such as recklessly ignoring the threat of sexually transmitted diseases in the pursuit of sexual gratification.

Inside the Brain

Many regions throughout the brain contribute to the male sexual response, ranging from centers in the hindbrain, which regulates basic body functions, to areas of the cerebral cortex, the organ of higher thought and intellect. The brain sites we have identified so far appear to be extensively interconnected. We now think the brain's control of sexual function works as a unified network, rather than as a chain of relay sites. In other words, the control of erection does not appear to be organized in a tightly linked chain of command centers but rather is distributed throughout multiple areas in the brain and spinal cord. Therefore, should injury or disease destroy one or more of these regions, the capacity for erections often remains intact.

One of the important brain regions regulating sexual behavior is the hypothalamus. This small area plays a vital role in linking the nervous and endocrine, or hormonal, systems and is involved in the control of certain basic behaviors, such as eating and aggression. A cluster of neurons in the hypothalamus, called the medial preoptic area, or MPOA, seems to have a crucial role in sexual function and, accordingly,

is being intensively studied at the moment.

Researcher François Giuliano of the Faculté de Médecine of the Université Paris-Sud and his colleagues have recently shown that electrical or chemical stimulation of the MPOA causes erections in rats. The MPOA appears to integrate stimuli from many areas of the brain, helping to organize and direct the complex patterns of sexual behavior. Some scientists speculate that the MPOA may also be involved in the recognition of a sexual partner.

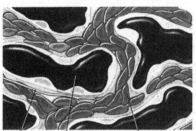

NERVE   SINUSOID   SMOOTH MUSCLE CELL CONTRACTED

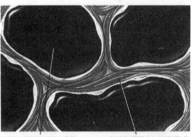

SINUSOID FILLED WITH BLOOD   SMOOTH MUSCLE CELL RELAXED

JOHN W. KARAPELOU

ENGORGEMENT begins when nerves release transmitters that diffuse into the smooth muscle cells around the arteries in the penis, causing the normally contracted cells to relax and blood to flow in (*top*). As they relax, the muscles elongate, pushing against the veins that drain blood from the penis. The blood becomes trapped in sinusoids—the chambers between muscle cells—and the penis becomes erect (*bottom*).

The hypothalamus also contains the paraventricular nucleus, another group of neurons with an important role in male sexual function. Like the MPOA, this nucleus is a processing center that sends and receives messages from different parts of the brain and spinal cord. During sexual arousal, the paraventricular nucleus releases oxytocin. This hormone has long been known to stimulate the release of milk in breast-feeding women and uterine contractions during delivery of a baby; in many species, oxytocin is a chemical "love" messenger that promotes bonding and social attachments. But it also proves to be a brain neurotransmitter that has a powerful proerectile effect in men. Like other neurotransmitters, oxytocin binds to target neurons and regulates the conduction of nerve impulses. In this case, oxytocin activates excitatory nerve pathways running from the spinal erection-generating center to the penis.

Higher brain centers are involved in male sexual response as well, but we know much less about them. Nevertheless, the few studies to date have provided some intriguing results. Researcher Serge Stoleru of Inserm in Paris recently used positron emission tomography (PET) to reveal which parts of the cerebral cortex are activated when men are sexually aroused. He compared PET scans in a group of men who were presented with three kinds of films: sexually explicit, humorous and emotionally neutral (such as a documentary on the Amazon). Stoleru found that when men were sexually aroused, specific parts of the cerebral cortex were activated, including regions associated with emotional experiences and control of the autonomic nervous system.

In addition, scientists are exploring how higher brain functions, such

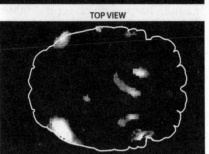
SIDE VIEW   FRONT VIEW

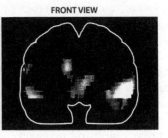
TOP VIEW

COURTESY OF SERGE STOLERU *Inserm*

AROUSAL has been mapped in these PET scans of men watching sexually explicit films. Although research on the sexual organization of the higher brain is just beginning, these scans show that several areas of the cerebral cortex are clearly involved.

as memory and learning, help to control erections. Psychologist Raymond Rosen of Robert Wood Johnson Medical School in New Brunswick, N.J., showed that healthy men can be taught to have erections on demand, in response to mental imagery or nonsexual cues. In one study, men were instructed to use their minds to arouse themselves in exchange for a financial reward. When they were given feedback on their performance via a light display, they rapidly learned to increase their erections—in the absence of direct physical stimulation—through the use of imagery and fantasy techniques. To keep their motivation high, the men earned financial bonuses that depended on the number and degree of erections they achieved.

This experiment was one of many that have shown that learning and memory strongly influence erections. Indeed, the ability of the brain to associate sexual arousal and orgasm with cues helps to explain why an astounding number of fetish objects—such as high-heeled shoes, leather whips and lingerie—can often enhance sexual arousal.

When Things Go Wrong

By understanding the role of the central nervous system in controlling erection and other sexual functions, we hope to set the stage for new therapies. Erectile dysfunction, which is defined as a consistent inability to get or keep an erection that is satisfactory for sexual performance, is an increasingly common health problem. A study we conducted a few years ago in the Boston area estimated that some degree of erectile dysfunction affects about 40 percent of men over age 40 and up to 70 percent of men 70 years old. As baby boomers grow old and the global population ages, we estimate that the number of men who have this condition will more than double in the next 25 years—ultimately affecting more than 330 million men worldwide.

If nerve stimuli cannot reach the penis for any reason, an erection problem is inevitable. Such dysfunction can also be an unfortunate complication of surgery to remove the prostate gland to treat prostate cancer, because this procedure can dam-

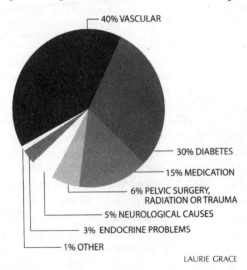
- 40% VASCULAR
- 30% DIABETES
- 15% MEDICATION
- 6% PELVIC SURGERY, RADIATION OR TRAUMA
- 5% NEUROLOGICAL CAUSES
- 3% ENDOCRINE PROBLEMS
- 1% OTHER

LAURIE GRACE

ERECTILE DYSFUNCTION has many causes, ranging from stress and other psychological concerns to purely physiological factors. This chart depicts the main physical causes of dysfunction and reveals that vascular problems underlie a vast number of cases.

age penile nerves. Diabetes can lead to nerve and blood vessel damage in the penis as well. Many neurological conditions—including spinal cord injury, Parkinson's disease, multiple sclerosis and stroke—can cause problems. And because a man's moods and mental well-being affect the flow of nerve messages to the penis, it is not surprising that stress, depression, anxiety or anger often underlies erection difficulties.

Using their growing knowledge of central nervous system control, researchers have begun to develop medications that target the central nervous system. A drug called apomorphine will most likely be the first in a new generation of therapies that acts directly on the brain as opposed to the penis, as Viagra does. Apomorphine—brand name Uprima—mimics the neurotransmitter dopamine, enhancing erections by binding to specific receptors on nerve cells in the paraventricular nucleus and the MPOA, thereby turning on proerectile pathways.

Apomorphine is under review by the U.S. Food and Drug Administration for approval, and a final decision is expected soon. Although the compound has been used in medicine for more than a century—for the treatment of Parkinson's disease, among other disorders—it was not until the mid-1980s that investigators, including R. Taylor Segraves, a psychiatrist at Case Western Reserve University, and Jeremy P. W. Heaton, a urologist at Queen's University in Ontario, began investigating it for the treatment of erectile dysfunction. Since then, clinical studies have evaluated apomorphine in more than 3,000 men and found that it can successfully treat those with many different types of erectile dysfunction.

Like all drugs, apomorphine can cause unwanted side effects. Whereas Viagra, the most widely prescribed drug for erectile dysfunction, can give rise to headaches, nasal stuffiness and facial flushing, apomorphine can induce nausea during its initial use. In the future, we may be able to treat some men more ef-

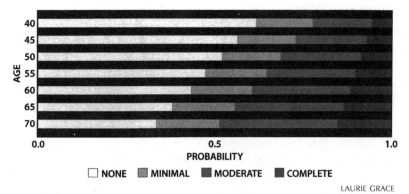

IMPOTENCE increases with age, according to several surveys. In 25 years, given the aging of the world's population, it is estimated that the condition may affect more than 330 million men.

fectively by combining apomorphine with therapies that act directly on the penis.

Sex and the Sexes

Until recently, most research on sexual function focused in large part on men and the control of penile erection. Fortunately, this is changing, as we increasingly recognize that sexual dysfunction is extremely common—and treatable—in both sexes. In fact, a recent survey of more than 3,000 Americans reported that the number of women with sexual complaints was greater than the number of men: 43 percent as opposed to 31 percent.

Many researchers are studying the mechanisms that control sexual function in women and are testing therapies to treat female sexual disorders. Our laboratory is conducting a clinical trial to determine whether apomorphine can enhance sexual arousal in women with such problems. We also are testing a new FDA-approved device called the EROS-Clitoral Therapy Device, which is used to provide gentle suction to the clitoris, causing engorgement. In women with sexual dysfunction, it has been shown to safely improve sexual sensation, lubrication, orgasm and sexual satisfaction.

This research has made us aware of some similarities between the sexes in the central nervous system's

control of arousal, orgasm and various sexual functions. Preliminary evidence suggests that the central control of sexual function in men and women is remarkably similar. For instance, as noted earlier, both sexes experience nocturnal arousal responses, and both are vulnerable to SSRI-induced sexual dysfunction.

Of course, there are also dramatic differences—as in the postorgasmic refractory period, the normal delay after an orgasm before arousal can occur again. Women can have multiple orgasms and therefore have virtually no refractory period, but most men have a refractory period that lasts from several minutes to many hours.

We have come a long way since da Vinci's discovery that the penis fills with blood—not air or spiritual essences—during an erection. The past decade has revolutionized not only the field of erection research but also our societal attitudes about sexual health. Only a few years ago erectile dysfunction went generally untreated.

Today this condition and other sexual problems are more openly recognized and discussed. Millions of men are receiving care for erection troubles, thanks to a burgeoning appreciation of the importance of sexual health and the availability of more effective and convenient treatments. In the near future we anticipate that there will be an even wide array of therapies for men and women. With our increasing insight into the brain's role in controlling our sexuality, we are also moving toward a more holistic view of sexual well-being—one that integrates mind and body and responds to the unique needs of both sexes.

The Authors

IRWIN GOLDSTEIN is a urologist at Boston University. He is a member of the Working Group for the Study of Central Mechanisms in Erectile Dysfunction, which was formed in 1998. The other members are John Bancroft of Indiana University; François Giuliano of the Faculté de Médecine, Université Paris-Sud; Jeremy P. W. Heaton of Queen's University, Ontario; Ronald W. Lewis of the Medical College of Georgia; Tom F. Lue of the University of California, San Francisco; Kevin E. McKenna of Northwestern University; Harin Padma-Nathan of the University of Southern California; Raymond Rosen of the Robert Wood Johnson Medical School; Benjamin D. Sachs of the University of Connecticut; R. Taylor Segraves of Case Western Reserve University; and William D. Steers of the University of Virginia. All the authors consult or investigate (or have done so in the past) for one or more pharmaceutical companies— among them Abbott, Eli Lilly, Merck, Pfizer and TAP; Sachs owns stock in Abbott; Heaton shares several patents on apomorphine.

Further Information

IMPOTENCE AND ITS MEDICAL AND PSYCHOLOGICAL CORRELATES: RESULTS OF THE MASSACHUSETTS MALE AGING STUDY. H. A. Feldman et al. in *Journal of Urology,* Vol. 151, No. 1, pages 54–61; January 1994.

NEURAL CONTROL OF PENILE ERECTION. F. Giuliano, O. Rampin, G. Benoit and A. Jardin in *Urology Clinics of North America,* Vol. 22, No. 4, pages 747–766; November 1995.

THE BRAIN IS THE MASTER ORGAN IN SEXUAL FUNCTION: CENTRAL NERVOUS SYSTEM CONTROL OF MALE AND FEMALE SEXUAL FUNCTION. K. McKenna in *International Journal of Impotence Research,* Vol. 11, Supplement 1, pages 548–555; 1999.

SEXUAL DYSFUNCTION IN THE UNITED STATES: PREVALENCE AND PREDICTORS. E. O. Laumann, A. Paik and R. C. Rosen in *Journal of the American Medical Association,* Vol. 281, No. 6, pages 537–544; February 10, 1999.

The Science of
Women & Sex

INSPIRED BY VIAGRA, researchers are rushing to unlock the mysteries of female desire. The answers are turning out to be much more complex than anyone expected.

BY JOHN LELAND

FOR ELLEN, A 45-YEAR-OLD COLLEGE professor in rural Maryland, the music of the bedroom has never been as harmonious as it is in magazines. She cannot reach orgasm with her husband, and has only tepid interest in sex. "Frankly, it's the one fly in the ointment of our marriage," she says. Sexual couples counseling didn't help; her gynecologist, "immanently unhelpful," told her nothing could be done. Then she heard about a Baltimore

How do we define sexual dysfunction in women?

It's both a mind and body thing, and many women have a problem at some point in their lives. Doctors saysexual woes rise to the level of dysfunction only when they are persistent and—most important—cause personal distress.

urologist named Toby Chai who was conducting a small trial of Viagra among women with sexual complaints. She'd read of the miraculous results in men and thought this might finally dispel the "iceberg" intruding on her marital life. "It's not

something we talk about every day, but it's always there." Returning home with six pills—three placebo, three Viagra—Ellen became a pilgrim in the increasingly frenzied search to unlock the mysteries of female desire.

Women's sexuality, Sigmund Freud opined, is the "dark continent" of the soul: an uncharted netherworld receding behind folds of flesh and muscle. Among the Big Ideas of the last century, few were as asinine as Freud's on sex and women, most notably his theory of penis envy. Yet in the decades that followed, science has continued to put forward as much ignorance as bliss. Until the late '20s, doctors manually stimulated women as a treatment for "pelvic disorder"; the vibrator, originally coal-fired, caught on as a way to shorten office visits.

In the 1950s and '60s, Alfred Kinsey and the team of Masters and Johnson began exploring female sexuality through the prism of its male counterpart. "We are still in a culture which has defined sexuality, sexual pleasure and [sexual goals] in male terms," says Dr. John Bancroft, current head of the Kinsey Institute. "Then we apply the same paradigm to women. That is a mistake." The

male paradigm is simple: erection and release. Women's satisfactions and drives are more complex, organized as much around the health of the relationship as the majesty that is orgasm.

How does loss of testosterone affect women?

Women produce testosterone in their adrenal glands and ovaries. Around the time of menopause, the amount produced declines, which may lead to a loss of desire, as well as fatigue and thinning hair.

Add science to this simple insight and it becomes a program for revolution. Sparked by the stunning success of Viagra, and the prospect that it might be duplicated with women, a new era of sexual experimentation is now taking shape—this time not in the bedroom, but in the laboratory. "It's such a Wild West frontier of new discovery," says Dr. Irwin Goldstein, the media-friendly Boston urologist and pioneer in research on men and women. (Like many doctors interviewed for this article, Goldstein is a paid consultant and gets research money from one or more of the drug companies, but does not own stock in any.)

As many as four in 10 American women experience some form of sexual dissatisfaction, a figure likely to grow as the 41 million women of the baby boom, for whom unencumbered sex seemed a birthright, make the passage through menopause. The shadow cast by dysfunction can spread far beyond the bedroom, darkening a woman's entire sense of well-being. "It was probably in some ways more devastating than breast cancer," says a 55-year-old college professor who lost her ability to become aroused after hysterectomy. "This huge piece of who I am had just gone." Drug companies, research clinicians and traditional therapists are all leaping into the fray. Their work, still in its embryonic stages, is already starting to yield a radical new understanding of anatomy, dysfunction—and even the evolutionary meaning of orgasm.

A dozen drug manufacturers, including Pfizer, the maker of Viagra, are rushing headlong into research and development, mostly on drugs originally intended to treat impotence in men. Both male and female genitals have smooth muscle tissue that engorges with blood during arousal. Researchers hope Viagra will relax this tissue in the clitoris, as it does in the penis, allowing the vessels in the organ to swell with blood. The early prognosis, though, is less than thrilling. In the most comprehensive female trial of Viagra to date, released this week, the drug proved no more effective than a placebo. Nonetheless, Cheryl Bourque, an analyst at Decision Resources, projects that by 2008, the market for treatments for women, including testosterone and estrogen (sidebar), could hit $1.7 billion. Drugs conceived specifically for women, still perhaps decades away, could make this figure seem minuscule.

The Risks of **Estrogen**

AFTER MENOPAUSE, changes in women's bodies can make sex painful. But new studies raise doubts about hormone therapy. BY SHARON BEGLEY

H OW MUCH RISK WILL A WOMAN ACCEPT IN RETURN FOR GOOD SEX? Many women approaching or past menopause view estrogen-replacement therapy (ERT) as a foundation of youth in a pill. By pumping up blood concentrations of estrogen to near-youthful levels, ERT vanquishes the hot flashes and night sweats responsible for libido-killing insomnia and irritability. It also prevents the thinning and drying out of vaginal tissue that comes with plummeting estrogen levels, notes Dr. Margery Gass, an Ob-Gyn at the University of Cincinnati College of Medicine. After menopause, thinner, less flexible vaginal tissue can make sex so painful that the body recoils even when the heart is willing. Virtually any form of estrogen—the pill Premarin, a patch, vaginal creams or vaginal rings kept in place for three months— "improves vaginal tissues," says Gass.

Because estrogen alone stimulates the uterine lining and increases the risk of endometrial cancer, women with an intact uterus are advised to pair estrogen with progestin—which blocks this effect—in a regimen called hormone-replacement therapy (HRT). Estrogen alone has long had a dark side: it is associated with an increased risk of breast cancer. Now, in one of those you-can't-win cases, it appears that progestin may increase the risk of breast cancer even more than estrogen alone, says Dr. Ronald Ross of the University of Southern California. Scientists now think that estrogen-progestin increases the risk of breast cancer 53 percent compared with not taking hormones; estrogen by itself raises the risk 34 percent. The longer a woman takes HRT, the greater her risk.

The standard retort to concerns about breast cancer has been, "Sure, but estrogen reduces the risk of osteoporosis." That remains pretty much unquestioned: estrogen decreases the amount of bone that is resorbed in the constant process of skeletal building and demolishing. But estrogen's killer app is supposed to be preventing heart disease. It lowers bad LDL cholesterol and raises good HDL. (Creams and rings are not effective because their estrogen is absorbed directly by the bloodstream, bypassing the liver, where cholesterol levels are adjusted.) That heart benefit was supposed to swamp the risk of breast cancer, especially since heart disease kills nine times as many American women every year as does breast cancer. But results of the newest, best-designed studies are dismaying. They find that HRT provides no heart benefits to women with existing cardiovascular disease; it may actually increase their risk of heart attacks. And it may not protect healthy women from developing heart disease: in April, researchers at the Women's Health Initiative, run by the National Institutes of Health, warned that HRT seems to raise the risk of heart attacks and stroke in healthy women, at least initially. "Women with heart disease should not take estrogen with the expectation that it will help their heart," says Dr. David Herrington of Wake Forest University. Not even great sex can fix a broken Heart.

Why do we know so little about sex and older women?

I n the past, women (and men) simply accepted dysfunction as a natural part of aging. After the spectacular success of Viagra, researchers began focusing on ways to help women remain sexually active.

Jennifer Berman is one of the few female urologists working on the cutting edge of this research. At the Women's Sexual Health Clinic in

Boston not long ago, Berman received a 54-year-old woman who, since menopause and a mastectomy, suffered vaginal dryness and pain

It's Really Not Just a Headache, Honey

As researchers learn more about the causes and types of female sexual dysfunction, they're uncovering new ways to help. There's no female equivalent to Viagra yet, but women have new reason to hope.

DYSFUNCTION TYPES

■ **Desire:** A lack of libido can have both physical and psychological roots. Stress and depression (as well as some medications) are major causes.

■ **Arousal:** Critical to sexual response, it may be expressed as a lack of subjective excitement or genital lubrication

■ **Lack of orgasm:** It's a more common problem than previously believed: a substantial number of women have never experienced the sensation

■ **Pain:** This condition can occur at any age, but it is especially troublesome after menopause, when natural lubricants dry up

DYSFUNCTION CAUSES

■ **Psychological:** These range from depression and past sexual abuse to unsatisfactory relationships and a bad body image

■ **Physical:** Factors include vaginal atrophy at menopause, nerve damage, diabetes, heart disease, smoking and obesity

TREATMENT OPTIONS

Researchers are looking at a wide range of medications and devices, most still in the experimental stage. For many women, the most effective treatment may combine drugs, hormones and counseling.

Viagra: The pill was no better than a placebo in women with a wide range of symptoms. new trials will target post menopausal women.

Prostaglandin E-1 cream: Still in early clinical trials, this 'vasodilator' dilates arteries, increasing blood flow to genital tissues.

Alprostadil cream: Another version of prostaglandin E-1 and still under study, this compound is being tested for improved arousal and lubrication

Dr. K's Dream Cream: Sold 'off label' by Dr. Jed Kaminetsky, this combination of vasodilators may increase genital engorgement and arousal

Clitoral device: Approved earlier this month by the FDA, this prescription device creates a 'genital suction' over the clitoris in order to increase blood flow and sensation

Testosterone patch: Women whose hormone levels have declined apply the patch (still in clinical trials) to their abdomen to increase libido

Natural aids are popular, but not subject to FDA oversight

For arousal L-arginine an amino acid
Yohimbe made from the bark of a tree

For libido DHEA helps fuel testosterone production

SOURCES: THE JOURNAL OF THE AMERICAN MEDICAL ASSOCIATION, NEWSWEEK REPORTING.

WHO SUFFERS

Problems* with physical intimacy affect more women than men and vary by age, education, race and marital status. The reasons are still unclear.

Sexual dysfunction

Women	Low sexual desire	22%
	Arousal problems	14
	Pain during intercourse	7
Men	Premature ejaculation	21%
	Erectile dysfunction	5
	Low sexual desire	5

*PROBLEMS THAT HAVE OCCURRED OVER THE LAST 12 MONTHS.

Health factors
These may contribute to sexual dysfunction
■ Poor health
■ Emotional problems or stress
■ Urinary-tract symptoms
■ A history of STDs

Low interest in sex

By age	Women	Men
18–29	32%	14%
30–39	32	13
40–49	30	15
50–59	27	17

By race	Women
White	29%
Black	44
Hispanic	30
Other	42

Painful intercourse

By age	Women
18–29	21%
30–39	15
40–49	13
50–59	8

By marital status	
Married	14%
Never married	17
Divorced, widowed, separated	16

Absence of orgasm

By age	Women	Men
18–29	26%	7%
30–39	28	7
40–49	22	9
50–59	23	9

High-school education	
Less than	34%
Graduate	29

College	
Some	24
Graduate	18

during intercourse, and lost all interest in sex. "I feel like I'm less than a woman," the woman says. Berman wanted to test the flow of blood to the woman's genitals. Supplied with a pair of 3-D glasses and a vibrator, the woman watched an erotic videotape while an ultrasound probe resembling an electronic tampon monitored her blood flow—an attempt to tease out the physical component of dysfunction. Berman and her sister, Laura, a sex therapist, have become the telegenic faces of female sexual dysfunction, a two-headed Oprah for the erotically aggrieved. Together they tag-team the mind and body, a synergy many doctors believe will provide the best relief for female sexual dysfunction. For women, more so than for men, simply "medicalizing" the problem is too reductive. While many Viagra-enhanced men are happy just to get erections, fixing women's blood flow will cure little if libido-killing stresses still assail

For women, the relationship and the context of sexuality can be even more critical to satisfaction than the majesty that is orgasm. Freud thought dysfunction was all in a woman's head. Now, high-tech tests reveal the role of physical causes.

the relationship, the home life and the woman's self-esteem. Women presenting identical complaints might require a drug, a weekend retreat or a sex toy, or some combination of the three.

Even so, medical advances promise important keys. Anatomists are finding that we haven't even mapped the basic body parts. In a conference room at Boston University, Trudy Van Houten stops an unsuspecting medical student. *The clitoris,* she challenges the young woman, a fourth-year med student: *how big is it?* The woman looks momentarily stunned. *Would you say it's one centimeter or 10?* By the fourth year of medical school, students should know the gross details of the body, but this seemingly simple question has the woman in a pickle. "It can't be as big as 10," she tries. Oh, but it is, it is. "It's here, it's here, it's here, it's here," says Van Houten, tracing a finger across an anatomical drawing. "Wow," says the student. "Thank you."

The new research borders on the macabre: Goldstein talks of "harvesting" clitorises, labia and vaginas from cadavers, surgery patients or animals to study the microprocesses of sexual response; Cindy Meston, a psychologist at the University of Texas at Austin, has reported that stimulating the same branch of the nervous system that shuts down sexual arousal in men seems to facilitate it in women. Researchers like Van Houten are only now starting to map the myriad nerves that spider through the pelvic region, hoping ultimately to spare hysterectomy patients from nerve damage, as surgeons do when they remove men's prostate glands.

As they learn about the body, scientists are also rethinking the types and roots of dysfunction. They have identified four sexual woes: a low sex drive or aversion to sex, difficulty becoming aroused, inability to reach orgasm and pain during sex.

Do female orgasms serve any biological function?

Evolutionary biologists haven't yet figured that one out, and it's a controversial subject. One possible theory: orgasms in women have no function and are just a development vestige, like male nipples.

Healthy women might experience any of these on occasion. They rise to the level of dysfunction only when they are persistent or recurring, and—most important—when they cause personal distress. Root causes can be physical (diabetes, obesity or other strain on the circulatory system), emotional (stress, fatigue or depression) or an interplay between the two. A cruel irony is that many drugs used to fight depression also dampen libido. For women now in middle age, the biggest threat to their sexual satisfaction may be social: after the age of 60 half of all women are without a partner.

Real help for many women is still far off. In his frenzied office at the New York Center for Human Sexuality, Dr. Ridwan Shabsigh proudly shows off a color photograph of

dense, tangled tubes. His lab team, he explains, injected a hardening resin into the bloodstream of a live rat, then dissolved the rodent in acid, leaving only the solidified resin where the blood vessels used to be. The image, created with an electron microscope, describes the vascular system of a rat vagina. "This is big," he said—one giant leap for science, one bad date for Queen Rat.

Shabsigh's team of head and body doctors uses an updated theoretical framework for female sexual response. In the 1970s, the influential psychiatrist Helen Singer Kaplan sorted women's responses into three successive phases—desire to arousal to orgasm—a one-way arrow pointing straight to nirvana. The arrow model, says Shabsigh, ignores the more reciprocal play between the various states of pleasure. "We think of female sexual function not as a line but as a circle" joining the four points of desire, arousal, orgasm and satisfaction. Turbulence or interruption at any point affects the weather at all the others. In other words, today's frustration about orgasm dampens next week's libido.

Though libido is the most common complaint, most of the drugs currently being tested target arousal. Many doctors think this will limit the pills' future impact. But for women like Ellen, the Maryland professor, this is splitting sexual hairs. The quiet disconnect of her marital bed, she says, caused emotional stress for both her and her husband. She was hoping Viagra would jumpstart her libido, but she wanted an orgasm, as well. "It'd be nice to have your cake and eat it, too," she says. Unfortunately, the pills did not work for her. "I haven't given up," she says.

Many of the drugs in development—VasoFem, Alista, FemProx—act a lot like Viagra, and this week's discouraging trial results are a potential wet blanket for the industry. "We're definitely continuing our research," says Heather Van Ness, a Pfizer rep. "We feel this [area] is significantly more complicated than erectile dysfunction." One researcher in the Viagra trials, Dr. Rosemary Basson, says the study may have incorporated too broad a range of ages and complaints to be definitive. Viagra may work for some conditions but not others. A more targeted study, limited to post-menopausal women, is now gearing up in the United States. Also being tested is a "dopamine agonist" called apomorphine, recently recommended for approval for use in men, which sends electrical impulses from the hypothalamus to the genitals to trigger increased blood flow.

Drugs, however, aren't the only potential stairway to heaven. Earlier this month the FDA approved an apparatus called EROS-CTD, a clitoral suction device the size of a computer mouse that draws blood to the organ. The device is available by prescription only and costs about $360. The best part of participating in the EROS trials, says a 35-year-old at-home mother in St. Paul, Minn., "is that we get one for free."

Hormone therapy is also promising, but can be a wild ride. Testosterone, for reasons no one quite understands, is involved in the sex drive of both men and women. In their 30s and 40s, most women experience a 15 percent drop in testosterone levels. Removal of the ovaries, often a part of hysterectomy,

reduces production to near zero. At the University of California, San Francisco, Dr. Louann Brizendine has been experimenting with testosterone replacement therapy, in both oral form and patches. This is the tricky end of the erotic medicine cabinet: side effects include increased risk of heart disease and liver damage, and long-term consequences are unknown. Also, the surges of biochemical desire can leave patients reeling. One woman unwittingly doubled her dosage and had to excuse herself every few hours just to seek relief.

As biologists expand their grasp of amatory nitty and gritty, the thorniest riddle may be more global: why, from an evolutionary point of view, do women have orgasms? Unlike the male O, women's climax does not appear to be necessary for reproduction. The traditional answer, phrased by anthropologist Don Symons in 1979, is that female orgasm is a relic of Darwinian sloppiness, like male nipples: evolution had no good motive specifically to cut one gender out of the fun. If you think this argument has passed unchallenged, you haven't breathed the air on campus lately. Proclaiming orgasmic empowerment, anthropologists speculated that the sweet paroxysm kept women supine after sex, facilitating insemination—a dubious argument, since nature did not design most women to climax reliably through intercourse, especially in the missionary position. The evolutionary biologist Sarah Blaffer Hrdy proposed that this skittishness was itself an evolutionary adaptation: our unsatisfied ancestresses would seek remedy from multiple

partners—in turn tapping each for protection and resources, and counting on confusion about paternity to multiply the generosity. Or maybe orgasm allows women to influence which mate will father their children. British biologists Robin Baker and Mark Bellis, who went so far as to attach micro video cameras to the ends of men's penises, found that women retained more of their partners' ejaculate if they reached orgasm as well. In an only-in-America study at the University of New Mexico, researchers Randy Thornhill and Steven Gangestad found that, other things being equal, women were more likely to climax when their partners' bodies were symmetrical, a marker of desirable genes. "It's all consistent with female choice," says Thornhill. Since competing explanations arise, you are free to accept this as gospel or just another reminder that the mysteries of sex won't be solved overnight.

The new science of sex, though, is not wholly academic. Revolutions in the lab will likely rearrange the bedroom, perhaps even the surrounding communities, in ways unforeseeable. As Jared Diamond describes in his book "Guns, Germs and Steel," new technologies often create societies' needs for them, rather than the other way around. Invention, in other words, can be the mother of necessity. Right now we are just approaching the cusp of that maternity. The dark continent is growing brighter and more electric with each turn of the circle.

With Claudia Kalb *and* Nadine Joseph

America: Awash in STDs

by Gracie S. Hsu

A "hidden epidemic" is stalking America, according to the Institute of Medicine, a branch of the National Academy of Sciences. More than 25 infectious diseases transmitted by unprecedented rates of promiscuous extramarital sexual activity are infecting at least 12 million Americans annually.

At current rates of infection, at least one in four Americans will contract a sexually transmitted disease (STD) at some point in life.

The United States bears the dubious distinction of leading the industrialized world in overall rates of STDs.

Two-thirds of the 12 million new cases a year are among men and women under age 25. Indeed, about 3 million teenagers—one in four sexually experienced adolescents—acquire an STD each year.

STDs should concern Americans because they can cause such serious consequences as cervical cancer, infertility, infection of offspring, and death. Most people are unaware that

- an estimated 100,000 to 150,000 women become infertile each year as a result of an STD;
- half of the 88,000 ectopic pregnancies that occur each year are due to a preexisting STD infection;
- 4,500 American women die each year from cervical cancer, which is almost always caused by an

STD called the human papilloma virus (HPV).

'STEALTH' DISEASE

"I don't think people understand how common some of these serious consequences are, particularly infertility," says Patricia Donovan, senior associate at the Alan Guttmacher Institute (AGI), a nonprofit research corporation specializing in reproductive health.

"Seventy-five percent of women with chlamydia don't have any symptoms. They don't know until 5 years later, when they have serious pelvic pain, or 10 years later, when they can't get pregnant, that they had this STD that would have been easily curable."

STDs such as chlamydia, gonorrhea, syphilis, and trichomoniasis are nonviral and therefore curable if detected early enough. Other STDs, however, are viral and have no cure. These include HPV, genital herpes, sexually transmitted hepatitis B, and the human immunodeficiency virus, or HIV, which is responsible for 90,000 cases of AIDS annually, a figure that was dramatically expanded in 1993 over previous years due to an official redefinition of AIDS.

As many as 56 million individuals—more than one in five Americans—may be infected with an incurable viral STD other than AIDS.

STDs are "a tremendous problem," says W. David Hager, president of the Infectious Diseases Society for Obstetrics and Gynecology.

"Last fall, a *New England Journal of Medicine* article found that slightly over 21 percent of Americans over age 12 are herpes simplex virus positive," Hager says. "That equals 45 million people.

"Furthermore, huge numbers of coeds on college campuses have HPV. Ninety-five percent of all cervical cancer and dysplasia [abnormal growth of organs or cells] are caused by HPV. And this may only be the tip of the iceberg."

The Institute of Medicine (IOM) estimates that the annual direct and indirect costs of selected major STDs, in addition to the human suffering associated with them, are approximately $10 billion. If sexually transmitted HIV infections are included, the total rises to $17 billion.

Medically, experts agree that the main risk factor for contracting an STD is promiscuity.

PROMISCUITY'S PERIL

"Having more than one lifetime sexual partner connotes risk," says Shepherd Smith, president of the Institute for Youth Development

This article originally appeared in *The World & I*, June 1998, pp. 56–61. Reprinted by permission of *The World & I*, a publication of The Washington Times Corporation. © 1998.

The Hidden Epidemic

→ The United States leads the industralized world in overall rates of STDs.

→ STDs can cause cervical cancer, infertility, infection of offspring, and death.

→ As many as 56 million Americans (more than one in five citizens) may be infected with an incurable viral STD other than AIDS, such as genital herpes or hepatitis B.

→ Annual costs of selected major STDs are about $10 billion. Including sexually transmitted HIV, the total rises to $17 billion.

COURTESY OF THE INSTITUTE
FOR YOUTH DEVELOPMENT

■ *Promiscuity skeptic:* Shepherd Smith, president of the Institute for Youth Development, says, "The more [sexual] partners, the more risk [for contracting STDs]. It's that simple."

Liberals usually argue that promiscuity already exists, that it results from legitimate personal choices, and that it is not necessarily something that can or should be prevented. Rather, people should be educated about their risks so that they can protect themselves with condoms if they choose to have more than one sexual partner.

CONSERVATIVES: PREVENT PROMISCUITY

To conservatives, America's STD epidemic is really a problem of promiscuity, a symptom of society's moral decline, which began with the 1960s sexual revolution.

Joe McIlhaney, president of the Medical Institute for Sexual Health in Austin, Texas, says that "the reason there are more [sexually transmitted] diseases now than 30 years ago is because the ethics and values of society have changed."

There has been, he says, "a weakening of values, not just those having to do with sex, but also of other values like respect, responsibility, integrity." He says parents are not teaching their children these values strongly anymore.

Hager concurs. "Family breakdown and the loss of a great deal of family identity," he says, have contributed to a problem he's seeing become more common among young women: "A majority of young women that we see with STDs come from a situation where they are seeking the love and intimacy that they have missed in their homes."

To reverse the moral decline, conservatives advocate reinstating the traditional values of abstinence until marriage and faithfulness within marriage.

First, "parents should give unambiguous messages regarding appropriate sexual conduct," says the IYD's Smith.

Research shows that parents have the biggest impact of anyone on kids' behavior. And, according to the National Longitudinal Study on

(IYD). "The more partners, the more risk. It's that simple."

Compared with men and women who have had only 1 partner, those who report 2–3 partners are 5 times as likely to have had an STD; those with 4–6 lifetime partners are 10 times as likely; and the odds are 31 times greater for those who report 16 or more partners.

But Americans today are far more promiscuous than in the past. One big reason is that people are initiating sexual intercourse at younger ages, which usually leads to a higher number of partners during their lifetime.

According to a national poll of more than 11,000 high-school-aged youths, 54 percent said they were sexually active, compared with 29 percent in 1970. The proportion of 15-year-olds who have had sex has risen from 4.6 percent in 1970 to 26 percent. And almost one-fifth of the sexually active teens say they have had four or more partners.

In urban areas, the percentage of sexually experienced women aged 15–19 who reported four or more sex partners increased from 14 percent in 1971 to 31 percent in 1988.

"Sexual behavior is putting a sizable portion of high school students at risk," says Richard Lowry, an adolescent-health expert at the federal Centers for Disease Control and Prevention (CDC).

Having several partners is especially dangerous for teenage girls, he says, because studies show that they often have an immature cervix, which may be more easily infected.

While experts agree that promiscuity is a major risk factor, liberals and conservatives generally hold very different values regarding promiscuity. Conservatives usually believe that promiscuity in and of itself is unhealthy and should be prevented by advocating abstinence until marriage and faithfulness within marriage.

The STD Tidal Wave

STD	Consequences of Infection	Estimated New Cases Annually	Estimated Costs (1990)
Pelvic Inflammatory Disease (PID)	Infertility, ectopic pregnancy	1 million	$4.2 billion
Chlamydia	PID, infertility, ectopic pregnancy; neonatal eye infections; infant pneumonia and chronic respiratory problems	4 million	$781 million
Gonorrhea	PID, infertility, ectopic pregnancy; in newborns causes blindness, septic arthritis, meningitis	1.1 million	$288 million
Genital Herpes*	Babies exposed at birth may die or suffer neurologic damage	200,000–500,000 (31 million currently infected)	$145 million
Trichomoniasis	Vaginal discharge	3 million	Unknown
Urethritis		1.2 million	Unknown
Human Papilloma Virus (HPV)*	Cervical cancer	500,000–1 million (24–40 million currently infected)	Unknown
Epididymitis	Fever, chills, groin pain	500,000	Unknown
Hepatitis B*	Liver cancer	100,000–200,000 (1.5 million currently infected)	Unknown
Syphilis	Stillborn children; in infants, congenital syphilis	120,000	Unknown
HIV*	Death, greater susceptibility to other diseases	40,000 (1 million currently infected)	Unknown

*NONCURABLE STDs

SOURCE: ALAN GUTTMACHER INSTITUTE

Adolescent Health, the largest-ever survey of American adolescents, kids were more likely to abstain from sex if their parents encouraged them to wait until marriage and discouraged birth control.

Kids also need to know that "sex within marriage is truly worth waiting for," Smith continues. "The NORC [National Opinion Research Center] study in Chicago found that the most sexually satisfied Americans are those who are in monogamous married relationships."

Second, "educators and medical professionals need to come around and help the parents to avoid dis-ease and have a consistent message," says McIlhaney. He suggests that schools teach a character-based sex education program, because "values are the foundation on which good character is built."

"Young people will behave at the level of greatest expectation," says Hager. "If your expectation of young people is that they will engage in sexual activity, you aren't teaching them appropriate restraints.

"If your expectation of young people is that they can abstain, your educational program and expectations will give them enough hope that they will be able to abstain."

LIBERALS: PREVENT UNPROTECTED SEX

Unlike conservatives, liberals think that preventing promiscuity is unrealistic and not even necessarily desirable.

Instead, they envision a culture where people are open and comfortable with their sexuality so each person would be able to negotiate with his sexual partner about what he wants or doesn't want from sex. Preventing promiscuity, therefore, is not the goal; preventing unprotected intercourse is.

■ *Advertising abstinence:* Various groups and localities have begun to run billboard ads, such as this one in Maryland, promoting abstinence as a way of stemming the STD epidemic.

To liberals, the problem of high STD rates stems from Americans' inability to talk about sexuality and provide factual sex education in the home, school, and health care setting.

Peggy Clarke, president of the American Social Health Association, the only nongovernmental organization devoted to fighting STDs, says that the reason STDs are flourishing is that "we, as a culture, have not been good at dealing with sexuality."

"We need to raise people's skills in talking about sexuality and becoming more comfortable with it," says Kent Klindera, director of the HIV/STD education department at Advocates for Youth. The message that humans are "sexual beings" has to come from all sectors of society, he says, including "schools, churches, the mass media."

For example, Klindera conducts a peer education program through the Episcopal Church. His workshops help young people build better communication skills around their sexuality, whether it be through condom negotiation or abstinence role playing. He says if young people can communicate better about their

sexuality, they'll be able to prevent the spread of STDs.

Liberals say that the best way to prevent STDs among the sexually active is to use condoms. They claim that condoms are "very effective" in preventing disease if used correctly every time. Thus, they want condoms to be distributed in schools, and they advocate increased funding for clinics that distribute condoms.

The AGI's Donovan says television networks should air condom ads to educate people about the risks of unprotected sex.

Planned Parenthood sums up the communication and condoms message this way: "Talk with your partners before the heat of passion, and use a condom every time!"

THE VALUES BATTLEFIELD

Conservatives say that the liberal approach is ultimately self-defeating, primarily because the underlying problem of promiscuity is not addressed. They also believe condoms are a poor substitute for true prevention, citing the following reasons:

1. Sending the implicit message that sex outside marriage is permis-

sible will increase the number of people choosing to have sex with multiple partners.

2. Talking explicitly about sexuality piques curiosity and increases the likelihood of sexual experimentation.

3. Condoms provide only partial protection at best. Studies show that condoms have a 12–16 percent failure rate at preventing pregnancy after one year of using the devices. And while pregnancy can only occur a few days during the month, an STD can be transmitted any time a person has sex. Studies also indicate that condoms provide no detectable protection against HPV, genital herpes, or chlamydia.

4. It is unrealistic to expect people to use condoms consistently and correctly with every act of intercourse for a long period of time. McIlhaney says that the highest rate of condom use is a little more than 50 percent, and this was among adults who knew their partners were HIV-positive and whose participation in a research study exposed them to constant encouragement to use condoms. He also cites a 1997 *CDC Update* that said that if people do not use condoms

effectively 100 percent of the time, the outcome would be the same as if they were not using condoms at all.

Liberals say that their approach is superior to the conservatives' for the following reasons:

1. Promiscuity exists, and a "just say no" message is an inadequate and unrealistic response. Conservatives have no response, liberals say, for those who choose to be sexually active outside marriage.

2. Condoms provide very effective protection against STDs. When asked about the 12–16 percent pregnancy failure rate of condoms, liberals respond that such a rate reflects "typical use." Perfect use of condoms, they say, results in an annual pregnancy rate of only 2 percent. They are also adamant about the effectiveness of condoms in preventing STDs. Planned Parenthood says that latex condoms offer "good protection" against many STDs, including gonorrhea, HIV, syphilis, and

> "Seventy-five percent of women with chlamydia don't have any symptoms. They don't know until . . . 10 years later, when they can't get pregnant," says an Alan Guttmacher Institute official.

chancroid, and "some protection" against HPV and genital herpes.

3. Their approach does not impose moral absolutes on people's sexual behavior. Choosing abstinence is just as fine an option as choosing to be sexually active using condoms. It is more important that people be open and comfortable with their own sexuality.

In the final analysis, liberals are right in saying that not everyone is going to practice abstinence until marriage and faithfulness within marriage.

Conservatives are also accurate in saying that far from everyone who engages in sex with multiple partners is going to use condoms consistently and correctly 100 percent of the time.

But ultimately, the debate is more about values than science. It's about whose ideas about human sexuality, family, and lifestyle will prevail.

And that is a question only the American public can answer.

Gracie S. Hsu is a policy analyst specializing in adolescent sexuality and life issues at the Family Research Council, a Washington, D.C.-based research and educational organization.

Prostate dilemmas

Early detection is forcing more men to weigh the difficult treatment options

By Susan Brink

"In the shower, you feel all soft, like a woman."

"I feel like my brain has been feminized."

"It's like the male hysterectomy."

"It's a delicate subject. There's a virility issue."

"Your wife ain't too happy."

"I was in the airport, nervous about flying and . . . whoosh. I lost control. Thank God I had clean clothes with me."

—Comments from prostate cancer survivors

Prostate cancer is an inglorious disease, rife with indignities that cut to the core of male sexuality and self-esteem, as these men suffering the aftermath of treatment attest. More and more men share that awareness. New York Mayor Rudolph Giuliani, 55, diagnosed with prostate cancer last month and still weighing his treatment options, is part of a generation of men in their 40s and 50s who are forced to understand the male body and its betrayals in a way never required of their fathers. "A lot of men who come to our meetings didn't even know they had a prostate. Even fewer know how to pronounce it," says Darryl Mitteldorf, who leads a Manhattan support group called Malecare.

The catalyst for this change is a blood test that can find cancer at earlier stages than ever before. The cancer mostly kills men over 65, but the test, called the prostate specific antigen (PSA) test, has forced it into the baby boom generation's consciousness, causing men as young as 40 to make a decision on whether or not to screen for early signs of this cancer. The test detects an enzyme made by the prostate, and its sensitivity to early cancer is both a blessing and a terrible burden. A series of wrenching options can begin to unfold if the PSA test gives a positive result that is confirmed as cancer, as is the case for 180,000 men each year. Treatments today are more effective and less debilitating than they once were, but they still carry a significant risk of impotence and incontinence, the result of damage to nerves or to the urethra, which the prostate straddles.

- Most men choose surgery to remove the prostate, the quickest route to a cure provided the cancer has not escaped the prostate. But even men in the best of health face three weeks or more of recovery.
- Standard radiation is an option for men too old or frail to withstand surgery. If it fails to eliminate the cancer, however, surgery is seldom possible. Radiation alters the gland, leaving it all but inoperable.
- Another treatment is implanting "seeds" of radioactive material directly in the prostate, in an outpatient procedure. Many men have short-term urinary problems following the implant, however, and while promising, this procedure is new enough to lack long-term results.

In skilled hands, surgery or radiation can cure 80 percent or more of early cancers. Yet paradoxically, some of the cancers detected by PSA might never pose a threat if untreated. The balance between lives saved by early detection and lives blighted by unnecessary treatments for harmless cancers is still so uncertain that the country's leading cancer research organization, the National Cancer Institute, is silent on whether or not men should get regular screening.

At each stage in a man's journey from a positive test result through treatment, doctors can come up with numbers that help point to the best course: the odds that surgery or radiation will lead to a cure, for example, and the chance that a man will emerge from treatment with his functions intact. The odds, many times, are good. But for each patient, every decision is a roll of the dice.

Most men get it. Next to skin cancer, prostate cancer is the most common cancer in American men. An estimated 37,000 men will die of the disease this year, and the lifetime risk of being diagnosed with prostate cancer—1 in 6—is higher than the 1-in-8 risk of breast cancer in women. (The breast cancer death toll is higher, however, at nearly 44,000 women a year.) Nearly every man shows evidence of prostate cancer if he lives long enough. Autopsies show that as many as 80 percent of men in their 80s probably have some prostate cancer cells when they die—cells that have never caused any harm. But the problem comes from those cancers that start early enough or are aggressive enough to eventually spread.

Finding those cancers early is the goal of the PSA test, and few researchers doubt that it is saving lives. The disease has no symptoms until after it has escaped from the prostate. The first sign can be the pain of cancer in the bones—at which point it is essentially incurable. "I would urge everyone to get the PSA test," Mayor Giuliani said unequivocally at the press conference disclosing his disease.

Many doctors would second Giuliani's call, at least for men whose genes put them at risk of the disease. A family history of prostate cancer can double a man's risk. The risk is even greater if more than one relative had the disease, and greater still if family members were diagnosed at relatively young ages—in their 50s, say.

The highest-risk families seem to carry genes that almost always lead to cancer. But other men may inherit normal genes in forms that are prone to turn cancerous when set off by some outside factor, perhaps a high-fat diet. Such genes may explain why African-American men are also at higher risk. They are diagnosed with the disease at least 50 percent more often than white men, and their death rate from it is nearly twice as high. The American Cancer Society, the National Comprehensive Cancer Network, and the American Urological Association all recommend that higher-risk men, including African-Americans and men with a family history of prostate cancer, talk with their doctors about annual PSA screening starting at age 40. For other men, these organizations suggest starting at 50.

But as the National Cancer Institute's silence about screening indicates, its benefits are still unproven. While prostate cancer death rates have dropped about 2.5 percent a year since widespread PSA screening began in the early 1990s, there's no conclusive evidence linking those improved outcomes to early detection. A clinical trial of 75,000 men, half screened and half not screened, was begun in 1993 to see if screening prolongs life. Results are years away.

What remains clear is that screening finds a large number of cancers that don't pose an immediate threat—and may not need immediate treatment. An analysis of about 300 patients at Johns Hopkins Hospital in Baltimore who most likely had early cancers and had their prostates removed found that between 25 percent and 33 percent had such small tumors that they were potentially insignificant. "In fact, 4 to 5 percent of tumors are so small, it's hard to

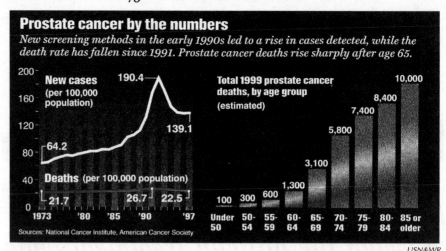

Prostate cancer by the numbers

New screening methods in the early 1990s led to a rise in cases detected, while the death rate has fallen since 1991. Prostate cancer deaths rise sharply after age 65.

New cases (per 100,000 population) 190.4 / 64.2 / 139.1
Deaths (per 100,000 population) 21.7 / 26.7 / 22.5
1973 '80 '85 '90 '97

Total 1999 prostate cancer deaths, by age group (estimated)
Under 50: 100 / 50-54: 300 / 55-59: 600 / 60-64: 1,300 / 65-69: 3,100 / 70-74: 5,800 / 75-79: 7,400 / 80-84: 8,400 / 85 or older: 10,000

Sources: National Cancer Institute, American Cancer Society

USN&WR

find them in pathology. We've seen that increasing over the years as a result of PSA screening," says Jonathan Epstein, professor of pathology, urology, and oncology at Johns Hopkins.

Whether to *begin* screening is controversial, but most experts agree on the wisdom of an age-related end to screening—though no one will pinpoint a specific age. Most suggest that if a man has a life expectancy of 10 years or less, he should not be tested. Patrick Walsh, chairman of urology at Johns Hopkins, says, "I won't test anyone in his 80s—unless he's brought in by both his parents."

Interpreting PSA. For men who opt for screening, the PSA count is not the last word. Ejaculation up to two days before the test can artificially raise the numbers (normal is below 4, high is above 10, and borderline is in between). Proscar or Propecia, two hair-growth drugs, can lower PSA numbers, as can certain herbs, including saw palmetto. And even if real, a high PSA can mean simpler, nuisance conditions rather than cancer: benign prostatic hyperplasia (BPH), an enlarged prostate that interferes with urination, for which Proscar can also be prescribed, or prostatitis, an infection that can be treated with drugs.

Prostate cancer is definitively diagnosed only after a biopsy, which entails probing a man from the rear. A biopsy gun shoots in a needle and removes prostate tissue in a fraction of a second, usually taking six to 18 samples from suspicious areas—a procedure most patients describe as, at best, highly uncomfortable. Those samples supply numbers that help determine how advanced any cancer is. The first is the stage of the tumor—how far it has spread. The second is the Gleason grade, a score of 1 to 10. A low score is given if the cancer

cells look largely similar to normal cells, a higher score if they move in angry swirls, indicating a more aggressive cancer.

Men with borderline PSA and low Gleason numbers sometimes choose to do nothing more than "watchful waiting," a strategy of closely monitoring PSA numbers and taking action only if they begin to rise. If the numbers are higher but still add up to a probable cure—an early-stage tumor with a Gleason grade of 7 or less, generally—surgery, external beam radiation, or radiation seed implants are the options. With higher numbers, suggesting an incurable cancer, a man might again opt to do nothing or try to limit its growth with radiation or hormonal therapy.

Yes, no, maybe. But again, the numbers aren't always accurate. "The [specimen on the] slide is not a black-and-white, yes-or-no answer," says Epstein. In a study at Johns Hopkins, researchers found that 1.5 percent of the slides pathologists called cancerous were benign, and 4 percent of the "benign" slides could well have been cancerous. And in more than a third of the samples, a second opinion resulted in a major change in the tumor grade or Gleason score. That could mean the difference between undergoing surgery or radiation in the hope of a cure, or undergoing those same treatments futilely because the cancer is incurable. Because so much depends on the results of the biopsy, experts recommend getting a second pathology opinion.

If the numbers suggest treatment, a man can start exploring his options. About 100,000 men a year with newly diagnosed cases opt for a radical prostatectomy—surgical removal of the prostate. Some 30,000 men choose external beam radiation, and a new tech-

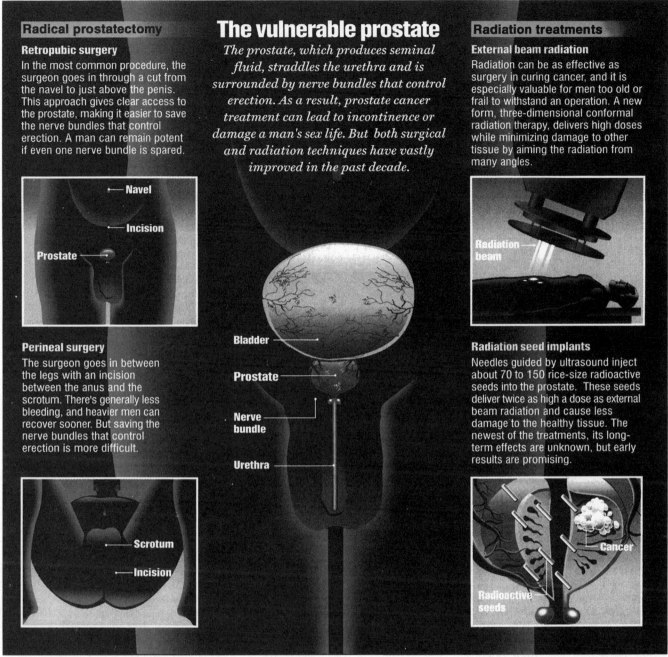

Radical prostatectomy

Retropubic surgery

In the most common procedure, the surgeon goes in through a cut from the navel to just above the penis. This approach gives clear access to the prostate, making it easier to save the nerve bundles that control erection. A man can remain potent if even one nerve bundle is spared.

Navel
Incision
Prostate

Perineal surgery

The surgeon goes in between the legs with an incision between the anus and the scrotum. There's generally less bleeding, and heavier men can recover sooner. But saving the nerve bundles that control erection is more difficult.

Scrotum
Incision

The vulnerable prostate

The prostate, which produces seminal fluid, straddles the urethra and is surrounded by nerve bundles that control erection. As a result, prostate cancer treatment can lead to incontinence or damage a man's sex life. But both surgical and radiation techniques have vastly improved in the past decade.

Bladder
Prostate
Nerve bundle
Urethra

Radiation treatments

External beam radiation

Radiation can be as effective as surgery in curing cancer, and it is especially valuable for men too old or frail to withstand an operation. A new form, three-dimensional conformal radiation therapy, delivers high doses while minimizing damage to other tissue by aiming the radiation from many angles.

Radiation beam

Radiation seed implants

Needles guided by ultrasound inject about 70 to 150 rice-size radioactive seeds into the prostate. These seeds deliver twice as high a dose as external beam radiation and cause less damage to the healthy tissue. The newest of the treatments, its long-term effects are unknown, but early results are promising.

Cancer
Radioactive seeds

ROD LITTLE *USN&WR*

nology, called three-dimensional conformal radiation therapy, allows the oncologist to more precisely aim the radiation at higher doses, improving cure rates with fewer side effects. But only about 40 percent of cancer centers have the required state-of-the-art equipment. An additional 10,000 men opt for radiation seed implants, called brachytherapy, in which a doctor guided by ultrasound imaging shoots pencil-lead-size radioactive pellets into the prostate, through the rectum.

But no matter how reliable a man's numbers and how careful his calcula-

tion, each step is clouded in uncertainty, as Richard Howe discovered. Howe's numbers, including a low PSA and Gleason score, made him a good candidate for watchful waiting. But the former president of Pennzoil Corp. chose surgery because he wanted an early shot at a cure. Physicians found his cancer was more aggressive than they had predicted. "I probably had a very close call," says Howe, who is not a physician but has studied prostate cancer enough to have had a paper published in 1994 in the *Journal of Urology* called "Prostate Cancer: A Patient's Perspective." Since

his surgery eight years ago, he has informally counseled nearly 3,000 men about their options.

For Steve Weglarz of Lynn, Mass., the predictive numbers proved accurate, but he gambled on favorable lifestyle odds—and lost. "The good news is my PSA is zero and has been since surgery" eight years ago, he says. That means the cancer has been cured. But the price the 72-year-old retired internist paid is incontinence. Weglarz was devastated. "I didn't expect to be incontinent. My urologist said the chances were 5 percent, so naturally I thought I'd be among

Milken accelerates cancer research

Mike Milken took his first PSA test in 1993, at age 46. A friend, Time Warner Chairman Steve Ross, had recently died of prostate cancer. Milken's results were stunning and devastating. "I had lymph nodes that were 100 to 500 times normal" size, he said in an interview with *U.S. News.* "My prognosis was so negative." Milken was given a life expectancy of 12 to 18 months; he went home and stayed in bed for 18 hours.

In the aftermath, he assessed his past. "I've lost 10 close relatives to cancer," he says. "My father was diagnosed [with malignant melanoma in 1976] at the height of my financial success." And he considered his future. "I had to conclude that every single one of my relatives had not won their fight against cancer and [ask] what I was going to do differently."

Milken became an impatient patient. He underwent radiation and hormone therapy. And he went public, one of the first in a line of celebrity prostate cancer patients, including Gen. Norman Schwarzkopf, Intel Corp. CEO Andy Grove, and Yankees Manager Joe Torre.

But Milken—once best known as the Wall Street junk-bond wizard who was jailed for securities violations and paid $1.1 billion in fines and settlements—

has done more than give the disease a face. He has used his connections, the news media, and a great deal of money to make science move faster. Seven years after his diagnosis, Milken has, through the Milken Family Foundation, invested some $50 million and raised another $70 million to bankroll his Association for the Cure of Cancer of the Prostate. Its mission is to fund research through "venture philanthropy," bringing together people with different skills and getting researchers to quickly share findings.

Business model. "He has applied a business model to research," says Howard Scher, a cancer researcher at Memorial Sloan-Kettering Cancer Center, whose work has been funded by Milken's group. "It is a very different philosophy." Typically, getting a cancer research grant is a time-gobbling process. Milken's group shrank applications to five pages and promised an answer in 60 to 90 days. The grants are often small—about $100,000—and designed to help scientists gather early data. And Milken is willing to twist some famous arms. When researchers needed a data storage system, he contacted Oracle CEO Larry Ellison. When scientists needed families with multiple cases of prostate cancer, he went on *Larry King*

Live to help launch a registry. They got 3,000 calls.

The work is making a difference. Research supported by the association has led to more than 70 treatments now being tested in human clinical trials. Among them: new chemotherapies, vaccines, and viruses designed to attack cancer cells.

Milken, who has been in remission for more than five years and has PSA readings of zero, credits his recovery to standard medical treatment, but he also embraces an anything-that-can't-hurt-is-worth-a-try approach. That includes meditation, sesame oil massages, ayurvedic medicine, aromatherapy, and nutrition. He has demonstrated recipes from his health cookbooks on his friend Martha Stewart's TV show. While lobbying in Washington, he temporarily replaced the Senate dining room menu with low-fat, high-soy food.

Some criticize the group's focus on late-stage disease. Milken's response? "No one ever died from having prostate cancer [confined] in their prostate.... Once we've solved late stage, we've solved everything." While he's pleased with the progress, he's a man used to getting things done fast. "It's just hard to believe that we're still working on this." —*Katy Kelly*

---

the 95 percent," he says. A study published in January in the *Journal of the American Medical Association* found that of 1,291 men who had undergone a radical prostatectomy, 8.4 percent were incontinent after 18 months and 60 percent were impotent. Both external beam radiation and radiation seed implants carry similar risks, though experienced surgeons and radiologists at centers that do a lot of prostate procedures report significantly lower rates.

No diapers. Weglarz found a way to cope. Two years after surgery, he went to a support group meeting and heard men tell similar tales. More important, he found out about a surgical procedure to implant an artificial sphincter, a device that releases urine only when triggered by external hand pumping. Weglarz no longer has to wear a pad.

Urologists can also counsel men on treatments to help overcome impotence following treatment, including the erec-

tile dysfunction drug Viagra if treatment has not damaged the nerve bundles surrounding the prostate, and various injectible drugs and vacuum devices. "You can do a lot to overcome the side effects," says Howe. "Would you rather be impotent and alive, or potent and dead?"

As Weglarz learned, even reassuring numbers are simply probabilities, and patients whose prospects look similar can fare very differently. When Mike Semenek of Downers Grove, Ill., found out four years ago that he had prostate cancer, he went to a support group, Us Too!, and met three other men who, like him, were recently diagnosed. Coincidentally, their PSA counts and Gleason scores were roughly the same. So, like businessmen with a lifesaving mission, they set about figuring their odds. "We tabulated survival rate charts by treatment types," says Semenek. "We used a decision analysis for deciding what treatment would be best for each of us.

We ended with a numerical value. All four of us ended up deciding that seed implant was the best for our particular objectives": surviving the cancer and preserving their quality of life.

Spasm. Semenek, 71, went to the Mayo Clinic in Scottsdale, Ariz., for his radiation seed implant, and his PSA numbers are very low and holding, with few troubling side effects. Bob Jackson, 74, of Chicago went to the Northwest Tumor Institute at Swedish Medical Center in Seattle, where John Blasko pioneered seed implant therapy, and his numbers are equally low. He was troubled by severe urinary problems for about two weeks following the procedure, however. "My experience of going to the bathroom was a spasm of the whole lower abdomen. I didn't know if I was urinating or defecating." When that difficulty subsided, he still had extreme difficulty urinating until he had a surgical procedure called transurethral

Greens (and reds) may cut your risk

Michael P. Semenek, 71, and Michael S. Semenek, 34, know just how much like Dad a son can be. Both men have three children, restore 1950s Chevrolets as a hobby, and treasure summer mornings fishing for trout. But when it comes to prostate cancer, the two hope their lives will differ by much more than their middle names.

The elder Semenek was diagnosed four years ago with prostate cancer, and *his* father had it, too. With two affected relatives, the younger Semenek is at least twice as likely to develop the ailment as other men are. So, the pair sifted through prevention information from a local support group, and a compelling message quickly emerged: Cut back on fatty foods, and feast on vegetables and fruits.

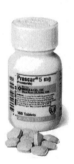

"I knew I should change," says Michael S. "Especially since I'm the first to throw a steak on the grill, come summertime."

Definitive evidence isn't in, but many researchers agree. "There doesn't seem to be a downside to that kind of eating," says Ian Thompson, chief of urology at the University of Texas Health Science Center at San Antonio. One of the first clues that diet influences the risk of prostate cancer came when scientists tracked men who had migrated from Japan to the United States and presumably adopted our fat-rich diet. A generation later, the same men came down with prostate cancer at four to nine times the rate of those who had stayed in Japan. More recently, at least 11 studies have linked high fat intake with a high risk of the disease.

And in a new study from Seattle, men who ate three half-cups of broccoli, brussels sprouts, or other cruciferous vegetables a week cut their risk by 41 percent.

Saturated fats, found in meats and dairy products, could lead to prostate cancer because digesting them generates cancer-causing molecules called free radicals. Conversely, many fruits and veggies are rich in antioxidants, which mop up the harmful molecules. Tomatoes, in particular, contain large amounts of a powerful antioxidant

called lycopene. And soy products contain genistein, which slows the growth of prostate cancer cells in lab animals.

Other leads. To most experts, the jury is still out on diet as prevention of prostate cancer because no one has conducted long-term clinical trials. But there are some other good leads. A Finnish study on lung cancer coincidentally found 32 percent less prostate cancer in men taking vitamin E. Another trial revealed a 63 percent drop in prostate cancer in men taking the mineral selenium. This fall, the National Cancer Institute will follow up with a 12-year, $100 million study of about 32,000 men. There's also a clue to prevention from an extended family in the Dominican Republic. Its males lack the hormone dihydrotestosterone, (DHT), a potent form of testosterone, and have virtually no prostate cancer. Now more than 18,000 healthy men are testing finasteride, a DHT blocker found in hair-growth drugs.

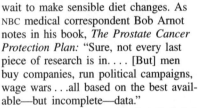

Doctors aren't yet ready to recommend pills or supplements for prevention. But men don't need to wait to make sensible diet changes. As NBC medical correspondent Bob Arnot notes in his book, *The Prostate Cancer Protection Plan:* "Sure, not every last piece of research is in.... [But] men buy companies, run political campaigns, wage wars . . .all based on the best available—but incomplete—data."

—*Rachel K. Sobel*

CLOCKWISE FROM TOP: JEFFREY MACMILLAN FOR *USN&WR* (3); MERCK

---

resection of the prostate to scrape away excess prostate tissue.

The two others, Bruce Sanfilippo, 61, and Dan Herman, 60, had treatment in the Chicago area. They both had only minor and temporary problems with urination, but their PSA numbers have fluctuated. Sanfilippo's are now low and stable, but Herman's are beginning to rise—a troubling sign that the cancer may return. None of them knows, of course, if the disease was simply more aggressive in the two men who are not doing as well or if an alternate procedure or institution would have made a difference. One thing the four friends have in common is that none became impotent following treatment.

Despite the agonizing trade-offs in making a treatment decision, the chilling reality is that cancer recurs in more than 35 percent of men, regardless of treatment. "For that group of people, the treatment options become pretty limited," says Erik Goluboff, director of urology at the Allen Pavilion of the Columbia-Presbyterian Medical Center in New York.

Bill Blair, 70, of Blue Island, Ill., went into surgery hoping for a cure. Instead surgeons found his cancer had spread farther than his doctor thought. He was sewn up with his prostate still inside. "My surgery was aborted. I was given the prophecy by all the experts that I would not live long and I should get my house in order," says Blair, who has already outlived predictions by two years.

Like other men whose cancer has advanced beyond the reach of the knife or the radiation beam, Blair faced some cruel choices. He could forgo any other medical treatments. Or he could try hormonal therapy, which he is doing. Hormonal therapy, a medical euphemism for surgical or chemical castration, drastically reduces testosterone, which slows the growth of the cancer. But the treatment also has profound side effects, including loss of the sex drive. "It makes an old man of you real fast. Anemia. Arthritis. Night sweats. Men finally figure out what women are going through," says Blair. "You lose muscle mass. You feel weak. I gained 15 pounds. You get depressed. You have a lot of mood swings. I was weepy." The side effects are troubling enough that Blair has chosen what he calls intermittent hormonal therapy, taking drugs to block testosterone when his PSA numbers are rising and getting off them when the numbers stabilize.

But where there is medical research, there is hope. Early this month, Goluboff presented a paper at the annual meeting of the American Urological Association with promising results about an experimental drug called Exisulind, which has been shown to kill prostate

cancer cells in mice. He followed 96 prostate patients who had had surgery but whose PSA levels continued to rise, indicating that their cancer had not been cured. Half received a placebo, and the other half got Exisulind, which seems to block an enzyme unique to cancer cells. PSA levels either stabilized or rose more slowly among the men taking the drug. And, unlike hormonal therapy, says Goluboff, it had "almost no side effects. It's like taking a vitamin pill."

It's a promising first step toward treating prostate cancer as a chronic disease that can be controlled. "People can live with an elevated PSA as long as they don't ever develop a metastasis," says Goluboff. The drug, still in clinical trials, may be approved by the Food and Drug Administration within a year.

For now, Giuliani and men like him can only juggle the numbers and come up with an educated guess about how

to cope with their cancer. Each decision is equal parts scientific logic and leap of faith.

With Josh Fischman

WHERE TO LEARN MORE

- **Books.** *Mayo Clinic on Prostate Health* explains the prostate from testing to treatment. *The Prostate: A Guide for Men and the Women Who Love Them,* by Patrick C. Walsh, explains the latest procedures and their side effects.
- **Decision help.** The National Comprehensive Cancer Network (*www.nccn.org*) offers an interactive decision tree for men deciding on tests and treatment.
- **Support.** Us Too! (*www.ustoo.com*) lists support groups in the United States and Canada.

too much
of a good
thing

Thanks to Bill Clinton, sex addiction is coming out of the closet. Thomas Beller visits the country's premier clinic for a firsthand dose of carnal knowledge

It was a bright Arizona day, and I was on my way to visit the sex addicts. The skies were blue, the vast desert was dotted with tumbleweed and cactus, and I was speeding down a narrow strip of pavement in a rented car, thinking about a particular kind of sex. Not good sex, or bad sex, but *overwhelming* sex. Sex: The Drug.

I was headed toward a private clinic called the Meadows, near Phoenix, that, under the direction of psychologist Patrick Carnes, has developed one of the leading programs in the country for the treatment of sex addiction. It was Carnes who initially coined the phrase, "sex addict" back in 1983, and who developed a system of treatment modeled after the twelve-step program of Alcoholics Anonymous. First, the patient has to admit he is powerless over his addiction. And then he has to appeal to a "higher power" for help.

So I was thinking, essentially, about sex and God. The vast desert around me didn't seem large enough to encompass all the possible variations on these two themes. Then, in the middle of nowhere (actually about forty miles south of a town called "Nowhere"), I saw a sign that made me smile.

It read: DETENTION CENTER. DO NOT PICK UP HITCHHIKERS.

I immediately imagined escaped sex addicts standing by the side of the road, next to a cactus, trying to wave down the passing cars. I should say very clearly that the sign didn't refer to the Meadows, which is *not* a detention center. People are there because their lives have spiraled out of control. They've lost their jobs or their marriages, been arrested, or come within a hair's breadth of those things happening. They want to be there. (A thirty-five-day

How about chocolate addiction? Golf addiction? People solemnly filing into Marx Brothers Anonymous declaring, "I am powerless to resist my desire to watch Zeppo"?

visit costs $35,000, so they have to *really* want to be there.) There is no chain-link fence. If you want to leave, you can take a cab.

But still, I liked imagining them lined up by the side of the road, and wondered what they might look like. Maybe they'd look like Kate Moss, whose recent rehabilitation for drink and drugs was rumored to include therapy

From *Elle* magazine, May 1999, pp. 170-179. © 1999 by Elle Magazine. Reprinted by permission.

for sex addiction. Or maybe like Michael Douglas, who reportedly sought treatment to avoid a divorce, or Aerosmith rocker Steven Tyler, a former Meadows patient. Or maybe they'd look like our president. You can't think about sex addiction for even a second without speculating about Bill Clinton, and vice versa. Now that the suspense of what will happen to him legally is over, we can return to the most fundamental question surrounding his behavior with Monica: why?

Carnes's books are laced with case histories. His simple prose has an almost incantatory quality: It's as though you are hiding behind the curtain in a doctor's office, or a confessional, a place where deep truths are laid bare. "Del was a lawyer. Brilliant, charming, and witty. His wife and three children were proud of his accomplishments. However, Del's public visibility was creating a problem because he was also a sexual addict. His double life included prostitution, porno bookstores, and affairs."

Or: "Chris . . . was an addict whose cruising was fused with her professional life as a consultant in urban planning. Her life was filled with seminars, conferences, and workshops. They served as a cover for her other life."

There is no question that there are men and women (according to Carnes, one of four sex addicts is female) whose relationship to sex has caused their lives to come undone. But then again, sex *addiction*? How about chocolate addiction? Golf addiction? People solemnly filing into Marx Brothers Anonymous declaring, "I am powerless to resist my desire to watch Zeppo"?

I imagined drivers anxiously speeding past the escaped sex addicts as they tried to hitch a ride. It made me laugh. Then I caught a glimpse of myself in the rearview mirror. I stopped laughing.

There are no meadows at the Meadows. The small cluster of bungalows and one-story buildings looks, at first glance, like a community-college campus, or a nursing home. There are a few patches of grass and a pine tree in its midst and from almost every vantage point there is a view of the desert. The very sight of it makes you feel meditative and small.

I'm greeted by John Ney, director of marketing. Although I don't ask him directly, I sense that, unlike all the other counselors here, he's not a reformed addict. He could well be marketing director for a consortium of podiatrists or a country club. But he has a sympathetic face, a sort of fixed expression of empathy that must be extremely useful as he spends his days among people who crave understanding.

The first thing we do is have lunch in the sunny cafeteria. The patients sit at tables chatting, a youngish bunch who are suffering from an assortment of ailments: drug addiction, alcohol addiction, sex addiction, eating disorders, with the odd gambling addict thrown in. I cast a longing gaze at them. I'd been told repeatedly that I would not

be able to talk with them, and John seems quite jumpy to see me even looking in their direction.

After lunch, John takes me to meet Bob Fulton and Maureen Canning, the primary sex-addict counselors. While John goes to tell them I'm here, I wander over to a small, forlorn gazebo known as the "smoking hut." A guy with a bandanna asks if I'm in the Survivors' group. I tell him I'm not, and he walks away. But, in Meadows-speak, I *am* a survivor—because the thing that Survivors have survived is their childhoods.

The first thing I notice when I walk into Maureen's office is something that resembles a large red Wiffle-ball bat, though this one is made of foam rubber and canvas, and seems designed more for bopping someone on the head

> ## "Say you walk into an ice-cream store and there are a hundred flavors," I say. "Is it all right to taste a few different ones?"

(in a cathartic, constructive way) than for hitting a ball.

Bob was a Catholic priest for seventeen years. Maureen has a nice smile, but as we talk I notice that every now and then her blink is a little delayed, as though something she has just said has triggered a powerful memory and caused her momentarily to freeze, the eyelid paused at half mast. When I ask what their respective addictions were, Bob says he was an alcoholic, and Maureen says she was a sex addict.

Bob and Maureen are in charge of the process by which patients look to their past to discover the origins of their behavior—the central tenet of sex addiction being that sex addicts suffered abuse as children. "We look at the underlying trauma," says Maureen. "Each patient starts by writing an autobiography up to age seventeen." Part of me thinks this is only slightly better than going to a palm reader, and part of me likes the idea of taking a thirty-minute synopsis of my life and handing it over to a couple of experts who can discern where, exactly, I got screwed up.

"When the patients present their autobiographies," says Maureen, "what I'm listening for are the trauma bonds. What messages did they get as children, and how are they playing them out today? And then, throughout treatment, I'm constantly tying their current behaviors back to their original wounding."

Whereas Eve may have committed original sin, sex addicts are apparently victims of an "original wound." Sometimes this is an explicit wound, such as sexual molestation. At other times it is more "covert," but has a similarly corrosive effect, though less like a hurricane than a wave slowly eroding the rock that it crashes against. An example of this might be the way that a father looks at his daughter's breasts, or his repeated requests for a massage. Or a mother who shames her son for masturbating. (Hanging out at the Meadows, one comes to feel that parenting is a near futile enterprise.)

"Once the patients start to draw correlations between the past and present, they begin to heal the trauma," says Maureen. She makes it sound easy. You figure out your trauma, and then it goes away. But, she adds, "It's not something we're going to be able to heal in thirty-five days. What we *can* do is bring up the consciousness around those issues, and then start to give them tools to deal with the addiction as they continue to work on the trauma."

The Meadows has a capacity for seventy patients at a time, of whom maybe a quarter are being treated for sex addiction. At the moment, only one member of the sex-addict group is a woman. "Probably as few as 10 percent of our sex-addiction patients are female," says Maureen, "which is disheartening, because that means that women are not getting the treatment they need."

What type of destructive behavior do women engage in? I ask.

"They have affairs," Maureen replies. "We're seeing more and more women going on the Internet, having romantic exchanges, and then meeting people and having sexual affairs. Usually what brings a woman here are the consequences: facing a divorce, losing her job, depression, suicidal thoughts, being unable to get up out of bed or take care of the children."

Whether male or female, sex addicts make sex—and their own sexuality—central to their self-image. "At the very core of a sex addict's being, they feel worthless," says Bob. "The sense of who they are is not fully developed, because the parents haven't been there to give it to them. And so what will undo the shame is the trauma resolution around the abandonment wounds."

I begin to despair. On one hand, I find this interesting: People who were traumatized by their formative experiences with their parents (a group which includes, I think it's fair to say, *everybody*, but I'll leave that alone for now) need to constantly reaffirm their worth by having sex with other people. But what Bob and Maureen are saying seems to be a New Age version of Philip Larkin's famous line, "They f___ you up, your mum and dad." And he didn't get $35,000 for that poem. So, in this uncharitable mood, I ask about the rubber bat.

"It's called a Bataka," says Maureen. "We use it for anger work. Many times a patient has a lot of anger that they have never been able to express to the perpetrator. We have them sit across from an empty chair, raise the bat, and say, "I'm really *angry* with you," and then beat the empty chair. And then once they're moving the anger out, the sadness and the pain will start to come up, and then the tears. And when that happens, you're really get-

ting down into the pain of that little kid and the healing can begin."

For the sex addict, shame is both wound and medicine. Sex takes you out of your feelings, but it works like a drug, and when the effect has worn off, the only thing that can placate the ensuing guilt is more sex. "It's almost like the addict is a separate part of yourself," says Bob. This, then, is the central metaphor: Dr. Jekyll and Mr. Hyde. The addict feels shame about his secret life, goes to great lengths to keep it a secret, yet has a strange, almost pathological desire to get caught. He doesn't so much engage in sex as enter it, as he would a secret chamber. But, I wondered, isn't this also an accurate description of the transformative power of sex itself? People lose themselves. They fall out of their own persona and

I ask about the President, whose aura is so strongly felt at the Meadows that they ought to have a portrait of him with a sign saying, THIS COULD BE YOU.

enter into another self, more wild and voracious or tender or angry or mirthful than their normal, real, walking-around-the-office self. And that wild metamorphosis is half the delight of sex, isn't it?

At the end of our meeting I pose the rather personal question that has been nagging at me throughout. It's the sort of question that is bound to creep into your thoughts if you're single and writing about sex addiction, namely: How much sex are you allowed to have before you have to start worrying about yourself?

"Say you walk into an ice-cream store and there are a hundred flavors," I say. "Is it all right to taste a few different ones?"

"Just because there are a hundred flavors doesn't mean you have to taste them all," responds Bob. "If you do, you've precluded the healthy intimacy that you get when you're not f___ the whole world. You can look at the one flavor that you have and get to know it in relationship to you."

"One?" I ask, somewhat grievously, suddenly feeling very literal-minded. "Should you marry the person you lose your virginity to?"

"I wouldn't press it into an absolute," says Bob.

"So what's the healthy area? Five flavors?"

"What's healthy is being in touch with one's own development; knowing what is motivating one's behavior. For me, it may be three flavors. For someone else, it may be twelve; for someone else, it may be one flavor."

"What about, say, twenty-five flavors?" I ask, apprehensively.

"For some people, twenty-five might be healthy. But if it's twenty-five, I would tend to think that there were things blocking—that many of those encounters were not a total engagement—that many of them were a way of self-medicating."

The one case study that I found truly persuasive did not appear in any of Carnes's books. It was a memoir by the poet Michael Ryan, called *Secret Life.* The only photograph of the author in the book appears on the back cover: a happy five-year-old boy sitting on the lawn. The picture was taken by a neighbor, a young man he calls "Bob Stoller," who abused Ryan regularly over the course of the following year. The bulk of the story is devoted to Ryan's youth and young adulthood—the bumbling but unremark-

What Bob and Maureen are saying seems to be a New Age version of Philip Larkin's line, "They f___ you up, your mum and dad." And he didn't get $35,000 for that poem.

able path of a rebellious Catholic boy with a loving mother and an alcoholic father. Apart from the description of his molestation, it might be called charming, and yet in its details one can see an insidious pattern of deviant, unhealthy sexuality develop, like a photograph slowly materializing in a darkroom.

Describing his groping encounters with an early girlfriend who wouldn't sleep with him, Ryan writes, "I did not find this (rolling around) erotic, but sex was only erotic when it was bad, and this was love, and love was good." This relatively innocent revelation made me think, Well, so what? Good sex has always been, somehow, bad.

But it's a short leap to this chilling passage: "I was certainly a magnet for some women, as some women were for me—suicidal women for whom sex was both validation and self-annihilation, an intense temporary escape from being themselves. Their hunger made them sexy to me and, no doubt, vice versa. We always at least half hated each other, the half that was a mirror."

And not long after that, he begins engaging in absurdly compulsive sex, his marriage falls apart, he is fired from his professorial job at Princeton University, and only when he finds himself in the midst of a road trip to seduce a friend's fifteen-year-old daughter does he pull off to the side of the road and have the epiphany that leads him into recovery. Ryan's evocative book convinced me that

Carnes is onto something in identifying certain patterns of sexual behavior, where they come from, and what might be done to stop them.

But then again, where do you draw the line? You can't help but look for echoes of your own experience among Carnes's case histories. And it's likely you'll find them. "The addict," he has written, "can transform even the most refined forms of nudity into his own particular fusion of loneliness and arousal." That's a nice phrase. As it happens, I'm prepared to admit that I can take many images—refined or nude or neither—and transform them into my own particular fusion of loneliness and arousal. But I don't know if that's such a bad thing. Sex is, by its very nature, a kind of counterattack on loneliness. That initial splitting of Adam and his rib, the ferocious desire to reconnect. It makes sense that the two are somehow entwined.

God, or its approximation, is a weird presence in twelve-step culture and, therefore, the Meadows. Joe Pack Arnold is the center's spiritual counselor, and his office is evidence of how a "higher power" could mean just about anything. The walls are festooned with a variety of religious objects: A cross hangs from a leather necklace, a brass menorah gleams in the afternoon light, a Buddha meditates in the corner, and there are quite a few Native American objects with feathers attached. His office is feathery.

"I try to get the patients in touch with their spirit, to help them experience intimacy as a spiritual experience," Arnold says in his Southern drawl. He has the strange transcendent vibe of someone whose concerns are more metaphysical than physical. Frizzy gray hair sprouts from beneath his fishing hat. He has sleepy, melancholy eyes—you could call them bedroom eyes, but given the setting, that might not be appropriate—that are enlarged by a pair of enormous glasses, and a face that reminds me (in a nice way) of a Cabbage Patch doll.

"If they're open to it, we talk a lot about a higher power outside the self, which is a source of energy beyond what we know in our mechanized society. God, if you will."

And what if you won't?

"Those are the patients I enjoy the most, because they don't bring a lot of baggage with them. We do simple things, like make eye contact with a mountain peak five minutes a day, something outside of ourselves. Or we take a walk—to listen, look, and smell, and see what happens. The desert is alive with a lot of things, and they become aware of that."

I ask about the President, whose aura is so strongly felt at the Meadows that they ought to have an oil portrait of him over the front door with a sign saying, THIS COULD BE YOU.

"Clinton is a textbook addict," says Arnold. "He grew up in a broken home, his father was an alcoholic, his mother practically raised him, he came from nothing. He's brilliant, which didn't work in his favor, because even though his sex addiction has been so obvious over the years, he's been able to rise above everything and there's been no intervention. I don't think he'll act out again while he's President . . . but I think he will act out again."

At long last I meet Patrick Carnes, PhD, the father, as it were, of sex addiction. He is a fine-looking man, with broad shoulders, a ruddy complexion, and a widow's peak that gives him a slightly roosterish aspect—he has the radiant good health of the early riser. His eyes are bright blue, slightly crossed, and gaze at me with a mixture of forbearance and suspicion. Journalists are not his favorite species.

For a long time, he and his speciality have suffered the slings and arrows of public ridicule. His books are littered with moments of frustration and exasperation with the media and the whole culture—sex addiction is his baby, and every snigger at its expense must have felt like a personal attack. So these post-Lewinsky days are a time of heady vindication for Patrick Carnes. The whole country has spent a solid year fixated on someone who does not seem in control of his sexual urges.

"Bill Clinton has helped a lot of people," he begins cautiously, " . . . inadvertently. Before the Monica Lewinsky stuff blew up, we were probably thirty years behind alcoholism in terms of public understanding. Now we're only fifteen years behind."

Throughout my readings of Carnes's books, I was always on the lookout for signs that he was, at heart, a kind of sex-negative scold; that the concept of sex addiction was really a way of turning the whole sexual revolution into a mental illness; that it was a cover for Puritanism. But whenever that seemed like the case, Carnes confounded my notion by advocating *more* sex, not less. "It is clear that sexual health should not be exploitative or judgmental or negative," he wrote. "Rather, the foundation for a healthy sexuality starts with acceptance, abundance, and exploration."

So how, I queried him now, is one to decipher where a healthy, lively sexuality ends, and an unhealthy, desperate, medicating sexuality begins?

"The question is whether the obsession is interfering with your life," Carnes replies.

"What about affairs?" I ask. "An affair will definitely interfere with your life. If there is an affair in a marriage, does that mean the unfaithful partner is a sex addict?"

"I would guess that 40 to 50 percent of relationships in this country end up with an affair somewhere," he says. "Asking how many affairs it takes to make a sex addict is like asking how many drinks it takes to make an alcoholic. It's more about a pattern of behavior over the long term, and about how you are living your life. Most people realize that they have a problem when they start making promises to themselves to stop their destructive behavior, and find that they can't. That's when people know they've crossed the line—when they can't stop having sex."

Sex is an instinct as fundamental to our existence as our appetite for food. I wondered how something necessary

to our survival as a species could be the basis for an addiction.

For clarification, I call Chester W. Schmidt, Jr., MD, chairman of the department of Psychiatry and Behavioral Sciences at Johns Hopkins. He and his colleagues were part of a special task force that deliberated whether to list Sex Addiction in the DSM-IV, the psychiatrist's diagnostic manual. They decided against it.

"In terms of pop psychology," explains Dr. Schmidt, "the term 'sex addiction' is very appealing. It intuitively makes sense to a lay person that certain individuals have an appetite for sex that is greater than the norm. How better to explain that in today's psychological terms than to call it an addiction?"

Of all our appetites, sex is the most anarchic. It's where we feel our keenest sense of sin.

"Carnes's method," he continues, "is to treat sex addiction with the same series of steps used for substance addiction: removal from stimulation, detox, a twelve-step program, and psychological support. But in medicine, the term *addiction* has a specific pharmacologic meaning, i.e., that substances taken into the body are active in the brain in such a manner that their removal causes a cascading effect of physiological symptoms known as withdrawal. We do not accept that excessive sexual activity is addictive, in the way we use that term."

The great mantra of the recovery movement is "whatever works." I ask Schmidt if he is being too pedantic, not seeing the forest for the trees.

"It's hard to say if Carnes's treatments are helpful, because he has never subjected his findings to a peer-review journal. He hasn't done controlled studies. Sex addiction is a facile explanation for an extraordinarily complex set of behaviors. If you can explain away certain disturbing acts with a 'diagnosis,' it literally catches your breath: 'I know my problem. I'm a sexual addict!' "

But when I mention this to Carnes, he points out that there are difficult ethical considerations when it comes to applying scientific methods to the real world. "Doing a controlled experiment would mean taking certain people—whose behavior puts them in a life-or-death situation—and giving them virtually no treatment at all," he says. "What we do instead is follow the behaviors of people who recover, as well as the behavior of people who relapse. It's a different way of profiling what works."

A desert sunset is a sight that will have you believing in a higher power almost instantly, and it is against this backdrop that Carnes and I say goodbye. He is smiling at me with that expertly beneficent smile, the smile of a minister or a doctor or a hustler. He is not a hustler, but there is something in the "If you're hurting, come to us" embrace of the Meadows that I distrust.

In a way, my problem is similar to Schmidt's: It's a question of language. But my objection is not so clinically specific, it's rather that I can't abide the exhausting phe- nomenon by which the recovery movement colonizes every aspect of human experience and makes it something that needs to be cured.

Of all our appetites, it seems to me, sex is the most anarchic. It's where we feel our keenest sense of sin. The sexual impulse rides roughshod over our ethics and our desire to be just to other people. All over the world, peo- ple build these fragile structures called relationships, and the single biggest fault line that can destroy nearly all that hard-won trust is the issue of sexual wantonness, of infi- delity—the idea that one of the partners will look outside the relationship to satiate a sexual appetite he or she can- not control.

Carnes's work is fascinating in its examination of the ways we misuse our sexuality—as a means of defining ourselves, of reliving childhood trauma, or simply as a narcotic to numb the discomforts of intimacy. The label "sex addiction," however, takes our lust and makes it something that needs *fixing*. It makes pathological that which is part of life. It makes, I suggest to Carnes, desire a disease.

"Sex addicts are not getting the sexual rewards they want," he responds. "They are not happy with what they are doing. If the only way for a woman to be orgasmic is for a man to hurt her, that is not a functional template. We want to help these people have more rewarding sex, encourage them to rewire themselves."

Standing against the distant mountains, Carnes has a kind of evangelical, John Wayne, last-good-man vibe. His voice is soothing. He just wants to help. He stands like a sexual Statute of Liberty amid an ocean of sand: give me your abused, your hurting, your sexually self-destructive bodies. We will rewire you. You won't have to hurt your- self anymore.

In truth, I'm lulled by his vision, comforted somehow. There is so much tumult, dissonance, fear, and despair out in the wide world of sex, but here the waters are calm. I have just one nagging qualm. "Couldn't you change the name?" I want to say. How about 'sex com- pulsion'? Sex obsession? Sex dependency?"

But I don't. Sex addiction by any other name just wouldn't be as sexy.

What Made Troy Gay?

By Deborah Blum

When Troy DeVore told his mother he was gay, his wife was with him.

The couple had driven eight hot sweaty hours in their little unair-conditioned car—470 near-silent miles—from the central California coast north to the dusty valley town of Redding. They reached Troy's mother's home near midnight, damp, exhausted, and anxious to get the words out and over with. They hadn't called to say they were coming.

As soon as Sandi DeVore opened the door, her son hauled her off to the back bedroom. For some time Sandi had felt that Troy was withdrawing into some unreachable distance. He wouldn't talk to her. She couldn't figure out why. All she knew was that she was worried to death about him. Now, without preliminaries, he blurted it out. "Mom, I'm gay." He had no idea what she would do or say. And then, he recalls, "My mother went and hugged my wife; well, she's my ex-wife now. And I thought, What? Shouldn't she be hugging me? But my mother said she thought my wife needed comforting more. Because she thought my wife was going to blame herself."

Mother and son both remember it that way: the first hug going to his wife, like a charm to be used against grief and guilt. Next Sandi DeVore turned to her son and took him in her arms and said, "Are you sure?" as if those words were another charm, against reality.

Today that question—"Are you sure?"—makes them both laugh. Since that breakaway moment in the summer of 1987, Troy has embraced homosexuality with exuber-

> **Scientists once would have pointed to his mother's personality. Now they think her DNA holds the strongest clue.**

ance. At age 32, he runs the public health program at Sacramento's Lambda AIDS Response, a gay nonprofit agency where he teaches safe sex to teenagers. He's cheerfully comfortable with himself, a big man (standing 6 foot 6 and weighing "too much and I'm not saying anything more") with a reddish beard, clear blue eyes, a quick laugh, and a style of dress that emphasizes jeans, T-shirts, and body piercing. He's filled his office with a furry mix of stuffed teddy bears. He wakes up every morning to a bear-shaped alarm clock playing Walt Disney's Winnie-the-Pooh theme song. Knowing what she now knows about Troy, Sandi wonders, How could I not have seen?

But she hadn't seen, and neither had Troy's wife or his father. And like any unwelcome secret unveiled within a family, this one rippled outward into a flood of blame. His father, long divorced from his mom and already on poor terms with Troy, was so furious when he heard about Troy's coming out that the two haven't spoken since. Meanwhile Troy's wife, Kathy, reacted just as Sandi had sensed she would, insisting that she'd somehow turned Troy toward men. As their marriage foundered, Sandi recalls, "Kathy was just so upset."

And Sandi? Sandi, as any mother might, blamed herself.

Sandi, now 50, shares much with her son. She's also tall, also red haired and blue eyed, and her enthusiasm for Troy's life now matches his. But in the months after

From *Health*, April 1998, pp. 82-86. © 1998 by Time Inc. Health, a division of Time Publishing Ventures, Inc. Reprinted by permission.

he came out, what she mainly felt was a profound sense of personal failure. Like most parents of her generation, she'd received the message that homosexuality was a mother's legacy. "I'm a real strong person. I have a strong personality. Was I so dominant that I pushed him into this?" she recalls wondering late at night, turning the circumstances over and over in her mind.

In hindsight, such worry looks painfully unnecessary. Over the past decade a new generation of researchers has uncovered evidence about what drives and shapes sexual orientation, particularly for men. And though there are still unanswered questions, this much seems certain: Sexual orientation is largely innate, dominated by genetics perhaps less powerful than the chromosomal information that dictates physical attributes, such as height, but strong compared with heredity's influence on other behaviors. Scientists estimate that a solid sense of self-worth is perhaps 30 to 40 percent inherited, which allows for powerful environment influence; shyness, perhaps 50 percent; height, perhaps 90 percent. Male sexual orientation, according to the new estimates, may be as much as 70 percent determined at birth.

There's a measure of comfort in this research. It has helped explain the uncomfortable feeling of difference experienced by many gays from an early age. It has raised hope that antigay sentiment can be relegated to the dustheap of prejudices. It has consoled mothers like Sandi DeVore. But it has not come without an irony attached. For if this research is correct, the genes that drive homosexuality are inherited from mothers.

NO ONE IS SURE, but the most reliable estimate—based on surveys of sexual behavior, which probably underestimate—is that 2 to 3 percent of men and not quite 2 percent of women have a same-sex orientation. That's 5 million Americans. Some hide it, desperately, from their parents. Some parents, with equal desperation, refuse to listen. Most gay children and their parents, though, do face the facts together. And from all accounts, one of the first questions parents ask themselves concerns blame: Was it something I did?

For decades scientists answered this question with a highly judgmental yes. Freud had posited that the cause was a domineering mother, an assertion that prompted millions of women over the years to wonder, as Sandi did, whether being a meeker person would have made the child grow up straight. Psychologists also theorized that gays were the product of weak or emotionally distant fathers, or of neurotic family life. Little tested, these explanations became popular wisdom; moreover, the American Psychiatric Association kept homosexuality in its diagnostic manual of mental disorders until 1973.

Such theories—no more than speculation, really—fell away when actually tested. In a study of 1,500 homosexuals and heterosexuals done by the Kinsey Institute in the 1970s, researchers found no evidence that a mother's personality or the quality of family life influenced sexual preference. Children of strong-willed mothers and timid mothers, from happy families and unhappy ones, were equally likely to turn out straight or gay. And while gay men tended to have more distant relationships with their fathers, the researchers theorized that fathers were more apt to turn away from gay sons.

The Kinsey study did more than discredit the myth of the "guilty" parent, however. It provided a compelling portrait of a group of people who were distinctive from an early age. The gays in the study reported playing differently from other children of their gender. Asked, "Did you specifically enjoy girls' activities, such as hopscotch, playing house, or jacks?" half of the gay men responded yes, compared to 12 percent of the straight men. Most gay men but few straight men reported disliking team sports, while 67 percent of the lesbians but only 18 percent of the straight women said they'd cringed at dolls and dress-up. Later studies involving interviews with the parents of gay subjects, conducted without telling them what their children had said, affirmed these childhood differences.

By chronicling such visible early behaviors, the Kinsey study suggested genetics was involved. But it took the pioneering work of psychologist Michael Bailey of Northwestern University and psychiatrist Richard Pillard of Boston University to put that notion on solid ground.

Working together in the early 1990s, they did a series of studies on families of gay men and women. Among identical twins, if one brother was gay, the other brother was gay 52 percent of the time. Among fraternal twins, the rate was 22 percent. The numbers were essentially the same for women. Homosexuality, Bailey and Pillard had found, fit the classic profile of inheritance: The more genetically alike someone was to a gay sibling, the more likely that person also was gay.

Inspired by these findings, Dean Hamer, a geneticist at the National Cancer Institute, wanted to tease out how the transfer might work. He knew that the men Bailey and Pillard studied had an unusually high number of gay male relatives on the mother's side. So he examined the genealogy of 40 families with at least two gay brothers to see if the same pattern emerged. It did: While the father's side showed no pattern, male cousins and uncles on the mother's side were two to three times more likely to be gay.

Whatever genes might be involved, Hamer figured, would be on the X chromosome—the one men get from their mothers. And when he scanned the X of the gay brothers, in 82 percent of his samples he found distinctive genetic markings in one region. He repeated the study, this time looking at the DNA of gay brothers, straight brothers, and lesbian women, and again got significant results: Sixty-seven percent of the gay brothers had the same markings on the X. But the surprise was that the straight men also shared telltale markings at that spot, only these imprints differed from those found in the DNA of gay men. On the lesbians' X chromosomes, however, the region showed no consistent marks.

Hamer couldn't say exactly what he'd found. It wasn't a "gay gene," and it didn't apply to women. Still, it was a genetic region clearly involved in setting male sexual preference. Put together with the work from Bailey, Pillard, and others, Hamer's study signaled a new era in the science of sexual orientation. BORN GAY, trumpeted the cover of *Time*.

TROY DEVORE'S CHILD-hood is the textbook case outlined by these researchers. He was a boy who—against everything in his environment—preferred dolls to trucks, girl playmates to boys, domestic games to sports. He was five, Troy recalls, when he developed a crush on television actor Chad Everett. "The signs were there," he says, "if anyone had known to look."

His first-grade teacher wrote on his report card that Troy was the type of boy who stopped to smell the flowers. "I ran into her years later, and she said she'd always suspected I was gay," he says. His female cousins remember that he would borrow their Barbies and other dolls, and wouldn't join backyard ball games. Says Sandi, "His friends were girls rather than boys. And the boys he did like were ones that needed some help. He had a blind friend. He had a friend in a wheelchair."

When he was a freshman in high school, he developed his first major crush. Feeling attracted to a boy terrified him. Beating up "faggots and queers" was a hot topic of discussion in the locker room after gym class. "In the showers it was always, you know, you show me yours, I'll show you mine, and then the topic of faggots would come up." He dated girls. He tried to be one of the guys. But he was different. And, in his mind, he couldn't do anything about it.

After Troy graduated from high school, he drifted, taking aimless and easy work until he fell into a friendship with a waitress at a fast-food restaurant. Kathy was pregnant and wasn't going to marry the father of her child. She seemed to be the answer to Troy's problems. "I asked her to marry me. I wanted kids. I really like kids. She wanted to be married. We both had ulterior motives, I guess." His stepdaughter was born in 1984, and he and his wife had a daughter together in 1986. The family moved to the central coast, where Troy and Kathy managed a small oceanfront motel.

By this time his mother was deeply concerned about him. "I couldn't put a finger on what was different about Troy," says Sandi. "But I was afraid he was going to die, to kill himself. He kept having these accidents, you

know? He hit a tree when he was driving. I kept thinking he wasn't going to make it."

Then a gay couple staying at the motel became estranged, and Troy found himself consoling the partners. Before long he was spending so much time with the men that his wife, in a fury, accused him of sleeping with male guests and, further, of being gay himself. "Yes, I guess I am," he said, shocked into telling the truth. Kathy insisted he tell his mother.

In the months and years after Troy came out to her, Sandi experienced the harrowing series of emotions familiar to many parents of gays. "The first six months were the hard ones," she says. "I even asked him if he thought he was going through a phase. I hear that lots of parents ask that question."

> When the "gay gene" made headlines, Troy called his mom. "I knew they'd find a way to blame you."

She found herself grieving the loss of the life she had hoped for him, terrified that he would contract AIDS, and ashamed that for all those years she'd failed to see her own son as he was. "I was going back through old photos, and I found a picture of him as a toddler, sitting on the floor playing with three Barbie dolls," she says. "But I just didn't look. Your mind just won't go there." On top of all that, the idea that her pushiness had driven her son from mainstream life wouldn't leave her alone.

"Then one day we were having an altercation, and he wasn't taking anything off me," she says. "And I realized that there was no way I was so overbearing that I could take away from him just being Troy." Finally she agreed with Troy. He was born different. She'd had nothing to do with it.

When Hamer's studies splashed across the newspapers, however, Sandi found she couldn't escape responsibility after all. "Troy called me right away," she remembers. "He said, 'I knew they'd find a way to blame you.'

"It's funny," she says. "I had always just thought, Is he gay because of me? I never thought about it being my family."

HOW MANY members of Sandi's family are gay can't be established; Troy is the only one who is out of the closet. Still, Troy and Sandi see a clear pattern. Across three generations of her large and far-flung family, they say, they've noted relatives who are both secretive about their sexual preferences and uneasy with them. The one relative who has come out to Sandi and Troy agrees with them. "There are many in our family that I believe to be gay that have never acknowledged it to anyone, not even themselves," says the relative, who has lived with a same-sex companion for years and who spoke on the condition of anonymity.

Despite the progress made by researchers, no one knows how the genes that help determine homosexuality work. One notion is that they are but slightly altered versions of the genes that propel most of us toward the opposite sex. Some scientists theorize that in males a testosterone release that starts around age four somehow organizes brain cells toward opposite-sex orientation. Perhaps, they say, the genes in homosexual boys prompt the same urge only in a different direction. Or the so-called gay genes could code for behaviors that in turn have an impact on sexual preference. Seen from that angle, the genes could be ones that encourage nonconformist behavior, say, or promote the flouting of authority. Or they could influence all of the above.

What's more, environmental or cultural triggers can't be ruled out. Scientists now know that nature and nurture push and tug at each other throughout our lives. Even something as genetically driven as height can be nudged by real-world factors—stunted by malnutrition or stress hormones. What in a child's life may sway his sexual preference? What he eats? His first playmate? No one has the foggiest idea. Even without answers to such questions, says Daryl Bem, a psychologist at Cornell University who studies the causes of homosexuality, all of us should accept that both environment and genes are at work—and that, when it comes to orientation, a parent's actions aren't the key.

"I don't think parents have very much to do with it," Bem says. "It may be that you have a boy with strongly feminine traits and that may mean he's likely to grow up gay. Really your only choice is whether you want him to grow up happy and well adjusted or miserable and neurotic."

THAT TROY grew up miserable is a truth neither Troy nor Sandi avoids. It is the motive, as if they need one, behind their respective struggles: in Troy's case to advocate for gay rights and in his mother's case to support Troy. "Troy was raised with three very macho stepbrothers," says Sandi, her voice flat with the sound of unwelcome memories. "There were rumors. That was really hard for him. He would never, never have wanted his brothers to think he was gay."

Hiding from his brothers wasn't even the most painful part of the past. Troy recalls a high school field trip to an amusement park during which his one good friend at the time declared that he'd heard the gossip that Troy was gay. "He said he wasn't going to mess around with any faggots and to leave him alone."

Troy sits in the courtyard of a Sacramento coffeehouse as he calls up this memory. A mimosa tree arches above

him. The bright morning filtered through the leaves makes a pattern on his face, a design of shadow and light. It doesn't disguise hurt. Troy likes to laugh, but he looks back now without even smiling. "It took years to get over that one," he says. "There isn't a choice in this. If I could have chosen, I would have chosen to be straight. Life is so much easier when you're straight."

"God," Sandi says, "Can you imagine how hard it was for Troy?"

Mother and son have become close in the years since Troy announced that he was gay. Sandi marches in gay pride parades and hosts parties for Troy's friends. Troy is engaged to a man he's been seeing for more than a year; Sandi is planning the wedding. She also helps out with his daughter and step-daughter, both of whom he is helping to raise. Sandi and Troy talk now about everything, including the family history and how his father blames them both for the shame, as he sees it, of having a gay son. Sandi and Troy have a tacit agreement: no more secrets, no more panicky confessions. It all comes out between them.

For his part, Troy hopes that the new scientific understanding of homosexuality will alter attitudes, allow for tolerance. In this he joins those who note how left-handedness, once considered a perversion to be weeded out, became quickly disconnected from a moral position once it was understood as a biological trait.

> Sandi, who's seen Troy hurt, challenges anyone who would change him. "God doesn't make junk," she says.

Sandi, like any mother who's seen a child hurt, is less trusting. She worries that people who hate the very idea of homosexuality will call for ways to "cure" the problem with some futuristic gene therapy or by injecting kids with hormones. The idea infuriates her. "God doesn't make junk," she says. "My son is not defective."

All around her she comes across minds in need of widening. In the small conservative California town where she lives, she challenges people who begin grumbling about gays. "I jump in right away, before they say something they're going to feel bad about. I tell them that my son is gay. And they, well, they usually say that it's okay, as long as he doesn't touch them." She begins to laugh, but it fades into a sigh.

"You know, it doesn't make any difference where the homosexuality came from," she says. "There is no sense looking for someone to blame. Troy is what he is. I just feel proud that he is a good parent, a good teacher, and not a judgmental person."

She smiles. "He learned that from me."

Deborah Blum is a professor of journalism at the University of Wisconsin at Madison and the author of Sex on the Brain.

OUT OF THE FOLD?

The debate over gay ordination and same-sex unions poses a critical choice for mainline Protestants: Embrace or schism?

By DAVID VAN BIEMA/CLEVELAND

It should have been a celebration of unity, but it turned into a shocking tableau of discord. Louisiana bishop Dan Solomon was presiding over the General Conference of the United Methodist Convention, a contentious but usually joyous quadrennial meeting to plot the future of America's second-largest Protestant denomination. Solomon had proved an amiable and unflappable moderator, but now his voice cracked. "I speak to you with anguish about what is about to unfold," he said. "I bury my head in prayer. I cannot witness what is about to occur." As 5,000 delegates looked on, Solomon's head did drop to the lectern. Minutes later, a squad of uniformed police entered from the wings of the Convention Center stage in Cleveland, Ohio, and arrested 27 gay-rights protesters, including two bishops, charging them with disrupting a lawful meeting. As the protesters filed out, many delegates, even those who had just voted three times against gay-rights proposals, watched in tears. Everyone knew the police had been at the ready and that the activists might force their hand by taking over the stage. But had it actually happened? After all, the Conference's logo is a picture of Jesus' embracing arms and the words of the Apostle Paul: WE WHO ARE MANY ARE ONE BODY.

There is hardly a religious group in America that is not beset by the issue that rent the Methodist meeting in May: the place of gay people in its pews. In March the organization of Reform Jewish rabbis agreed that its members could perform gay-holy-union ceremonies if they chose. The group was then castigated for it by other Jewish branches. Last month the Vatican, which had earlier ordered an American nun and priest

to end a ministry to gays and their families because it did not stress the "intrinsically disordered" nature of homosexuality, further prohibited the nun and priest from talking about what they used to do. Even the small Mennonite and General Conference Mennonite churches, for years planning a merger, came within 10 votes of scuttling it, in part because they couldn't agree on the combined church's position on gays.

But the most wrenching expression of the dilemma is playing out in the mainline, a process that will intensify this week as the Presbyterian Church (USA) convenes in Long Beach, Calif. Few expect the Southern Baptists to ordain gays or the Reform Jews to legislate against them, but the traditional liberal denominations are almost violently torn. The three proposals whose passage prompted the civil disobedience and arrests in Cleveland—bans on gay ministers and holy unions, as well as a clause stating that homosexuality is "incompatible with Christian teaching"—prevailed by votes of roughly 2 to 1. That kind of majority is satisfying in electoral politics, but alarming in groups that regard themselves as constituting the body of Christ. Mainline Evangelicals and some gay-rights advocates have threatened to abandon their denominations, and the specter of full-blown schism looms in the future. Even in the bosom of the relatively unruffled Episcopal Church, whose representatives will meet in Denver on July 14, the issue can wreak havoc. When a Seattle-area rector told his 300-person Episcopal congregation some time ago that he was a celibate gay, 100 of them walked out.

The issue is impossible to ignore and yet maddening to be stuck on. Says a Presbyterian lesbian who has done hundreds of hours

of advocacy on the issue: "This is the church I grew up in and was nurtured in and found my faith in. I can't believe we are doing this to each other. Presbyterians don't talk a lot about [the end of the world], but when the Last Judgment comes . . . surely this is not what God wants us to waste our time on." But she cannot let it go.

This controversy is two-sided, and its conservative participants engage it with a passion and a devotion to the Gospel that equals that on the left. Says Claire Dargill, 38, a Presbyterian from Bridgeport, Conn.: "A sin is a sin, and you can't just change that because it's popular or politically correct. I just don't see how we can welcome gays into the church in the face of that." But as these portraits from the left-to-moderate wing of the discussion indicate, the issue is so divisive that it can foster bitterness and, at the very least, soul searching, even among those of apparently like mind.

TRACEY LIND: NO MORE PASSING

On the day last week when she donned the stole and the chasuble of her new office, on the day when her Episcopal bishop installed her as the dean of Cleveland's grand Trinity Cathedral, the Very Rev. Tracey Lind took a moment to think back on Sunday School, which in her case took place in a Reform synagogue. As a child, she had been half-Jewish, half-Christian, and the rabbi, who was teaching about the Holocaust at the time, glanced up shrewdly and asked, "Tracey, you could have passed. Would you have died for your faith or denied it?"

"You could have passed." The line haunted her in more ways than one. It took decades to settle the rabbi's implied religious query. It was only in 1984 that Lind stood on a Manhattan corner and heard what she describes as "the voice of God" calling her to the Episcopal ministry, into which she was ordained in 1987. But there was a second challenge the rabbi hadn't intended. On that same curbside, Lind promised herself, "I won't let the church use my sexuality as an excuse for not hearing God's voice through me." She was gay. And at that time, in a church with a distinct live-and-let-live-but-don't-rock-the-boat attitude, she felt that a dramatic coming-out would be a distraction. For the noblest of reasons, she was still passing.

That changed in 1995. Lind felt a special empathy for the oppressed; she attracted national attention for a series of dynamic social programs she had introduced as pastor to St. Paul's Episcopal Church in inner-city Paterson, N.J. But then a storm brewed in her backyard. Former Newark assistant bishop Walter Righter was charged with heresy for having knowingly ordained an open homosexual named Barry Stopfel.

Stopfel was Lind's good friend, she told her flock in a powerful, high-risk sermon; "It could have been me." She recounted the rabbi's challenge. Here was her answer. "I am not coming out because I want to flaunt my sexuality, [but] because the Gospel demands it," she said. "To exist in a homophobic society in fear and collaboration . . . causes moral insanity and moral death. To state clearly who one is and who one loves is to claim life in the midst of death."

At which point, oddly enough, everything fell into place. Her congregation rose and applauded. Ecclesiastical judges threw out the Righter case. Episcopal bishops have since ordained dozens of gay priests. "There is still work to do in this church, but for gays the tide has turned," says Lind. She was offered the high-profile job as cathedral dean, often a stepping stone to a bishop's post. Says Wiley Cornell, Trinity's senior lay leader: "Sexual orientation was a nonissue for the search committee."

Or close to one. In fact, the church omitted mention of Lind's sexuality when it announced her hire in February. "We didn't want that to become the defining vision everyone had of her," says Cornell.

And so begins a more subtle stage in Lind's development. She no longer passes. But her prominence sometimes demands a new discretion. "If you've spent your life banging on a door to get in, what do you do when you get inside?" she asks. "My job is to continue to engage people. As any good politician knows, there are no permanent enemies and no permanent allies."

The installation ceremony ends, and the bands strike up. Lind throws herself gamely into the bluegrass and polkas. Then as evening falls, a deejay comes on. And the newly invested dean, beaming, boogies down to the Village People's *YMCA*.

MEL WHITE: THE LURE OF SCHISM

Slender, California-breezy and prone to corny gay humor, the Rev. Mel White, co-head of the roving protest group Soulforce, seems a bit lightweight at first. But he has a powerful life saga, and was willing to get arrested not just in Cleveland in May and in Orlando, Fla., in June (Baptists), but plans to do likewise in Long Beach in July (Presbyterians) and possibly in Denver a week later (Episcopalians). The only transdenominational figure on the scene, he will establish the nightly-news rat-tat-tat for the entire season of contention. His attitude toward the various denominations? "We don't debate anymore. You change your policies, or we're going to split you apart and leave."

White's is a transformation that begs for comparison with Saul's on the road to Damascus. Grandson of a tent revivalist, White was ghostwriter of choice in the 1980s to the Evangelical élite, co-authoring books with Billy Graham, Jerry Falwell and Pat Robertson. One day, sitting with Falwell in a car surrounded by gay protesters, he realized he should be on the outside. After 25 years of clandestinely trying to "cure" himself via exorcism, electroshock and prayer, the father of two divorced and settled down with a man named Gary Nixon. Then he began searching for a way to expiate sins committed in the service of "homophobic haters."

That turned out to be Soulforce. For six years, White steeped himself in the confrontational nonviolence taught by Mohandas Gandhi and Martin Luther King Jr. He courted the heirs and icons of his newfound field—Gandhi's grandson Arun, King's daughter Yolanda and his strategist James Lawson—and they joined him in Cleveland, along with several hundred multidenominational gays, lesbians and transgendered persons wearing T shirts emblazoned with THIS DEBATE MUST END—WE ARE GOD'S CHILDREN TOO. Of these, 191 helped White block a Convention Center exit and went to jail, an act of "redemptive suffering" intended as a Christian witness to the perceived injustice of the Methodist position on homosexuality.

Humdrum as such activism might be in big-city streets, it can still shock the church world. Since the 1970s, mainline homosexual church activists have worked within the system, assuming that their quest for inclusion would begin as a minority cause but triumph when their brothers and sisters in Christ saw the justice of their plea. Only recently have some reached the conclusion that they are no match for Evangelical forces

THE CHURCHES

Where They Stand Now

UNITED METHODIST CHURCH
■ **GAY ORDINATION:** Banned, but will be defied by some congregations
■ **GAY-HOLY-UNION CEREMONIES:** Banned, but will be defied by some congregations
■ **LIKELIHOOD OF SCHISM:** The New England Conference is the most rebellious. Yet, save among radicals, there is little serious talk of schism

PRESBYTERIAN CHURCH (USA)
■ **GAY ORDINATION:** Effectively banned in 1997, but a church court has allowed a gay seminarian to continue his studies
■ **GAY-HOLY-UNION CEREMONIES:** Banned, but a church court allows commitment ceremonies as long as they are not called marriages
■ **LIKELIHOOD OF SCHISM:** Conservatives have a "take-a-hike" resolution, encouraging congregations that want to ordain and marry gays to leave, allowing them to take funds and church property

EPISCOPAL CHURCH
■ **GAY ORDINATION:** Openly gay priests and cathedral deans
■ **GAY-HOLY-UNION CEREMONIES:** Has refrained from coming up with a specific liturgy, but many ministers perform unions
■ **LIKELIHOOD OF SCHISM:** The American church is at odds with its parent Anglican Church. Bishops from around the world voted against gay marriage and ordination and declared that active homosexuality is "incompatible with Scripture." However, the statement was advisory

campaigning fervently from the right and that after rejecting gay ordination and marriage at convention after convention, denominational consensus was only hardening. In this context, White's attitude makes a certain harsh sense.

His campaign has predictably attracted ire from the right. Says James Heidinger II, publisher of *Good News,* a conservative Methodist journal: "We don't feel good about outsiders coming in and using intimidation and pressure on our delegates for something that ought to be a family affair."

In fact, even some in-house gay activists feel trampled on. "He's just like Falwell in his own way," says an Episcopalian.

White claims to understand. Of the gay Methodist activists who met him when he arrived in Cleveland (and who were themselves eventually arrested, to Bishop Solomon's dismay), he says, "They're thinking, 'Mel, we've worked four years for this moment. Don't screw it up for us.' " But to the extent that they are worried that he may mar their dialogue with their denominations, he really doesn't care. "Schism? Yes, we are calling for a personal schism. I don't think there's any chance for reconciliation in these churches. We're pushing people to say, Either you change the policies, or we will leave and get someplace where we *can* be spiritually fed. We're calling gay, lesbian, bi- and transgendered people to leave these churches . . . And then let them try to find an organist."

A NEW SUNDAY LESSON

Jane Wise was worried about gays in her church. Not about their being there. But that they might walk out the door and she might have to decide whether or not to go with them.

Wise, who is 73 and straight, recently arrived at her usual pew in Trinity United Methodist Church in Austin, Texas, for a special meeting of the congregation. In front of her was her friend Carolyn Dietrich, 39. At the pulpit was Trinity's pastor, Sid Hall, recapping: the Methodist General Conference's 65% vote calling homosexuality incompatible with Christian teaching was even higher than the tally four years before. Where did that leave Trinity? Eight years ago, it became a reconciling congregation,

one that "welcomes all people regardless of race . . . age [or] gender identity." But didn't the General Conference's emphatic, repeated rejection of homosexuality make that an empty pledge? Could Trinity in good faith stay in the Methodist fold? A woman stood and declared with some heat, "Whether you are gay or lesbian, black or white or transgendered, we're all part of God's family and should be accepted as that." "Very well put," muttered Wise.

Things have come a long way since 1988. That was the year Trinity hired Pastor Hall at age 30, hoping a young minister could revive a congregation shrunk to a mere 120 members, mostly old; they joked that anyone under 70 should join the youth group. Hall proved dynamic alright, but not in a way the solidly middle-class, overwhelmingly straight congregation had expected. Over three years he explicitly campaigned to extend fellowship to gays. This caused considerable whispering. "People said, 'Sid's not going to last very long, and we can always get another minister,' " recalls Wise. "One friend of mine said she thought if gays came to church, Sid's children would be molested. I told her I didn't think so."

When Trinity finally voted in 1992, reconciliation passed by a 4-to-1 vote. And the church thrived. This year it counted 350 members, a full third of whom are gay (plus one transgendered person, a Mary Kay beauty-products saleswoman). For Wise, the transformation was a joy and a challenge. A joy because people like Carolyn Dietrich returned to the church. Thirty-five years ago, Wise had taught Carolyn in Sunday School. Since then, Dietrich had gone off into the world, become a teacher and then a funding consultant, lived in Dallas, and wooed and wed her partner Lisa Dalton in a nondenominational ceremony. On the day Dietrich arrived at Trinity for the first time in nearly 30 years, Wise gave her a big hug.

Dietrich and Dalton also represented Wise's challenge. Issues like same-sex marriage still trouble her. "I don't know how to put it," she puzzles. "My own marriage meant so much to me . . . I'm sure it would mean the same to others, but we haven't approved such things in the church."

Today, however, she is worried that as a result of the Conference vote, Pastor Hall—who has already stopped performing any weddings at all because of the ban on gay nuptials—may feel called to lead Trinity out of the church altogether. That would put Wise in a terrible place. "I've grown so accustomed to the [Methodist] rules and regulations," she says nervously. Luckily, the meeting flows another way. One by one, congregants declare that they will continue to struggle for gay initiatives within the Convention. Alice Crabtree, a heterosexual mother of three, rises and says, "This church is a place where you can bring your most-honest-to-God-awful self or your most magnificent self," she says. "And people know you and love you. You watch people die. But you can come here because this is a safe place. For some people it's all the family we've got."

Dietrich, weeping, turns to her old Sunday School teacher. "Do you have a Kleenex?" she asks. Wise, as if the 35 years had never happened, calmly opens her beige pocketbook and hands her a tissue. Then she leans forward and gives Dietrich a couple more. "Just in case," she says.

—With reporting by Wendy Cole/ Cleveland and Austin and Lisa McLaughlin/New York

The Five Sexes, Revisited

*The emerging recognition that people come in bewildering
sexual varieties is testing medical values and social norms*

By Anne Fausto-Sterling

As Cheryl Chase stepped to the front of the packed meeting room in the Sheraton Boston Hotel, nervous coughs made the tension audible. Chase, an activist for intersexual rights, had been invited to address the May 2000 meeting of the Lawson Wilkins Pediatric Endocrine Society (LWPES), the largest organization in the United States for specialists in children's hormones. Her talk would be the grand finale to a four-hour symposium on the treatment of genital ambiguity in newborns, infants born with a mixture of both male and female anatomy, or genitals that appear to differ from their chromosomal sex. The topic was hardly a novel one to the assembled physicians.

Yet Chase's appearance before the group was remarkable. Three and a half years earlier, the American Academy of Pediatrics had refused her request for a chance to present the patients' viewpoint on the treatment of genital ambiguity, dismissing Chase and her supporters as "zealots." About two dozen intersex people had responded by throwing up a picket line. The Intersex Society of North America (ISNA) even issued a press release: "Hermaphrodites Target Kiddie Docs."

It had done my 1960s street-activist heart good. In the short run, I said to Chase at the time, the picketing would make people angry. But eventually, I assured her, the doors then closed would open. Now, as Chase began to address the physicians at their own convention,

> *Much has changed since 1993. Intersexuals have materialized before our very eyes.*

that prediction was coming true. Her talk, titled "Sexual Ambiguity: The Patient-Centered Approach," was a measured critique of the near-universal practice of performing immediate, "corrective" surgery on thousands of infants born each year with ambiguous genitalia. Chase herself lives with the consequences of such surgery. Yet her audience, the very endocrinologists and surgeons Chase was accusing of reacting with "surgery and shame," received her with respect. Even more remarkably, many of the speakers who preceded her at the session had already spoken of the need to scrap current practices in favor of treatments more centered on psychological counseling.

What led to such a dramatic reversal of fortune? Certainly, Chase's talk at the LWPES symposium was a vindication of her persistence in seeking attention for her cause. But her invitation to speak was also a watershed in the evolving discussion about how to treat children with ambiguous genitalia. And that discussion, in turn, is the tip of a biocultural iceberg—the gender iceberg—that

continues to rock both medicine and our culture at large.

Chase made her first national appearance in 1993, in these very pages, announcing the formation of ISNA in a letter responding to an essay I had written for *The Sciences,* titled "The Five Sexes" [March/April 1993]. In that article I argued that the two-sex system embedded in our society is not adequate to encompass the full spectrum of human sexuality. In its place, I suggested a five-sex system. In addition to males and females, I included "herms" (named after true hermaphrodites, people born with both a testis and an ovary); "merms" (male pseudohermaphrodites, who are born with testes and some aspect of female genitalia); and "ferms" (female pseudohermaphrodites, who have ovaries combined with some aspect of male genitalia).

I had intended to be provocative, but I had also written with tongue firmly in cheek. So I was surprised by the extent of the controversy the article unleashed. Right-wing Christians were outraged, and connected my idea of five sexes with the United Nations–sponsored Fourth World Conference on Women, held in Beijing in September 1995. At the same time, the article delighted others who felt constrained by the current sex and gender system.

Clearly, I had struck a nerve. The fact that so many people could get riled up by my proposal to revamp our sex and gender system suggested that change—as well as resistance to it—might be in the offing.

Indeed, a lot has changed since 1993, and I like to think that my article was an important stimulus. As if from nowhere, intersexuals are materializing before our very eyes. Like Chase, many have become political organizers, who lobby physicians and politicians to change current treatment practices. But more generally, though perhaps no less provocatively, the boundaries separating masculine and feminine seem harder than ever to define.

Some find the changes under way deeply disturbing. Others find them liberating.

WHO IS AN INTERSEXUAL—AND how many intersexuals are there? the concept of intersexuality is rooted in the very ideas of male and female. In the idealized, Platonic, biological world, human beings are divided into two kinds: a perfectly dimorphic species. Males have an X and a Y chromosome, testes, a penis and all of the appropriate internal plumbing for delivering urine and semen to the outside world. They also have well-known secondary sexual characteristics, including a muscular build and facial hair. Women have two X chromosomes, ovaries, all of the internal plumbing to transport urine and ova to the outside world, a system to support pregnancy and fetal development, as well as a variety of recognizable secondary sexual characteristics.

That idealized story papers over many obvious caveats: some women have facial hair, some men have none; some women speak with deep voices, some men veritably squeak. Less well known is the fact that, on close inspection, absolute dimorphism disintegrates even at the level of basic biology. Chromosomes, hormones, the internal sex structures, the gonads and the external genitalia all vary more than most people realize. Those born outside of the Platonic dimorphic mold are called intersexuals.

In "The Five Sexes" I reported an estimate by a psychologist expert in the treatment of intersexuals, suggesting that some 4 percent of all live births are intersexual. Then, together with a group of Brown University undergraduates, I

set out to conduct the first systematic assessment of the available data on intersexual birthrates. We scoured the medical literature for estimates of the frequency of various categories of intersexuality, from additional chromosomes to mixed gonads, hormones and genitalia. For some conditions we could find only anecdotal evidence; for most, however, numbers exist. On the basis of that evidence, we calculated that for every 1,000 children born, seventeen are intersexual in some form. That number—1.7 percent—is a ballpark estimate, not a precise count, though we believe it is more accurate than the 4 percent I reported.

Our figure represents all chromosomal, anatomical and hormonal exceptions to the dimorphic ideal; the number of intersexuals who might, potentially, be subject to surgery as infants is smaller—probably between one in 1,000 and one in 2,000 live births. Furthermore, because some populations possess the relevant genes at high frequency, the intersexual birthrate is not uniform throughout the world.

Consider, for instance, the gene for congenital adrenal hyperplasia (CAH). When the CAH gene is inherited from both parents, it leads to a baby with masculinized external genitalia who possesses two X chromosomes and the internal reproductive organs of a potentially fertile woman. The frequency of the gene varies widely around the world: in New Zealand it occurs in only forty-three children per million; among the Yupik Eskimo of southwestern Alaska, its frequency is 3,500 per million.

INTERSEXUALITY HAS ALWAYS BEEN to some extent a matter of definition, and in the past century physicians have been the ones who defined children as intersexual—and provided the remedies. When only the chromosomes are unusual, but the external genitalia and gonads clearly indicate either a male or a female, physicians do not advocate intervention. Indeed, it is not clear what kind of intervention could be advocated in such cases. But the story is quite different when infants are born with mixed genitalia, or with external

genitals that seem at odds with the baby's gonads.

Most clinics now specializing in the treatment of intersex babies rely on case-management principles developed in the 1950s by the psychologist John Money and the psychiatrists Joan G. Hampson and John L. Hampson, all of Johns Hopkins University in Baltimore, Maryland. Money believed that gender identity is completely malleable for about eighteen months after birth. Thus, he argued, when a treatment team is presented with an infant who has ambiguous genitalia, the team could make a gender assignment solely on the basis of what made the best surgical sense. The physicians could then simply encourage the parents to raise the child according to the surgically assigned gender. Following that course, most physicians maintained, would eliminate psychological distress for both the patient and the parents. Indeed, treatment teams were never to use such words as "intersex" or "hermaphrodite"; instead, they were to tell parents that nature intended the baby to be the boy or the girl that the physicians had determined it was. Through surgery, the physicians were merely completing nature's intention.

Although Money and the Hampsons published detailed case studies of intersex children who they said had adjusted well to their gender assignments, Money thought one case in particular proved his theory. It was a dramatic example, inasmuch as it did not involve intersexuality at all: one of a pair of identical twin boys lost his penis as a result of a circumcision accident. Money recommended that "John" (as he came to be known in a later case study) be surgically turned into "Joan" and raised as a girl. In time, Joan grew to love wearing dresses and having her hair done. Money proudly proclaimed the sex reassignment a success.

But as recently chronicled by John Colapinto, in his book *As Nature Made Him*, Joan—now known to be an adult male named David Reimer—eventually rejected his female assignment. Even without a functioning penis and testes (which had been removed as part of the reassignment) John/Joan sought masculinizing medication, and married a woman with children (whom he adopted).

Since the full conclusion to the John/Joan story came to light, other individuals who were reassigned as males or females shortly after birth but who later rejected their early assignments have come forward. So, too, have cases in which the reassignment has worked—at least into the subject's mid-twenties. But even then the aftermath of the surgery can be problematic. Genital surgery often leaves scars that reduce sexual sensitivity. Chase herself had a complete clitoridectomy, a procedure that is less frequently performed on intersexuals today. But the newer surgeries, which reduce the size of the clitoral shaft, still greatly reduce sensitivity.

THE REVELATION OF CASES OF failed reassignments and the emergence of intersex activism have led an increasing number of pediatric endocrinologists, urologists and psychologists to reexamine the wisdom of early genital surgery. For example, in a talk that preceded Chase's at the LWPES meeting, the medical ethicist Laurence B. McCullough of the Center for Medical Ethics and Health Policy at Baylor College of Medicine in Houston, Texas, introduced an ethical framework for the treatment of children with ambiguous genitalia. Because sex phenotype (the manifestation of genetically and embryologically determined sexual characteristics) and gender presentation (the sex role projected by the individual in society) are highly variable, McCullough argues, the various forms of intersexuality should be defined as normal. All of them fall within the statistically expected variability of sex and gender. Furthermore, though certain disease states may accompany some forms of intersexuality, and may require medical intervention, intersexual conditions are not themselves diseases.

McCullough also contends that in the process of assigning gender, physicians should minimize what he calls irreversible assignments: taking steps such as the surgical removal or modification of gonads or genitalia that the patient may one day want to have reversed. Finally, McCullough urges physicians to abandon their practice of treating the birth of a child with genital ambiguity as a medical or social emergency. Instead, they should take the time to perform a thorough medical workup and should disclose everything to the parents, including the uncertainties about the final outcome. The treatment mantra, in other words, should be therapy, not surgery.

I believe a new treatment protocol for intersex infants, similar to the one outlined by McCullough, is close at hand. Treatment should combine some basic medical and ethical principles with a practical but less drastic approach to the birth of a mixed-sex child. As a first step, surgery on infants should be performed only to save the child's life or to substantially improve the child's physical well-being. Physicians may assign a sex—male or female—to an intersex infant on the basis of the probability that the child's particular condition will lead to the formation of a particular gender identity. At the same time, though, practitioners ought to be humble enough to recognize that as the child grows, he or she may reject the assignment—and they should be wise enough to listen to what the child has to say. Most important, parents should have access to the full range of information and options available to them.

Sex assignments made shortly after birth are only the beginning of a long journey. Consider, for instance, the life of Max Beck: Born intersexual, Max was surgically assigned as a female and consistently raised as such. Had her medical team followed her into her early twenties, they would have deemed her assignment a success because she was married to a man. (It should be noted that success in gender assignment has traditionally been defined as living in that gender as a heterosexual.) Within a few years, however, Beck had come out as a butch lesbian; now in her mid-thirties, Beck has become a man and married his lesbian partner, who (through the miracles of modern reproductive technology) recently gave birth to a girl.

Transsexuals, people who have an emotional gender at odds with their physical sex, once described themselves in terms of dimorphic absolutes—males trapped in female bodies, or vice versa. As such, they sought psychological relief through surgery. Although many still do, some so-called transgendered people today are content to inhabit a more ambiguous zone. A male-to-female transsexual, for instance, may come out as a lesbian. Jane, born a physiological male, is now in her late thirties and living with her wife, whom she married when her name was still John. Jane takes hormones to feminize herself, but they have not yet interfered with her ability to engage in intercourse as a man. In her mind Jane has a lesbian relationship with her wife, though she views their intimate moments as a cross between lesbian and heterosexual sex.

A person who projects a social gender at odds with his or her genitals may die for the transgression.

It might seem natural to regard intersexuals and transgendered people as living midway between the poles of male and female. But male and female, masculine and feminine, cannot be parsed as some kind of continuum. Rather, sex and gender are best conceptualized as points in a multidimensional space. For some time, experts on gender development have distinguished between sex at the genetic level and at the cellular level (sex-specific gene expression, X and Y chromosomes); at the hormonal level (in the fetus, during childhood and after puberty); and at the anatomical level (genitals and secondary sexual characteristics). Gender identity presumably emerges from all of those corporeal aspects via some poorly understood interaction with environment and experience. What has become increasingly clear is that one can find levels of masculinity and femininity in almost every possible permutation. A chromosomal, hormonal and genital male (or female) may emerge with a female (or male) gender identity. Or a chromosomal female with male fetal hormones and masculinized genitalia—but with female pubertal hormones—may develop a female gender identity.

THE MEDICAL AND SCIENTIFIC communities have yet to adopt a language that is capable of describing such diversity. In her book *Hermaphrodites and the Medical Invention of Sex,* the historian and medical ethicist Alice Domurat Dreger of Michigan State University in East Lansing documents the emergence of current medical systems for classifying gender ambiguity. The current usage remains rooted in the Victorian approach to sex. The logical structure of the commonly used terms "true hermaphrodite," "male pseudohermaphrodite" and "female pseudohermaphrodite" indicates that only the so-called true hermaphrodite is a genuine mix of male and female. The others, no matter how confusing their body parts, are really hidden males or females. Because true hermaphrodites are rare—possibly only one in 100,000—such a classification system supports the idea that human beings are an absolutely dimorphic species.

At the dawn of the twenty-first century, when the variability of gender seems so visible, such a position is hard to maintain. And here, too, the old medical consensus has begun to crumble. Last fall the pediatric urologist Ian A. Aaronson of the Medical University of South Carolina in Charleston organized the North American Task Force on Intersexuality (NATFI) to review the clinical responses to genital ambiguity in infants. Key medical associations, such as the American Academy of Pediatrics, have endorsed NATFI. Specialists in surgery, endocrinology, psychology, ethics, psychiatry, genetics and public health, as well as intersex patient-advocate groups, have joined its ranks.

One of the goals of NATFI is to establish a new sex nomenclature. One proposal under consideration replaces the current system with emotionally neutral terminology that emphasizes developmental processes rather than preconceived gender categories. For example, Type I intersexes develop out of anomalous virilizing influences; Type II result from some interruption of virilization; and in Type III intersexes the gonads themselves may not have developed in the expected fashion.

WHAT IS CLEAR IS THAT SINCE 1993, modern society has moved beyond five sexes to a recognition that gender variation is normal and, for some people, an arena for playful exploration. Discussing my "five sexes" proposal in her book *Lessons from the Intersexed,* the psychologist Suzanne J. Kessler of the State University of New York at Purchase drives this point home with great effect:

> The limitation with Fausto-Sterling's proposal is that . . . [it] still gives genitals . . . primary signifying status and ignores the fact that in the everyday world gender attributions are made without access to genital inspection. . . . What has primacy in everyday life is the gender that is performed, regardless of the flesh's configuration under the clothes.

I now agree with Kessler's assessment. It would be better for intersexuals and their supporters to turn everyone's focus away from genitals. Instead, as she suggests, one should acknowledge that people come in an even wider assortment of sexual identities and characteristics than mere genitals can distinguish. Some women may have "large clitorises or fused labia," whereas some men may have "small penises or misshapen scrota," as Kessler puts it, "phenotypes with no particular clinical or identity meaning."

As clearheaded as Kessler's program is—and despite the progress made in the 1990s—our society is still far from that ideal. The intersexual or transgendered person who projects a social gender—what Kessler calls "cultural genitals"—that conflicts with his or her physical genitals still may die for the transgression. Hence legal protection for people whose cultural and physical genitals do not match is needed during the current transition to a more gender-diverse world. One easy step would be to eliminate the category of "gender" from official documents, such as driver's licenses and passports. Surely attributes both more visible (such as height, build and eye color) and less visible (fingerprints and genetic profiles) would be more expedient.

A more far-ranging agenda is presented in the International Bill of Gender Rights, adopted in 1995 at the fourth annual International Conference on Transgender Law and Employment Policy in Houston, Texas. It lists ten "gender rights," including the right to define one's own gender, the right to change one's physical gender if one so chooses and the right to marry whomever one wishes. The legal bases for such rights are being hammered out in the courts as I write and, most recently, through the establishment, in the state of Vermont, of legal same-sex domestic partnerships.

NO ONE COULD HAVE FORESEEN such changes in 1993. And the idea that I played some role, however small, in reducing the pressure—from the medical community as well as from society at large—to flatten the diversity of human sexes into two diametrically opposed camps gives me pleasure.

Sometimes people suggest to me, with not a little horror, that I am arguing for a pastel world in which androgyny reigns and men and women are boringly the same. In my vision, however, strong colors coexist with pastels. There are and will continue to be highly masculine people out there; it's just that some of them are women. And some of the most feminine people I know happen to be men.

Anne Fausto-Sterling is a professor of biology and women's studies at Brown University. Portions of this article were adapted from her recent book SEXING THE BODY *(Basic Books, 2000).*

Unit Selections

Key Points to Consider

❖ What makes male-female intimacy difficult to achieve? Have you learned any lessons about yourself and the opposite sex "the hard way"?

❖ Do we as a society focus too little or too much on sexual mechanics—sexual parts and acts? List at least six adjectives you find synonymous with *great* sex.

❖ How do you feel about flirting? What would be different about establishing contact and relationships if people spoke directly and objectively to one another instead of flirting? How well do you think you know the "rules" of flirting?

❖ If you had to lose one of your senses *for sex only*, which would it be and why? Is this the same sense you would choose to do without if it were all-encompassing? Why or why not?

❖ Which do you think is harder—finding a partner or keeping a relationship strong? Why?

❖ Why does intimacy seem more difficult to achieve now than in previous generations? If you had a time machine, would you prefer to go back in time, forward in time, or stay where you are as you search for intimacy? Explain your reasons.

 **Links** **www.dushkin.com/online/**

These sites are annotated on pages 4 and 5.

Most people are familiar with the term "sexual relationship." It denotes an important dimension of sexuality—interpersonal sexuality, or sexual interactions occurring between two (and sometimes more) individuals. This unit focuses attention on these types of relationships.

No woman is an island. No man is an island. Interpersonal contact forms the basis for self-esteem and meaningful living. Conversely, isolation results in loneliness and depression for most human beings. People seek and cultivate friendships for the warmth, affection, supportiveness, and sense of trust and loyalty that such relationships can provide.

Long-term friendships may develop into intimate relationships. The qualifying word in the previous sentence is "may." Today many people, single as well as married, yearn for close or intimate interpersonal relationships but fail to find them. Despite developments in communication and technology that past generations could never fathom, discovering how and where to find potential friends, partners, lovers, and soul mates is reported to be more difficult today than in times past. Fear of rejection causes some to avoid interpersonal relationships, others to present a false front or illusory self that they think is more acceptable or socially desirable. This sets the stage for a game of intimacy that is counterproductive to genuine intimacy. For others a major dilemma may exist—the problem of balancing closeness with the preservation of individual identity in a manner that satisfies the need for both personal and interpersonal growth and integrity. In either case, partners in a relationship should be advised that the development of interpersonal awareness (the mutual recognition and knowledge of others as they really are) rests upon trust and self-disclosure—letting the other person know who you really are and how you truly feel. In American society this has never been easy, and today some fear it may be more difficult than ever.

These considerations in regard to interpersonal relationships apply equally well to achieving meaningful and satisfying sexual relationships. Three basic ingredients lay the foundation for quality sexual interaction: self-awareness, understanding and acceptance of the partner's needs and desires, and mutual efforts to accommodate both partners' needs and desires. Without these, misunderstandings may arise, bringing anxiety, frustration, dissatisfaction, and/or resentment into the relationship. There may also be a heightened risk of contracting AIDS or another STD (sexually transmitted disease), experiencing an unplanned pregnancy, or experiencing sexual dysfunction by one or both partners. On the other hand, experience and research show that ongoing attention to these three ingredients by intimate partners contributes not only to sexual responsibility, but also to true emotional and sexual intimacy and a longer and happier life.

As might already be apparent, there is much more to quality sexual relationships than our popular culture recognizes. Such relationships are not established by means of sexual techniques or beautiful/handsome features. Rather, it is the quality of the interaction that makes sex a celebration of our sexuality. A person-oriented (as opposed to genitally oriented) sexual awareness, coupled with a whole-body/mind sexuality and an open, relaxed, even playful, attitude toward exploration make for equality in sexuality.

The subsection *Establishing Sexual Relationships* opens with "Why We Fall In Love," an article that explores the biological and genetic issues and processes that have the potential to increase attraction, kindle romance, lead to exciting and fulfilling relationships, or undermine all of these. The next article, "The New Flirting Game," discusses the conscious, planful side of flirting, with examples of the rules of today's flirting game for men, women, heterosexuals, gays, and lesbians, as well as what happens when one is unaware of or violates the rules. Finally "What's Your Love Story?" looks at how the story or script each person develops consciously and unconsciously—often beginning in early childhood—predicts the successful or unsuccessful outcome of his or her love life.

The subsection *Responsible Quality Sexual Relationships* opens with an article whose title is an intriguing question: "Are You Connecting on the Five Levels of Sex?" After studying the article, readers will understand erotic, sensual, intimate, push-the-envelope, and spiritual sex and how to add or enhance any missing levels. Although how-to-improve-your-sex-life advice is not hard to find in today's more open culture and media, the next article "Eight Sizzling Sex Secrets" is an especially "hot" one written by "hot" lovers from the tropics. The final unit article, "Celibate Passion: The Hidden Rewards of Quitting Sex," provides a thought-provoking challenge to our often complex and contradicting cultural beliefs about sex and intimacy. Readers are encouraged to use the articles in this unit as a backdrop of perspectives and experiences that can assist all of us in considering, comparing, and improving our interpersonal and/or sexual relationships.

Why We Fall in Love

It may be a many-splendored thing, but romance relies on Stone Age rules to get started

BY JOSH FISCHMAN

The woman in the spaghetti-strap dress has the attention of not one but three guys at a cocktail table. Head tilted to the side, her hand reaching up to brush back her dark hair, she's talking and laughing, and the guys are laughing along with her. Except for one. He's heading up to the bar to buy her a drink.

"She's doing very well," says David Givens. "The head tilt, showing the bare arms–these are all signs of approachability." Givens, sitting about three tables away in Havanas Club–Spokane, Wash.'s hottest bar–is watching with a practiced eye. An anthropologist and head of the Center for Nonverbal Studies in Spokane, he has been in and out of bars and lounges to watch people flirt for over two decades now, driven to answer one basic question about the survival of a species. "People don't trust one another at first. Heck, fish don't either. So the issue is: How do two bodies get close enough together to procreate?"

They flirt. Eyes try to connect with other eyes across a room. People move closer, and then attempt opening lines that, however clumsy, somehow work. He buys her that drink; she laughs at his joke. She studies his face. He guesses her intentions. Someone summons up the nerve to ask for a telephone number, and later the nerve to dial it. "Hi. We met the other night, and I was wondering. . . ." A date: a bite of lunch, a cup of coffee, maybe a movie. They talk about where they work, where they live, about shared friends, shared interests, shared values. And perhaps another date.

And then the talk flows more easily, the laughs come comfortably. He talks about his family, she about hers. Evenings out and parties at friends' become shared memories, and a growing familiarity gives way to fondness. To liking. Even to love. And to promises to have and to hold, forever and ever.

This is all well and good. But beneath love's ineffable mysteries and majesty, there lie some basic principles of biology and genetics. Mother Nature casts her strong shadow over much of that initial activity that sparks the cascade of events leading to love. Flirting, for example, has rules that cross cultures and countries, based on gestures that seem anchored deep within our evolutionary history. And those gestures, scientists are now discovering, follow codes of attraction and beauty that may be millions of years old. Those codes, in turn, have evolved because they point us–like Cupid's fleet arrows–toward the healthiest mate. Why? Because attraction to a healthy person gives us

 From *U.S. News & World Report*, February 7, 2000, pp. 42-48. © 2000 by U.S. News & World Report. Reprinted by permission.

our best chance to have babies and pass our genes to the next generation. "You cannot talk about beauty without talking about health," says psychologist Devendra Singh of the University of Texas-Austin.

Men, for instance, have been drawn to certain-size hips and waists for more than 20,000 years. Artie Butler, a 28-year-old Los Angeles cop, for instance, admires the intelligence and self-esteem of his fiancée, Janel Lenox, a 29-year-old schoolteacher. But her figure made a big first impression. "She has a very small waist, small arms, big butt, and nice long legs," he says frankly. "I love the waist area."

Butler's reaction, researchers contend, has some deeply rooted biology behind it: that waist and hip size is better linked to having babies than is a less curvaceous figure. Women, scientists reported several weeks ago, seem drawn to tall men, who in turn father more babies than shorter men.

SECOND TIME A CHARM.

Artie Butler, 28, and Janel Lenox, 29, were set up by friends but didn't connect. On a second try, she thought Butler was the nicest man she'd ever met. And he was struck by Lenox's dignity and beauty.

- *"She has a very small waist and nice long legs."*

So, though true love may be deep, complex, and sculpted by individual psychology, that first tug of desire has a face and shape driven by that need to reproduce. After all, the name of the game of life—in the long run—is to move your genes into succeeding generations. Millions of years ago, human ancestors had to find a mate to do this without help from Internet dating services, DNA analysis, social clubs, or village matchmakers. All they had to go on was outside appearance. Men looked for signs that women would have healthy children, such as fat around the hips that could

nourish a pregnancy; women looked for signs that men had good genes, such as height or a strong build.

THE LOOK OF LOVE.

Eugenia Kang, 22, met Joe Herger, 21, when the two were students at Harvard. He didn't make much of an impression on her at first, but a few years and his more mature body and mind made a world of difference to her eyes.

- *"He was older and better looking . . . not the skinny freshman anymore."*

A case of immunity

Eugenia Kang, who just graduated from Harvard, didn't see much of this when she met Joe Herger, who is a year younger and had been chasing her since he hit campus. "When I first met him I had no impression because he was just some freshman volleyball player," Kang remembers. "No" impression isn't quite accurate. Herger really made a bad one. He was drunk and handcuffed to another guy at a college party, and dragged them both over to talk to Kang. Bad move; it took him until last year to really get her attention. By that time, says Kang, "he was older and better looking. He was working out, not the skinny freshman anymore. And he was more mature." So, she says, she "chased" someone for the first time in her life.

What Kang probably started chasing, according to Randy Thornhill, a biologist at the University of New Mexico in Albuquerque, were hormonal changes to the body, and the disease-fighting potential these hormones reveal. After all, mating with a creature who produces sickly children, or who dies before raising them, is a fast trip down an evolutionary dead end.

Birds, with their elaborate plumage, actually figured this one out long before humans did. Pretty feathers take a lot of energy to grow and maintain; the most famous example

is the peacock's tail. Naturalists have asked: Why bother? This is energy that could be used for finding and eating food, for instance, or fighting off disease. To use it to grow a long ornamental tail—well, you'd want something pretty big in return.

That return comes in the form of more opportunities to mate. It works because the tail is not just a demonstration of beauty but of toughness. The bird is saying to potential mates, in effect, "I'm strong enough, and have a powerful enough immune system, that I can fight off parasites and fight for food even while dragging this huge tail behind me. So I've got the genes that would make for a great mate."

Showoffs, sure. But people do essentially the same thing, says Thornhill, author of the forthcoming book *A Natural History of Rape*. In humans, hormones can mark a strong immune system, particularly the male sex hormone testosterone and the female sex hormone estrogen. But since hormones cannot easily be examined for potency, people have to look for outer signs. In men, testosterone leaves its mark on the face. Adolescent boys with the highest testosterone levels, Thornhill has found, have bigger chins and craggier brows as adults—think John Wayne or Jack Palance, think the opposite of Woody Allen. So like the peacock's tail, the craggy face is sending a message about the robust constitution of its owner: His immune system is tough enough to withstand infectious assault, and probably other kinds of assault as well. These would be good genes to have in your baby.

Testosterone is also linked to muscle buildup, a signature of the transition from boy to man—something Kang picked up on—and an obvious evolutionary advantage. Height is a similar feature: Last month researchers reported that out of about 3,200 men, once confounding elements like education and age were accounted for, the taller men were much more likely to have children.

What men notice is when estrogen starts creating a womanly figure, chiefly by depositing fat around the hips and shrinking the size of her waist relative to her hips. The magic proportion, according to Austin's Singh, is a waist that is between 60 percent and 70 percent of hip size. The reason this particular waist-to-hip configuration is attractive isn't certain, but Singh suspects it's because of a strong evolutionary connection between that body type and fertility. Millenniums ago, food was an irregular commodity; you had to catch as catch can. So when scarcity overlapped with pregnancy, fat on the hips, rear, and thighs was invaluable, especially during the third trimester and when nursing. Even today this waist-hip ratio is one of the best predictors of a successful conception.

FAMILY TIES.

Daozheng Lu, 61, and Li-Lo Lu, also 61, first met near Shanghai where their parents lived in the 1950s. Young intellectuals, married and then repeatedly tossed about by the political storms of China, they ended up living in Tampa Bay, Fla.
• *"She basically looked healthy. A lot of the girls in China . . . were pretty skinny."*

Daozheng Lu, a 61-year-old technology researcher in Tampa Bay, Fla., remembers that his wife's shape made a big impression when they met in the mid-1950s near Shanghai. "She basically looked healthy," he says. "A lot of the girls in China at that time were very skinny." But Li-Lo Hsu, soon to become Li-Lo Lu, was more well-rounded. And her first impressions of her future husband? "He was pretty handsome. He was taller than me."

Double your pleasure

Another outside clue to the genes within is symmetry: a good match between both sides of the face as well as arms, hands and wrists. In several studies, Thornhill and his colleague Steven Gangestad have found that both sexes think symmetry is stimulating. Again, the researchers theorize that it is a sign of a strong constitution. Two copies of a gene are usually better than one, should one copy turn defective; and this idea of a backup carries out to eyes, hands, and arms. Symmetry is so important that women, apparently, can not only see it but smell it as well. The New Mexico researchers found that women, at the time in their monthly cycle when they're most likely to conceive, rated T-shirts that had been worn by symmetrically faced men as smelling more attractive than other shirts. (Men, reinforcing their reputation for insensitivity, had no nose for symmetrical women.)

The evolution of attraction has an interesting twist, however. Women, though drawn to symmetrical and testosterone-marked males for mating, prefer other facial types when it comes to raising a family. Researchers at the University of St. Andrews in Fife, Scotland, found that women—except when they are most likely to conceive—rated male faces as more attractive if they showed *feminine* features: a smaller jaw and bigger eyes, for example. Such guys, the researchers speculate, may be more likely to stick around and help raise a family. Women, evolutionary psychologists argue, spend more of their energy in pregnancy and have fewer mating opportunities than do men. So to make the most of things, women may want both the hardy genes for the family tree and the responsible behavior of someone who will help it grow.

This is, apparently, what Laura Bernstein felt she got in her husband, Stan Ikonen. When the East Coast public relations executive met the Texas firefighter, she was turned off by the fact that he was a hunter. But she was attracted to his cowboy image, and also because he was bright and responsible. And at age 51, 14 years after they met, she still is.

Men take almost the direct opposite approach. Victor Johnston, a psychobiologist at New Mexico State University in Las Cruces, found the heart-shaped face, small at the jaw and wide eyes, combines elements that are particularly desirable to men. This is because of men's historical mating habits. Over the Internet, Johnston had people vote in a kind of "face breeding" program that took the most popular female faces in categories such as attractiveness and youthfulness and merged them to form composites. What he found was that beauty—that heart-shaped face—overlapped with youth most often around age 22. That's during the peak fertility years, Johnston says, and it's no accident. Fertile women give men the best chance of passing their genes down the line. So it makes sense, from the long-term view of evolutionary success, to be most attracted to fertile youth.

Getting into someone's genes

It also makes sense to get some genetic diversity into the family tree—it gives creatures from guppies to people a better shot at beating diseases that decimate one genetic blueprint but can't knock out a slight variation. Inbreeding, on the other hand, lays bare that vulnerability. And again people seem to have evolved ways to spot mates with healthy genetic differences without calling in the DNA analysts.

Carole Ober, a geneticist at the University of Chicago, has studied one group that should be especially prone to inbreeding: the Hutterites, a close-knit religious community in South Dakota, all descended from 64 founders. She examined genes that make up the group's immune systems. Surprisingly, couples showed many more differences in these genes than one might have expected given the small starting population and close contact of the present group. That's good for group survival, because couples who did have close matches on these genes also had higher miscarriage rates. Swiss researchers, also studying immune system genes, found women were most attracted to the scent of men whose genes were most distinct from their own.

And indeed, people may be led by the nose to make these genetic choices, Ober thinks. "Odor is really important for kin recognition in rodents; that's been proven," she says. It's not just smell. Odorless chemicals known as pheromones, wafting from one animal to the nose of another, strongly affect sexual behavior. It could be true in humans, too. That notion got a big boost when Ober's Chicago colleague, psychologist Martha McClintock, finally discovered pheromones in humans in 1998. One of these compounds lengthens the menstrual cycle; the other one shortens it. It's the first clear sign that humans use chemical communication that can affect sexual activity. In animals, pheromones determine which hamsters mate, which male elephants dominate others; female monkeys in heat even release a pheromone that works as an aphrodisiac. McClintock cautions that pheromone effects in people are not likely to be as strong or clear-cut, since human behavior is more complex than that of lower animals. But chemical effects are doubtless there; that, Thornhill suspects, is how women are able to sniff out symmetry.

Safe sex

Women—and men—also need to sniff out something else about a potential partner: danger. No matter how attractive the plumage, approaching someone who will thwack you in the head is no way to ensure the future of your genes. And that's where behavior comes in, to signal safety as people begin to get to know one another.

"Courtship is like a never-ending series of permissions that you have to get, all the way down the line," David Givens says as he strains to be heard above the pounding beat in Havanas Club. One person signals a little interest, the other person doesn't rebuff, and the first person then tries a stronger signal to see what happens. The key is that both men and women need to appear harmless.

A fight over the evolution of rape

They're saying men evolved to be rapists?" Teri Gutierrez cries incredulously. The advocacy coordinator at Sexual Support Services in Eugene, Ore., is thunderstruck. "That's absurd. Women are getting seriously hurt and they're saying that it's evolution?"

In a word, yes. Biologist Randy Thornhill and anthropologist Craig Palmer, in a new book that's become a lightning rod for controversy, argue that rape has evolved, over millions of years, as a strategy to help men reproduce. *A Natural History of Rape*, soon to be published by the MIT Press, is a far cry from most recent thinking on the topic. Susan Brownmiller, in *Against Our Will* in 1975, argued that rape is about power and domination, and today it's hard to find a rape crisis center that disagrees.

A brutish alternative. But Thornhill and Palmer contend that rape is a way for males to spread their seed, increasing the chance that their genes will be passed to future generations. They don't endorse rape, the scientists say emphatically; they just want to point out that it's a brutish alternative males might use when flowers and candy fail. Other animals—from scorpion flies to dolphins—certainly do. And this sexual perspective has implica-

tions for protection, the scientists argue. Women, for instance, should not dress provocatively to inflame desire.

The idea hasn't been universally derided. "On the one hand, I think it's a hypothesis, carefully put forward, that needs to be taken seriously," says David Buss, author of another new book that deals with coercion and reproduction, *The Dangerous Passion*. "On the other hand, I don't think the evidence is truly there."

For one thing, he says, rape is much less common in tribal societies than it is in modern ones. "Traditionally, women live with lots of brothers and uncles around, and retribution would be swift if a rapist tried anything. He'd get seriously hurt. And that hardly seems like the path to evolutionary success."

Meredith Small, an anthropologist at Cornell University, adds that Thornhill and Palmer haven't shown that "raped women bear their rapists' children. If not, the strategy is a reproductive failure."

Finally, Carolyn Ford, director of the Albuquerque Rape Crisis Center in New Mexico, scoffs at the idea of dressing for protection: "We saw 464 victims here last here," she says. "Most were wearing jeans. They're not provoking anything."

—*J.F.*

That's how it was for Gordon Arnold, a banker in Plano, Texas. He felt completely comfortable with his wife, Julie, when they first met. The couple, both 56, remember quickly reaching a sense of ease with one another. It wasn't a total accident. On their first date, Gordon particularly recalls being quiet because he didn't want to dominate the conversation and scare Julie away.

There are several signals about safety that remain constant from Spokane to Bali, and from people to apes, indicating their evolutionary importance, Givens says. The shoulder shrug is a prime example. The reflex is a sign of uncertainty, part of an age-old startle response intended to pro-

tect the vulnerable neck. A chagrined Bill Clinton did it on national television when he apologized for his illicit relationship with Monica Lewinsky, the anthropologist notes.

A tilted head uses some of these same muscles and nerve circuits. Both gestures, using muscles and nerve circuits that can be traced back through millions of years of animal history and seen in animals today, are signs of withdrawal, not what you'd see in a prelude to an attack. Nor is holding your hands palm up, as one of the men talking to the dark-haired woman in Havanas does. The gesture is controlled by neural circuits found in anatomy as simple as fish brains and spinal cords, so it even predates

OPPOSITES ATTRACT.

Cartoonist Ellen Slingerland, 52, thought that her husband Rudy, 45, sitting in the shadows when they first met, was a haughty intellectual. He, a geologist at Pennsylvania State University, thought Ellen was extremely flamboyant.
• *"We met, we hated each other, and then we got married."*

palms. It's a muscle reflex that bends the body and neck back, away from danger, Givens says; as those muscles contract they also rotate the forearms and palms up.

The signals run from the hands down to the feet. Givens, who consults for corporations, asks, "Have you ever looked at a boss talking to employees? Look at the feet position. His are pointed out, which is a gesture of dominance, while everyone gathered around him has feet pointed in." The same foot position showed up on many videotapes Givens made of men approaching women in bars, in parks, in restaurants.

What goes on without words can even overcome verbal faux pas. "Rude Rudy" is what Ellen Slingerland called her husband when they first met—though she did it behind his back. To his face, the Philipsburg, Pa., cartoonist voiced a vigorous analysis of Shakespeare, which led Rudy, a geologist, to call her stubborn and opinionated. She decided he was condescending. But her first impression of him, sitting in the shadows on a porch, an intriguing, mysterious intellectual, never left. And he liked her flamboyant gestures. So they went out again, and again. That was 18 years ago. "We met, we hated each other, and then we got married," says Rudy.

Mind over body

Still, despite all this foot shuffling and symmetry sniffing, people are not total prisoners of ancient instincts. There are a wide variety of couples out there. And the reason is that a lot of personal experience gets layered on top of all this biology and pulls people in different directions, says psychologist Ayala Malach Pines of Ben-Gurion University in Israel and author of the recent book *Falling in Love: Why We Choose the Lovers We Choose.* "Parts of our romantic code are shared with other cultures and people. But parts are very individual."

Early experiences, in particular, seem very powerful. In Pines's surveys of American and Israeli couples, more women than men described

KEYSTROKES AND HEARTBEATS.

Skipping visual first impressions, Bruce and Ronni Keller of Las Vegas, ages 34 and 30, met over the Internet. A face-to-face meeting heightened their interest and their attraction, and eventually led to a proposal.
• *On the Net "it's a lot easier to open yourself up, to put yourself out there."*

their partners as similar to their fathers. And men described their partners as similar to their mothers.

And today's technology allows couples to sidestep the physical world completely—at least for a while. Ronni and Bruce Keller met in a chat room on the Internet. Bruce, 34, struck Ronni, 30, as "naively honest," a pleasant contrast, she says, to her ex-husband. And he found, by chatting online, that "it's a lot easier to open yourself up, to put yourself out there." Chats turned into phone calls, which turned into actual visits. Last August it all turned into a marriage for the Las Vegas couple.

This should give hope to those without lantern jaws or the perfect proportions of waist to hips. "People bring different things to the mating market," Thornhill says. "You can compensate for looks." A man who doesn't look as if he stepped from a Marlboro ad can, for instance, show he's a good, caring partner, with all the evolutionary advantages that entails. The same is true for a woman without those extra-wide eyes. The trick is to somehow pack those sentiments into initial contact. And remember that things like symmetry have their limits: Supermodel Cindy Crawford has a beauty spot, but it's on just one side of her face.
With Jia-Rui Chong and Roberta Hotinski

For more on evolution, genetics, and attraction, visit www.usnews.com.

THE NEW
Flirting Game

*IT MAY BE AN AGES-OLD, BIOLOGICALLY-DRIVEN ACTIVITY,
BUT TODAY IT'S ALSO PLAYED WITH ARTFUL SELF-AWARENESS
AND EVEN CONSCIOUS CALCULATION.*

By Deborah A. Lott

To hear the evolutionary determinists tell it, we human beings flirt to propagate our genes and to display our genetic worth. Men are constitutionally predisposed to flirt with the healthiest, most fertile women, recognizable by their biologically correct waist-hip ratios. Women favor the guys with dominant demeanors, throbbing muscles and the most resources to invest in them and their offspring.

Looked at up close, human psychology is more diverse and perverse than the evolutionary determinists would have it. We flirt as thinking individuals in a particular culture at a particular time. Yes, we may express a repertoire of hardwired non-verbal expressions and behaviors—staring eyes, flashing brows, opened palms—that resemble those of other animals, but unlike other animals, we also flirt with conscious calculation. We have been known to practice our techniques in front of the mirror. In other words, flirting among human beings is culturally modulated as well as biologically driven, as much art as instinct.

In our culture today, it's clear that we do not always choose as the object of our desire those people the evolutionists might deem the most biologically desirable. After all, many young women today find the pale, androgynous, scarcely muscled yet emotionally expressive Leonardo DiCaprio more appealing than the burly Tarzans (Arnold Schwartzenegger, Bruce Willis, etc.) of action movies. Woody Allen may look nerdy but he's had no trouble winning women—and that's not just because he has material resources, but because humor is also a precious cultural commodity. Though she has no breasts or hips to speak of, Ally McBeal still attracts because there's ample evidence of a quick and quirky mind.

In short, we flirt with the intent of assessing potential lifetime partners, we flirt to have easy, no-strings-attached sex, and we flirt when we are not looking for either. We flirt because, most simply, flirtation can be a liberating form of play, a game with suspense and ambiguities that brings joys of its own. As Philadelphia-based social psychologist Tim Perper says, "Some flirters appear to want to prolong the interaction because it's pleasurable and erotic in its own right, regardless of where it might lead."

Here are some of the ways the game is currently being played.

TAKING The Lead

When it comes to flirting today, women aren't waiting around for men to make the advances. They're taking the lead. Psychologist Monica Moore, Ph.D. of Webster University in St. Louis, Missouri, has spent more than 2000 hours observing women's flirting maneuvers in restaurants, singles bars and at parties. According to her findings, women give non-verbal cues that get a flirtation rolling fully two-thirds of the time. A man may think he's making the first move because he is the one to literally move from wherever he is to the woman's side, but usually he has been summoned.

Who determined that baring the neck is a sign of female submissivness? It may have a lot more to do with the neck being an erogenous zone.

By the standards set out by evolutionary psychologists, the women who attract the most men would most likely be those with the most symmetrical features or the best hip-to-waist ratios. Not so, says Moore. In her studies, the women who draw the most response are the ones who send the most signals. "Those who performed more than 35 displays per hour elicited greater than four approaches per hour," she notes, "and the more variety the woman used in her techniques, the more likely she was to be successful."

SEXUAL Semaphores

Moore tallied a total of 52 different nonverbal courtship behaviors used by women, including glancing, gazing (short and sustained), primping, preening, smiling, lip licking, pouting, giggling, laughing and nodding, as if to nonverbally indicate, "Yes! yes!" A woman would often begin with a room-encompassing glance, in actuality a casing-the-joint scan to seek out prospects. When she'd zeroed in on a target she'd exhibit the short darting glance–looking at a man, quickly look-

ing away, looking back and then away again. There was something shy and indirect in this initial eye contact.

But women countered their shy moves with other, more aggressive and overt tactics. Those who liked to live dangerously took a round robin approach, alternately flirting with several different men at once until one responded in an unequivocal fashion. A few women hiked their skirts up to bring more leg into a particular man's field of vision. When they inadvertently drew the attention of other admirers, they quickly pulled their skirts down. If a man failed to get the message, a woman might parade, walking across the room towards him, hips swaying, breasts pushed out, head held high.

WHO'S Submissive?

Moore observed some of the same nonverbal behaviors that Eibl-Eibesfeldt and other ethologists had deemed universal among women: the eyebrow flash (an exaggerated raising of the eyebrows of both eyes, followed by a rapid lowering), the coy smile (a tilting of the head downward, with partial averting of the eyes and, at the end, covering of the mouth), and the exposed neck (turning the head so that the side of the neck is bared).

But while many ethologists interpret these signs as conveying female submissiveness, Moore has an altogether different take. "If these behaviors serve to orchestrate courtship, which they do, then how can they be anything but powerful?" she observes. "Who determined that to cover your mouth is a submissive gesture? Baring the neck may have a lot more to do with the neck being an erogenous zone than its being a submissive posture." Though women in Moore's sample used the coy smile, they also maintained direct eye contact for long periods and smiled fully and unabashedly.

Like Moore, Perper believes that ethologists have overemphasized certain behaviors and misinterpreted them as signifying either dominance or submission. For instance, says Perper, among flirting American heterosexual men and women as well as homosexual men, the coy smile is less frequent than direct eye contact and sustained smiling. He suggests that some cultures may use the coy smile more than others, and that it is not always a sign of deference.

In watching a flirtatious couple, Perper finds that a male will perform gestures and movements that an ethologist might consider dominant, such as sticking out his chest and strutting around, but he'll also give signs that could be read as submissive, such as bowing his head lower than the woman's. The woman may also do both. "She may drop her head, turn slightly, bare her neck, but then she'll lift her eyes and lean forward with her breasts held out, and that doesn't look submissive at all," Perper notes.

Men involved in these encounters, says Perper, don't describe themselves as "feeling powerful." In fact, he and Moore agree, neither party wholly dominates in a flirtation. Instead, there is a subtle, rhythmical and playful back and forth that culminates in a kind of physical synchronization between two people. She turns, he turns; she picks up her drink, he picks up his drink.

Still, by escalating and de-escalating the flirtation's progression, the woman controls the pace. To slow down a flirtation, a woman might orient her body away slightly or cross her arms across her chest, or avoid meeting the man's eyes. To stop the dance in its tracks, she can yawn, frown, sneer, shake her head from side to side as if to say "No," pocket her hands, hold her trunk rigidly, avoid the man's gaze, stare over his head, or resume flirting with other men. If a man is really dense, she might hold a strand of hair up to her eyes as if to examine her split ends or even pick her teeth.

PLANNING It Out

Do women make these moves consciously? You bet. "I do these things *incidentally* but not *accidentally*," one adept female flirter told Perper. She wanted her movements and gestures to look fluid and spontaneous but they were at least partly planned. In general, says Perper, women are more aware than are men of exactly what they do, why they do it and the effect it has. A man might simply say that he saw a woman he

Men are able to recite in enormous detail what they do once they are in bed with a woman, but it is women who remember each and every step in the flirtation game that got them there.

was attracted to and struck up a conversation; a woman would remember all the steps in the flirtation dance. "Men can tell you in enormous detail what they do once they are in bed with a woman," declares Perper. But it is the women who know how they got there.

LEARNING The Steps

If flirting today is often a conscious activity, it is also a learned one. Women pick up the moves early. In observations of 100 girls between the ages of 13 and 16 at shopping malls, ice skating rinks and other places adolescents congregate, Moore found the teens exhibiting 31 of the 52 courtship

signals deployed by adult women. (The only signals missing were those at the more overt end of the spectrum, such as actual caressing.) Overall, the teens' gestures looked less natural than ones made by mature females: they laughed more boisterously and preened more obviously, and their moves were broader and rougher.

The girls' clearly modeled their behavior on the leader of the pack. When the alpha female stroked her hair or swayed her hips, her companions copied quickly. "You never see this in adult women," says Moore. "Indeed, women go to great lengths to stand out from their female companions."

Compared with adults, the teens signaled less frequently–7.6 signs per hour per girl, as opposed to 44.6 per woman–but their maneuvers, though clumsy, were equally effective at attracting the objects of their desire, in this case, teen boys.

BEYOND The Straight and Narrow

Flirting's basic purpose may be to lure males and females into procreating, but it's also an activity indulged in by gays as well as straights. How do flirting rituals compare?

Marny Hall, a San Francisco-area psychologist who's been an observer and participant in lesbian courtship, recalls that in the 1950s, gay women adhered to rigid gender-role models. Butches did what men were supposed to do: held their bodies tight, lit cigarettes with a dominating flourish, bought drinks, opened doors and otherwise demonstrated strength and gallantry. "Butches would swagger and wear chinos and stand around with one hip cocked and be bold in their gazes," she observes. "Femmes would sashay and wiggle their hips and use indirect feminine wiles."

Beginning in the late 1960s, such fixed role-playing began to dissolve. Lesbians meeting in consciousness-raising groups rejected gender as-

sumptions. It was considered sexually attractive, says Hall, to "put yourself out without artifice, without deception." In the 90s, however, the butch-femme distinction has returned.

But with a difference. Today's lesbians have a sense of irony and wit about the whole charade that would do Mae West proud. "A butch today might flirt by saying to a femme, 'Can I borrow your lipstick? I'm trying to liberate the woman within,' " she says with a laugh. "The gender roles are more scrambled, with 'dominant femmes' and 'soft butches.' There's more plurality and less polarization."

In San Francisco, gay men are learning the flirting repertoire used by straight women.

Male homosexuals also exhibit a wide range of flirting behaviors. In his studies, Perper has observed two gay men locked in a stalemate of sustained eye contact for 45 minutes before either made the next move. At the other end of the spectrum, he's seen gay dyads go through the entire flirtation cycle–"gaze, approach, talk, turn, touch, synchronize"–and be out the door on the way to one or the other's abode within two minutes.

The advent of AIDS and the greater societal acceptance of long-term gay attachments are changing flirtation rituals in the gay community. A sign of the times may be a courtship and dating course currently offered at Harvey Milk Institute in San Francisco. It instructs gay men in the repertoire of gestures long used by straight women seeking partners–ways of slowing down the flirtation, forestalling physical contact and assessing the other's suitability as a long-term mate. In short, it teaches homosexuals how to employ what the ethologists call a "long-term strategy."

FLIRTING Bi-Ways

When you're a crossdresser, all possibilities are open to you," says a male heterosexual who goes by the name Stephanie Montana when in female garb. In feminine persona, says Montana, "I can be more vulnerable, more animated and use more intermittent eye contact."

On one occasion Montana discovered what women seem to learn early on. A man was flirting with her, and, giddy with the attention, Montana sustained eye contact for a bit too long, gave too many overt sexual signals. In response, the man started acting in a proprietary fashion, frightening Montana with "those voracious male stares." Montana had learned the courtship signals but not the rejection repertoire. She didn't yet know how to put on the brakes.

Bisexuals have access to the entire panoply of male and female gestures. Loree Thomas of Seattle, who refers to herself as a bisexual non-op transsexual (born male, she is taking female hormones and living as a woman, but will not have a sex-change operation), has flirted *four* ways: dressed as a man interacting with men or with women, and dressed as a woman in encounters with women or men.

As a man flirting with a woman, Thomas found it most effective to maintain eye contact, smile, lean close, talk in a low voice and offer sincere compliments about the woman's best features. Man to man, says Thomas, the progression to direct physical contact accelerates. As a woman with a woman, Thomas' flirting has been "more shy, less direct than a man would be." As a woman with a man, she's played the stereotypical female role, "asking the man questions about himself, and listening as if totally fascinated." In all cases, eye contact and smiling are universal flirtation currency.

What the experience of crossdressers reinforces is the degree to which all flirtation is a game, a careful charade that involves some degree of deception and role-playing. Evolutionists talk about this deception in terms of men's tendency to exaggerate their wealth, success and access to resources, and women's strategic use of cosmetics and clothing to enhance their physical allure.

Some of the exhilaration of flirting, of course, lies in what is hidden, the tension between what is felt and what is revealed. Flirting pairs volley back and forth, putting out ambiguous signals, neither willing to disclose more than the other, neither wanting to appear more desirous to the other.

To observers like Moore and Perper, flirtation often seems to most resemble the antics of children on the playground or even perhaps the ritual peek-a-boo that babies play with their caregivers. Flirters jostle, tease and tickle, even sometimes stick out a tongue at their partner or reach around from behind to cover up their eyes. As Daniel Stern, researcher, psychiatrist, and author of *The Interpersonal World of the Infant* (Karnac, 1998), has pointed out, the two groups in our culture that engage in the most sustained eye contact are mothers and infants, and lovers.

And thus in a way, the cycle of flirting takes us full circle. If flirting sets us off on the road to producing babies, it also whisks us back to the pleasures of infancy.

What's Your Love Story?

In your relationship, are you a cop, a comedian, a prince or a martyr? Robert J. Sternberg, Ph.D., reveals how you can use your "love story" to find your perfect match.

BY ROBERT J. STERNBERG, PH.D.

Relationships can be as unpredictable as the most suspense-filled mystery novel. Why do some couples live happily ever after, while others are as star-crossed as Romeo and Juliet? Why do we often seem destined to relive the same romantic mistakes over and over, following the same script with different people in different places, as if the fate of our relationships, from courtship to demise, were written at birth?

Perhaps because, in essence, it is. As much as psychologists have attempted to explain the mysteries of love through scientific laws and theories, it turns out that the best mirrors of the romantic experience may be *Wuthering Heights,*

Casablanca and *General Hospital.* At some level, lay people recognize what many psychologists don't: that the love between two people follows a story. If we want to understand love, we have to understand the stories that dictate our beliefs and expectations of love. These stories, which we start to write as children, predict the patterns of our romantic experiences time and time again. Luckily, we can learn to rewrite them.

I came up with the theory of love as a story because I was dissatisfied—not only with other people's work on love, but also with my own. I had initially proposed a triangular theory of love, suggesting that it comprises three elements: intimacy, passion and commitment. Different loving relationships have different combinations of these elements. Complete love requires all three elements. But the theory leaves an important question unanswered: what makes a person the kind of lover they are? And what attracts them to other lovers? I had to dig deeper to understand the love's origins. I found them in stories.

My research, which incorporates studies performed over the past decade with hundreds of couples in Connecticut, as well as ongoing studies, has shown that people describe love in many ways. This description reveals their love story. For example, someone who strongly agrees with the statement "I believe close relationships are like good partnerships" tells a business 'story; someone who says they end up with partners who scare them—or that they like intimidating their partner—enacts a horror story.

Couples usually start out being physically attracted and having similar interests and values. But eventually, they may notice something missing in the relationship. That something is usually story compatibility. A couple whose stories don't match is like two characters on one stage acting out different plays—they may look right at first glance, but there is an underlying lack of coordination to their interaction.

This is why couples that seem likely to thrive often do not, and couples that seem unlikely to survive sometimes do. Two people may have similar outlooks, but if one longs to be rescued like Julia Roberts in *Pretty Woman* and the other wants a partnership like the lawyers on the television show *The Practice,* the relationship may not go very far. In contrast, two people with a war story like the bickering spouses in *Who's Afraid of Virginia Wolf* may seem wildly incompatible to their friends, but their shared need for combat may be what keeps their love alive.

More than anything, the key to compatibility with a romantic partner is whether our stories match. To change the pattern of our relation-

ships, we must become conscious of our love stories, seek people with compatible tales, and replot conclusions that aren't working for us.

The Beginning of the Story

We start forming our ideas about love soon after birth, based on our inborn personality, our early experiences and our observations of our parents' relationships, as well as depictions of romance in movies, television and books. We then seek to live out these conceptions of love ourselves.

Based on interviews I conducted in the 1990s, asking college students to write about their romantic ideals and expectations, I have identified at least 25 common stories which people use to describe love. (There are probably many more.)

Some stories are far more popular than others. In 1995, one of my students, Laurie Lynch, and I identified some of the most common tales by asking people to rate, on a scale of one to seven, the extent to which a group of statements characterized their relationships. Their highest-ranked statements indicated their personal love story. Among the most popular were the travel story ("I believe that beginning a relationship is like starting a new journey that promises to be both exciting and challenging"), the gardening story ("I believe any relationship that is left unattended will not survive") and the humor story ("I think taking a relationship too seriously can spoil it"). Among the least popular were the horror story ("I find it exciting when I feel my partner is somewhat frightened of me," or "I tend to end up with people who frighten me"), the collectibles story ("I like dating different partners simultaneously; each partner should fit a particular need") and the autocratic government story ("I think it is more efficient if one person takes control of the important decisions in a relationship").

Another study of 43 couples, conducted with Mahzad Hojji, Ph.D., in 1996, showed that women prefer the travel story more than men, who pre-

fer the art ("Physical attractiveness is the most essential characteristic I look for in a partner"), collectibles and pornography ("It is very important to be able to gratify all my partner's sexual desires and whims," or "I can never be happy with a partner who is not very adventurous in his or her sex life") stories. Men also prefer the sacrifice story ("I believe sacrifice is a key part of true love"). Originally, we had expected the opposite. Then we realized that the men reported sacrificing things that women did consider significant offerings.

No one story guarantees success, our study showed. But some stories seem to predict doom more than others: the business, collectibles, government, horror, mystery, police ("I believe it is necessary to watch your partner's every move" or "My partner often calls me several times a day to ask what I am doing"), recovery ("I often find myself helping people get their life back in order" or "I need someone to help me recover from my painful past"), science fiction ("I often find myself attracted to individuals who have unusual and strange characteristics") and theater stories ("I think my relationships are like plays" or "I often find myself attracted to partners who play different roles").

How Stories Spin Our Relationships

When you talk to two people who have just split up, their breakup stories often sound like depictions of two completely different relationships. In a sense they are. Each partner has his or her own story to tell.

Most important to a healthy, happy relationship is that both partners have compatible stories—that is, compatible expectations. Indeed, a 1998 study conducted with Mahzad Hojjat, Ph.D., and Michael Barnes, Ph.D., indicated that the more similar couples' stories were, the happier they were together.

Stories tend to be compatible if they are complementary roles in a single story, such as prince and princess, or if the stories are similar enough that they can be merged into a new and unified story. For example, a fantasy story can merge with a gardening story because one can nourish, or garden, a relationship while dreaming of being rescued by a knight on a white steed. A fantasy and a business story are unlikely to blend, however, because they represent such different ideals–fate-bound princes and princesses don't work at romance!

Of course, story compatibility isn't the only ingredient in a successful relationship. Sometimes, our favorite story can be hazardous to our well-being. People often try to make dangerous or unsatisfying stories come true. Thus, someone who has, say, a horror or recovery story may try to turn a healthy relationship into a Nightmare on Elm Street. People complain that they keep ending up with the same kind of bad partner, that they are unlucky in love. In reality, luck has nothing to do with it: They are subconsciously finding people to play out their love stories, or foisting their stories on the people they meet.

Making Happy Endings

Treating problems in relationships by changing our behaviors and habits ul-timately won't work because crisis comes from the story we're playing out. Unless we change our stories, we're treating symptoms rather than causes. If we're dissatisfied with our partner, we should look not at his or her faults, but at how he or she fits into our expectations.

To figure out what we want, we need to consider all of our past relationships, and we should ask ourselves what attributes characterized the people to whom we felt most attracted, and what attributes characterized the people in whom we eventually lost interest. We also need to see which romantic tale we aim to tell–and whether or not it has the potential to lead to a "happily ever after" scenario (see box, "Find Your Love Story").

Once we understand the ideas and beliefs behind the stories we accept as our own, we can do some replotting. We can ask ourselves what we like and don't like about our current story, what hasn't been working in our relationships, and how we would like to change it. How can we rewrite the scenario? This may involve changing stories, or transforming an existing story to make it more practical. For example, horror stories may be fantasized during sexual or other activity, rather than actually physically played out.

We can change our story by experimenting with new and different plots. Sometimes, psychotherapy can help us to move from perilous stories (such as a horror story) to more promising ones (such as a travel story). Once we've recognized our story–or learned to live a healthy one of our choosing–we can begin to recognize elements of that story in potential mates. Love mirrors stories because it is a story itself. The difference is that we are the authors, and can write ourselves a happy ending.

Robert J. Sternberg is IBM Professor of Psychology and Education in the department of psychology at Yale University.

READ MORE ABOUT IT

Love Is a Story, Robert J. Sternberg, Ph.D. (Oxford University Press, 1998)

A Natural History of Love, Diane Ackerman (Random House, 1994

Find Your Love Story

Adapted from *Love Is a Story* by Robert J. Sternberg, Ph.D.

Rate each statement on a scale from 1 to 9, 1 meaning that it doesn't characterize your romantic relationships at all, 9 meaning that it describes them extremely well. Then average your scores for each story. In general, averaged scores of 7 to 9 are high, indicating a strong attraction to a story, and 1 to 3 are low, indicating little or no interest in the story. Moderate scores of 4 to 6 indicate some interest, but probably not enough to generate or keep a romantic interest. Next, evaluate your own love story. (There are 12 listed here; see the book for more.)

STORY #1

1. I enjoy making sacrifices for the sake of my partner.
2. I believe sacrifice is a key part of true love.
3. I often compromise my own comfort to satisfy my partner's needs.
Score:__
The *sacrifice story* can lead to happy relationships when both partners are content in the roles they are playing, particularly when they both make sacrifices. It is likely to cause friction when partners feel compelled to make sacrifices. Research suggests that relationships of all kinds are happiest when they are roughly equitable. The greatest risk in a sacrifice story is that the give-and-take will become too out of balance, with one partner always being the giver or receiver.

STORY #2

Officer:
1. I believe that you need to keep a close eye on your partner.
2. I believe it is foolish to trust your partner completely.
3. I would never trust my partner to work closely with a person of the opposite sex. **Score:__**

Suspect:
1. My partner often calls me several times a day to ask exactly what I am doing.
2. My partner needs to know everything that I do.

3. My partner gets very upset if I don't let him or her know exactly where I have been. **Score:__**

Police stories do not have very favorable prognoses because they can completely detach from reality. The police story may offer some people the feeling of being cared for. People who are very insecure relish the attention that they get as a "suspect," that they are unable to receive in any other way. But they can end up paying a steep price. As the plot thickens, the suspect first begins to lose freedom, then dignity, and then any kind of self-respect. Eventually, the person's mental and even physical well-being may be threatened.

STORY #3

1. I believe that, in a good relationship, partners change and grow together.
2. I believe love is a constant process of discovery and growth.
3. I believe that beginning a relationship is like starting a new journey that promises to be both exciting and challenging. **Score:__**

Travel stories that last beyond a very short period of time generally have a favorable prognosis, because if the travelers can agree on a destination and path, they are already a long way toward success. If they can't, they often find out quite quickly that they want different things from the relationship and split up. Travel relationships tend to be dynamic and focus on the future. The greatest risk is that over time one or both partners will change the destination or path they desire. When people speak of growing apart, they often mean that the paths they wish to take are no longer the same. In such cases, the relationship is likely to become increasingly unhappy, or even dissolve completely.

STORY #4

Object:
1. The truth is that I don't mind being treated as a sex toy by my partner.
2. It is very important to me to gratify my partner's sexual desires and whims, even if people might view them as debasing.

3. I like it when my partner wants me to try new and unusual, and even painful, sexual techniques. **Score:__**

Subject:
1. The most important thing to me in my relationship is for my partner to be an excellent sex toy, doing anything I desire.
2. I can never be happy with a partner who is not very adventurous in sex.
3. The truth is that I like a partner who feels like a sex object. **Score:__**

There are no obvious advantages to the **pornography story.** The disadvantages are quite clear, however. First, the excitement people attain is through degradation of themselves and others. Second, the need to debase and be debased is likely to keep escalating. Third, once one adopts the story, it may be difficult to adopt another story. Fourth, the story can become physically as well as psychologically dangerous. And finally, no matter how one tries, it is difficult to turn the story into one that's good for psychological or physical well-being.

STORY #5

Terrorizer:
1. I often make sure that my partner knows that I am in charge, even if it makes him or her scared of me.
2. I actually find it exciting when I feel my partner is somewhat frightened of me.
3. I sometimes do things that scare my partner, because I think it is actually good for a relationship to have one partner slightly frightened of the other. **Score:__**

Victim:
1. I believe it is somewhat exciting to be slightly scared of your partner.
2. I find it arousing when my partner creates a sense of fear in me.
3. I tend to end up with people who sometimes frighten me. **Score:__**

The horror story probably is the least advantageous of the stories. To some, it may be exciting. But the forms of terror needed to sustain the excitement tend to get out of control and to put their participants, and even sometimes those around them, at both psychological and

physical risk. Those who discover that they have this story or are in a relationship that is enacting it would be well-advised to seek counseling, and perhaps even police protection.

STORY #6

Co-dependent:
1. I often end up with people who are facing a specific problem, and I find myself helping them get their life back in order.
2. I enjoy being involved in relationships in which my partner needs my help to get over some problem.
3. I often find myself with partners who need my help to recover from their past. **Score:__**

Person in recovery:
1. I need someone who will help me recover from my painful past.
2. I believe that a relationship can save me from a life that is crumbling around me.
3. I need help getting over my past. **Score:__**

The main advantage to the **recovery story** is that the co-dependent may really help the other partner to recover, so long as the other partner has genuinely made the decision to recover. Many of us know individuals who sought to reform their partners, only to experience total frustration when their partners made little or no effort to reform. At the same time, the co-dependent is someone who needs to feel he or she is helping someone, and gains this feeling of making a difference to someone through the relationship. The problem: Others can assist in recovery, but the decision to recover can only be made by the person in need of recovery. As a result, recovery stories can assist in, but not produce, actual recovery.

STORY #7

1. I believe a good relationship is attainable only if you spend time and energy to care for it, just as you tend a garden.
2. I believe relationships need to be nourished constantly to help weather the ups and downs of life.
3. I believe the secret to a successful relationship is the care that partners take of each other and of their love. **Score:__**

The biggest advantage of a garden story is its recognition of the importance of nurture. No other story involves this amount of care and attention. The biggest potential disadvantage is that a lack of spontaneity or boredom may develop. People in garden stories are not immune to the lure of extramarital relationships, for example, and may get involved in them to generate excitement, even if they still highly value their primary relationship. In getting involved in other relationships, however, they are putting the primary relationship at risk. Another potential disadvantage is that of smothering—that the attention becomes too much. Just as one can overwater a flower, one can overattend a relationship. Sometimes it's best to let things be and allow nature to take its course.

STORY #8

1. I believe that close relationships are partnerships.
2. I believe that in a romantic relationship, just as in a job, both partners should perform their duties and responsibilities according to their "job description."
3. Whenever I consider having a relationship with someone, I always consider the financial implications of the relationship as well. **Score:__**

A **business story** has several potential advantages, not the least of which is that the bills are more likely to get paid than in other types of relationships. That's because someone is always minding the store. Another potential advantage is that the roles tend to be more clearly defined than in other relationships. The partners are also in a good position to "get ahead" in terms of whatever it is that they want. One potential disadvantage occurs if only one of the two partners sees their relationship as a business story. The other partner may quickly become bored and look for interest and excitement outside the marriage. The story can also turn sour if the distribution of authority does not satisfy one or both partners. If the partners cannot work out mutually compatible roles, they may find themselves spending a lot of time fighting for position. It is important to maintain the option of flexibility.

STORY #9

1. I think fairy tales about relationships can come true.
2. I do believe that there is someone out there for me who is my perfect match.
3. I like my relationships to be ones in which I view my partner as something like a prince or princess in days of yore. **Score:__**

The **fantasy story** can be a powerful one. The individual may feel swept up in the emotion of the search for the perfect partner or of developing the perfect relationship with an existing partner. It is probably no coincidence that in literature most fantasy stories take place before or outside of marriage: Fantasies are hard to maintain when one has to pay the bills, pack the children off to school and resolve marital fights. To maintain the happy feeling of the fantasy, therefore, one has to ignore, to some extent, the mundane aspects of life. The potential disadvantages of the fantasy relationship are quite plain. The greatest is the possibility for disillusionment when one partner discovers that no one could fulfill the fantastic expectations that have been created. This can lead partners to feel dissatisfied with relationships that most others would view as quite successful. If a couple can create a fantasy story based on realistic rather than idealistic ideals, they have the potential for success; if they want to be characters in a myth, chances are that's exactly what they'll get: a myth.

STORY #10

1. I think it is more interesting to argue than to compromise.
2. I think frequent arguments help bring conflictive issues into the open and keep the relationship healthy.
3. I actually like to fight with my partner. **Score:__**

The **war story** is advantageous in a relationship only when both partners clearly share it and want the same thing. In these cases, threats of divorce and worse may be common, but neither partner would seriously dream of leaving: They're both having too much fun, in their own way. The major disadvantage, of course, is that the story often isn't shared, leading to intense and sustained conflict that can leave the partner without the war story feeling devastated much of the time. People can find themselves in a warring relationship without either of them having war as a preferred story. In such cases, the constant fighting may make both partners miserable. If the war continues in such a context, there is no joy in it for either partner.

STORY #11

Audience:
1. I like a partner who is willing to think about the funny side of our conflicts.
2. I think taking a relationship too seriously can spoil it; that's why I like partners who have a sense of humor.
3. I like a partner who makes me laugh whenever we are facing a tense situation in our relationship. **Score:__**

Comedian:
1. I admit that I sometimes try to use humor to avoid facing a problem in my relationship.
2. I like to use humor when I have a conflict with my partner because I believe there is a humorous side to any conflict.
3. When I disagree with my partner, I often try to make a joke out of it. **Score:__**

The **humor story** can have one enormous advantage: Most situations do have a lighter side, and people with this story are likely to see it. When things in a relationship become tense, sometimes nothing works better than a little humor, especially if it comes from within the relationship. Humor stories also allow relationships to be creative and dynamic. But the humor story also has some potential disadvantages. Probably the greatest one is the risk of using humor to deflect important issues: A serious conversation that needs to take place keeps getting put off with jokes. Humor can also be used to be cruel in a passive-aggressive way. When humor is used as a means of demeaning a person to protect the comedian from responsibility ("I was only joking"), a relationship is bound to be imperiled. Thus, moderate amounts are good for a relationship, but excessive amounts can be deleterious.

STORY #12

1. I think it is okay to have multiple partners who fulfill my different needs.
2. I sometimes like to think about how many people I could potentially date all at the same time.

3. I tend and like to have multiple intimate partners at once, each fulfilling somewhat different roles.
Score:__

There are a few advantages to a collection story. For one thing, the collector generally cares about the collectible's physical well-being, as appearance is much of what makes a collection shine. The collector also finds a way of meeting multiple needs. Usually those needs will be met in parallel—by having several intimate relationships at the same time—but a collector may also enter into serial monogamous relationships, where each successive relationship meets needs that

the last relationship did not meet. In a society that values monogamy, collection stories work best if they do not become serious or if individuals in the collection are each viewed in different lights, such as friendship or intellectual stimulation. The disadvantages of this story become most obvious when people are trying to form serious relationships. The collector may find it difficult to establish intimacy, or anything approaching a complete relationship and commitment toward a single individual. Collections can also become expensive, time-consuming, and in some cases illegal (as when an individual enters into multiple marriages simultaneously).

ARE YOU CONNECTING ON
THE FIVE LEVELS OF
SEX?

YOU MAY THINK YOU'RE REACHING SEXUAL PEAKS OF PLEASURE, BUT HAS YOUR BEDROOM BONDING SCORED A HIGH-FIVE? PUT YOUR RELATIONSHIP TO THE TEST TO SEE IF YOUR ACTS OF AMOUR GO TO ALL LIMITS. AFTER ALL, WHY EXPERIENCE JUST A FRACTION OF THE FUN?

BY LESLIE YAZEL

HOW ADORABLE. Now that you're solidly with your boyfriend, who everyone—including you!—agrees is amazing, all your friends feel perfectly free to tell you what they really thought of your past sex partners "Ugh, White Bread Boy?" says one. "No one had ever told him that women could have orgasms!" They all shriek with laughter. "Then there was the New Agey yoga guy who meditated to the goddess of virility," recalls another. "And don't forget that macho bartender who could only get off if he called you Mommy!" Aren't you glad you were so open with your girlfriends?

Thankfully, those days are over. You, sister, are currently creating mattress magic with a stunningly normal—yet totally sexy—man who completely adores you. The lovemaking is as amazing as he is. But now's your chance to make it even better. Since you're in such a solid and exciting matchup, you can push your sexual ticket to make your bedtime the most spontaneous, orgasmic, fantasy-fulfilling, explosively intimate sex you've ever had.

How? By exploring all five levels of sex. Experts now believe that incorporating five dimensions—erotic, sensual, intimate, daring and spiritual—into your sexual menu can make a huge difference in your relationship. "Hitting all five levels not only keeps sex feeling fresh and new, it makes you feel more emotionally connected," explains Tracey Cox, author of *Hot Relationships: How to Know What You Want, Get What You Want, and Keep It Red Hot* (Bantam Doubleday Dell)

"With a little effort, all couples have the capacity to reach all five."

To score a sexual high-five with your man, read on to identify which levels you're currently connecting on and which ones need a little buffing up. Then try our suggestions to help take your lovemaking from pretty good to peel-me-off-the-ceiling status.

SEX LEVEL 1
EROTIC SEX

The last time you watched a movie lovemaking scene where a couple knocks over lamps, breaks museum-caliber Ming vases and rips expensive underwear off each other's body just to get carnal quickly, you thought (a) Looks like my sex life, or (b) Uh-oh, I hope they have a replacement bag for their Dirt Devil Hand Vac.

If you picked (b), it's probably been awhile since you had real-life erotic sex—obstacle-free horizontal hula to enjoy simply for pleasure's sake. "When I'm with my boyfriend, I feel this hunger for him that's so strong, I have to go wherever my instincts take me: I'll lick his neck or dig my fingers into his back," says Julie, 29, a sales rep in Tulsa. "The best part of this feeling is that I never worry about anything; I'm too far gone on sexual autopilot."

Julie's primal passion bubbled to the surface once she was able to ditch her inhibitions about how she might look, sound or even smell during sex. "But too many women still have their deepest instincts blocked by superficial fears—they think, If I do that, I'll look fat," observes Cox. "Others are afraid that their man will think they're dirty or sleazy, so they hold back in bed."

To unleash your erotic side, Cox recommends taking a sex sabbatical for a week or two. During that time, you and your man should agree not to have any physical contact, but you should seek out daily sex-you-up triggers, like steamy movies, flirty gestures, even racy e-mails hinting at a torrid get-together in the very near future. "After a week or two of building up sexual tension without providing for a release, your desire will be so strong, it'll overcome any self-consciousness that may be holding you back," assures Cox.

SEX LEVEL 2
SENSUAL SEX

Ask yourself: Each time you get busy, do you get naked, kiss kiss, fondle fondle, and then move on to the actual act? Or is your bedroom experience a sonic boom of sensory overload that has you practically speaking in tongues? "Sensual sex is the latter—it's lovemaking that incorporates all five senses, during which you slowly and steadily stimulate each other to intense peaks of sexual pleasure," says Cox. The advantage to your relationship? Since all that sensual exploration leads you to know his body as intimately as you know your own (and vice versa), you learn new ways to send him to Ecstasy-ville while becoming emotionally closer, too.

But before you automatically do unto him what you would like him to do to you, bear in mind that sensual sex is the one level where gender differences matter. "Ongoing research shows that women become aroused with their ears and men with their eyes," asserts Linda Banner, Ph.D., a sex therapist in San Jose, California.

That's not to say all guys only get aroused by images of Pamela Anderson Lee leaking out over her bustier, but visual stimulation is a surefire route to getting his mind off the Yankees game and on to, well, your playing field. In addition to doing the tried-and-true eye-candy tricks like undressing slowly with the lights on and giving him a show when you're on top, you might want to try a more offbeat approach like the flashlight game. Turn out all the lights, take off your clothes, then shine your flashlight on his private parts—and he'll do the same to you. Or take both flashlights and shine them on yourself. The close-up view of your body illuminated by the light will make him think he's being treated to his own private peep show.

And when it comes to the aural aspect of sex, you don't need him to imitate Barry White on Viagra to reap the benefits—many women get turned on by tuning in to their own moans and groans, says Banner. This is how Rachel, a 26-year-old researcher from Indianapolis, encourages herself to have bigger, better orgasms while making love with her live-in boyfriend. "The first time we were together, I couldn't help but let out these throaty *oohs* and *ahhs*," recalls Rachel. "Now

whenever I hear myself moaning like that, I'm turned on in an almost out-of-body way—it's as if I'm listening to some other, totally uninhibited woman getting closer and closer to orgasm—plus, it reminds me of that first night."

SEX LEVEL 3
INTIMATE SEX

The word *intimate* has gotten a bad rap. It now implies being so comfortable that he'll show you that nasty boil on his back, and you'll go to bed with zit medicine on. And the words *intimate sex* are couple code for same-old sex, the kind that long-term sweethearts gripe about and brand-new daters pray that they can avoid like an incurable STD. "But preconceptions aside, intimate sex is actually one of the most passionate types two people can experience, since it's all about deep connection and trust," explains Cox. And this dimension of lovemaking does not have to depend on how long you've been together. "My current boyfriend and I have only known each other for six months, but we're incredibly close in bed—a kind of closeness I now realize I never achieved with the live-in boyfriend

CELEBRITY SEX MATCH

We rate the carnal chemistry of five film couples on a scale from 1 to 10. **by Sarah Copeland**

FROM HERE TO ETERNITY

Deborah Kerr and Burt Lancaster turn a deserted beach into a steamy, slippery, full-sensory playground. EROTIC: **1**; SENSUAL: **9**; INTIMATE: **8**; PUSH-THE-ENVELOPE: **2**; SPIRITUAL: **6**

GHOST

Nothing could stop the clay-smeared passion of Demi Moore and Patrick Swayze—not even his death. EROTIC: **6**; SENSUAL: **7**; INTIMATE: **8**; PUSH-THE-ENVELOPE: **3**; SPIRITUAL: **9**

THE ENGLISH PATIENT

Ralph Fiennes and Kristin Scott Thomas have a love affair steamier than the desert backdrop on their mapmaking expedition. EROTIC: **7**; SENSUAL: **4**; INTIMATE: **9**; PUSH-THE-ENVE-LOPE: **7**; SPIRITUAL: **8**

REINDEER GAMES

Ben Affleck's caged-up desire is finally freed when he and Charlize Theron engage in some fall-out-of-bed savage shagging. EROTIC: **10**; SENSUAL: **6**; INTIMATE: **5**; PUSH-THE-ENVE-LOPE: **7**; SPIRITUAL: **0**

COMMITTED

The sensual synergy of Goran Visnjic's hands-only approach leaves Heather Graham shivering in the front seat of her car. EROTIC: **3**; SENSUAL: **9**; INTIMATE: **4**; PUSH-THE-ENVE-LOPE: **2**; SPIRITUAL: **8**

I had all through my twenties," remarks Juliette, 30, a paralegal from Washington, D.C.

Although adding an intimate facet to your sex life doesn't require a long-term bond, it does take a fairly unguarded heart. To get emotions to rise to the surface, think of things only the two of you share, like relationship rituals or goofy jokes. Or concentrate on the character quirks that made you fall for him in the first place. "Before my boyfriend and I began dating, he would come into the ice cream store where I worked and order cup after cup of ice cream, never getting up the nerve to ask me out," recalls Heather, a 24-year-old M.B.A. student. "Every time I remember his shy, geeky way of getting to know me, I feel this intense rush of love for him and a need to be physically close."

But just because you're craving physical contact doesn't mean you should drag him straight to the bedroom and jump his bones. Instead, translate your feelings into touches with small, simple gestures—brushing his hair with your fingertips while you two are entwined on the couch; holding him in bed as he blows off steam about his ogre of a boss. Once you've fully connected—and your libidos are ready for lift-off—try sex positions that closely align your bodies, like missionary or spooning. Cox also suggests licking hands and pausing mid-passion just to hug and kiss. It may seem kind of corny, but it'll keep you on the same "I'm so glad we're together" wavelength.

SEX LEVEL 4
PUSH-THE-ENVELOPE SEX

If you don't remember the last time you giggled to yourself in the heat of the horizontal moment thinking, I can't believe we're doing this crazy thing, you may lack a little envelope-pushing in your love life. But that doesn't mean one of you has to don a rubber suit while the other swings from the ceiling trying to press record on the video camera. Push-the-envelope sex is about pushing your own sexual boundaries with a sense of playfulness and humor—not about acting out someone else's definition of kinky.

But even in this age of anything-goes-as-long-as-it's-legal loving, many women are afraid their partner will view them as weird if they propose a night of role-playing, sex in a public place or renting a softcore porno flick. "Women are still raised with this sense that 'good girls don't' when it comes to anything outside what's considered 'normal' sex," explains Banner. "But guys love it when a woman suggests something

new—he won't think you're weird, he'll be turned on by your boldness and sense of adventure."

Jamie, a 30-year-old writer from New Jersey, learned this firsthand when she finally gathered the courage to hint to her fiancé about her longtime silk-scarf fantasy. "I'd always thought that the most sexually thrilling thing would be to be blindfolded with a silk scarf and then slowly licked and teased to orgasm," recalls Jamie. "Finally, I'd met a man I trusted enough to indulge in that fantasy with me. So I brought it up one day by musing, 'You won't believe the crazy dream I had last night. . . .' Then I described exactly what I wanted him to do to me. He got the hint—and later that night, I got my fantasy fulfilled."

SEX LEVEL 5
SPIRITUAL SEX

If you're like most women, you associate the word *spiritual* more with receiving communion than with tireless carnality. But spiritual sex has nothing to do with organized religion or even New Agey things like chanting or creating a shrine at the foot of your bed. "Incorporating spirituality into your sex life means you transcend concerns and worries about your physical selves to focus on the mingling of your inner selves, your souls," explains Rabbi Shmuley Boteach, author of *Dating Secrets of the Ten Commandments* (Doubleday).

"I know this sounds kind of hokey, but right before I reach orgasm, my body begins to open up in such a way that I feel like it's uniting with my husband's body," marvels Kelly, 32, a nurse in New York City. "Joined to him for a few moments like that, I feel this sense of blissful inner peace—as if everything is right with the world. I'm not a religious person, but I would definitely describe this feeling as otherworldly."

To prime your bodies for this divine type of passion, first clear your mind of nagging, day-to-day clutter. Next, Boteach recommends having sex in positions that afford plenty of eye contact—like missionary and girl-on-top. "Our eyes are the windows to our souls," he says, "so locking them with your lover's is critical to spiritually connecting." Boteach also advises lots of kissing: "Kissing is an opening up of one person's body to another's, a sharing of life breath." Finally, settle into one or two or three lovemaking positions that press your bodies close together—like missionary—so that as your passion grows, your bodies truly begin to feel as if they're melding into one, he says.

8 sizzling sex secrets (only lovers in the tropics know)

By Susan Crain Bakos

IT REALLY IS HOTTER IN THE TROPICS—SEX, THAT IS. HERE, HOW TO TURN UP THE HEAT AT HOME.

TROPICAL ISLANDS ARE THE SEXIEST PLACES ON EARTH. Every scented breeze feels like a caress, and life moves at a slow, languorous pace that leaves you free to follow the rhythms of your own desire. It's too hot to wear heavy clothing, so you become deliciously body-conscious, aware of the movement of legs and torsos under thin fabric. No wonder so many couples choose to honeymoon in Hawaii and other tropical paradises: The minute the plane touches down, all you want to do is make love. Slowly.

In tropical sex, a couple's erotic defenses come down. Orgasms (while very, very nice) are not the ultimate goal, but part of a long continuum of pleasure given and received–and getting there is more than half the fun.

So why–assuming you're not on a plane to Hawaii or Tahiti or the Caribbean at this very moment–are we tantalizing you with all this?

Because even if you live in Skwentna, AK you can make love as though you were in the tropics right in your own bedroom. Peel a mango, pull up a chair, and let us tell you how.

1. TURN UP THE HEAT

Most Americans are so accustomed to air-conditioning that they've forgotten how sexy a sultry night can be. Remember that classic steamy film *Body Heat,* with William Hurt and Kathleen Turner making it in Florida (in summer, yet) in a luxurious house that, inexplicably, was not air-conditioned? Total climate control is boring, so open the bedroom window and let some heavy summer air inside. Or indulge in foreplay in a steamy shower or whirlpool. Feel the lust oozing out of every pore.

"My husband always told me I look sexy after a workout. But I never want to make love then

From *Redbook*, July 2000, pp. 108–109, 134–135. © 2000 by Susan Crain Bakos. Reprinted by permission.

because I don't smell all that sexy—and besides, I exercise in the morning before work, so there's no time for sex. So one night I filled the bathroom with scented candles (lots of exotic florals) and took a long, hot shower. I didn't shampoo, so my hair was damp around the edges and curly. I sprayed my body lightly with gardenia oil. When my husband came into the bathroom, he inhaled deeply, took one appreciative look, and said, 'I want to ravish you.' Then he did."
—Michele, 28

"When my wife and I bought our first house, we couldn't afford central air-conditioning. Our window unit in the bedroom didn't work very well, but we didn't want to spend the money to replace it. I remember that summer as the hottest in our marriage, and I'm not just talking about the air temperature. We couldn't get enough of each other. The sex was hot, sweaty, and uninhibited. She said she felt like a bad girl."
—Dennis, 33

2. PILE ON THE FLOWERS AND FRUIT

Flowers are a plant's sex organs, and in the tropics, where the air is heavy with their scent, you never forget it. Bring that feeling home. Don't stop with a tight bouquet and a few scented candles. Scatter petals on the bed. Crush them with your bodies. And then . . . add fruit. Bananas, pineapples, papayas, and mangoes add atmosphere while imparting a natural energy boost. Instead of dinner, make a pitcher of piña coladas (easy on the alcohol), cut tropical fruits into bite-size pieces, and move your feast into the bedroom.

"When I was stationed at the U.S. Consulate in the Philippines, I had the good fortune to have an affair with an older Filipino woman. She would sprinkle flower petals on my body and massage me so that her fingertips felt like they were covered in velvet. When I tried to reciprocate, I tore the petals up the first time. She taught me how to have a gentle touch, to propel the petals across her skin with the slightest pressure from the pads of my fingertips. (It helps to work a small amount of oil into the skin first.) She always had flowers in her hair. Sometimes they fell out when she was on top of me and leaning forward. I've never had a better lover. And I know she made me a better lover than I would have been without her."
—Bruce, 36

"I turned the bedroom into a tropical paradise for a night. I even put on a CD of rain-forest sounds. We fed each other pieces of fruit. The juice spilled from our lips, ran down our fingers. We licked each other clean. That led to passionate kissing—and more."
—Carrie, 27

3. START IN THE MORNING, FINISH AT NIGHT

Stroking and caressing are open-ended pleasures in the islands, not just foreplay. So forget the end and concentrate on the means: Think of erotic contact with your partner as play. Couples who arouse but don't satisfy each other in the morning are likely to find time to make love that night.

"We got into the tropical mind-set through role-playing. I pretended I was a Polynesian woman who wanted to be seduced but, according to the dictates of her culture, had to make her beloved work for the prize. I put single stems of flowers in small vases around the tub. In the morning I took a bath rather than my customary shower. He 'spied' on me as if I were bathing in a lagoon. I allowed him a few kisses and caresses, then I got out of the tub and hurried away from him. We called each other during the day, leaving suggestive messages. At home that evening I put on a floral skirt and tank top, no underwear. By the time I took his hand and led him to the bedroom, we were hotter for each other than we'd been in months."
—Jessica, 31

"When my wife suggested that we tease each other in the morning, I thought, When will we fit that in between getting ready for work and the kids set for day care? We sacrificed the minutes we usually spent arguing about whose turn it was to take out the garbage, drop off the cleaning, and so forth. Best trade-off we ever made."
—Sean, 33

4. ADORN YOUR BODY

Western women buy sexy lingerie, put it on when they're feeling seductive, and take it off far too soon—to the point where getting naked can feel like getting down to business. In the tropics, women leave their flowers, ankle bracelets, and toe rings on, and sometimes their sarongs too. A wispy piece of clothing, an adornment or two, can make you feel freer and sexier than wearing nothing at all.

"I once saw a stunning photo in a gallery of a woman wearing sheer black stockings, elbow-length black gloves, a strand of pearls, and nothing else. Years later I convinced my fiancée to pose like that for me and let me take her picture. Though almost completely naked, she projected erotic power, not vulnerability. On our honeymoon in Hawaii, she let me photograph her in our room posed suggestively behind a large potted banana palm, naked except for a lei and a hibiscus flower behind her ear. Again she held the power, but in a different way: She was Eve in the garden, without the snake or the apple—lush, inviting, promising intense pleasure, not eventual punishment."
—Mark, 32

"My husband and I spent three weeks in Bali, where the men wear sarongs. He started wearing one, and we both came home with the sarong habit. I love it when he wears his around our bedroom. I can reach inside the fold of the cloth and touch his genitals. When I'm turning him on, it's very obvious. A man in a sarong is hot."
—Marilyn, 35

5. USE YOUR MOUTH—LESS

Islanders kiss less often than Western lovers do; when they kiss during lovemaking, they kiss deeply, with eyes open. They also perform oral sex for shorter periods of time. Instead of using it in a goal-oriented way (to give the woman an orgasm, for example, so the man can have his without guilt), they simply savor the experience.

"We had fallen into a lovemaking rut. He gave me an orgasm via cunnilingus, then we had intercourse and he came. I didn't think I would come if we varied the routine. But I did, because we took the time to give each other pleasure in slower, more varied ways. We've learned to use oral sex less as a means to an end—and now we enjoy it more than we used to."
—*Dawn, 31*

"I was continually monitoring Dawn's progress toward orgasm. When she took that pressure away, I approached her differently. I love the way she feels and tastes. She's like sweet velvet under my tongue. Making oral love to her feels decadent." —*Scott, 30*

6. TRY THE PALM-TREE TRICK

In the Hawaiian islands, according to a local erotic legend, the palm trees have been planted a uniform distance apart to facilitate a popular lovemaking position: A man and a woman sit with their backs against the trees. She opens her legs, and he strokes her clitoris with the underside of his penis. Obviously, you don't need palm trees for this. Try placing stacks of pillows at your backs. Or experiment with other positions that allow mutual genital pleasuring without deep pene-

tration—for example, lying face-to-face on your side, or in spoon fashion with your back against his chest.

"My wife and I have found that the secret to prolonging the genital connection is starting before I have an erection, then not letting it take over when I do get one. I rub my not-yet-erect penis back and forth across her clitoris, which she finds very arousing. We play with shallow penetration. When I get hard, I pull back and massage her with my thumb until the erection subsides again. What's the payoff for this? Heightened arousal, stronger orgasms for both of us." —*Alan, 36*

"Making love this way helped me focus more on my genitals. I always thought my breasts were more sensitive than my vulva. I was wrong."
—*Jennie, 34*

7. EXPAND YOUR ORGASMS

An expanded orgasm is one that feels stronger, deeper, and longer, and seems to spread from the genitals into other parts of the body. A quick way to learn the art of orgasm expansion (which is called "high sex" in the islands): While masturbating (or having your partner touch you), use the other hand to lightly massage your vulva, inner thighs, and groin. Imagine that you are spreading the arousal through those areas. Stay on the verge as long as possible. Continue massaging throughout your orgasm and imagine you are spreading the orgasm throughout your entire body.

"When you learn how to do this, you understand that sex truly does begin in the brain, because it's a mind trick. You convince yourself that you are

spreading the fire through your fingertips. It does work, but I recommend learning the technique through masturbation. Otherwise you have to disconnect from your partner to focus so intently on yourself and your own pleasure. Once you've learned the expansion technique, you can do it whenever you want." —*Angela, 32*

"I really enjoy masturbating Angela. She feels disconnected from me, but I feel very connected to her. I don't know why she thinks she's being selfish when all the erotic attention is focused on her. It excites me to excite her that much. I feel like a stud." —*Paul, 30*

8. FORGET ABOUT AFTERPLAY

In the islands, a man is expected to fall asleep in his lover's arms, and she in his, after they have had their fill of lovemaking. The very American concept of afterplay—talking about your intimacy and actively cuddling in order to reinforce the relationship—is regarded with some amusement by people of tropical cultures. Give their way a try by putting off the conversation and the requisite number of reassuring hugs. After all, what could be more intimate than shared erotic exhaustion?

"It was too hot to cuddle afterward. So I took a shower; and we turned on the air-conditioner. If we had a pool, we would have gone for a naked midnight swim." —*Janelle, 28*

"Afterplay has always seemed like homework to me. Sometimes I've wondered if my wife agreed to have sex that night because she thought we needed the 'intimacy.' Being let off that hook makes me feel more affectionate." —*Paul, 33*

Celibate Passion

The hidden rewards of quitting sex

Kathleen Norris
The Christian Century

Kathleen Norris is the author of Dakota *(Ticknor & Fields, 1993).*

Celibacy is a field day for ideologues. Conservative Catholics tend to speak of celibacy as if it were an idealized, angelic state, while feminist theologians such as Uta Ranke-Heinemann say, angrily, that celibate hatred of sex is hatred of women. That celibacy constitutes the hatred of sex seems to be a given in popular mythology, and we need only look at newspaper accounts of sex abuse by priests to see evidence of celibacy that isn't working. One could well assume that this is celibacy, impure and simple. And this is unfortunate, because celibacy practiced rightly is not at all a hatred of sex; in fact it has the potential to address the troubling sexual idolatry of our culture.

One benefit of the nearly ten years that I've been affiliated with the Benedictines as an oblate, or associate, has been the development of deep friendships with celibate men and women. This has led me to ponder celibacy that works, practiced by people who are fully aware of themselves as sexual beings but who express their sexuality in a celibate way. That is, they manage to sublimate their sexual energies toward another purpose than sexual intercourse and procreation. Are they perverse, their lives necessarily stunted? Cultural prejudice would say yes, but I have my doubts. I've seen too many wise old monks and nuns whose celibate practice has allowed them to incarnate hospitality in the deepest sense. In them, the constraints of celibacy have somehow been transformed into an openness. They exude a sense of freedom.

The younger celibates are more edgy. Still contending mightily with what one friend calls "the raging orchestra of my hormones," they are more obviously struggling to contain their desire for intimacy and physical touch within the bounds of celibacy. Often they find their loneliness intensified by the incomprehension of others. In a culture that denies the value of their striving, they are made to feel like fools, or worse.

Americans are remarkably tone-deaf when it comes to the expression of sexuality. The sexual formation that many of us receive is like the refrain of an old Fugs song: "Why do ya like boobs a lot—ya gotta like boobs a lot." The jiggle of tits and ass, penis and pectorals assaults us everywhere—billboards, magazines, television, movies. Orgasm becomes just another goal; we undress for success. It's no wonder that in all this powerful noise, the quiet tones of celibacy are lost.

But celibate people have taught me that celibacy, practiced rightly, does indeed have something valuable to say to the rest of us. Specifically, they have helped me better appreciate both the nature of friendship and what it means to be married. They have also helped me recognize that celibacy, like monogamy, is not a matter of the will disdaining and conquering the desires of the flesh, but a discipline requiring what many people think of as undesirable, if not impossible—a conscious form of sublimation. Like many people who came into adulthood during the sexually permissive 1960s, I've tended to equate sublimation with repression. But my celibate friends have made me see the light; accepting sublimation as a normal part of adulthood makes me more realistic about human sexual capacities and expression. It helps me better respect the bonds and boundaries of marriage.

Any marriage has times of separation, ill health, or just plain crankiness in which sexual intercourse is ill advised. And it is precisely the skills of celibate friendship—fostering intimacy through letters, conversation,

From *Utne Reader,* September/October 1996, pp. 51–53. Originally from *The Christian Century,* March 20, 1996. Adapted from *The Cloister Walk* by Kathleen Norris. © 1996 by Kathleen Norris. Reprinted by permission of Riverhead Books, a division of The Putnam Publishing Group.

performing mundane tasks together (thus rendering them pleasurable), savoring the holy simplicity of a shared meal or a walk together at dusk—that help a marriage survive the rough spots. When you can't make love physically, you figure out other ways to do it.

The celibate impulse in monasticism runs deep and has an interfaith dimension. It is the Dalai Lama who has said, "If you're a monk, you're celibate. If you're not celibate, you're not a monk." Monastic people are celibate for a very practical reason: The kind of community life to which they aspire can't be sustained if people are pairing off. Even in churches in which the clergy are often married—Episcopal and Russian Orthodox, for example—their monks and nuns are celibate. And while monastic novices may be carried along for a time on the swells of communal spirit, when that blissful period inevitably comes to an end the loneliness is profound. One gregarious monk in his early 30s told me that just as he thought he'd settled into the monastery, he woke up in a panic one morning, wondering if he'd wake up lonely for the rest of his life.

Another monk I know regards celibacy as the expression of an essential human loneliness, a perspective that helps him as a hospital chaplain when he is called upon to minister to the dying. I knew him when he was still resisting his celibate call. The resistance usually came out as anger directed toward his abbot and community, more rarely as misogyny. I was fascinated to observe the process by which he came to accept the sacrifices that a celibate, monastic life requires. He's easier to be with now; he's a better friend.

This is not irony so much as grace: In learning to be faithful to his vow of celibacy, the monk developed his talent for relationship. It's a common story. I've seen the demands of Benedictine hospitality—the requirement that all visitors be received as Christ—convert shy young men who fear women into monks who can enjoy their company.

Celibates tend to value friendship very highly. And my friendships with celibate men, both gay and straight, give me some hope that men and women don't live in alternate universes. In 1990s America, this sometimes feels like a countercultural perspective. Male celibacy, in particular, can become radically countercultural insofar as it rejects the consumerist model of sexuality that reduces a woman to the sum of her parts. I have never had a monk friend make an insinuating remark along the lines of "You have beautiful eyes" (or legs, breasts, knees, elbows, nostrils), the kind of remark women grow accustomed to deflecting. A monk is supposed to give up the idea of possessing anything, including women.

Ideally, in giving up the sexual pursuit of women (whether as demons or as idealized vessels of purity)

the male celibate learns to relate to them as human beings. That many fail to do so, that the power structures of the Catholic Church all but dictate failure in this regard, comes as no surprise. What is a surprise is what happens when it works. For when men have truly given up the idea of possessing women, a healing thing occurs. I once met a woman in a monastery guest house who had come there because she was pulling herself together after being raped, and she needed to feel safe around men again. I've seen young monks astonish an obese and homely college student by listening to her with as much interest and respect as to her conventionally pretty roommate. On my 40th birthday, as I happily blew out four candles on a cupcake ("one for each decade," a monk in his 20s cheerfully proclaimed), I realized that I could enjoy growing old with these guys.

As celibacy takes hold in a person, as monastic values supersede the values of the culture outside the monastery, celibates become people who can radically affect those of us out "in the world," if only because they've learned how to listen without possessiveness, without imposing themselves. In talking to someone who is practicing celibacy well, we may sense that we're being listened to in a refreshingly deep way. And this is the purpose of celibacy, not to attain some impossibly cerebral goal mistakenly conceived as "holiness," but to make oneself available to others, body and soul. Celibacy, simply put, is a form of ministry—not an achievement one can put on a résumé but a subtle form of service. In theological terms, one dedicates one's sexuality to God through Jesus Christ, a concept and a terminology I find extremely hard to grasp. All I can do is catch a glimpse of people who are doing it, incarnating celibacy in a mysterious, pleasing, and gracious way.

The attractiveness of the celibate is that he or she can make us feel appreciated, enlarged, no matter who we are. I have two nun friends who invariably have this effect on me, no matter what the circumstances of our lives on those occasions when we meet. The thoughtful way in which they converse, listening and responding with complete attention, is a marvel. And when I first met a man I'll call Tom, I wrote in my notebook, "Such tenderness in a man . . . and a surprising, gentle, kindly grasp of who I am."

I realized that I had found a remarkable friend. I was also aware that Tom and I were fast approaching the rocky shoals of infatuation—a man and a woman, both decidedly heterosexual, responding to each other in unmistakably sexual ways. We laughed a lot; we had playful conversations as well as serious ones; we took delight in each other. At times we were alarmingly responsive to one another, and it was all too easy to fantasize about expressing that responsiveness in physical ways.

The danger was real but not insurmountable; I sensed that if our infatuation were to develop into love, that is, to ground itself in grace rather than utility, our respect for each other's commitments—his to celibacy, mine to monogamy—would make the boundaries of behavior very clear. We had few regrets, and yet for both of us there was an underlying sadness, the pain of something incomplete. Suddenly, the difference between celibate friendship and celibate passion had become a reality; at times the pain was excruciating.

Tom and I each faced a crisis the year we met—his mother died, I suffered a disastrous betrayal—and it was the intensity of those unexpected, unwelcome experiences that helped me to understand that in the realm of the sacred, what seems incomplete or unat-tainable may be abundance after all. Human relationships are by their nature incomplete—after 21 years my husband remains a mystery to me, and I to him, and that is as it should be. Only hope allows us to know and enjoy the depth of our intimacy.

Appreciating Tom's presence in my life as a miraculous, unmerited gift helped me to place our relationship in its proper, religious context, and also to understand why it was that when I'd seek him out to pray with me, I'd always leave feeling so much better than when I came. This was celibacy at its best—a man's sexual energies so devoted to the care of others that a few words could lift me out of despair, give me the strength to reclaim my life. Celibate love was at the heart of it, although I can't fully comprehend the mystery of why this should be so. Celibate passion—elusive, tensile, holy.

Unit Selections

Key Points to Consider

❖ In your opinion, what are the most important characteristics of a contraceptive? Why?

❖ What personal feelings or expectations make you more likely to use contraception regularly?

❖ Under what circumstances might a person not use contraception and risk an unintentional pregnancy?

❖ Do you agree that it should be easier to develop, test, and market new contraceptive methods and that incentives should be offered to companies willing to do so in order to lower America's very high rate of unplanned pregnancies? Defend your answer.

❖ Should contraceptive responsibilities be assigned to one gender or be shared between men and women? Defend your answer.

❖ Have you found a fairly comfortable way to talk about contraception and/or pregnancy risk and prevention with your partner? If so, what is it? If not, what do you do?

❖ In the situation of an unplanned pregnancy, what should be the role of the female and the male with respect to decision making? What if they do not agree?

❖ Should there be some kind of proficiency test or license required in order to be a parent? Why or why not? If you had the responsibility for setting forth the requirements—age, marital status, knowledge of child development, emotional stability, income level, or anything you choose—what would they be and why?

 **Links** **www.dushkin.com/online/**

18. **Ask NOAH About Pregnancy: Fertility & Infertility**
    http://www.noah.cuny.edu/pregnancy/fertility.html
19. **Childbirth.Org**
    http://www.childbirth.org
20. **Medically Induced Abortion**
    http://www.nejm.org/content/1995/0333/0009/0537.asp
21. **Planned Parenthood**
    http://www.plannedparenthood.org

These sites are annotated on pages 4 and 5.

While human reproduction is as old as humanity, many aspects of it are changing in today's society. Not only have new technologies of conception and childbirth affected the *how* of reproduction, but personal, social, and cultural forces have also affected the *who*, the *when*, and the *when not*. Abortion remains a fiercely debated topic, and legislative efforts for and against it abound. Unplanned pregnancies and parenthood in the United States and worldwide continue to present significant, sometimes devastating, problems for parents, children, families, and society.

In light of the change of attitude toward sex for pleasure, birth control has become a matter of prime importance. Even in our age of sexual enlightenment, some individuals, possibly in the height of passion, fail to correlate "having sex" with pregnancy. In addition, even in our age of astounding medical technology, there is no 100 percent effective, safe, or aesthetically acceptable method of birth control. Before sex can become safe as well as enjoyable, people must receive thorough and accurate information regarding conception and contraception, birth, and birth control. However, we have learned that information about, or even access to, birth control is not enough. We still have some distance to go to make every child one who is planned for and wanted.

Despite the relative simplicity of the above assertion, abortion and birth control remain emotionally charged issues in American society. While opinion surveys indicate that most of the public supports family planning and abortion, at least in some circumstances, there are certain individuals and groups strongly opposed to some forms of birth control and to abortion. Within the past few years, voices for and against birth control and abortion have grown louder, and, on a growing number of occasions, overt behaviors, including protests and violence, have occurred. Some Supreme Court and legislative efforts have added restrictions to the right to abortion. Others have mandated freer access to abortion and reproductive choice and have restricted the activities of antiabortion demonstrators. Voices on both sides are raised in emotional and political debate between "we must never go back to the old days" (of illegal and unsafe back-alley abortions) and "the baby has no choice."

The nature and scope of the questions raised about the new technologies of reproduction from contraception and abortion through treatments for infertility, or what has become known as "assisted reproduction," have become very complex and

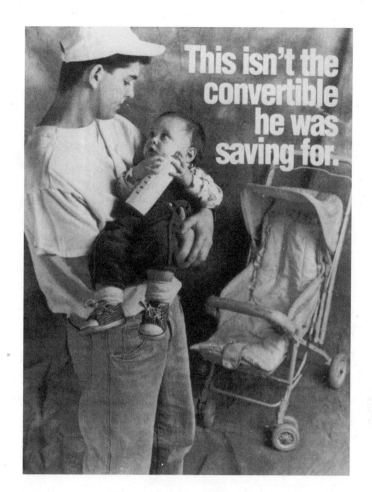

This isn't the convertible he was saving for.

far-reaching. Medical, religious, political, and legal experts, as well as concerned everyday people, are debating basic definitions of human life as well as the rights and responsibilities not only of men, women, and society, but of eggs, sperm donors, and surrogates. The very foundations of our pluralistic society are being challenged. We will have to await the outcome.

The article in the *Birth Control and Abortion* subsection is designed to inform and update readers on available birth control methods as well as on the myriad of factors that go into individuals' and couples' choices and uses of them. "Protecting Against Unintended Pregnancy: A Guide to Contraceptive Choices," covers the full range of prescription and nonprescription methods in a factual, yet easy-to-read style.

The second subsection opens with "How Old Is Too Old to Have a Baby?" an article that suggests that in the not-too-distant-future there may be no scientific upper limit to fertility. The second article "What Mother Nature Teaches Us About Motherhood" is likely to surprise all readers with its description of research findings that conclude parenting-related behaviors of "working" mothers are the same over the full range of the species— humans, animals, birds, insects, and fish. The subsection closes with "Pregnant Pleasures" a fact-filled, yet reassuring, guide to staying intimate during pregnancy.

Protecting Against
Unintended Pregnancy
A Guide To Contraceptive Choices

by Tamar Nordenberg

*I am 20 and have never gone to see a doctor about birth control.
My boyfriend and I have been going together for a couple of years and have
been using condoms. So far, everything is fine. Are condoms alone safe enough,
or is something else safe besides the Pill? I do not want to go on the Pill.*
—Letter to the Kinsey Institute for Research in Sex, Gender, and Reproduction

This young woman is not alone in her uncertainty about contraceptive options. A 1995 report by the National Academy of Sciences' Institute of Medicine, *The Best Intentions: Unintended Pregnancy and the Well-being of Children and Families,* attributed the high rate of unintended pregnancies in the United States, in part, to Americans' lack of knowledge about contraception. About 6 of every 10 pregnancies in the United States are unplanned, according to the report.

Being informed about the pros and cons of various contraceptives is important not only for preventing unintended pregnancies but also for reducing the risk of illness or death from sexually transmitted diseases (STDs), including AIDS.

The Food and Drug Administration has approved a number of birth control methods, ranging from over-the-counter male and female condoms and vaginal spermicides to doctor-

From *FDA Consumer,* April 1997, pp. 20-26. Reprinted by permission of *FDA Consumer,* the magazine of the U.S. Food and Drug Administration.

prescribed birth control pills, diaphragms, intrauterine devices (IUDs), injected hormones, and hormonal implants. Other contraceptive options include fertility awareness and voluntary surgical sterilization.

"On the whole, the contraceptive choices that Americans have are very safe and effective," says Dennis Barbour, president of the Association of Reproductive Health Professionals, "but a method that is very good for one woman may be lousy for another."

The choice of birth control depends on factors such as a person's health, frequency of sexual activity, number of partners, and desire to have children in the future. Effectiveness rates, based on statistical estimates, are another key consideration (see "Birth Control Guide"). FDA is developing a more consumer-friendly table to be added to the labeling of all contraceptive drugs and devices.

Barrier Methods

• *Male condom.* The male condom is a sheath placed over the erect penis before penetration, preventing pregnancy by blocking the passage of sperm.

A condom can be used only once. Some have spermicide added, usually nonoxynol-9 in the United States, to kill sperm. Spermicide has not been scientifically shown to provide additional contraceptive protection over

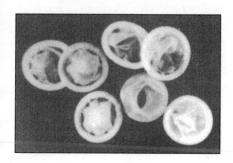

the condom alone. Because they act as a mechanical barrier, condoms prevent direct vaginal contact with semen, infectious genital secretions, and genital lesions and discharges.

Most condoms are made from latex rubber, while a small percentage

are made from lamb intestines (sometimes called "lambskin" condoms). Condoms made from polyurethane have been marketed in the United States since 1994.

Except for abstinence, latex condoms are the most effective method for reducing the risk of infection from the viruses that cause AIDS, other HIV-related illnesses, and other STDs.

Some condoms are prelubricated. These lubricants don't provide more birth control or STD protection. Non-oil-based lubricants, such as water or KY jelly, can be used with latex or lambskin condoms, but oil-based lubricants, such as petroleum jelly (Vaseline), lotions, or massage or baby oil, should not be used because they can weaken the material.

• *Female condom.* The Reality Female Condom, approved by FDA in April 1993, consists of a lubricated polyurethane sheath shaped similarly to the male condom. The closed end, which has a flexible ring, is inserted

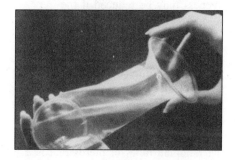

into the vagina, while the open end remains outside, partially covering the labia.

The female condom, like the male condom, is available without a prescription and is intended for one-time use. It should not be used together with a male condom because they may not both stay in place.

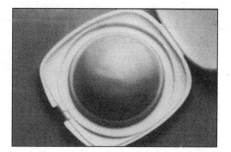

• *Diaphragm.* Available by prescription only and sized by a health professional to achieve a proper fit, the diaphragm has a dual mechanism to prevent pregnancy. A dome-shaped rubber disk with a flexible rim covers the cervix so sperm can't reach the uterus, while a spermicide applied to the diaphragm before insertion kills sperm.

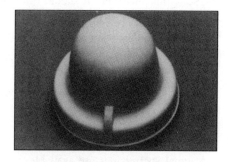

The diaphragm protects for six hours. For intercourse after the six-hour period, or for repeated intercourse within this period, fresh spermicide should be placed in the vagina with the diaphragm still in place. The diaphragm should be left in place for at least six hours after the last intercourse but not for longer than a total of 24 hours because of the risk of toxic shock syndrome (TSS), a rare but potentially fatal infection. Symptoms of TSS include sudden fever, stomach upset, sunburn-like rash, and a drop in blood pressure.

• *Cervical cap.* The cap is a soft rubber cup with a round rim, sized by a health professional to fit snugly around the cervix. It is available by prescription only and, like the diaphragm, is used with spermicide.

It protects for 48 hours and for multiple acts of intercourse within this time. Wearing it for more than 48 hours is not recommended because of the risk, though low, of TSS. Also, with prolonged use of two or more days, the cap may cause an unpleasant vaginal odor or discharge in some women.

• *Sponge.* The vaginal contraceptive sponge has not been available since the sole manufacturer, Whitehall Laboratories of Madison, N.J., voluntarily stopped selling it in 1995. It remains an approved product and could be marketed again.

The sponge, a donut-shaped polyurethane device containing the spermicide nonoxynol-9, is inserted into the vagina to cover the cervix. A woven polyester loop is designed to ease removal.

The sponge protects for up to 24 hours and for multiple acts of intercourse within this time. It should be left in place for at least six hours after intercourse but should be removed no more than 30 hours after insertion because of the risk, though low, of TSS.

Vaginal Spermicides Alone

Vaginal spermicides are available in foam, cream, jelly, film, suppository, or tablet forms. All types contain a sperm-killing chemical.

Studies have not produced definitive data on the efficacy of spermicides alone, but according to the authors of *Contraceptive Technology,* a leading resource for contraceptive information, the failure rate for typical users may be 21 percent per year.

Package instructions must be carefully followed because some spermicide products require the couple to wait 10 minutes or more after inserting the spermicide before having sex. One dose of spermicide is usually effective for one hour. For repeated intercourse, additional spermicide must be applied. And after intercourse, the spermicide has to remain in place for at least six to eight hours to ensure that all sperm are killed. The woman should not douche or rinse the vagina during this time.

Hormonal Methods

• *Combined oral contraceptives.* Typically called "the pill," combined oral contraceptives have been on the market for more than 35 years and are the most popular form of reversible birth control in the United States. This form of birth control suppresses ovulation (the monthly release of an egg from the ovaries) by the combined actions of the hormones estrogen and progestin.

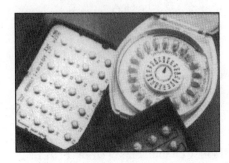

If a woman remembers to take the pill every day as directed, she has an extremely low chance of becoming pregnant in a year. But the pill's effectiveness may be reduced if the woman is taking some medications, such as certain antibiotics.

Besides preventing pregnancy, the pill offers additional benefits. As stated in the labeling, the pill can make periods more regular. It also has a protective effect against pelvic inflammatory disease, an infection of the fallopian tubes or uterus that is a major cause of infertility in women, and against ovarian and endometrial cancers.

The decision whether to take the pill should be made in consultation with a health professional. Birth control pills are safe for most women— safer even than delivering a baby—but they carry some risks.

Current low-dose pills have fewer risks associated with them than earlier versions. But women who smoke—especially those over 35—and women with certain medical conditions, such as a history of blood clots or breast or endometrial cancer, may be advised against taking the pill. The pill may contribute to cardiovascular disease, including high blood pressure, blood clots, and blockage of the arteries.

One of the biggest questions has been whether the pill increases the risk of breast cancer in past and current pill users. An international study published in the September 1996 journal *Contraception* concluded that women's risk of breast cancer 10 years after going off birth control pills was no higher than that of women who had never used the pill. During pill use and for the first 10 years after stopping the pill, women's risk of breast cancer was only slightly higher in pill users than non-pill users.

Side effects of the pill, which often subside after a few months' use, include nausea, headache, breast tenderness, weight gain, irregular bleeding, and depression.

Doctors sometimes prescribe higher doses of combined oral contraceptives for use as "morning after" pills to be taken within 72 hours of unprotected intercourse to prevent the possibly fertilized egg from reaching the uterus. In a Feb. 25, 1997, *Federal Register* notice, FDA stated its conclusion that, on the basis of current scientific evidence, certain oral contraceptives are safe and effective for this use.

• *Minipills.* Although taken daily like combined oral contraceptives, minipills contain only the hormone progestin and no estrogen. They work by reducing and thickening cervical mucus to prevent sperm from reaching the egg. They also keep the uterine lining from thickening, which prevents a fertilized egg from implanting in the uterus. These pills are generally less effective than combined oral contraceptives.

Minipills can decrease menstrual bleeding and cramps, as well as the risk of endometrial and ovarian cancer and pelvic inflammatory disease. Because they contain no estrogen, minipills don't present the risk of blood clots associated with estrogen in combined pills. They are a good option for women who can't take estrogen because they are breast-feeding or because estrogen-containing prod-

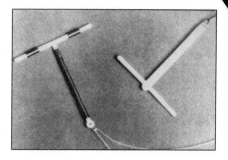

ucts cause them to have severe headaches or high blood pressure.

Side effects of minipills include menstrual cycle changes, weight gain, and breast tenderness.

• *Injectable progestins.* Depo-Provera, approved by FDA in 1992, is injected by a health professional into the buttocks or arm muscle every three months. Depo-Provera prevents pregnancy in three ways: It inhibits ovulation, changes the cervical mucus to help prevent sperm from reaching the egg, and changes the uterine lining to prevent the fertilized egg from implanting in the uterus. The progestin injection is extremely effective in preventing pregnancy, in large part because it requires little effort for the woman to comply: She simply has to get an injection by a doctor once every three months.

The benefits are similar to those of the minipill and another progestin-only contraceptive, Norplant. Side effects are also similar and can include irregular or missed periods, weight gain, and breast tenderness.

(See "Depo-Provera: The Quarterly Contraceptive" in the March 1993 *FDA Consumer.*)

• *Implantable progestins.* Norplant, approved by FDA in 1990, and the newer Norplant 2, approved in 1996, are the third type of progestin-only contraceptive. Made up of matchstick-sized rubber rods, this contraceptive is surgically implanted under the skin of the upper arm, where it steadily releases the contraceptive steroid levonorgestrel.

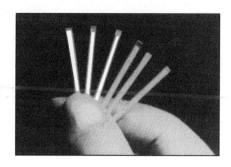

The six-rod Norplant provides protection for up to five years (or until it is removed), while the two-rod Norplant 2 protects for up to three years.

Norplant failures are rare, but are higher with increased body weight.

Some women may experience inflammation or infection at the site of the implant. Other side effects include menstrual cycle changes, weight gain, and breast tenderness.

Intrauterine Devices

An IUD is a T-shaped device inserted into the uterus by a health-care professional. Two types of IUDs are available in the United States: the Paragard CopperT 380A and the Progestasert Progesterone T. The Paragard IUD can remain in place for 10 years, while the Progestasert IUD must be replaced every year.

It's not entirely clear how IUDs prevent pregnancy. They seem to prevent sperm and eggs from meeting by either immobilizing the sperm on their way to the fallopian tubes or changing the uterine lining so the fertilized egg cannot implant in it.

IUDs have one of the lowest failure rates of any contraceptive method. "In the population for which the IUD is appropriate—for those in a mutually monogamous, stable relationship who aren't at a high risk of infection—the IUD is a very safe and very effective method of contraception," says Lisa Rarick, M.D., director of FDA's division of reproductive and urologic drug products.

The IUD's image suffered when the Dalkon Shield IUD was taken off the market in 1975. This IUD was associated with a high incidence of pelvic infections and infertility, and some deaths. Today, serious complications from IUDs are rare, although IUD users may be at increased risk of developing pelvic inflammatory disease. Other side effects can include perforation of the uterus, abnormal bleeding, and cramps. Complications occur most often during and immediately after insertion.

Traditional Methods

• *Fertility awareness.* Also known as natural family planning or periodic abstinence, fertility awareness entails not having sexual intercourse on the days of a woman's menstrual cycle when she could become pregnant or using a barrier method of birth control on those days.

Because a sperm may live in the female's reproductive tract for up to seven days and the egg remains fertile for about 24 hours, a woman can get pregnant within a substantial window of time—from seven days before ovulation to three days after. Methods

to approximate when a woman is fertile are usually based on the menstrual cycle, changes in cervical mucus, or changes in body temperature.

"Natural family planning can work," Rarick says, "but it takes an extremely motivated couple to use the method effectively."

• *Withdrawal.* In this method, also called *coitus interruptus,* the man withdraws his penis from the vagina before ejaculation. Fertilization is prevented because the sperm don't enter the vagina.

Effectiveness depends on the male's ability to withdraw before ejaculation. Also, withdrawal doesn't provide protection from STDs, including HIV.

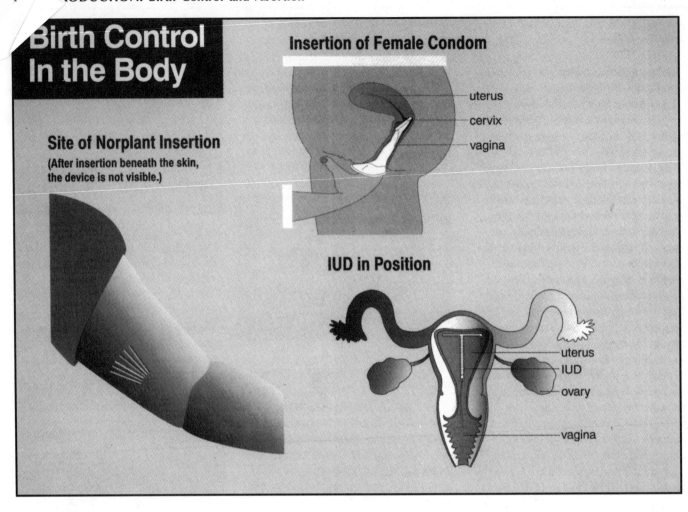

Birth Control In the Body

Insertion of Female Condom

- uterus
- cervix
- vagina

Site of Norplant Insertion
(After insertion beneath the skin, the device is not visible.)

IUD in Position

- uterus
- IUD
- ovary
- vagina

Birth Control Guide

Efficacy rates in this chart are based on Contraceptive Technology (16th edition, 1994). They are yearly estimates of effectiveness in typical use, which refers to a method's reliability in real life, when people don't always use a method properly. For comparison, about 85 percent of sexually active women using no contraception would be expected to become pregnant in a year.

This chart is a summary; it is not intended to be used alone. All product labeling should be followed carefully, and a health-care professional should be consulted for some methods.

Type	Estimated Effectiveness	Some Risks[d]	Protection from Sexually Transmitted Diseases (STDs)	Convenience	Availability
Male Condom	88%[a]	Irritation and allergic reactions (less likely with polyurethane)	Except for abstinence, latex condoms are the best protection against STDs, including herpes and AIDS.	Applied immediately before intercourse; used only once and discarded.	Nonprescription
Female Condom	79%	Irritation and allergic reactions	May give some STD protection; not as effective as latex condom.	Applied immediately before intercourse; used only once and discarded.	Nonprescription

Type	Estimated Effectiveness	Some Risks[d]	Protection from Sexually Transmitted Diseases (STDs)	Convenience	Availability
Diaphragm with Spermicide	82%	Irritation and allergic reactions, urinary tract infection	Protects against cervical infection; spermicide may give some protection against chlamydia and gonorrhea; otherwise unknown.	Inserted before intercourse and left in place at least six hours after; can be left in place for 24 hours, with additional spermicide for repeated intercourse.	Prescription
Cervical Cap with Spermicide	64–82%[b]	Irritation and allergic reactions, abnormal Pap test	Spermicide may give some protection against chlamydia and gonorrhea; otherwise unknown.	May be difficult to insert; can remain in place for 48 hours without reapplying spermicide for repeated intercourse.	Prescription
Sponge with Spermicide (not currently marketed)	64–82%[b]	Irritation and allergic reactions, difficulty in removal	Spermicide may give some protection against chlamydia and gonorrhea; otherwise unknown.	Inserted before intercourse and protects for 24 hours without additional spermicide; must be left in place for at least six hours after intercourse; must be removed within 30 hours of insertion; used only once and discarded.	Nonprescription; not currently marketed.
Spermicides Alone	79%	Irritation and allergic reactions	May give some protection against chlamydia and gonorrhea; otherwise unknown.	Instructions vary: usually applied no more than one hour before intercourse and left in place at least six to eight hours after.	Nonprescription
Oral Contraceptives—combined pill	Over 99%[c]	Dizziness; nausea; changes in menstruation, mood, and weight; rarely, cardiovascular disease, including high blood pressure, blood clots, heart attack, and strokes	None, except some protection against pelvic inflammatory disease.	Must be taken on daily schedule, regardless of frequency of intercourse.	Prescription
Oral Contraceptives—progestin-only minipill	Over 99%[c]	Ectopic pregnancy, irregular bleeding, weight gain, breast tenderness	None, except some protection against pelvic inflammatory disease.	Must be taken on daily schedule, regardless of frequency of intercourse.	Prescription
Injection (Depo-Provera)	Over 99%	Irregular bleeding, weight gain, breast tenderness, headaches	None	One injection every three months	Prescription
Implant (Norplant)	Over 99%	Irregular bleeding, weight gain, breast tenderness, headaches, difficulty in removal	None	Implanted by health-care provider—minor outpatient surgical procedure; effective for up to five years.	Prescription
IUD (Intrauterine Device)	98–99%	Cramps, bleeding, pelvic inflammatory disease, infertility, perforation of uterus	None	After insertion by physician, can remain in place for up to one or 10 years, depending on type.	Prescription
Periodic Abstinence	About 80% (varies, based on method)	None	None	Requires frequent monitoring of body functions (for example, body temperature for one method).	Instructions from health-care provider

Type	Estimated Effectiveness	Some Risks[d]	Protection from Sexually Transmitted Diseases (STDs)	Convenience	Availability
Surgical Sterilization —female or male	Over 99%	Pain, bleeding, infection, other minor postsurgical complications	None	One-time surgical procedure	Surgery

a Effectiveness rate for polyurethane condoms has not been established.
b Less effective for women who have had a baby because the birth process stretches the vagina and cervix, making it more difficult to achieve a proper fit.
c Based on perfect use, when the woman takes the pill every day as directed.

Infectious diseases can be transmitted by direct contact with surface lesions and by pre-ejaculatory fluid.

Surgical Sterilization

Surgical sterilization is a contraceptive option intended for people who don't want children in the future. It is considered permanent because reversal requires major surgery that is often unsuccessful.

• *Female sterilization.* Female sterilization blocks the fallopian tubes so the egg can't travel to the uterus. Sterilization is done by various surgical techniques performed under general anesthesia.

Complications from these operations are rare and can include infection, hemorrhage, and problems related to the use of general anesthesia.

• *Male sterilization.* This procedure, called a vasectomy, involves sealing, tying or cutting a man's vas deferens, which otherwise would carry the sperm from the testicle to the penis.

Vasectomy involves a quick operation, usually under 30 minutes, with possible minor postsurgical complications, such as bleeding or infection.

Research continues on effective contraceptives that minimize side effects. One important research focus, according to FDA's Rarick, is the development of birth control methods that are both spermicidal and microbicidal to prevent not only pregnancy but also transmission of HIV and other STDs.

Tamar Nordenberg is a staff writer for FDA Consumer.

How Old Is Too Old to Have a Baby?

Fertility technology is advancing at such an astonishing pace that couples who fail to have children in their forties could realistically wait until their sixties to try again

BY JUDITH NEWMAN

TO BECOME A FATHER at 52 is unusual. To become a mother at 52 is to defy nature. Alan and Deirdre, both 52, don't want to let many of their friends and colleagues in on their secret yet, in case something goes wrong. But they are doing everything in their power to have a baby. They have the money, and they have the will. Deirdre, a trim, athletic researcher at a medical school in Connecticut, has three adult children from a previous marriage; Alan, a college English professor, has never had kids. "I always wanted children," he says. "Three years ago, when I found this woman I loved who was my own age, I thought, 'Well, that's one dream I'll have to relinquish.' "

Deirdre had already gone through menopause. By supplying the correct amounts of estrogen and progesterone via hormone therapy, it is relatively easy to make the uterus of a post-menopausal woman hospitable to a fetus. But even then, the chance of a woman Deirdre's age getting pregnant with her own eggs is nonexistent. So doctors suggested the couple consider implanting a donor egg fertilized with Alan's sperm. Egg donation is no longer considered cutting-edge medicine, but using the procedure to impregnate a woman over 50 is. Still,

Alan and Deirdre were overjoyed. "I thought, 'Isn't science great?' " Alan says.

In a few weeks, Machelle Seibel, a reproductive endocrinologist at the Fertility Center of New England, will mix the eggs of a much younger woman with Alan's sperm and introduce the resulting embryos to Deirdre's uterus. Her chances of giving birth will then rocket from less than 1 percent to 50 percent. "I would have considered doing this even if I hadn't remarried," Deirdre says with a lopsided grin. "The idea of having another child at this stage is compelling."

Not that Deirdre and Alan are unaware of the problems of being older parents. They worry about how they'll function with little sleep—"although I needed a lot of sleep even when I was in college," Alan says—and they are concerned that they might not be around to see their child come of age. If Deirdre gets pregnant, they plan to move to the Midwest to be near Alan's four brothers and sisters. "As a hedge against possible early death, we want our child to be surrounded by as much family as possible," Alan says.

Deirdre's three children, all in their twenties, are trying to be supportive. But

they're skeptical. "Independently they came to me and said they thought it would be weird to be their age and have parents in their late seventies," Deirdre says. "But I look at it like this: Our definition of 'family' has expanded. Now there are gay and adoptive and single-parent families who've used assisted technology. So although an 'older-parent family' is what we'll be, it's only one of several variations."

Twenty-two years after the world's first test-tube baby was conceived through in vitro fertilization, science is giving men and women—at least those who can afford the steep medical fees—increasing flexibility to alter the seasons of their lives. Infertility treatments once considered revolutionary are now commonplace: If a man has a low sperm count, sperm cells can be retrieved from a testicle for direct injection into an egg's cytoplasm. If the shell of an egg has hardened because of age, doctors can hatch it in the lab and then implant it on the uterine wall. If a woman has stopped producing eggs, she can avail herself of drugs to induce ovulation, as well as donor eggs or donor embryos. These days, the science of assisted reproductive technology is advancing at such a rapid rate that laboratory researchers say it will soon be medically possible for even a centenarian to give birth. But such tinkering with the biological clock begs a commonsense question: How old is too old to have a baby? And this seemingly straightforward question trickles into a cascade of other questions: How old is too old for parents? For children? For society?

When it comes to treating women for infertility, the American Society for Reproductive Medicine would like to draw its line in the sand at menopause. "Around 50, that's when reproductive processes have physiologically stopped, and therefore the intervention and treatment by physicians should also stop," says Robert Stillman, a former member of the society's board of directors. "Infertility is a medical disorder, affected by the reproductive life span. Just as we wouldn't consider inducing a prepubescent individual to conceive—although we could—we shouldn't induce pregnancy in someone who's gone through menopause."

In recent years, an increasing number of women have chosen to spend more time building a career, or looking for the right mate, before having children. Some have been shocked to belatedly discover there is no denying a fact of nature. Without any scientific intervention, childbearing is out of the question for most women by the time they reach their early forties. Between the ages of 35 and 40, fertility tapers off, and after 43 it pretty much plummets off the cliff. That is because something about the aging process upsets the process of meiosis, the nuclear division of the ovum or sperm in which chromosomes are reduced to half their original number. Sex cells do not divide properly, and there are too many or too few chromosomes in the egg or sperm. For women in their mid-forties, there is a dramatic increase in the risk that their eggs will have the wrong number of chromosomes after ovulation. Hence the difficulty in getting, and staying, pregnant. And unlike a man, whose sperm supply is constantly renewing itself, a woman is born with all the eggs she'll ever have. In fact, ovaries start aging before a woman's birth. A 20-week-old fetus has about 7 million eggs. Eighteen weeks later, at birth, that number has been decimated to less than 2 million. Even though the eggs remain unused throughout childhood, by puberty the egg supply has dropped to 400,000—less than

Double Trouble

Since the advent of in vitro fertilization two decades ago, there has been an explosion in the number of multiple births, particularly among women over 40. Statistics released last September by the Centers for Disease Control reveal a 52 percent increase overall in twin births between 1980 and 1997. Among women between 40 and 44, the increase in the number of twins born was 63 percent, and among women between 45 and 49 it was a staggering 1,000 percent. The ages of the mothers had less effect on the health or survival of the infants than the pregnancy complications generally associated with multiple births. For example, the risk of a very low birth weight is eight times higher for twins than for single births. The ultimate impact of multiple births on the lives of older parents is immeasurable. "Keeping up with two kids instead of one is a real challenge," says Machelle Seibel. "The increase in energy required is exponential rather than additive."

6 percent of what the child started with. By menopause, the egg larder is close to empty.

Even when an older mother manages to get pregnant, she and her baby face additional medical hurdles. With mothers over 35, there is a greater risk of hypertension and diabetes for themselves, and likely a greater risk of juvenile diabetes for the children. A 1995 Swedish study found that women born to mothers age 45 or older had a slightly higher chance of developing breast cancer than women born to younger mothers. Most well known is the increased risk of certain chromosomal abnormalities such as Down's syndrome, in which there is an extra set of genes in each cell.

Studies suggest that being the child of an older father also carries risk. Because older sperm tend to have more chromosomal mutations—ranging in seriousness from harmless to lethal—there is among older fathers a higher rate of kids born with certain rare tumors, neural-tube defects, congenital cataracts, and upper limb defects. Curiously, there's also a higher rate of homosexual children born to older dads.

While men experience some decline in the number of sperm, motility, and morphology—the number of normal sperm—after age 40, it's generally not enough to prevent them from becoming fathers. There are typically 150 to 300 million sperm released in one ejaculation. Even if the number drops by 50 percent, there are still pretty good odds there will be some keepers.

And now, technology has advanced to the point where even men with extremely poor sperm quality can father

children. With intracytoplasmic sperm injection, an embryologist can inject a single sperm into the cytoplasm of an egg with a microscopic needle while bypassing the normal cascade of chemical reactions necessary for fertilization. The procedure, which has only been around since 1992, is a primary reason for the speed-of-light development of fertility treatment for aging would-be parents—because it's not only sperm that can be injected into the egg. The processes of microinjection and micromanipulation of egg and sperm are making a wider array of new treatments possible.

For example, embryologist Jacques Cohen, scientific director at the Institute for Reproductive Medicine and Science of Saint Barnabas in Livingston, New Jersey, has developed a procedure called cytoplasmic transfer that shows promise for assisting women approaching their early forties who either can't get pregnant through in vitro fertilization or have embryos of such poor quality they don't survive. Doctors take the cytoplasm of a youthful and healthy egg—containing not the DNA but the proteins and enzymes for healthy cell growth—and inject it into the problematic egg to boost its quality. Possible health risks with the procedure have not yet been conclusively studied and there are troubling ethical questions. (See box "Can a Baby Have Three Parents?") But out of 26 attempts, the technique has resulted in 12 live births.

Jamie Grifo, director of New York University's reproductive endocrinology unit, is further refining another technique to assist women between 42 and 45, whose chances of having a child with their own eggs hover around 5 per-

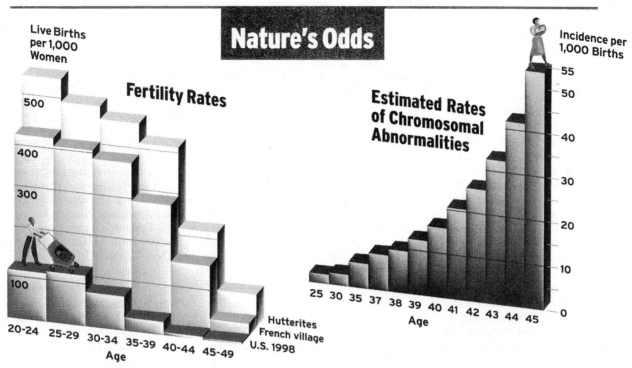

Dale Glasgand

LEFT: Contemporary birth records of the Hutterites, a religious sect in the western U.S. and Canada that does not practice birth control, and seventeenth-century birth records from a French village reveal a similar pattern: Natural fertility rates among women drop off precipitously around age 40. The latest available overall birthrates for U.S. women follow the same downward trend but are lower across the board because of the prevalence of birth control and a tendency of women to marry later in life. RIGHT: Statistics indicate that the risk of women having children with chromosomal abnormalities, including Down's syndrome, rises steadily from 2.1 per thousand births at age 25 to 53.7 per thousand births at age 45.

cent. He takes an older woman's egg and extracts the nucleus, which contains the DNA. Then he removes the nucleus from the donor egg of a much younger woman and in its place microinjects the genetic material of the older woman. The procedure, attempted on two women last year, resulted in fertilized embryos but not babies. Grifo and his team went back to the lab, perfecting the process on mice. The result: baby mice.

Grifo's groundbreaking work could provide the answer women like Alison Carlson are looking for. Carlson is a golden girl: blond, sunny, a former professional tennis coach in San Francisco. When she got married last year to a younger man and started trying to get pregnant at 42, she assumed she'd succeed quickly. "I was an athlete," she says. "I felt the normal rules wouldn't apply to me." At first it seemed she would be right. In her initial round of in vitro fertilization, Carlson produced an impressive 27 eggs, and 25 were fertilized: "I was a champ." She got pregnant but quickly miscarried. Forty-five percent of women over 40 do, usually

because of chromosomal abnormalities in their eggs. "Suddenly I felt like I should buy one of these T-shirts that say 'I Can't Believe I Forgot to Have Children.'" Carlson says that when she tried again, she failed to get pregnant at all.

Intellectuallly, Carlson knows the problem is age, but emotionally she cannot accept it. Like so many men and women over 40 who begin fertility treatments, she feels pressure to keep trying. "I'm embarrassed because, first, I felt I was being so arrogant," she says. "Like, here we all are, a bunch of baby boomers who went to college in the second wave of feminism, dedicated to having important careers before having babies, and then paying gobs of money so science can give us what we want. I'm appalled at my own sense of entitlement."

Given the anguish many aging baby boomers now experience trying to get pregnant, it's hard to fathom that the future holds no less than the end of infertility. Doctors recently discovered how to freeze a woman's eggs when she's young and then thaw them when she's ready to get pregnant. A woman could

finish college and graduate school, launch a career, and then start a family with eggs she parked on ice at age 18.

Banking individual eggs is just the beginning. Recently Kutluk Oktay, the chief of reproductive endocrinology and infertility at New York Methodist Hospital in Brooklyn, has been experimenting with freezing and transplanting swatches of ovarian tissue. Each bit of tissue contains thousands of immature follicle eggs. While individual, already-developed eggs die easily when frozen, immature follicle eggs embedded in the ovarian tissue fare a lot better. Oktay has already tried the technique on a 30-year-old dancer from Arizona who'd had her first ovary removed at 17 because of cysts but had the foresight to have her second ovary frozen. Last fall, Oktay sewed 80 small pieces of the tissue back into her pelvis and revived her menstrual cycle. The woman is not trying to conceive. But Oktay's colleague, Roger Gosden, now reproductive biology research director of McGill University's Royal Victoria Hospital in Montreal, has removed the ovaries of sheep, frozen them, thawed them, sutured them back in the sheep—and gotten lambs aplenty.

Of course cryopreservation will not help those whose eggs are already sitting on the porch in little rocking chairs. But researchers have found ways to keep old eggs alive. Jon Tilly, the director of the Vincent Center for Reproductive Biology at Massachusetts General Hospital in Boston, has been studying genetically altered mice to better understand the process of apoptosis, or natural cell death. Cells are programmed to die: Fifty or sixty genes, maybe more, regulate their expiration. One specifically involved in the death of immature eggs in the ovaries is known as the bax gene. When Tilly and his researchers studied mice that lacked the bax gene, they found that 24-month-old females—the equivalent of 80- to 100-year-old humans—still have functioning, estrogen-producing ovaries. "We were pretty amazed," says Tilly. "And the bax gene has a precise counterpart in humans that appears to be responsible for the decimation of eggs during menopause." Silencing of one of the "cell death" genes may be the first step in finding treatments to help woman delay menopause or avoid the health problems—osteoporosis, heart disease—associated with the cessation of estrogen production. Tilly also believes that in the not-wildly-distant future the ability to suppress the bax gene in women's ovaries may prolong their fertility too. He is quick to add, however, that even though the old female mice with newly viable eggs were allowed to cavort with young, studly mice, they did not produce offspring. This is because older mice lose the capacity to excrete adequate levels of two hormones: one that stimulates egg follicles to grow and mature and another that causes the ripened egg to be released from the ovary into the reproductive tract.

Another approach to ending infertility involves beating the numbers game. What if a woman had an unlimited number of eggs? This may someday be possible if researchers can get somatic cells—that is, cells from anywhere in the body—to act like sex cells. Normal cells are diploid, with 46 chromosomes—23 from one's father and 23 from one's mother. The gonads (testicles and ovaries) divide the chromosomes to create haploid cells, namely spermatozoa and eggs. As the eggs age, most suffer from aneuploidy, the uneven division

Can a Baby Have Three Parents?

One new fertility treatment called cytoplasmic transfer involves taking a younger woman's "egg white," which contains the proteins and enzymes necessary for proper growth, and microinjecting it into the egg of an older woman. The idea is to restore healthy components to the older woman's egg, making fertilization and pregnancy more likely. The problem, says Machelle Seibel, is that mitochondria—tiny football-shaped structures in the cytoplasm that are the energy powerhouses of a cell—also contain some DNA. And scientists know that there are a number of inherited mitochondrial DNA diseases, resulting in health problems that range from the mild to the fatal. (Problems as varied as sudden infant death syndrome and Alzheimer's are thought to stem from genetic defects in the mitochondria.) Theoretically, the young woman giving her cytoplasm becomes the third parent, capable of passing along some genetic information, including her family diseases. "I don't think this component of the procedure is completely appreciated by the providers or the receivers," says Seibel. "Cytoplasmic transfer may be fine, but its safety is unproven. This makes me a little uncomfortable."

of the chromosomes. Anything other than 23 sets of chromosomes makes the egg either entirely unviable, or viable but resulting in abnormalities like Down's syndrome. It is not that the eggs, in their undeveloped state, are abnormal; it's that something about the machinery of meiosis—the chromosomal division at ovulation—goes awry as women age. The key to fixing this problem is to make faux eggs—normal body cells that behave like eggs by undergoing meiosis. Thus, anyone 18 to 100 would have an unlimited supply of easily harvested "sex cells."

This is exactly what Cohen and some other researchers are working on now. Bioethicists balk, because the process sounds like a kissing cousin to cloning. But it's not. The resulting cell has half its mother's chromosomes and, when united with sperm, could be expected to create a bona fide, half-his, half-hers human. The catch is that the parents could theoretically be 100 or more years old. "This is going to involve some major discussions about what's clinically acceptable and what's socially acceptable," Cohen says.

Of course, even if they have all the financial resources in the world, most couples past the age of retirement probably won't want to start raising children. "This won't be some huge public policy issue," says Arthur Caplan, director of the University of Pennsylvania's Center for Bioethics. "It's not like you'll see all these people running from nursing homes to birthing centers." But, Caplan adds, the very fact that 50-year-old

mothers and fathers could become relatively commonplace raises another issue. "One of the ethical questions becomes: What's in the best interest of the child? And the answer is simple: It's good not to be an orphan. A good, loving environment requires one parent. So if a father is 20 and a mother 80, that's not a problem. If the father is 60 and the mother 40, well, one should think about the implications of depriving a child of grandparents. It's not morally reprehensible, but it's an issue. Now, if both parents are in their sixties"—as was the case in 1996 with Arceli Keh, the 63-year-old Filipino who gave birth after lying about her age to her fertility specialists in California—"that's a problem."

Contemplating their own untimely demise won't deter truly determined older parent wanna-bes, like Eileen and Charles Volz of Millbury, Massachusetts. Eileen, a certified public accountant, was 42 and had just married Charles, a digital commerce executive, in 1992 when she was diagnosed with breast cancer. Radiation and chemotherapy put her into immediate menopause, but she overcame the cancer. Four years passed before she and her husband heard about egg donation. "People thought we were a little nuts," says Charles Volz. "I mean, I already had three children, and she had survived breast cancer—why should we tempt fate?"

One look at their son, C.J., answers the question. On her first try at Machelle Seibel's clinic, she got pregnant with a donor egg and had C.J. at 48. "I never for a moment felt he wasn't mine,"

Eileen says. "Genetics is the smallest part of being a mother."

Eileen Volz is now 50; her husband is 48. They tried a second round of egg donation, which failed, but they are contemplating a third. Sure they'll be collecting Social Security by the time C.J. is ready to head off to college. But Charles Volz speaks for older parents everywhere when he offers this Pollyannaish view of his midlife adventure: "It's not a problem at all. Hey, I'm going to live forever."

Perhaps the biggest question for science and society will not be answered for a number of years, until the first generation of children born to older parents through assisted reproductive technology enters their teenage years: What happens when children nature did not intend to create become adults? Already there are some troubling questions about the 20,000 children conceived throughout the world by intracytoplasmic sperm injection. Aggressively injecting a sperm into an egg manually has been found to change a whole sequence of molecular events in fertilization; for example, the DNA packaged in the head of the sperm unravels more slowly than in normal fertilization, throwing off the timing of the process. Scientists worry that although there hasn't been an obvious increase in birth defects so far, sex chromosome abnormalities may show up when the children reach puberty. One 1998 study in Belgium showed that of 1,082 prenatal tests on intracytoplasmic sperm injection pregnancies, one in 120 had sex chromosome abnormalities, as compared to a general population figure of one in 500 pregnancies.

"Fertility is a unique field in some respects," says Massachusetts General's Jon Tilly. "In most fields of scientific inquiry, most of the problems are worked out in animal models. But here, technology is moving so fast, and people are so desperate for answers, that work on humans is paralleling work on animals. That may turn out to be good, because we are accelerating the application of our knowledge. But it may be bad, because we don't know what's safe. We don't know about unforeseen problems. There may be reasons the body is not designed to be reproducing after its early forties."

WHAT MOTHER NATURE TEACHES US ABOUT
Motherhood

By JEFFREY KLUGER

WITH SQUALLING INFANTS in tow, she works back-breaking shifts—as long as 17 hours a day—to feed her growing family. Then she drags herself home, where she is greeted by her equally demanding older children, who expect her to referee their squabbles as they roughhouse and play. When the kids finally fall asleep, she has only a few hours to eat, clean up and grab some shut-eye before the sun rises and she must do it all again.

Typical working mom? No, a wild baboon living on the plains of Kenya. But in ways that are deeper and more resonant than most people realize, female baboons and other nonhuman primates *are* typical working moms. They struggle with the same challenges that human mothers face and work out surprisingly similar solutions. Tamarin mothers in the Amazon Basin rely on aunts and grandmothers to tend the young while the mothers forage for food. Moms and dads among Brazil's titi monkeys take turns minding the kids and bringing home the bacon, just as in any well-adjusted two-income human family.

And it is not just primates whose parenting strategies echo our own. More and more, scientists have come to realize that among creatures as diverse as mice and seals, birds and spiders, mothering is a surprisingly consistent, remarkably familiar business. If there is a Mother's Day message in all this, it's that the more we understand the animals' behavior, the better we can understand our own.

For scientists studying the business of parenting, parting the curtain on the animal world helps explain not only how mothering strategies work but also how they sometimes break down. Confused teens aren't the only mothers who abandon their babies; other mammals do it too. Parents may recoil when a Susan Smith drowns her sons in a South Carolina pond, but scientists routinely observe infanticidal animals—apparently driven by similarly dark demons—committing similarly black acts.

Certainly, not everyone is pleased with this new research. Looking to animals to study something as complex as motherhood, critics say, is little more than anthropology by analogy, relying on the worst kind of scientific reductionism to explain the highest kind of human impulses. But anthropologists view matters differently, seeing in animal and human mothers a striking commonness of purpose—and a striking commonness of grace. "All mothers face similar dilemmas," says anthropologist Sarah Blaffer Hrdy of the University of California at Davis, "no matter what their ambitions or circumstances."

There are few challenges the animal families of Africa or the Amazon face that the Banzer family of Houston, wouldn't understand. Stephanie Banzer, 31, is a marketing manager for Compaq Computers as well as the mother of 19-month-old Matthew. When Stephanie gave birth, she and her husband knew they would need her income to keep the household running. Full-time mothering was thus not an option—and full-time baby-sitters were too expensive. Instead, she turned to a team of child-care providers she knew could do the job: her mother and two aunts. The three older women look after Matthew when Banzer and her husband are at work, returning the toddler well cared for at the end of the day. "These are the women who raised me," Banzer says. "He is in very loving hands."

While the Banzers may think of the work Matthew's grandmother and great-aunts do as mere baby-sitting, anthropologists know it is part of a far more primal practice called alloparenting. In all manner of animals, including bees, elephants, lions, lemurs, bats and birds, creatures with no parental investment in offspring routinely expend enormous amounts of energy caring for their relatives' young. Alloparents are not unconditional caretakers; they won't devote scarce resources to other offspring at the expense of their own. But when conditions allow an alloparenting deal to be made, it's a good bargain all around, with adults protecting their genetic legacy and the infant getting a team of surrogate moms in return. "Babies can learn to be quite satisfied with any of a select group of caretakers," says Hrdy, whose book *Mother Nature* is the most notable and artful of a flock of new studies re-examining motherhood.

Of course, even with a parade of alloparents, offspring will have little chance of reaching maturity if there isn't sufficient food to keep them nourished. In the game of survival, there is nothing more critical than keeping babies' bellies full, and mothers go to great lengths to get the job done. After one type of Australian spider lays her eggs, she lives barely long enough to see her young mature. Then she positions herself among them and slowly liquefies, transforming herself into an edible goo that gives her babies a nutritional kick start in life. The very idea of mammalian metabolism is a subtler case of maternal self-sacrifice. An organism taking in precious calories and then giving them away in the form of milk directly defies the me-first rule of all animal survival, yet mammal mothers do it willingly.

Often animals don't have to go to such nurturing extremes. For all creatures, one key to successful parenting is not merely reproducing but also knowing when not to reproduce—timing births so that the supply of food and other resources stay ahead of the babies to tend.

Heather Knotts, 35, of Chicago, a career mom, walks just this kind of parenting tightrope. Holding down a demanding job in an advertising agency, she works even harder at home, rearing a daughter, 5, and a son, 2. If Knotts and her husband had their way, she would set aside being adwoman and work full time as a mom. That was what they had planned. "After our first child was born, we knew I'd have to keep working," she says, "but we thought it would be for only a couple of years."

Three years after the Knottses had their first child, however, the second came along, and the idea of halving the household income while doubling the number of children it had to support was out of the question. The best Knotts could do was cut her workweek from five days to four, taking herself out of the running for promotions she had coveted but still not getting the round-the-clock time she wants with her kids.

As procreative strategies go, this seems an odd one. If you want to devote yourself exclusively to parenting, it's better to take your reproductive chips off the table after having one child so you can maximize the resources you have to do the job. If you want a multichild family, you'd better make sure that the family bank account is full to bursting.

When it comes to reproduction, though, nothing is quite so easy. Nature abhors deficits and surpluses, and successful parenting often involves spacing births far enough apart so no offspring go hungry but not so far apart that resources go unused. Many mammals nurse a pup or cub or child far longer than necessary because lactation shuts down ovulation and a new pregnancy can be put off until circumstances are right for it. Only when they are will the mother conceive again. "All mother mammals are forced to make the most of the resources available while making trade-offs compatible with their own survival," says Hrdy.

But what happens when this resource-management system breaks down? What if the mother gambles wrong and an offspring comes along when there are no resources to support it, or what if she is too young to care for it? What if the infant is sickly and seems likely to languish no matter how well it's looked after? Humans agonize over these situations, but mothers throughout the animal kingdom show a surprising willingness to abandon or even kill such luckless young rather than pour energy down a bottomless reproductive well.

An American black bear, which normally gives birth to two or three cubs at a time, may walk away from one born alone, calcu-

lating that it's better to wait for a multiple birth next year than exhaust herself with a singleton now. Mice will examine offspring after they're born and eat undersize young, improving the overall fitness of the litter and giving themselves a valuable dose of protein in the process.

Things become truly troubling when human beings facing the same difficult circumstances start making equally brutal choices. Anthropologists report that during a three-year period of social upheaval in Bolivia in the 1930s, nearly every mother in an Ayoreo Indian village committed infanticide at least once. In India and China, selective infanticide of baby girls is still commonly, if quietly, practiced. And while there may be less of a history of such killing in the U.S., periodic cases of high-schoolers secretly giving birth and then murdering their infant are proof that such practices know no cultural boundaries.

If an impulse to commit infanticide is indeed part of our genetic legacy, can it be forgiven? Or does such a crime remain a crime no matter how strong the primal drives behind it? Anthropologists take the long view—at least when the crime is abandonment and not murder. "I think we have to re-examine the harsh penalties we place on young, uneducated women who abandon infants," says anthropologist Helen Fisher of Rutgers University. "They were dancing to primitive, natural rhythms, and they got out of synch."

The problem with such scientific forgiveness is that it may give human beings, with their much celebrated free will, too little credit. Most mothers will love and nurture even an unwanted infant because, well, it seems the right thing to do. Most will stretch their resources to the breaking point in order to have a second child not because that's what their genes drive them to do but because they love having children. Critics of the work of Hrdy and others resist drawing too many parallels between human and animal parents, insisting that the few traits that distinguish us from other species are far more important than the many things we share.

"The argument goes that in the highest primates, 99% of DNA is the same as human DNA," says Lawrence Cunningham, a theologian at the University of Notre Dame. "But what's significant is that 1% difference. It is a kind of moral evolution that takes place within humans."

Surprisingly, many scientists agree. "There's a history in primatology of looking at primate species as if they were models for humans," says evolutionary psychologist Leda Cosmides of the University of California at Santa Barbara. "But that's not really the way to do it, because humans are not baboons or chimps, just as baboons are not chimps or humans."

Just what distinguishes the higher species of primates from the very highest one is not always clear, but one of the most important differences seems to be the delight humans take in challenging their primitive urges—and even flat-out defying them. Hrdy writes that when her children were babies, she often cooed to them nonsensical endearments that were oddly evocative of food. "Sweet potato," "muffin," "cutie-pie," she would call them. "I could eat you up," she'd gush. Why she chose those words to babble, she couldn't say, but after a period of what she calls "Darwinian self-analysis," she realized that she might actually be hearing the echo of some genetic programming buried deep within the carnivorous parts of her brain.

Hrdy, of course, never had any real inclination to consume her children with anything other than affection. In fact, she became consumed *by* them—by their needs, by their demands, by her own impulse to protect them. In human mothers—indeed, in all animal mothers—there has always been tension between much that is sublimely good and at least a few things that aren't so good. It is humans alone, however, who have the ability to contemplate those choices—and then know which ones to make.

—Reported by Dan Cray/Los Angeles, Unmesh Kher/New York and Maggie Sieger/Chicago

Pregnant *pleasures*

Your sex life will change . . . maybe for the better.

BY CAREN OSTEN GERSZBERG

The question of whether a woman is sexy during pregnancy was never debated on CNN—until actress Hunter Tylo sued the makers of *Melrose Place* for pregnancy discrimination last year. The actress had been fired after becoming pregnant; the producers felt that she couldn't realistically play the role of a seductress (even if her belly was hidden from view). A jury of ten women and two men sided with Tylo, awarding her almost $5 million.

Although Tylo felt confident about the fact that she was as alluring as ever, it's hard for most pregnant women to feel like sex symbols. Plagued by fatigue and morning sickness in her first trimester, Trish Ratliff, of Fort Eustis, Virginia, for example, says that making love was the last thing on her mind. She also had visible stretch marks on her breasts, hips, and thighs, which made her feel self-conscious about her body. On the other hand, Laurie Greenberg, of New York City, was surprised to find that she constantly seemed to be in the mood. Everything seems to take on a new shape during pregnancy—your body, your future, and, inevitably, your sex drive.

It would be remarkable, in fact, if pregnancy had no effect on sexual desire, because your libido is linked to both the physical and emotional changes you're experiencing, notes Christiane Northrup, M.D, assistant clinical professor of obstetrics and gynecology at the University of Vermont, in Burlington. In a normal pregnancy, sexual intercourse is safe and healthy right until the very end, even in a slightly modified version of the man on top. Many women actually find that it's the most enjoyable sex

they've ever had, according to Northrup, who is the author of *Women's Bodies, Women's Wisdom* (Bantam).

For many expectant mothers, pregnancy is a rare opportunity to have spontaneous sex. "It's very exciting not having to worry about birth control or trying to get pregnant," says Lee Dannay, of New York City. "Without either concern, I can just relax and enjoy the moment."

When your partner takes delight in your changing appearance, it can help alleviate anxiety you may feel about your burgeoning body. Once her morning sickness subsided, Trish Ratliff liked the way her husband watched her as she dressed or undressed. "He wanted to make love as much as he always had, and he particularly loved touching my breasts, because they were twice as big as they used to be."

Laurie Greenberg's husband, Ira, however, admitted that he was less turned on, even though he responded whenever she initiated lovemaking. "It didn't really bother me," says Laurie, "because the thought of a beautiful baby growing inside of me made me feel very good about my body."

Of course, in addition to raising emotional issues in bed, your changing shape also poses physical ones. Nausea can make any sexual position uncomfortable if pressure is placed on your abdomen. And your size may keep you from feeling either agile or alluring.

However, sexual desire returns to normal for most women during the middle trimester, when their bodies have adjusted to pregnancy and size isn't a major obstacle. In fact, increased blood flow to the pelvic area caused by hormonal changes can produce a heightened sensitivity, explains Northrup, allowing

some pregnant women to experience orgasm more easily and more frequently—or maybe even for the first time in their life.

Don't worry—you won't hurt the baby

Both of you may be concerned that intercourse could harm the baby, but it is well protected by the amniotic sac and the mucous plug, which blocks the cervix and guards against infection. Some couples even have the irrational notion that the baby seems to be "watching" them.

As your pregnancy progresses, you may have to experiment with different positions. Some doctors suggest having vaginal intercourse facing each other side by side, or in the spooning position, in which your partner lies behind you; this prevents excess pressure from being placed on your belly.

"Positions that might be dangerous are going to be very uncomfortable," says Linda Hughey Holt, M.D., director of the Institute for Women's Health at Evanston Northwestern Healthcare, in Evanston, Illinois, and coauthor of *The Pregnancy Book* (Little, Brown & Co.). "A woman in her ninth month, for example, shouldn't lie with her full weight on her belly, but she wouldn't be able to anyway." Similarly, a man should use his arms to support himself when he's lying on top.

Sex has been shown to speed up labor only when a woman is at term or past her due date. In normal pregnancies, there is no direct link between intercourse earlier on and the start of labor. Sometimes, however, a doctor may rec-

Too embarrassed to ask your doctor?

Q: Sometimes urine trickles out during sex. Is this normal?
A: Yes. This can happen during intercourse if there's pressure put on your belly. The muscles in the bladder also tend to relax during pregnancy, causing small amounts of urine to leak in some women when they laugh, cough, or sneeze.

Q: Is it okay for my partner to perform oral sex on me?
A: Generally, yes. In very rare instances, forcefully blowing air into the vagina can cause an amniotic fluid embolism—air enters the uterus and forces amniotic fluid into the mother's circulatory system—which could be fatal to both mother and baby.

Q: Why do my breasts leak when my husband touches them?

A: When the nipples are stimulated during the last weeks of pregnancy, they may leak colostrum, a protein-filled liquid produced for the baby before the milk comes in. (Nipple stimulation also can cause the uterus to contract, but there's no reason to avoid it in a healthy pregnancy.)

Q: In my last pregnancy, I was overdue, and having sex finally started my labor. I'm worried that sex may cause me to go into labor early this time. Is that possible?
A: Although sexual intercourse can trigger uterine contractions that may lead to labor, it's not a cause of premature labor. However, if you are at risk for preterm labor because of a prior history, if you're carrying twins, or if your cervix has started to dilate, your doctor may suggest that you abstain.

ommend limiting or abstaining from sex after a certain point if you have a prior history of early contractions or preterm labor, since nipple stimulation and orgasm may trigger contractions. Sex also should be avoided by women who have placenta previa, a condition in which the placenta covers the cervix.

If you've had a prior miscarriage, your doctor may suggest abstaining from sex during the first trimester, just to be on the safe side. Although there is no causal connection between intercourse and miscarriage, it's possible that your uterus may be especially sensitive. Lynn Gallop, of Wilmington, North Carolina, had six first-trimester miscarriages before getting pregnant with her son, Jack. "My doctor told us we could start having sex after four months, but I was always too scared," she says. If you notice any spotting or bleeding, have pain during intercourse, or if your water breaks, stop having sex immediately and call your doctor.

This is also the perfect time to experiment with alternative ways to express your affection, from foot rubs to taking baths together. Your comfort level—both physical and emotional—should determine how often you have sex and when. Whether it's a question of general anxiety or a specific technique, communication is the best way for you and your partner to maintain a healthy sex life. "Once I explained to my husband that my nipples were very sensitive but I still enjoyed it when he touched the rest of my breast, he changed his technique, and it felt good," says Ratliff. And if the two of you can talk openly about your sex life now, you'll also feel more comfortable discussing it after the baby arrives.

Caren Osten Gerszberg is a freelance writer in Larchmont, New York.

Unit Selections

Key Points to Consider

❖ Do you remember trying to get answers about your body, sex, or similar topics as a young child? How did your parents respond? How did you feel? Do you hope your children will ask you questions about sex? Why or why not? Which topics or questions do you expect will be hardest for you to handle and answer?

❖ Would you like to be a junior or senior high school–aged young person today? Why or why not? In what ways is being a young teen easier than when you were that age? How is it more difficult? In what ways is being a young male different? A young female? A young person discovering that she or he is not heterosexual?

❖ How do you view sex and sexuality at your age? In what ways is it different from when you were younger? How do you perceive the changes—positively, negatively, not sure—and to what do you attribute them? Are there things you feel you have missed? What are they?

❖ Close your eyes and imagine a couple having a pleasurable sexual interlude. When you are finished, open your eyes. How old were they? If they were younger than middle age, can you replay your vision with middle-aged or older people? Why or why not? How does this relate to your expectations regarding your own romantic and/or sexual life a few decades from now?

❖ Do you ever think about your parents as sexual people? Your grandparents? Was considering these two questions upsetting for you? Embarrassing? Explain your answers as best you can.

 **Links** **www.dushkin.com/online/**

These sites are annotated on pages 4 and 5.

Individual sexual development is a lifelong process that begins at birth and terminates at death. Contrary to popular notions of this process, there are no latent periods during which the individual is nonsexual or noncognizant of sexuality. The growing process of a sexual being does, however, reveal qualitative differences through various life stages. This section devotes attention to these stages of the life cycle and their relation to sexuality.

As children gain self-awareness, they naturally explore their own bodies, masturbate, display curiosity about the bodies of the opposite sex, and show interest in the bodies of mature individuals such as their parents. Exploration and curiosity are important and healthy aspects of human development. Yet it is often difficult for adults (who live in a society that is not comfortable with sexuality in general) to avoid making their children feel ashamed of being sexual or showing interest in sexuality. When adults impose their ambivalence upon a child's innocuous explorations into sexuality, fail to communicate with children about this real and important aspect of human life, or behave toward children in sexually inappropriate ways, distortion of an indispensable and formative stage of development occurs. This often leaves profound emotional scars that hinder full acceptance of self and sexuality later in the child's life.

Adolescence, the social stage accompanying puberty and the transition to adulthood, proves to be a very stressful period of life for many individuals as they attempt to develop an adult identity and forge relationships with others. Because of the physiological capacity of adolescents for reproduction, sexuality tends to be heavily censured by parents and society at this stage of life. Societal messages, however, are powerful, conflicting, and confusing: "Just Say No" . . . "Just Do It"; billboards and magazine ads using adolescent bodies provocatively and partially undressed; "romance" novels, television shows, movies with torrid sex scenes; and Internet chat rooms. In addition, individual and societal attitudes place tremendous emphasis on sexual attractiveness (especially for females) and sexual competency (especially for males). These physical, emotional, and cultural pressures combine to create confusion and anxiety in adolescents and young adults about whether they are okay and normal. Information and assurances from adults can alleviate these stresses and facilitate positive and responsible sexual maturity if there is mutual trust and willingness in both generations.

Sexuality finally becomes socially acceptable in adulthood, at least within marriage. Yet routine, boredom, stress, pressures, the pace of life, work or parenting responsibilities, and/or lack of communication can exact heavy tolls on the quantity and quality of sexual interaction. Sexual misinformation, myths, and unanswered questions, especially about emotional and/or physiological changes in sexual arousal/response or functioning, can also undermine or hinder intimacy and sexual interaction in the middle years.

Sexuality in the later years of life has also been socially and culturally stigmatized because of the prevailing misconception that only young, attractive, or married people are sexual. Such an attitude has contributed significantly to the apparent decline in sexual interest and activity as one grows older. As population demographics have shifted and the baby boomer generation has aged, these beliefs and attitudes have begun to change. Physiological changes in the aging process are not, in and of themselves, detrimental to sexual expression. A life history of experiences, good health, and growth can make sexual expression in the later years a most rewarding and fulfilling experience, and today's aging population is becoming more vocal in letting their children and grandchildren know that as we age we don't grow out of sex, but that, in fact, like fine wine, it can get better with age.

The opening article "Sexuality and Young Children" matter-of-factly explains that babies and young children are sexual beings while helping parents and other caregivers understand normal versus cause-for-concern behaviors. The next two articles focus on sex education for youth in their schools in Taiwan and the United States. Although it seems that children are more alike than different with respect to their reactions, interest, questions, and so forth, despite being a half a world apart. Taiwan has a comprehensive and mandatory program the likes of which few American children receive. The final article in this subsection focuses on a special population of youth—gay, lesbian, and bisexual adolescents—that is becoming increasingly open and acknowledged in our society and schools and, thereby, "Teaching Schools a Lesson."

The article in the "Sexuality in the Adult Years" subsections looks realistically at lifelong sexuality and sexual satisfaction as natural, desirable, but, at times, hard to manage life goals in today's world. "Married With Children" confronts the age-old dilemma faced by parents of young children—not having enough time or energy to have sex as often as they would like, but still wanting to maintain their intimacy and connection. It offers a wealth of expert advice and real-life experiences designed to help anyone, regardless of age or the particular dilemma facing them, to increase their capacity for a full, healthy, and satisfying sex life for each and every decade of their lives.

Sexuality Through the Life Cycle

Understanding Normal Sexual Behavior

Sexuality and Young Children

by Alice Sterling Honig

nfants and young children are very sensual creatures. Carry a baby in arms and he may happily lean down and lick your salty arm. Croon sweet nothings lovingly as you change a young toddler's diaper, and as you clean his skin gently, he may well thrust his legs orgiastically and joyfully in response to intimate and tender ministration. Babies have passionate feelings. They suck greedily, drool, lick, squeeze, bang, listen to lullabies, and respond with relaxation to massage and loving touch.

Sexuality is part of a young child's sensual repertoire. Directors need to know what kinds of sexual behaviors are normal to observe in child care and what sexual behaviors should raise concerns so that plans for addressing those concerns can be made with teachers and parents.

Dr. Alice Sterling Honig, professor emerita of child development at Syracuse University, is the author of numerous books and articles on infancy, child care, prosocial behavior, language development, and parenting in different cultures. Annually in June, she conducts QIC—a one-week quality infant/toddler caregiving workshop. Her most recent books are *Behavioral Guidance for Infants and Toddlers* and (with H. Brophy) *Talking With Your Baby: Family As the First School.*

Normal Aspects of Sexuality in the Early Years

Masturbation is very normal in infants and young children. As soon as a caregiver takes off a diaper, many boys poke and pull at their penis. Little girls may pat their vulva and even confide to a beloved caregiver, "This is my best feeling part."

When young children are given correct body part names, they are more likely to use them very matter of factly. For example, an older toddler, having been put down for a nap, climbed out of her crib and marched into the room where the adults were quietly preparing for afternoon activities. "I hurt my 'gina climbin' out of the crib," she announced indignantly. The caregiver reassured her, reminded her that it was nap time, and carried her gently and firmly back to her crib.

When children hear correct names for body parts, they will be direct and not secretive about sexual parts. Bath time is a fine time to label every part of the body as one washes a young child. Penis, scrotum, vulva, vagina, nipples, anus—these are good clear words to use. Calling a penis a *faucet* or *tinkle* gives a young child the feeling that although ears and hands can be correctly labeled there is something not okay about sexual parts.

When does masturbation normally occur in the classroom? When preschoolers or kindergarten children are trying hard to concentrate on a long story, they may well put their hands inside their pants and pat their genitals. Somehow this gesture soothes the child and even helps him or her concentrate more attentively on the teacher's reading of the story! Such behaviors are entirely normal.

Nap time is another time when patting of genitals under the covers helps some children relax. Tugging on labia or rubbing one's penis seems to relieve stress and tension and may help a child settle into sleep more easily. Teachers need to think of occasional masturbation as a form of self-soothing, albeit a sexual form, that little ones use to help themselves relax into sleep.

When is masturbation worrisome? If a child masturbates constantly in the child care facility, this is a strong sign of tension and worry. This can happen when a child comes into a new care environment and temperamentally has a difficult adjustment time. One young toddler had moved several thousand miles when his mom left his father abruptly and moved back home with Grandma. Placed in center care, he firmly kept one hand inside his pants on his penis; the thumb of the other hand remained firmly in his mouth. After a couple of months, he gained enough trust to free up his hands to play with toys and play dough and to climb the slide on the playground.

When teachers build basic trust, a child is less likely to hang onto genital patting and thumb sucking as if they are desperate lifelines to security. Tolerance and low-key acceptance are teacher techniques that reveal their empathy for a tense child who is bewildered by too many changes and losses in life.

When masturbation is compulsive and frenzied and does not seem to bring relief of tension, this may well reflect abuse or maltreatment in the child's home life. Unremitting masturbation is a way for the child to try to relieve his or her own tension and a way to reenact traumatic sexual episodes. A second-grade youngster would stand on the table in the classroom, take out his penis, and masturbate while staring at the teacher. This child was in foster care. His biological father had made him witness and participate in sexual abuse of this younger sister. The child's behavior was disturbed.

Compulsive and obsessive sex behaviors need urgent attention from a mental health professional. Other compulsive sexual behaviors may include furtively asking other preschoolers daily to take down their pants and show off their genitals. Be sure that in your care facility children do toilet together in groups so that quite casually they become knowledgeable about the fact that boys have a penis and girls have a vulva.

When sexual differences are kept strictly secret for the first years, a five year old can be quite traumatized, for example, by inadvertently seeing a little girl sitting on a toilet. Once such child ran screaming to report, "Teacher, teacher, Denise lost her weewee!" Children are indeed curious. They may want to *see* the differences between boys and girls. But after noticing that there are only two sexes with much the same equipment for each person of the same sex, they will go on to become curious about other things such as bellybuttons, how toes wiggle, and how toys work.

Fanciful sexual ideas. Many young children have hazy ideas about science and how bodies work. their mistaken beliefs lead them occasionally to express bizarre ideas that do not reflect worrisome sexual abuse but simply a strong imagination. One five year old, when his new baby sister was born, watched his dad give the baby a bottle. Then he cheerfully informed his parents that he too could feed the baby. He could give her pretend milk from his penis! Since he was used to seeing liquid come out of his penis during toileting, he figured he could have milk come out, too, and thus feed his new little sister. The parents simply nodded and did not respond with anger or tension to this creative offer. The child made no further comments of this nature. There was no reason to suspect premature knowledge of some adult sexual practices. A director's calmness and awareness of the child's current circumstances boosts his or her ability to handle such an episode.

Inappropriately Mature Sexual Knowledge: A Danger Sign

Exposure to explicit adult sexuality in toddlerhood or early childhood can lead children to discuss intimate details of intercourse or oral or anal relations far beyond the knowledge that they need to have in early childhood. A parent who was having illicit sexual relations on the couch during the day while the toddler was fully present felt that there was no risk since the toddler "could not talk much yet." If a child is disturbed or frightened by uninterpretable adult sexual behaviors and vocalizations, you may see acting out behaviors in the classroom. These could include trying to reproduce intercourse actions in a play situation away from where the teacher is looking. Such a case would have to be handled quite judiciously.

At a parent meeting, you will want to talk easily about how important it is for parents (even when toddlers have limited vocabulary) to be careful not to use scatological words or engage openly in sexual actions that can bewilder or even scare children.

Sometimes preschoolers act out their anguish at loss or physical violence in the home by inappropriate sexual touching or actions. One preschooler had just lost her beloved grandfather, the only male figure in her life. She took children into the closet to "hump" them, as she called it. This behavior was her response to loss and upset feelings, rather than a compulsive reenactment of sexual behaviors experienced at home. Each case needs to be judged individually by the teachers and by the director.

What Should Teachers Tell Children About Sexuality?

Children need to know the names of all their body parts. They also need to know that their sexual parts belong to them. These are their private parts. Nobody except a parent, a doctor, a nurse, or a trusted caregiver may touch their private parts.

Be sure that your caregivers are *askable* adults. One six year old confided that his older stepbrothers were sticking pebbles into his anus. He was even too scared to tell his father, whose girlfriend's sons were responsible for the actions. Nobody should be allowed to hurt anyone in your classrooms. So if an episode of inappropriate behavior occurs, this rule of *no hurting* can be firmly invoked without exploding in anger because the particular aggression involved sexual body parts.

Another kindergarten-age child confided to her teacher that some boys did not have a penis and that a girl could have a penis. It turned out that the child had seen a boy sitting on the toilet with his penis so tucked between his legs that the girl thought he had no penis. Staff need to be cheerfully clear and matter of fact with young children about the anatomical differences between a little boy and a little girl.

Many published materials can be very helpful. Directors should provide staff with books to read in class, such as Gordon's (1983) book *Girls Are Girls and Boys Are Boys: So What's the Difference?* Other useful materials for staff reading are suggested in the "References."

Teach Staff About Sexual Identity and Gender Role

When planning curricular workshops on block building or children's temperament styles, be sure to include a workshop on young children and sexuality. Help your staff learn some of the basic terminology. For example, the term *sexual identity* refers to the biological reproductive patterns of a person's behavior. *Gender identity* is the self-awareness and acceptance of being either a female or a male. *Gender role* refers to a person's acceptance and adoption of behaviors socially defined as belonging to one sex or the other (Honig, in press). Thus, "a little boy may know that he is a boy, and feel comfortable about it, but still enjoy some activities such as playing house or pretending to nurse a doll tenderly" (Honig, 1983, p. 58). A little girl may love to climb trees and dream of becoming a tractor driver but be very glad she is a girl.

Teachers can tell children that some children are boys; some are girls. Social reasoning is facilitated by knowing the two categories of persons. Maccoby (1990) has even suggested that it is possible that single sex play groups, so typical from about five to ten years old, may occur because children strive to get more cognitive clarity regarding which group they belong to.

Conclusions

Young children show behaviors that indicate awareness of sexual organs and pleasuring very early. Some of these behaviors are quite normal developmentally and are part of young children's passionate curiosity about their bodies, their caregivers, and their world. Other sexualized behaviors reflect exposure to violence and possibly to adult sexuality or sexual abuse. Directors will need to make careful decisions about how to handle each concern that teachers bring to them. Calm acceptance that children are curious and sensual creatures and good adult observation skills to be alert to signs of sexual or other abuse will make staff feel confident and at ease in responding to young children's sexuality as well as all other aspects of their personhood.

References

Brooks-Gunn, J., & Matthews, W. S. (1979). *He and she: How children develop their sex-role identity.* Englewood Cliffs, NJ: Prentice Hall.

Child Study Association of America (1970). *What to tell your children about sex.* New York: Simon & Schuster.

Golombok, S., & Fivush, R. (1994). *Gender development.* New York: Cambridge University Press.

Gordon, S. (1983). *Girls are girls and boys are boys: So what's the difference?* Fayetteville, NY: Ed-U Press.

Honig, A. S. (1983). Research in review: Sex role socialization in young children. *Young Children, 38,* 57–70.

Honig, A. S. (1998). Sociocultural influences on sexual meanings embedded in playful experiences. In D. P. Fromberg & D. Bergen (Eds.), *Play from birth to twelve and beyond: Contents, perspectives, and meanings* (pp. 338–347). New York: Garland Press.

Honig, A. S. (in press). Psychosexual development in infants and young children: Implications for caregivers. *Young Children.*

Maccoby, E. E. (1990). Gender and relationships: A developmental account. *American Psychologist, 45,* 513–520.

Sex in School?
It's Required!
Sex Education Comes
to Taiwan

Is *"intercourse" the be-all and end-all of youth sex? Of course not. Sex education, guided by the principle of "accepting yourself and understanding the opposite sex," is being strongly promoted on campuses at all levels of education in Taiwan. What is its content? And how effective is it?*

Just waking up from their lunch-time siestas, fifth-grade girls at the Minchuan Primary School in Taipei City follow their teachers to the audiovisual room. Today, the topic in health class is "growing up with confidence."

The film begins. The cartoon figure of a naked girl appears on the screen, and she begins to grow. Her breasts enlarge, her thin waist grows into hips, and she begins to sprout pubic hair. The girls begin to giggle and laugh, as if they're looking at some kind of freak show. Then the cartoon boy begins to grow, his Adam's apple protrudes, and he grows facial and pubic hair. Finally, when his penis becomes erect and ejaculates sperm, the screams and laughter of the girls reach such a pitch that the room is shaking. Many girls cover their eyes, and shouts of "Disgusting!" and "What the heck is this?!" fill the air.

The most welcome
"shock education"

Don't misunderstand, this isn't a showing of a pornographic film. This is the school helping children who are about to enter puberty. The school has asked a nurse from a sanitary napkin company to come to the school to instruct fifth-grade girls in understanding the changes they and their male classmates are soon to experience, and how to handle menstruation.

Judy Hsiao, a professional affairs representative for Proctor and Gamble who is giving the class, says that less than two years ago, this type of "shock education" could only be shown to students in middle school or above. However, since nutrition these days is much better, children mature faster. They experience menstruation and nocturnal emissions at an earlier age. Thus in the past two years the audience for this type of class has been extended to include fifth-grade students. The lecture ended, the teacher gives out beautifully printed health handbooks, as well as sanitary napkins for the girls to try. Because this type of class is sorely needed in schools, Hsiao is busy all year-round. She has given more than 200 classes in primary schools around northern Taiwan.

It is the same week, and male and female students at the Affiliated Senior High School of National Taiwan Normal University (NTNU) enter the main lecture hall in groups of two or three. The theme of today's lecture—sponsored by a condom company in cooperation with the Mercy Memorial Foundation—is "safe sex." This is the first such lecture at the school, and students are participating voluntarily during weekend "extracurricular activity" period.

After a brief five-minute play, the main speaker, Wang Jui-chi, a lecturer from the Mercy Memorial Foundation, broaches the main topic: "Students, if you keep a condom in the pocket of a pair of tight-fitting jeans, what will happen?" Students shout guesses in reply: "It will become misshapen!" "It will break!" "Someone will get pregnant!"

"Do boys have to be like the guys in porn movies and keep going strong for 30 minutes in order to be considered real men? How is it that porn stars can be so 'virile'?" Again there are answers:

"Because they don't insert in the first place!" "Because the scenes are shot separately and spliced together!" "It's computer animation!" "Because these guys are just doing a job, and are so numb to what they are doing they can't 'finish it off!'"

Amidst the sounds of laughter the lecture ends. Then, several upright models of erect penises are placed on a table for the students to try putting condoms on. Girls who have never seen one before cover their mouths and giggle. Boys on the other hand rush to take their turn. Off to one side you can hear the instructor's voice of caution: "Don't underestimate the knowledge required to use condoms. Last time there was one studly guy who put the condom on inside out!"

Between repression and
licentiousness

Many parents still refer to children's sexual organs as "the little chickie" or "younger sister." They say things like "children come from their mummy's belly-button" or "it's better to die than lose your virginity." It is with such euphemisms and outdated views that they (mis)guide their children.

Meanwhile, in schools at all levels, these obstacles to open discussion are being transcended and sex education is being strongly promoted. Through various channels, topics covering everything from the use of condoms and sanitary napkins to reproductive biology, sexual psychology, and sexual attitudes (including gender identity, sexual morality, and so on) are being introduced onto the campus. These subjects are being discussed openly in the halls of knowledge, and questions are being asked and answered frankly and freely.

For millennia, parents and teachers have seen sexual knowledge as "forbidden fruit." They have been deeply afraid that once their children know about sex, they will become over-stimulated and seek to try it. Are such worries exaggerated? It is clear that different people and schools have very different answers to this question.

When asked whether she would really like to have a boyfriend and try sex, a girl who had just witnessed the condom lecture at NTNU Affiliated High School said decisively: "Definitely not. I don't want to consider anything like that until after I pass the university entrance exam." At another school where a similar class had been arranged, the guidance director stated that the school asked teachers to urge students "in need"—i.e. those who already had friends of the opposite sex—to go to the lecture, "because they would be much more likely to need this knowledge."

Edwin Yen was a pioneer who was studying and promoting sex education for schoolchildren as long as 20 years ago; he is now director of the Health Education Department at NTNU and executive director of the Mercy Memorial Foundation. He points out that in the past the education system was conservative. Sex was considered to be dirty and vulgar, not worthy of the halls of knowledge. Children were left to find out for themselves as best they could.

Fortunately, over the past ten years or so, society has opened up considerably and the barriers to sex education have been greatly reduced. On the other hand, sex education faces a new and even stronger challenge: The market is filled with ridiculous distortions about sex, with unrestrained sexual activity being encouraged in sexual publications, pornographic programs on cable TV, reporting of sex scandals in the news media, and encouragement of sexual liberation by some feminists.

Today, the goal is to keep children from being affected by the two extremes of repressed desire or ignorant promiscuity, and to help them establish correct sexual attitudes as early as possible. Thus the Ministry of Education has begun to promote sex education in schools under the name of "sex and gender equality education." It has been discussed and seminars have been held continually at schools at all levels. Sexual education has gone from being a taboo subject on campuses to being one of the most prominent aspects of educational reform.

Accept yourself, appreciate others

In that case, what exactly is being taught in sex education?

Ho Chin-tsai, who is a member of the Ministry of Education committee in charge of promoting sex education, describes its guiding principles: "Sex education begins from understanding and appreciating one's own body, and progresses to appreciating the opposite sex with which one interacts. In addition, it encourages understanding and tolerance of oneself and others, and of different modes of sexual expression and sexual values in society."

Take "understanding one's own body." Judy Hsiao says, for example, that you should not assume that everyone knows about sexual biology just by experiencing it. Didn't people in the past just muddle their way through in growing up regardless of whether they were taught or not? In September of this year, just after schools reopened, she heard the following tale about one girl in a primary school in Taipei County experiencing her first menstrual cycle.

This fifth-grade girl took sick leave for a week. When her teacher went to visit her, the girl cried despondently, "I can't stop bleeding. I'll probably die!" It turns out that the girl's parents were divorced, and her single parent father was busy working, and had no time or energy to look after his daughter during this fearful and embarrassing time.

Differences in nutrition and inheritance mean that some children grow up more quickly or more slowly than others. Children at that age most fear falling behind others. Middle-school girls worry greatly that they are "washboards" (flat chested), and are too embarrassed to broach the subject of buying a bra with their moms. Boys fear that they are not "hung" enough. Ignorant as they are, they take totally unrelated things like the size of their noses as the basis for comparison of their "manhood." The sense of inferiority of slight and short boys can become so serious that it becomes a learning impediment.

"These types of worries that arise from individual differences must be dealt with through correct education. Moreover, children must be encouraged to improve and develop themselves through sports and nutrition, so that they can have confidence that they are in charge of their own bodies," says Chung Chu-chen, a volunteer lecturer at the Hsinchu family services center, who has had a great deal of experience in education.

Nocturnal emissions and masturbation

Another point to consider is that, seeing as puberty is "mating season," young people are especially sensitive about their appearances or any dissimilarities with other kids. Many things that in the eyes of adults may be trivial can deeply affect a child's self-respect and self-confidence.

Chou Li-yu, principal of the Wanfang Middle School, relates that once a boy sent her a letter asking that he be permitted not to wear the summer uniform (with short pants) because he had especially hairy legs. Also, many young girls who develop quickly, in order to hide their all-too-noticeable breasts, wear their winter school jackets all year round, even in the worst summer heat. This is why Chou, who deeply understands the concerns of young people in their early teens, has never made seasonal uniform changes compulsory.

Another common phenomenon which young guys worry about is nocturnal emissions. The testicles mature during early puberty, and begin to manufacture sperm. If it is not released, it will spill out when it reaches a certain saturation level. Though this is completely normal, many people in Taiwan have tremendous misconceptions. There are giant advertisements in the newspapers, using sinister or frightening language, offering "cures" for so-called "loss of control at the sperm gate" or "leaking of essence." Even many adults spend lots of time and money trying to compensate for a so-called "kidney deficiency" that is connected to ejaculation (the kidneys are supposed to govern sexual activity). If no one explains things to children, they can easily jump to wild surmises on their own.

Masturbation is another important element of sex education for boys in puberty. Just as there is unfounded fear of "kidney deficiency" with nocturnal emissions, many boys who play the "forbidden game" worry that they may be "sex-crazed." And since masturbation is ordinarily accompanied by sexual fantasizing—perhaps about girl classmates or even one's own sisters—boys can suffer from feelings of guilt.

"In fact, masturbation is the best way of taking care of the onrush of sexual desire in puberty. So long as children do not become obsessed, parents don't need to interfere," says Chiang Han-sun, head of the Department of Urology at Taipei Medical College and a director of the Chinese Association of Sexuality Education.

It should be noted, however, that masturbation is not exclusively an issue for teens. Children from age 3 to 6 commonly play with their own reproductive organs. Sadly, many adults who don't understand that this is normal will, as soon as they see a child doing this, beat them or tie their hands. There have even been nursery schools which have forced children to strip and "show the class" in order to humiliate them into stopping. "This type of violent and repressive technique, though it may prevent the behavior for a short time, could very well lead to all kinds of sexual problems for that person in the future," says Chiang.

Studies abroad suggest that adult sexual problems such as exposure, fetishes, impotence, or premature ejaculation are all related to repression of sexuality in early childhood. Sufferers of these problems find it impossible to have normal adult sexual relationships, which leads to a terrible loss of happiness over their entire lives.

Don't test the high notes

Besides the understanding and acceptance of one's own body, sexual education also emphasizes understanding and respecting the opposite sex. Take for example menstruation. Judy Hsiao points out that many girls feel ill at ease about menstruation, mainly because they fear being laughed at by their male classmates. She has seen cases in which co-ed classes have been taken to lectures on sanitary-napkin use, and the boys protest: "These things that girls use are disgusting. Why do we have to look at them?"

When she runs across such situations, Hsiao always asks: "Is your mother not a girl? How about your future wife? Is it possible you don't love them, and don't want to understand their needs?"

Chou Li-yu says: "Sex ed need not always be about sexual relations between boys and girls. It can in fact be related to things that are very much a part of the daily routine." For example, she says, everyone agrees that girls having their periods can be excused from gym class. By the same token, music teachers can try to understand the problems of boys who are at the age when their voices begin to break, and not test them on singing songs that have high notes or may harm their voices. This would be an excellent "sex education" model.

Of course, the foundation of sex education is still sexual behavior, because puberty is after all a time when young people begin to seek out partners. At what age and under what conditions should children be allowed to engage in

sexual activity? This is the problem that most concerns parents.

According to a 1996 survey by the Taiwan Provincial Family Planning Center, 8.5% of high school students had engaged in sexual behavior. Although current sex education does not directly touch on sexual behavior, two of the main points are contraception and prevention of sexually transmitted disease. Thus there are now lectures on condom use in high schools.

Assault and identity

There's also the problem of sexual assault. Since the passage of the new sexual assault prevention law last year, middle and primary schools have been required to devote four class hours per academic year to instructing children in preventing sexually related crimes. Many schools have begun self-defense classes, and put on little anti-kidnapping dramas such as "Little Red Riding Hood and the Big Bad Wolf." The problem is that this is a rather unusual angle from which to approach relations between the sexes, especially since children are being taught how to fight off the opposite sex even before they have learned how to get along with them. Although for various reasons these classes were considered urgent, there is some concern that they may have bad side effects.

Edwin Yen explains that "sexual assault prevention education is essential," in light of the large number of sexual assault cases (including incestuous rape) in Taiwan. While all children are taught self-defense, boys are also taught how to give release to their growing desire and how to avoid using sex as a weapon to hurt others as a way of venting the frustrations of daily life. These all fall within the scope of sex education.

Looking farther down the road, to cope with an increasingly open and pluralistic society, sex education should also include acceptance and understanding of "non-mainstream" sexual expression. Homosexuality is one example. Unfortunately, little research has been done in Taiwan on this subject, and there are few ready-made teaching materials for teachers to use in class.

Su Chien-ling, a board member of the Awakening Foundation, points out that "sissy" boys and "tomboy" girls are often looked down upon by teachers and classmates. There are cases of middle school boys ganging up to "teach" tomboy girls "a lesson," and of feminine boys being beaten up by their male classmates or even being "sexually harassed" by female classmates. These are not rare problems. Therefore, in the plan for

"gender equality education" which is being promoted as part of sex education, strong efforts will be made to break through gender stereotypes and to encourage children to have a broader sexual outlook.

Starting from the beginning

Chiang Han-sun says education can be roughly divided into the two areas of "knowledge and technical education" on the one hand and "life education" (how to live an appropriate and beautiful life) on the other. Sex ed is the most fundamental aspect of life education.

Chiang emphasizes that, while knowledge and technical education can be life-long, without any age limitations, the situation is different with life education. "Life education follows age. From infancy to childhood to puberty, there are biological and psychological needs that develop with age. If these needs are not adequately satisfied or guided in the right direction, once the opportunity is missed and a person's character is formed, it is extremely difficult to turn things around." Chiang emphasizes the urgency of sexual education, and takes for example the idea that "if a girl can get correct information about menstruation before age 10, she can understand better how to cope with her periods and reduce the physical and psychological distress they may bring."

There's already a consensus on the importance of sex education. However, teacher training and class design are still at the embryonic stage.

"Sex education in fact begins right from childbirth. Moreover, sexual attitudes begin to take shape very early in life. Thus, primary school is an important period for introducing sex education," says Huang Yawen, chairperson of the department of health education at Taipei Teachers' College. Frustratingly, in the current primary school curriculum, the only thing related to sex education is the "morality and health" class which is taught two periods a week. Sex education constitutes only an extremely small part of that class. It is very difficult for kids to build a comprehensive outlook on sex from the occasional lectures they get.

Even more disappointing is that, of the nine teachers' colleges in Taiwan, few make health courses required. Some don't even have a professor specializing in health education. "Primary school teachers have never studied the subject themselves, so how can they teach it to their students?" sighs Huang Ya-wen.

With sex education just getting started, primary school teachers must rely as much as they can on outside resources. They need the help of such organizations as the Mercy Memorial Foundation and its lecturers, the family education services centers in various locations, women's groups, and private industries making feminine-hygiene and sex-related products.

What about middle and high schools, whose kids are hitting puberty? The only sex ed in middle schools is the stuff on "secondary sexual characteristics" in "health education" texts in the first and second years of middle school. At the high school level, girls at least can attend health care classes where they can discuss issues related to women's biology. But boys don't even have this.

Under these circumstances, schools must scramble and find their own way. For example, the private Chiangju High School has a "sex education week" for boys every December. The school shows a sex-ed film every day at noon during this week, and boys are asked to write an essay on what they have learned from the film; there is also a health teacher on hand to answer questions.

Lacking any definite curriculum or teacher training, most schools invite outside specialists to give lectures during the time set aside for weekend extra-curricular activities. However, the lectures are not linked together—this time the topic may be biology, next menstruation, and the next time sexual assault—so the knowledge imparted remains superficial and unsystematic.

An inglorious "first place" in Asia

Sex education is something that is brand new in Taiwan's post-repressive society, and for many senior teachers it is still a vulgar subject. Many of these teachers muddled through their own very naive youths, and they are unable to answer the kinds of in-depth questions that young kids today can pose. For example, as feminists raise high the banner of "Orgasms, not harassment!" students may ask the teacher: "What is an orgasm? "How can you achieve orgasm?" Some teachers think these students are being deliberately provocative and give them a demerit.

The Ministry of Education's Ho Chintsai says that today many parents complain that schools don't teach their children to be diligent at the books, but teach too much trash that only "distracts" them from studying. No wonder, with the undercurrent of conservatism still flowing strong, that many teachers prefer to live by the rule "the less taught, the less trouble," says Ho.

Taiwan's long-term inadequacy in sex ed is most obvious in one of Taiwan's inglorious "top rankings in Asia." Among the newly industrialized countries of Asia, Taiwan ranks first in pregnancy among girls aged 15–19. Taiwan has a rate of 17 per thousand, much higher than the figures for Japan (4) and Korea (11). Though the statistics do not say how many of these are unwed mothers, in any case pregnancy at an age before the uterus is fully mature is highly dangerous, and should be avoided.

Liu Tan-kui, a specialist in the Bureau of Health Promotion and Protection at the Department of Health, says that the 16,000 babies born to "little mothers" each year are a great burden for society. Statistics indicate that "80% of 'little mothers' know nothing about contraception, which demonstrates a tremendous shortcoming in sex education in Taiwan."

School and families link up

The chance for improving this dismal record has arrived. Edwin Yen explains that of the seven core areas in the new nine-year standard curriculum that will go into effect in 2001, "health and physical education" (including sex education) is ranked right up there as an equal with languages, the humanities, social studies, natural sciences, technology, and mathematics. It will receive 10 to 15% of total class time.

Under this structure, in the future sex ed will naturally receive its share of teachers, budgets, and attention to class design. Yen sees this as the greatest accomplishment of his more than 20 years of "plowing the ground" for sex ed.

Nevertheless, Chiang Han-sun, who has worked hand-in-hand with Yen these many years to promote sex ed, offers a cautionary reminder: "Sex is the most intimate of human relationships, so sex education should be led by those closest to the children—parents are the best guidance counselors."

Chiang says that there is no other road to successful education than "love" and "setting a proper example." Parents are the most important models for their children's sex education, and the example of a loving marital relationship is more important than a thousand classroom lectures. It's just that most parents don't know how to take the next step and explicitly teach their children, so the schools must help them out.

Sex is part of human nature, right from infancy. It is not a bad thing. Now that sex education has entered its infancy, it also needs lots of attention from all concerned.

(Laura Li/tr. by Phil Newell)

From pleasure to power to pregnancy prevention,
the surprising truth about what kids learn
—and don't learn—
from school-based sex education

SEX ED
how do we
score?

By Carolyn Mackler

he 12:55 bell rings at Ridgewood High School and a flock of freshman filter into Evelyn Rosskamm Shalom's Health 9 class. Greeting the sea of navy blue baseball caps and Capri pants, Shalom announces that today's lesson will commence with the "question box" and instructs students to proceed as quietly as possible to the Magic Carpet. In a stampede evocative of July in Pamplona, 25 pairs of Nikes and clunky sandals clamor onto a dingy gray rug at the back of the room and, with one brave male exception, self-segregate by gender: girls on one side, boys on the other, a puerile triad huddled in the back. Shalom, joking about her recent fiftieth birthday, treats herself to a metal chair at the mouth of the circle and produces slips of folded, white paper.

"Any more to add before I begin?" she asks, casually tucking a wayward strand of auburn hair behind one ear.

Braces-revealing smirks ripple through the crowd, especially among the Peanut Gallery trio, who menacingly ooze "spitball" from every pore of their bodies.

Shalom quickly scans a crumpled selection. "Have I already answered: 'Why do people have oral sex?' "

The Peanut Gallery erupts and a handful of mid-pubescents dutifully nod their heads. Shalom, a 16-year veteran of Ridgewood High School who has been described as someone who rules a class with velvet-gloved discipline, allows the rascals a heartbeat to blow off steam before skillfully channeling their discomfort into a lively debate in response to the next question: "What is the right age to have sex?" Once Shalom takes the floor to address the query, a hush falls over the Magic Carpet.

The only discernable sound is the buzzing of florescent lights above. Fifty eyes are intent on Shalom. Even the Peanut Gallery is hooked.

So goes a typical health class at Ridgewood High School in suburban New Jersey. The Ridgewood school district is renowned for its comprehensive and thorough family-life education curriculum. Following a 1980 statewide mandate that all New Jersey school-children were to have sex education, Ridgewood Public Schools formed an advisory committee to consult with the school regarding its ever-evolving curriculum. Ridgewood students receive health education every year of their public school careers, beginning with instruction from a certified nurse specialist in elementary school and progressing to classes taught by high school teachers, such as Shalom, who has a master's degree in health education.

"Ridgewood takes it seriously," Shalom explains, sipping a raspberry Snapple after class. "We have a minister, a pediatrician, someone from the YMCA, several parents, and two students, among others, serving on the committee, which reviews everything that will go on in my class, from lessons to controversial videos. I'm under more scrutiny than the English teacher, but by the same token, I have a support network. If a parent calls to complain—which happens infrequently—I'm not out on a limb by myself."

And then there's the question box, or anonymous questions, as they're often referred to in health-education circles. Shalom operates her question box—a pushing-the-envelope trade tool that gives the teacher jurisdiction to answer any inquiry—by

In a country where a mere 6.9 percent of men and 21 percent of women hold out for their honeymoon, force-feeding "Just Say No" to teenagers sends them scurrying to the playground or onto the Web in search of information—usually to find misinformation—and frolicking under the covers all the same.

first distributing identical slips of paper and then requiring that all students write one to three lines. (If a student has no question, she or he must thrice scribble "I have no questions at the present time.") And finally, Shalom makes good on her promise to honor every question, which in any given session can produce such gems as "Do teenagers have sex?" "Is it right to have an abortion if you get pregnant by mistake?" and "What exactly do guys do when they masturbate?" Shalom notes, "In any class, if someone is asking a question, you know that at least a few other people were wondering the same thing." She informs her students from the start not to waste time devising outrageous queries just to get a reaction; she's been at this too long to get embarrassed. And with no further ado, she plows into the explanation minefield with nary a blush.

Perhaps it's the ubiquitous florescent lights that stir up decade-old memories of my eleventh-grade health class, where the beefy, small-town wrestling coach slapped transparencies of the chlamydia bacterium onto the overhead projector and recited a litany of drippy symptoms, in a lesson that bore a greater resemblance to the previous year's fetal pig dissection than to my forays in the back of minivans. As I recount my tale of sex ed woe, Shalom shakes her head. "If kids are going to change their behavior, we need to teach them the facts before they engage, but that alone is not sufficient. We must give them time to talk about their attitudes and practice communication skills." Pushing her wire-rimmed glasses up on her nose, she adds, "Anyway, Ridgewood would never make a physical education teacher cover chlamydia, just as they wouldn't expect me to coach volleyball."

fade from the Magic Carpet to a school district in Franklin County, North Carolina, where, in the fall of 1997, a scissors-toting parent-volunteer was summoned to the high school to slice chapters 17, 20, and 21 out of ninth-graders' health textbooks. The culpable text—covering contraception, sexually transmitted disease (STDs), and relationships—didn't comply with the statewide abstinence-only curriculum, ruled the school board. Apparently, in a state where in 1996 there were 25,240 recorded pregnancies among 15- to 19-year-olds, the board hoped that if they obliterated a discourse on condoms, getting down wouldn't dawn on youngsters.

Unfortunately, this sort of scene is business as usual with the politically explosive issue of school-based sex education. While a uniform national curriculum does not exist, barrels of federal money are being siphoned into abstinence-only-until-marriage programs, frequently laden with wrath-of-God scare tactics. Comprehensive sexuality education the likes of Ridge-

wood's, designed to reinforce sexuality as a positive and health part of being human, is available to only about 5 percent of school-children in the United States. Sexuality education is an across-the-school-boards contentious subject, bound to generate controversy, even among well-meaning feminists; sexuality is not a one-size-fits-all equation, and the messages appropriate for one kid may not work for the girl or boy at the adjacent desk.

And then there's the Great Antipleasure Conspiracy. Translation: adults swindling kids (especially girls) by trying to convince them that sex is no fun, in the hope that they won't partake, a practice exemplified by the shocking omission of the clitoris—whose sole function is to deliver female pleasure—from most high school biology textbooks. The notion of women experiencing erotic pleasure—or possessing full sexual agency—clearly scares the boxer shorts off conservative educators. Analogous to attempting to eradicate pizza by withholding Italy from a map of Europe, not including the clitoris in a textbook depiction of female genitalia is a frighteningly misleading excuse for education.

Tiptoeing around any of these issues—from pleasure to power to pregnancy prevention—is denying youngsters their basic right to health information. It is catapulting them into life-threatening sexual scenarios without sufficient tools to protect themselves. It is jeopardizing their chance to lay sturdy foundations for a sexually healthy adulthood. It's time to wake up and smell the hormones.

Ridgewood boasts one of the most progressive school districts in a "mixed landscape," explains Susan N. Wilson, the executive coordinator of the Network for Family Life Education, a nonprofit organization based at the Rutgers School for Social Work in Piscataway, New Jersey, that promotes comprehensive sexuality education in schools and communities. Wilson, whom Shalom calls a "crusader for sexuality education," explains that over the past several years there has been progress in the quantity of sex education in the schools. "In most places, it exists; something is being taught," she says, "but there are many school districts where students receive the bare minimum—HIV education—and very, very late in their school lives." Wilson points out that many politicians have embraced AIDS education with open arms. "In a true intertwining of church and state, they've jumped at the chance to reveal that sex does, in fact, equal death."

Debra Haffner, president of the Sexuality Information and Education Council of the United States (SIECUS), a nonprofit group that advocates for sexuality education and sexual rights, describes how most young people in this country get hurried through sex-abuse prevention in early grade school, the Pu-

SEX ED The Art of Peer Education

In the mid-seventies, Cydelle Berlin, then a drama teacher in Princeton, New Jersey, would sit aghast in the junior high school auditorium as local physicians manhandled the sex education program, aversion-therapy style. "A proctologist would flash these huge blown-up slides of penises infected with all sorts of things and say 'This is what would happen if you had sex,'" she recounts. "And the students would be doing spontaneous testimonials like, 'Oh my God, I will never do that!'"

Convinced that something was rotten in the state of sex education, Berlin began taking human-sexuality courses at New York University, which eventually led to the completion of a doctorate in 1988 with a specialty in adolescent sexuality. The AIDS epidemic was threatening large numbers of teenagers, and Berlin feared that "if we didn't talk about sex in a context young people responded to, understood, and felt empowered by, we were going to lose all our young people." Also aware that we can't "teach AIDS prevention without letting adolescents know that sexuality is a powerful and positive force in their lives," Berlin married her message to her art and developed the NiteStar program (originally called STAR Theatre).

Operating out of St. Luke's-Roosevelt Hospital Center in New York City, NiteStar, now in its eleventh year, uses young actors to perform an array of psychodramas that tackle sexuality, homophobia, gender equity, masturbation, and every "ism" known to teen-kind. Members of the NiteStar company, ranging in age from the teens to early twenties and with a diversity of ethnic, racial, cultural, and socioeconomic backgrounds, undergo intense health-education training. The actor-educators then hit stages, schools, and community centers, performing humorous, musically enriched skits that waltz the gamut from sexual limit-setting scenarios to zany condom demonstrations. One sketch glimpses a heterosexual couple debating whether to have an abortion or a baby; another presents two young men miming a game of hoops and conferring on a mutual buddy who, one snickers, "has sugar in his tank," referring to the suggestion that he may be gay. The other contends that he will befriend him regardless of his sexual orientation.

"At first, kids act like they already know everything," describes a company member, Alice, referring to the post-performance Q & A where the actors, remaining in their roles, field questions from the audience. "But once they realize that we will answer absolutely anything, their guard melts away and they really open up." The skits, born of improvisation, are designed to relate to youth on their own level. "We look like the kids in the audience. We speak their language," says 18-year-old Karyn, "and we don't wear cheesy uniforms. We just wear what we wore to school that day."

NiteStar, performing primarily in New York City and the surrounding suburbs, has reached about 800,000 people and was the subject of a PBS documentary, *Sex and Other Matters of Life and Death,* which has aired regularly nationwide since 1996. Berlin, who believes sexuality education should begin long before adolescence, says, "I wish we didn't have to call what NiteStar does revolutionary. I wish we lived in a climate where it could just be important in the way that a lot of work is important."

—C.M.

---

berty Talk in fifth grade, a lesson on HIV and STDs in middle school, and possibly a health elective in high school. "There's currently a great emphasis on abstinence in this country," she adds, "partially driven by federal programs, but partially driven by the conservative influence in communities."

Seasoned feminist sexuality educators consistently encourage teenagers to postpone intercourse until they're prepared for a mature sexual relationship. But the puritanical monsoon of fear-based abstinence education swamping the country is a different matter. As part of welfare reform in 1996, Congress passed, and President Clinton signed into law, a federal program that allocates cash—a total of $50 million per fiscal year—to states that teach abstinence-only-until-marriage as the expected standard for school-age children. The modus operandi of these programs is to highlight the "harmful psychological and physical effects" of premarital and extramarital sexual activity and erase any discourse on contraceptives—which curiously ignores the notion that abstainers-until-marriage may, in fact, want to utilize birth control once they've tied the connubial knot.

Abstinence-only lessons, though varying from classroom to classroom, often revolve around a "pet your dog, not your date" theme. One resoundingly sexist message is that the onus of restricting foreplay should fall on the girl, encouraging her to use "self-control" rather than "birth control." A pseudoscientific chart from Sex Respect, a fear-based abstinence curriculum, depicts how male genitalia become aroused during "necking," while female genitalia lag behind until "petting."

The girl-cum-gatekeeper's pleasure gets swept to the side, leaving her to ward filthy, boys-will-be-boys paws off her silky drawers.

In many fear-based abstinence lessons, misinformation abounds. One curriculum emphasizes the "danger" of French kissing by falsely implying that the concentration of HIV in saliva is high enough to be transmitted via spit-swapping. Mum is the word from teachers in response to students whose queries flirt with anything other than the abstinence-only model. In a public-school-aired video entitled *No Second Chance* (Jermiah Films), a student demands of a nurse: "What if I want to have sex before I get married?" Her chilling response: "I guess you just have to be prepared to die . . . and take your spouse and one or more of your children with you."

The overwhelming bulk of scientific research underscores the failure of abstinence-only education in doing anything but eclipsing the erotic with the neurotic. A recent report by the National Campaign to Prevent Teen Pregnancy revealed that "the weight of the current evidence indicates that these abstinence programs do not delay the onset of intercourse." In a country where a mere 6.9 percent of men and 21 percent of women ages 18 to 59 hold out for their honeymoon, force-feeding "Just Say No" to teenagers sends them scurrying to the playground or onto the Web in search of information—usually to find misinformation—and frolicking under the covers all the same. But the risks of leaving kids without sufficient skills and facts range from the obvious—pregnancy and STDs—to sexual abuse, date rape, and sexual powerlessness.

Then there's the Great Antipleasure Conspiracy: adults swindling kids (especially girls), by trying to convince them that sex is no fun, in the hope that they won't partake, a practice exemplified by the shocking omission of the clitoris from most high school biology textbooks.

Reducing adolescent pregnancy and the risk of sexually transmitted diseases is clearly paramount. But Susan Wilson, who's convinced that the right wants to "stamp out" teen sexuality altogether, wonders whether the effort is "on a collision course with healthy sexuality."

Debra Haffner echoes similar sentiments. "My mentor from 20 years ago used to call that 'Sex is dirty. Save it for someone you love,'" she scoffs. "We cannot ingrain in young people the message that sexual intercourse violates another person, kills people, and leaves you without a reputation, and then expect that the day they put a wedding band on their finger they're going to forget all that."

She pauses and adds wryly, "It just creates adults who are in sex therapy because they can't have fulfilling relationships with their spouses and partners."

hearing the term 'sex ed,' people think of plumbing lessons and organ recitals," proclaims Haffner. "They envision anatomy and physiology and disaster prevention. Sexuality education, on the other hand, underscores that sexuality is about who we are, as women and men, not what we do with one certain part of our bodies."

In 1996, SIECUS published the second edition of its *Guidelines for Comprehensive Sexuality Education: K–12*, which it had originally developed earlier in the decade with a task force that included the Centers for Disease Control and Prevention, Planned Parenthood Federation of America, and the National School Boards Association. The guidelines serve as a framework to facilitate the development of a comprehensive sex education program arising from the belief that "young people explore their sexuality as a natural process of achieving sexual maturity." Accordingly, emphasis should be placed on informed decision-making about intercourse by acknowledging—not condemning—the broad range of adolescent sexual behaviors.

The SIECUS sexuality education model is designed to spiral through the school years, with age-appropriate lessons at all grade levels. Starting in early elementary school, children would learn, among many things, proper terminology for female and male genitalia. "When I tell this to my seniors," Shalom explains, referring to the students in her elective course on parenting, "they are shocked. They say, 'But then you'll have little kids singing "vulva, vulva" all day long.' And I point out that three-year-olds don't run around saying 'shoulder, shoulder, shoulder.' It should just be part of their whole repertoire."

The philosophy behind comprehensive sexuality education is to start small with all concepts relating to sexuality and add on as children's developmental capabilities mature. If the topic is sexual identity, in upper elementary school, 9- to 12-year-olds (already having defined homosexuality in previous grades) would learn about anti-gay discrimination and add bisexuality to the mixing pot. By junior high, students learn theories behind the determination of sexual orientation and discuss same-sex fantasies. Unfortunately, this approach to homosexuality is to sex education what simultaneous multiple orgasms are to sex—rare. Even in progressive school districts, discourse on sexual orientation remains painfully patchy, often providing little insight and appearing very late.

Proponents of comprehensive sexuality education believe that by high school, teenagers should have processed enough information to make responsible choices surrounding sex. And the research is on their side: studies reveal that teenagers who partake in discussions that include all options, from chastity belts to condoms, often delay sexual intercourse or reduce its frequency. By cultivating in adolescents a sense of sexual self-determination—with empowerment and gratification and honest communication being central—things tend to fall into place; unwanted pregnancy and sexually transmitted diseases remain on the periphery, not at the hub of their ideas about human sexuality.

Back to the Great Antipleasure Conspiracy. There's reluctance even among liberal adults—most likely due to their own discomfort surrounding sexuality—to acknowledge that the majority of sex is for recreation, not procreation. Scarier still is the notion of pleasuring oneself. Wilson points out that masturbation is a subject "avoided assiduously by teachers." It is essential for schools to employ educators who will not blanch at the mention of, say, a clitoris (and who, like Shalom, boycott clitoris-free textbooks). "Nobody invests money in training," says Wilson, who points out that often sex ed teachers hit the chalkboard with only a weekend workshop under their belt. "A basic course in human sexuality for everyone in the helping professions should be commonplace."

Sex education can even send shivers up feminist spines when it comes to handling a controversial issue like abortion. It seems easy if the teacher is pro-choice; explosive if she or he boasts a bumper sticker broadcasting "Abortion Stops a Beating Heart!" The safest way to navigate this tangled terrain is for teachers to acknowledge the range of values surrounding issues such as homosexuality, abortion, or masturbation in the hope that students will ultimately develop their own, educated opinions. "If there were a school-based program that only presented the pro-choice point of view, that would be wrong," says Haffner, who has recently published a SIECUS monograph, *A Time to Speak: Faith Communities and Sexuality Education,* in which she emphasizes the role of religious institutions in the education of their young congregants and encourages churches and synagogues to coordinate their curricula with those of the schools.

Another key means for schools to negotiate the values quagmire is to give credence to SIECUS' omnipresent message that parents should be the primary sexuality educators. Envisioning a proliferation of parent nights, when parents could meet the health teachers and review the material, Haffner encourages educators to solicit parental support, all in the hope that the classroom will serve as a catalyst for domestic dialogue.

"Most Americans are terrified of this subject," says Wilson. "We teach people to read and we expect them to read. We teach people about numbers and we expect them to be able to do mathematical equations. So then we're saying we don't want to teach kids about human sexuality, but we're hoping they make sensible decisions?"

"I know I've done my job well," explains Shalom, "when a kid articulates to me, 'I never realized sex was so complicated until I took your class.' Not that it's bad. Not that it's evil. Not that it's nasty. But it's complicated, and maybe more than you want to get into at 14."

the 2:55 bell rings, signaling the end of the day at Ridgewood High School. A gaggle of spankingly clean-cut students, ranging from a ninth-grader to seniors, cluster in Shalom's small, windowless office. All alums of Health 9, they've gathered to share knowledge garnered from the Magic Carpet.

Before my tape recorder can begin rolling, phrases like "outercourse" and "the abstinence jar" bounce off the walls, which are dotted with colorful posters and photos of Shalom's grown children. Shalom has already introduced me to the aforementioned abstinence jar that she displays in class. It is empty, thus stimulating a discussion about what needs to fill it in order for abstinence to thrive, things like alternatives to intercourse and developing a vocabulary that includes yes, no, and every possible shade of maybe.

"If you're going to teach abstinence, you've at least got to teach masturbation," pipes in Jennifer, an intrepid senior.

"But," she adds, "if a girl knows how to please herself without the help of a guy, it goes against women's traditionally passive sex role, and people are intimidated by that."

Clearly the Great Antipleasure Conspiracy has not gone as smoothly as planned.

But then again, these teenagers are not the norm. Products of comprehensive sexuality education that encourages them to become their own sexual agents, they display at once a level-headed ease regarding sexuality and a keen awareness of the risks involved in indulging.

"Kids know better than to believe sex is just bad," says Peter, another senior, "so the only thing that happens when teachers push abstinence is we don't take teachers as seriously."

"If sex is such a bad thing, then why is it all over movies and television?" Greg, the lone first-year student, chimes in.

"If you've had sex education, you can watch movies and understand what's realistic and what's not," comments jeans-clad Irene, in response to Jennifer's sardonic description of Hollywood heat-of-the-moment, candlelit smooching scenes, where neither women say stop nor men whip out condoms.

SEX ED I Read You Loud and Clear

When I was 11, I used to crouch in the back of the Life Bridge Book Shop in Brockport, New York, thumbing through Peter Mayle's then-radical nuts, bolts, and orgasms book, *Where Did I Come From?* (Carol Publishing Group). In the ensuing years, the market has seen a proliferation of coming-of-age resources, most targeted squarely at women-in-training, such as Karen and Jennifer Gravelle's *The Period Book* (Walker and Company) and Mavis Jukes's *It's a Girl Thing* (Knopf). While her/his sexuality education books, such as Cynthia Akagi's *Dear Larissa: Sexuality Education for Girls Ages 11–17* (Gylantic Publishing) and *Dear Michael: Sexuality Education for Boys Ages 11–17* dot the shelves. Resources for boys lag behind what's available for girls. "I don't think anyone's paying attention to boys in that sense," says Elizabeth Debold, a developmental psychologist and founding member of the Harvard Project on Women's Psychology and Girls' Development. "Boys are supposed to inherently know what they're doing—know where to put it—when in reality they end up feeling horribly uncomfortable and awkward in their bodies."

That said, here are a few of the quality resources available, several of which are useful for both girls and boys:

Caution: Do Not Open Until Puberty: An Introduction to Sexuality for Young Adults with Disabilities, by Rick Enright. Illustrated by Sara L. Van Hamme (Devinjer House)

Originally a booklet for the Thames Valley Children's Centre in Ontario, Canada, it breaks the "conspiracy of silence" around disabled teens' sexuality in a fearless and funny fashion.

Deal With It! A Whole New Approach to Your Body, Brain, and Life as a gURL, by Esther Drill, Heather McDonald, and Rebecca Odes (Pocket Books)

Marketed as "the *Our Bodies, Ourselves* for teenagers" and inspired by the interactive Web site gURL.com, this lively book is packed with frank, practical information.

Girltalk: All the Stuff Your Sister Never Told You, by Carol Weston (HarperPerennial)

Includes an extensive discussion about sex with sections that plunge into "Do-It-Yourself Orgasms" and "To Do It or Not to Do It: That is the Question."

It's Perfectly Normal: Changing Bodies, Growing Up, Sex & Sexual Health, by Robie H. Harris. Illustrated by Michael Emberley (Candlewick Press)

Intended for the junior-high set, reader-friendly fodder on sexuality, sexual orientation, and pubescent idiosyncrasies, with visuals that leave *National Geographic* in the dust.

Out With It: Gay and Straight Teens Write About Homosexuality, edited by Philip Kay, Andrea Estepa, and Al Desetta (Youth Communication)

An anthology of articles authored by teens with titles such as "Coming Out to Mom," "Straight but Not Narrow-Minded," and "Minority Within a Minority."

SEX, ETC.: A Newsletter by Teens, for Teens, published by the Network for Family Life Education (Rutgers University)

Distributed to nearly 500,000 teens nationwide, mostly via schools, with straight (and gay and bi) off-the-cuff editorials and interviews.   —C.M.

"Actually, you can appreciate the movies more," Dana softly adds, "because you're less impressionable."

Before long, the conversation wends its way to yesterday's senior elective, where a former Ridgewood student, now openly gay and in his third year of medical school, reminisced on the closets of his alma mater. "The class was intimidated at first," says Jennifer, "but after a while people started asking things like 'Do you go to gay bars?' and 'Do you march in parades?' and 'Do you agree with gay men being flamboyant?' it was interesting to hear about it."

Some would maintain that high school is already too late to introduce such a discussion. But even though a large-scale study of junior and senior high school students revealed that a booming 10.7 percent were unsure of their sexual orientation, homosexuality is still up there with the best of the taboos, snagging minimal airtime in most classrooms. Academy Award-winning director Debra Chasnoff's groundbreaking documentary *It's Elementary: Talking About Gay Issues in School* (Women's Educational Media) peeks into a handful of U.S. classrooms where teacher-warriors are braving the odds and discussing homosexuality. The film skillfully demonstrates that the earlier such conversations begin, the more open and understanding kids become.

It doesn't take a logician to deduce that the future of sex education is in serious jeopardy, but perhaps it's going to take feminists to do something about it. With a paucity of children receiving comprehensive sexuality education and gobs of federal money flying into reactionary, fear-based instruction, there's plenty of action to be taken, in the form of rallying school districts, educators, politicians, and parents to support education designed to empower, enlighten, and yes, even excite youth about sexuality. And while we'll be sorry to see sex therapists hard-pressed for clients, we can envision a world where girls and boys grow into adults who regard their sexuality as anything but a one-way ticket to disease and unplanned pregnancy.

As I lean across Shalom's metal desk to hit the off-button on my tape recorder, she interjects one final comment. "I see how kids respond to this stuff every single day," she reports. "They are just waiting for adults to share the tools with them. And it's not 'share the tools so I can go out and do it,' it's 'please help me learn how to grow up.'"

Carolyn Mackler is a "Ms." contributing editor. Her first young-adult novel will be published by Delacorte Press in 2000.

TEACHING SCHOOLS A LESSON

Undaunted by the opposition, gay students are giving their schools a lesson in tolerance BY DAVID KIRBY

Morgan Frieden, a 15-year-old girl in Huntsville, Ala., developed a "huge crush" as a sixth-grader on an eighth-grade girl just out of the closet, sending the entire school "into an uproar." By the time Frieden got to high school, she was even gutsier. Only a few teachers and students knew she was a lesbian when she arrived, but in the fall of her ninth-grade year, she took her girlfriend to the homecoming dance. "It was a blast!" says Frieden, who is now a sophomore. "We got a few evil looks, a few 'Ooh, can I butt in?' looks, and many 'Way to go!' looks."

Huntsville may not seem the most likely place to find an openly lesbian student, let alone one who would show up at a dance with her girlfriend. But increasingly across the nation, gay and lesbian students are coming out in their schools with a sense of confidence that would have seemed impossible just a few years ago. And if a flourishing gay student culture seems extraordinary to gay and lesbian adults, it's downright disturbing, even shocking, to many straight ones. Almost overnight school districts, youth centers, clergy, counselors, and parents have found themselves dealing with demands for gay-straight alliances (GSAs) at school and with same-sex dating, including at the prom. The "problem" that teachers and administrators have for years been too frightened to confront is suddenly walking through the schoolhouse door every weekday morning.

For thousand of gay teens, life is still hellish. But more and more, gay and lesbian students are out, brave, and happy despite the obstacles they still face. Mostly they are normal American teenagers complete with all the joy and drama that come with their age. The closet seems at most a temporary stop. Lamar Lottie (who spoke on the condition that his real name not be used) is a 17-year-old jock at a private school in the Dallas suburbs who says if he were outed, "it'd be OK. But it would make things more difficult." But, he adds quickly, "I'm considering coming out next year, when I'm a senior."

In fact, many students seem equally at ease with their orientation, even if being honest about it causes them problems. For Justin Ruben Irizarry, a 17-year-old senior in Elizabeth, N.J., coming out was more difficult, partly because his parents are dead. He realized he was gay "at the tender age of 8" and told his extended family a few years later. His uncle promptly threw him out of the house. Irizarry now lives with other relatives.

Other students tell more innocent stories. Jascie Williams, a 16-year-old junior at Philadelphia's High School for Creative and Performing Arts, remembers having little girlfriend "bathroom buddies" she would get caught making out with. Then, at age 13, while reading her favorite book, Rita Mae Brown's *Six of One,* Williams discovered what a lesbian was and liked it. Nick Fulcher, a 17-year-old junior from Maple Grove, Minn., says his friends, mostly girls, "were very accepting. They all wanted details about my gay friends and the guys I was dating."

The presence of out gay students is changing schools. Speeding that change are national groups such as the Gay, Lesbian, and Straight Education Network that brings information, contacts, and resources to even the most isolated young people. As a sign of just how much schools are being transformed by the demands of gay and lesbian students, gay-straight alliances are popping up at an astonishing rate, sometimes in the most conservative of places, such as Orange County, Calif., and Baton Route, La.

These alliances "have exploded in this country in the last several years," says Kevin Jennings, GLSEN's founder and executive director. "Just a short while ago, there was a general denial that there even were gay teens."

Jennings notes that the movement has succeeded in spite of, not because of, the education system: "What we see happening is a real grassroots movement led by students and isolated faculty." The schools' response, he says, "has ranged from indifference to overt hostility. Active support at least at the initial stages, is frankly, virtually unheard of." One reason: The median age of public school teachers is 47. "They started college the year of the Stonewall riots," Jennings says. Even today, most teacher training programs offer nothing about gay kids at all.

Virginia Uribe, who in 1984 founded Los Angeles's Project 10, the first on-campus gay group in the country, says the prospect of out gay kids terrifies administrators. "There is a great fear of parents, especially at the administrative level," she says. "They are afraid of controversy, of opposition, that they will look bad. And the higher up you get in education the more cowardly you become. But we are making some progress." In Los Angeles, for example, at least 40 of the city's 49 high schools, along with several alternative schools, have some form of gay group on campus. But not every place is like Los Angeles. In most of the country, Uribe points out, teachers still fear, "whether justified or not, that they will lose their job if they even talk about gay and lesbian issues or allow a group to form."

Not surprisingly, there are still no gay-straight alliances in the Huntsville school system, but that's not because Frieden's not trying. "I'm doing my best, slowly, but surely, to open people's eyes," she says.

However, acceptance in many schools is still hard-won, both from peers and teachers. Gina Russell, a 17-year-old senior from Ames, Iowa, has made a point of becoming a beacon for other gay kids: "I've been as blatantly out as possible, so people sort of

YOUTH QUAKE

A glimpse at gay-youth struggles on high school campuses around the country

BY JON BARRETT

Every so often a student uprising—like that at Calfornia's El Modena High School—catches the nation's attention and, therefore, newspaper headlines. But it's impossible for those headlines to illustrate the battles gay and lesbian youth face every day. This box, as a result, just scratches the surface of recent antigay attacks and the subsequent struggles of gay youth on campuses across the country.

OREGON

• **August 1998:** The far-right Oregon Citizens Alliance files an initiative for the November 2000 ballot that would prohibit public schools from discussing homosexuality and bisexuality "in a manner which encourages, promotes, or sanctions such behaviors."
• **February 2000:** A junior at Sam Barlow High School in Gresham is told he can't cross-dress or war a T-shirt that reads, SORRY, GIRLS, I'M GAY.

CALIFORNIA

• **April 1999:** Five students file a lawsuit against the Morgan Hill Unified School District claiming that officials at Live Oak High and Murphy Middle schools did nothing to stop anti-gay harassment between 1994 and 1997. One of the plaintiffs, a seventh-grader, was hospitalized after a group of boys repeatedly beat him at a school bus while shouting antigay epithets. The bus driver, the suit says, did nothing.
• **October 1999:** The state provides gay-inclusive nondiscrimination protections to students.
• **February 2000:** A judge rules that a gay-straight alliance at El Modena High School must be allowed to meet while a court case against the Orange Unified School District, which prohibited the club, proceeds.
• **February 2000:** A proposal to start a gay-straight alliance at Mission Viejo

High School is shot down because of the school district's policy against all noncurricular clubs.

NEVADA

• **January 2000:** Derek Henkle, a former Reno student, sues the school district for failing to protect him from antigay harassment, including an incident in which a lasso was thrown around his neck and he was threatened with being dragged from a pickup truck.

UTAH

• **November 1999:** A U.S. district judge rules that the Salt Lake City School District did not violate high school students' First Amendment rights by preventing them from forming a gay-straight alliance.
• **November 1999:** Two female students at Ogden's Weber High School are suspended after kissing in the school hallway.

WISCONSIN

• **August 1985:** The state enacts gay-inclusive nondiscrimination protections for students.

LOUISIANA

• **February 2000:** At least 36 students are suspended for protesting the formation of a gay-straight alliance at McKinley High School in Baton Rouge.

MASSACHUSETTS

• **1993:** The state provides gay-inclusive nondiscrimination protection to students.
• **May 1999:** Two students at Northfield Mount Hermon School corner a 17-year-old fellow student and carve HOMO in five-inch block letters across his back with a pocketknife. They say they tar-

geted the boy because he likes the British rock band Queen, who lead singer, Freddie Mercury, died of AIDS complications in 1991.
• **January 2000:** A Boston High School student is sexually assaulted and beaten unconscious on a subway by a trio of female classmates who assumed she's gay because she holds hands with girls. The victim, a Morrocan, grew up in a culture where hand-holding among schoolgirls is customary.

NEW HAMPSHIRE

• **July 1999:** Two students at Manchester High School file a lawsuit against their school district and the school principal for denying them the right to form a gay-straight alliance. The board later agrees to recognize the GSA rather than fight the lawsuit.

CONNECTICUT

• **1997:** The state provides gay-inclusive nondiscrimination protections to students.

NEW YORK

• **September 2000:** After many days of being subjected to antigay harassment, a 16-year-old gay student at Shenendehowa High School in Clifton Park is "ganged up" on by five students. After he hits one of his tormentors on the head with a stick, he is suspended. School officials allegedly take no action against the assailants. The incident prompts school officials to add the words *sexual orientation* to the school's antiharassment policy.

FLORIDA

• **March 1999:** An 18-year-old male student at Taylor High School in Pierson is told he can't wear a dress to the prom. Officials capitulate when the student threatens to sue.

flock to me if they're unsure." She founded the first alliance in Iowa as a freshman, saying "it was relatively easy." The hard part though, "has been maintaining the energy

to not only keep things going but also fight back against the antiqueer mentality of the student body." She also took her then-girlfriend to the prom last spring and reports

it was "fantastic." There were no harsh words, "but we did get some strange looks. I wrote a column about it for our school paper, actually." Still, like most gay teens,

Russell does get harassed sometimes. "I've been called a 'queer' and a 'f_____ dyke' in the hallway, but only twice," she says. "I reported them, and it was dealt with."

Once out, gay students are often quickly stereotyped to the exclusion of the rest of their personalities. "I'm known as the 'gay guy' at school," says 18-year-old Galen Newton, a senior in Clive, Iowa. "Although the intent is more likely descriptive than hurtful, I am assigned this title with little thought or consideration." The words, says Newton, who is Asian-American, "could never justify my personality. They could never show the depth of my character. For some reason, they rank my orientation before my character, benevolence, and hard work. My sexuality is even ranked before my race, which I consider to be much more obvious."

More disheartening is the response from some teachers, who are supposed to be concerned primarily with their students' well-being. Not all teachers know how to handle having gay students around. Russell says that days after she came out, a teacher at her school "spent the day telling his classes how sick and wrong gay people were and that he would hate to have a gay student in his class." When she heard about it Russell told her counselor, who told her the teacher was retiring and "we should just let it go." Other teachers have been better, Russell says. Some have put up signs for the group she founded, and a few even come to meetings. But others ignore gay slurs in the classroom, "and that's

strained my relationships with them," she says.

Newton says he can tell his relationship with a faculty member "has surpassed that of mere teacher-student to friendship when I disclose that I am gay." Still, it's not easy: "I'm terribly frightened that if I just come out and tell all my teachers, they'll stereotype me immediately. I am more than my sexuality, and I have to make that clear before I am open with a teacher. It would be nice to think that a teacher leaves his or her prejudices out of the classroom, but this would not be realistic."

Even in the face of obvious harassment, some school officials prefer to keep their heads in the sand. Jascie Williams, who was recently selected as one of 20 outstanding teens in *Teen People* magazine, was outed one day by a fellow student, and the harassment began. "I'd spent so much time being free in my home, and suddenly people were banging me up against walls," she says. "Word got around fast, and I couldn't walk down the hallway without being called a dyke. I didn't know what to do," Finally Williams saw a counselor. "He said, 'Things like that don't happen at this school.' He made me feel like I was crazy, like my problems weren't valid," says Williams, who began cutting classes and feeling sick about her life. "I had a stress sickness, the harassment was so bad."

But with the help of her parents, she fought back. Philadelphia schools have no-harassment policies, including harassment based on sexual orientation. "We reminded

the school that they could be sued for this," Williams says. After considering a transfer, she decided to stay and went on to become coordinator of the school's gay-straight alliance.

Fighting back helped check the physical and emotional stress all that harassment had engendered. "I had a big talk with the principal," Williams says matter-of-factly. "I really started demanding things."

As a result, Williams has begun to change attitudes of school officials and other students. She got involved with a GSA-sponsored program to make public schools safer for sexual minorities, and she helped expand her school's alliance to make it a more comfortable place for a larger number of students, specifically bisexuals. "There really are so many bisexual kids out there," she says, "and they are too often excluded."

Williams also started a speakers' bureau for gay kids to talk in high school classes, a pretty gutsy move. "Sometimes kids are uncool, but I allow them to ask any question they want," she says. "They think it's all about sex but I teach them there's a culture and history, that we are a people, not just a sex act. My message to them is important, and some of them really get it. I hope it makes them think twice before they harass someone. Only they are the ones who can put a stop to harassment."

Kirby is a regular contributor to The New York Times.

Married with Children

A husband and wife on what happens to passion when kids enter the picture.

by Mark Harris and Theresa Dougal

MARK: It's daybreak, a school morning. Both girls are in the family room, simultaneously scarfing down a plate of waffles, watching an Arthur video they could recite by heart, and drawing pictures in old bluebooks. At the moment it seems they're deepest in their flow. Theresa and I make our break. With freshly poured coffees in hand, we sneak up the stairs behind them and settle back into bed for fifteen minutes of peace before the day's activities are launched.

It's often our most—and sometimes only—intimate moment of the day. Though there are no guarantees. More mornings than not, Sylvie, age seven, and three-year-old Linnea trail us into the bedroom before we've even had a chance to readjust the pillows. And with an alacrity that's noticeably absent when, say, they've been asked to pick up their bedroom, both girls have wedged themselves between us, sometimes snuggling in quietly, but more often burrowing into the covers to play House, Whining Baby, or the highly interactive Pretend You're This, I'll be That.

In my better moods, when the girls haven't bumped my coffee mug, sloshing java into the bedcovers, or kneed me once again below the bathrobe belt, I embrace what's a truly beautiful family moment. At other times, I see it as just another intrusion into what's left of the intimacy Theresa and I share.

Kids. They've come between us, in bed and otherwise. That's been true from the beginning, of course. From the moment Theresa was first pregnant we naturally began to focus less on each other and more on the growing bulge that was Sylvie, the family we were becoming. So, willingly, we took in stride the changes in intimacy that followed—massages that once eased into

lovemaking were now begged to ease the lower back ache of a third trimester: candle-lit table talk now turned on such romantic themes as diapering systems and the mechanics of breastfeeding.

When the kids came on, and with a vengeance it seemed, they tugged us further apart. The sheer effort and time it takes to keep them fed, clothed, marginally well groomed, happily engaged, and out of the emergency room draws straight from time in which we could connect, lend an ear, offer a hug. And when bedtime stories have been read, last potty parades marched, and the girls are finally asleep, our first impulse is to turn not to each other but to our other pressing needs. Which are legion, from unfinished writing assignments and ungraded student essays to grocery shopping and the ritual shoveling out of the family room.

Some nights we're so wiped from it all that we've been known to check the clock and calculate the value of sex with all the passion of a government economist. And when it's well past midnight, we're deep in sleep deficit, and Linnea's cough medicine is sure to wear off just when we're slipping into R.E.M., we've easily chosen more Z's over Big O's.

This won't always be so (I'm hoping); at least the parenting lit says these early childhood years are among the hardest on moms and dads. I'm certainly planning on some of our labor lessening when Linnea walks into that first-grade classroom (1,247 days from this date, but who's counting?). Our choice to live away from family members who could take the kids for a Sunday afternoon, or to limit our in-home day care, hasn't helped our cause either.

We could do more to close the gap between us that the kids have opened. But

that would require a closer meeting of the minds than Theresa and I have arrived at. I'd be more willing than she to take the advice of the marriage counselors who extol the value of the weekly parents' night out, and I'm the one who attempts to set more of the kinds of limits between parent and child my own mother and father established.

By her own admission, Theresa, a full-time professor at the local college, isn't inclined to part with the girls for an evening date after she's been in the classroom and office all day. It's the working mother's guilt, I know, and I wouldn't deny her the bonding that's so vital to her, even if I could. To the extent I'm able, I understand—and accept—her need to mother.

But I'm not always happily resigned to it. I often nudge Theresa to carve out more time for us—and for herself. Like the kids, I want some of her attention too. An involved father, I've been home half the day with the kids, and when she walks in the door, I'm ready to disengage from them and connect with her. And I'll admit that when Theresa chooses them over me, I sometimes resent it and withdraw, taking refuge in the diversions of my bachelorhood, the movies, beers out with friends, my own work. Some days I feel I'm just waiting for the kids to get older, for them to need her less, to make her more available for us.

Our solid past has helped us weather this lean period, for sure. We'd been together eight years before Sylvie arrived, time to forge a strong marriage well before we created a family. And while we may connect less often, less deeply than we used to, we still do make time for us. We just squeeze more from less to do it. Before kids, connecting meant birthdays that would take days to celebrate, a Friday night out that would take in dinner, a movie, and a late morning rising. Today, intimacy is a ritualistic glass of wine we share in bed every night, or the odd twenty minutes of snuggling on the couch while the kids are lost in play up in their bedroom. These doses of intimacy are smaller, sure, but still meaningful, powerful, and restorative.

I'm just now beginning to accept the fact that Theresa and I, both together and alone, will forever struggle for more intimacy, to balance the incessant demands of the family life with those of the husband and the wife who created it. We accepted that challenge, knowingly or not, at that heart-stopping moment on a sunny May afternoon seven years ago when Sylvie was first laid in our arms.

Still, the struggle to balance the needs of the lovers with the needs of the parents has not been without its unexpected rewards. Like how watching Theresa as a mother—the woman who jumps out of a deep slumber to comfort a crying child, who at midnight can be found icing a birthday cake for Sylvie she's fashioned into a magic kingdom, and then marches into a classroom at 9:00 the next morning to lead a discussion of Thoreau—has only increased, not diminished, my love for her. Or how our kids have drawn Theresa and me closer together. They're our joint creation, after all. Because of them, we spend even more time together, struggle and enthuse even more, and talk more than ever, even if it is about Linnea's disinclination to ever comb her hair, or how to get Sylvie to tell off the school chum who's stealing her morning snack. For that and a million other reasons, this husband, this father, is willing—if not always happy—to move over when little girls arrive to turn our marital bed into a raucous playhouse.

THERESA: The scene was both cute and annoying. Sylvie, then age three and enthralled with dress-up play, had come downstairs to parade her latest ensemble. She sported something new yet vaguely familiar—long and pink, silky, and embroidered with flowers. It was my sole surviving wedding-shower negligee, which Sylvie had rooted out of my pajama drawer. I opened my mouth to protest—"Hey, wait a minute, that's not yours!"—and then I sighed and succumbed. "Oh well. I don't use it anyway."

The significance of Sylvie's triumph was not lost on me. The child of our dreams, she had become much the center of our lives, a place of honor she would soon

share with her little sister Linnea. Her contentment was paramount to me, and the negligee incident underscored that fact. But the symbolism nagged at me and forced me to address an important question: Could there be room in my life for children, with their myriad physical and emotional needs and desires, and for a loving, intimate relationship with my husband? What happens to the passion when a twosome becomes a threesome?

The years Mark and I shared before Sylvie was born were full of excitement and the sheer enjoyment of being together. We had a wealth of leisure time, and we made the most of it. Our favorite pastimes revolved mostly around talk—watching a movie and then hashing it out, discussing books, taking long walks in our neighborhood, lounging in bed while ruminating over a morning cup of coffee or an evening glass of wine. We have come to know each other so well through these self-revelatory conversations, creating a deep and intimate bond.

With the arrival of Sylvie, the tectonic plates of our existence shifted. Sylvie, so welcome and so loved, bonded us, but she also demanded most of our time and attention, as babies do. While we willingly and happily cared for her, we couldn't help but notice how little time we had left to focus on each other. We still laugh ruefully over a particularly telling incident. Mark was holding the baby, and from another room I heard a thump and a groan. "What happened!?" I cried. "I bumped my head," Mark said. "Oh, good," I replied in sincere relief. "I was afraid it was the baby." "Thanks a lot," he muttered.

If Sylvie's infancy challenged our previous absorption in one another, how much more so does our busier life now. Mark and I both have fulfilling careers, and we also take almost sole care of our two children. We've worked hard at "having it all," but in the process we've stretched ourselves thin. Something has to go, and often it's the time we devote to each other. If we can barely make it through a chock-full day, how on earth are we going to have the energy at night to light the candles, warm the massage oil, dwell on each other the way we used to do?

While we both bemoan this state of affairs, reminding each other on particularly hard days, as we sneak a hug, that "I'm still in here," it's clear that we come at the issue from somewhat different perspectives. I easily yield to the demands of my daughters. Sometimes, their needs get in the way of my closeness with Mark, especially when I let myself become just too tired to devote real energy to our intimacy. This problem

frustrates me, but I have a hard time getting around it. Sometimes Mark encourages me to "set more limits"—to preserve a little more space for myself and for "us," but I am torn.

Fortunately, though, Mark and I have begun to find ways to carve out more moments for ourselves. The girls play together more now, which gives us a little more time to reconnect. And at night we make time—even if it comes out of our sleep—to sit in bed together and talk. This evening ritual has been a constant in our relationship, making our bedroom the locus of an intimacy that is still deep and multi-faceted. When we turn out the lights, we still turn to each other with love and desire, whether we act on it or not.

Still, I have been longing to return ourselves to the center stage a little more often, so two weeks ago I secretly orchestrated our very first, luxurious night away alone together since Sylvie was born. Mark's birthday called for something special, so I planned an outing to approximate the "old days" of life before kids. I could have predicted that Mark would enjoy himself—once he got over the shock—but I wasn't quite prepared for the eagerness with which I embraced the opportunity to feed a flame that has admittedly been serving somewhat as a pilot light. When Mark asked me if I wanted to make a checkup call home, I declined. I didn't want to alter the tender mood that had been deepening in us since the moment we entered the hotel. I knew perfectly well that the girls were fine. I also knew that I liked what was happening between Mark and me; I liked our intensifying and prolonged awareness and enjoyment, both emotionally and physically, only of each other.

I guess our time away crystallized for me what I had long sensed but not fully acknowledged—that although motherhood reaps many rewards, the kind of passion that brings and keeps two people together is not necessarily one of them. If I want to have such intimacy, I must create it with Mark alone, and that's what this night was all about. Our little second honeymoon was so gratifying, in so many ways, that we won't wait another seven years to try it again. And in the end, we had no use for that pink negligee; Sylvie and Linnea can keep it. Such props are for newlyweds.

Mark Harris is a frequent contributor to Hope. *Theresa Dougal is a professor of English at Moravian College in Bethlehem, Pennsylvania.*

Unit 6

Key Points to Consider

❖ What does your college or university do about date or acquaintance rape? Are there education or prevention programs? How is a report of an assault handled? How do you think these issues should be handled on campuses?

❖ Are birth control (contraceptive prescriptions, emergency contraception, and sterilization), abortion, and infertility services available at the clinics and hospitals in your community? If not, why and how far would someone have to travel to get them?

❖ Have you overheard or participated in formal or informal discussions about potential or real sexual harassment at your job or school? How do you, your classmates, or coworkers feel about it? How would you rate your school or employer regarding awareness, prevention programming, and response to complaints?

❖ How do you feel about laws restricting sexual behaviors (for example, age limits, marital requirements for engaging in sex, or laws making specific sexual behaviors illegal)? Which laws would you add or change related to sexual issues or behaviors?

❖ Where do you believe "personal freedom" or "choice" about sexually related behaviors begins to collide with the "greater good" of society? How about sex online?

❖ If you had a magic wand, what would you change about sexuality and how American society affects it? (Go ahead and dream, you're not being asked to identify if and how it could really happen.)

 **Links** **www.dushkin.com/online/**

These sites are annotated on pages 4 and 5.

This final unit deals with several topics that are of interest or concern for different reasons. Also, as the title suggests, it combines "old" or ongoing topics and concerns with "new" or emerging ones. In one respect, however, these topics have a common denominator—they have all taken positions of prominence in the public's awareness as social issues.

Tragically, sexual abuse and violence are long-standing occurrences in society and in some relationships. For centuries, a strong code of silence surrounded these occurrences and, many now agree, increased not only the likelihood of sexual abuse and violence, but the harm to victims of these acts. Beginning in the middle of this century, two societal movements helped to begin eroding this code of silence. The child welfare/child rights movement exposed child abuse and mistreatment and sought to improve the lives of children and families. Soon after, and to a large extent fueled by the emerging women's movement, primarily "grass-roots" organizations that became known as "rape crisis" groups or centers became catalysts for altering the way we looked at (or avoided looking at) rape and sexual abuse.

Research today suggests that these movements have accomplished many of their initial goals and brought about significant social change. The existence and prevalence of rape and other sexual abuse is much more accurately known. Many of the myths previously believed (rapists are strangers that jump out of bushes, sexual abuse only occurs in poor families, all rapists are male and all victims are female, and so on) have been replaced with more accurate information. The code of silence has been recognized for the harm it can cause, and millions of friends, parents, teachers, counselors, and others have learned how to be approachable, supportive listeners to victims disclosing their abuse experiences. Finally, we have come to recognize the role that power, especially unequal power, plays in rape, sexual abuse, sexual violence, and, a term coined more recently, sexual harassment.

The articles in the first subsection, *Sexual Abuse and Harassment*, seek to highlight several ongoing and emerging issues with respect to sexual abuse, violence, and harassment. Despite some progress, such abuse still occurs, and the damage to victims can be compounded when they are not believed or, worse yet, they, rather than the perpetrator are blamed. The first, "Christy's Crusade" follows the courageous fight—all the way to the Supreme Court—for justice by a college student rape victim. The next two focus on emerging complexities surrounding sexual abuse, and, in turn, all sexual behavior. As we as a society have sought to expose and reduce abusive sex, it has become increasingly clear that all of society and each of us as individuals/potential partners must grapple with the broader issue of what constitutes consent: What is non-abusive sexual interaction? How can people communicate interest, arousal, desire, and/or propose sexual interaction, when remnants of unequal power, ignorance, misinformation, fear, adversarial sex roles, and inadequate communication skills still exist? Finally, another layer of perplexing questions that confront the proactive/reactive dilemma: What is, or should be, the role of employers, school personnel, or simply any of us who may be seen as contributing on some level due to awareness or complicity to an environment that allows uncomfortable, abusive, or inappropriate sexual interaction? Is it possible that we are so "sensitive" to the potential for abuse that combined with our discomfort, anger, and fear we have become hysterical vigilantes pushing an eager legal system to indict "offenders" who have not committed abuse or harassment?

The second subsection, *Legal and Ethical Issues Related to Sex*, delves into some current legal and ethical dilemmas associated with sexuality and sexual behavior. All societies have struggled with the apparent dichotomy of freedom versus protection when it comes to enacting laws about human behavior. In addition, the pace of technological advances (infertility treatment, AIDS, and nonsurgical abortion methods, to name just a few) has far outstripped society's attempts to grapple with the legal, ethical, and moral issues involved. At the present time, a variety of laws about sexual behaviors exist. Some are outdated, apparently in conflict with evolving social norms, even majority behaviors. Some laws are permissive, seeking to protect individual freedoms. Others are restrictive, seeking to protect society and allowing the intrusion of legal representatives into the private, even consensual, sexual behaviors of otherwise law-abiding citizens. The first article, "Legislative Morality," takes as a given that laws about behavior, including sexual behavior, will legislate morality, but what is uncertain is "whose morality" will reign. The next two articles, "Pregnant? You're Fired!" and "The Hidden Health Threat That Puts Every Woman at Risk," address pregnancy and reproduction-related rights, laws and services, and include information we all, regardless of gender or life stage, need to know. "Criminal Injustice" illustrates how even when ground-breaking legislation is passed, the goal sought—in this case reduction of sexual assault—may not be realized. The final article "Porn.con?" focuses on today's computer-age version of the thorny freedom-of-speech/expression versus pornography issue by chronicling the rise to fame of Seth Warshavsky, the millionaire founder of a panorama of sexually-explicit Web sites.

Each year *Annual Editions: Human Sexuality* closes with a final Focus section that is designed to give readers "food for thought" about an emerging trend in the "big picture" of sexuality or to raise very broad questions that do not have current or simple answers. Last year's turn-of-the-century Focus section merged both of these alternatives with the question, "Will sexuality in the new century be better or worse?" At the time of the writing of the 00/01 edition, we acknowledged that not only would an answer to the question take some time to become evident, but that there existed significant conflict as far as what people considered better (or worse). Mindful that these two statements are still quite true as the 01/02 edition goes to press we have retained the same concluding subsection. The first two articles address what had been predicted one or more decades ago to be the exciting future of sex: virtual sex. The remaining three discuss evidence of trends away from dichotomies to possible middle ground in three areas of sexuality: gender roles or male versus female; sexuality and religion or sexual versus sacred; and sexuality and philosophy or East versus West. Because today's readers are present and future trend makers, we challenge you to confront and discuss these complex personal and societal issues in order to conceptualize a better future for all of us. A future of sex that finds a balance between complete freedom for the individual and subjugation or homogenization of human diversity to a narrow definition of the common good. Only by so doing can humankind's quest for joyful, healthy, and fulfilling sexuality be realized.

Old/New Sexual Concerns

CHRISTY'S
CRUSADE

WHEN WOMEN VICTIMS OF VIOLENT crimes do not find justice in state courts, do they have the right to sue for damages in federal court? For one young woman, attempting to gain that right took her all the way to the United States Supreme Court.

by Patrick Tracey

IN SEPTEMBER OF 1994, THE CONFLUENCE OF TWO EVENTS—ONE IN the United States Congress and one in a college dorm room—would provide the backdrop for a U.S. Supreme Court case of crucial importance to women. On September 13 of that year, Congress passed the Violence Against Women Act (VAWA). The law, which women's groups had lobbied Congress to pass, was created to provide federal protections for women on the grounds that states were not vigorously pursuing cases involving violence against women. In addition to the equal protection component, Congress inserted an economic component to the law, based on evidence that violence against women impairs their ability to earn a living. Among other things, VAWA put federal muscle into prosecuting abusers who cross state lines or violate orders of protection. Under its civil rights remedy, it also allowed victims of gender-motivated violence to sue their attackers for damages. It was this last provision that brought the case of then 19-year-old Christy Brzonkala (pronounced bron-KA-la) before the U.S. Supreme Court.

Just one week after the passage of VAWA, Brzonkala was allegedly raped in a dorm room at Virginia Polytechnic Institute, in Blacksburg, Virginia, by two university football players. After two university disciplinary hearings failed to adequately address the charges, Brzonkala sued her attackers for damages in federal court under the still untested Violence Against Women Act. This prompted state prosecutors to open an investigation. A grand jury was called but refused to indict Brzonkala's alleged attackers. The case wound its way through the federal court system until March of 1999, when the U.S. Fourth Circuit Court of Appeals, in Richmond, ruled against Brzonkala, finding that Congress exceeded its constitutional authority when, in enacting VAWA, it claimed that violence against women affected interstate commerce. The court also ruled against Brzonkala on the equal protection front, finding that VAWA was not an appropriate response to the failure of state criminal courts to treat female and male victims of violence equally. VAWA supporters countered both points, arguing that violence against women does affect commerce by undermining a woman's ability to get and keep a job. (The Bureau of National Affairs found that domestic violence costs U.S. employers $3–$5 billion annually. And according to the Department of Justice, the cost of rape to society is $127 billion annually.) Supporters also argued that the civil rights remedy was an appropriate response to bias in the state courts because it gave women another option for redress—the chance to litigate their claims in federal court. After the Richmond appeals court rejection, Brzonkala's attorneys took the case to the U.S. Supreme Court, where it was heard on January 11 of this year. A decision is expected by June.

—The Editors

THE 23-YEAR-OLD PLAINTIFF IS SUFFERING FROM BATTLE FATIGUE. For five years, she has shunned the media spotlight. But on this blustery January morning, at the foot of the wide marble steps of the United States Supreme Court, it isn't easy. Christy Brzonkala lowers her head, running the gauntlet to the back entrance of the courthouse. Hordes of reporters staked out to film her arrival have missed her completely.

Brzonkala v. *Morrison; Crawford;* and *Virginia Polytechnic Institute and State University* began as a university disciplinary hearing at Virginia Tech in Blacksburg, a rural town nestled in the New River Valley of the Blue Ridge Mountains. One of the football players whom Brzonkala had accused of rape,

"IT WAS OBVIOUS THAT RAPE VICTIMS WEREN'T GOING TO GET ANY JUSTICE ON CAMPUS."

James Crawford, was acquitted by the disciplinary panel. The other, Antonio Morrison, after initially being found guilty of sexual assault then later acquitted, was only required to attend a one-hour session with a university affirmative-action counselor. "It was obvious," Brzonkala says, "that rape victims weren't going to get any justice on campus, so I decided to get my own attorney."

Eileen Wagner, an English professor turned lawyer, had close ties to the academic world. She was a member of the American Association of University Women (AAUW), an organization to which Brzonkala's mother also happened to belong. Mary Ellen Brzonkala was referred to Wagner by an AAUW member who assured her that Wagner was not afraid to take on a large university and was well-equipped to handle her daughter's case.

Wagner told her young client that she didn't stand much of a chance in criminal court because rape cases were not always vigorously pushed by state police and prosecutors. Not only that, there was no physical evidence. And indeed, a state grand jury later failed to indict, partly because, as in the vast majority of rape cases in the U.S., Brzonkala's physical evidence had literally swirled down the drain when she bathed that night. However, Wagner told her client that there was one possibility: Congress had passed VAWA just one week before Brzonkala was allegedly raped, and she could be one of the first to sue under it. She could file a suit in federal civil court even without physical evidence because there is a lower burden of proof there than in criminal courts.

Brzonkala recalls Wagner saying to her that no one had yet sued for damages under VAWA and "we might get some justice from it." Brzonkala says, "[Wagner] and I talked for about five hours that day. Three days later, I said I'd do it." What tipped the balance for Brzonkala was the fact that Wagner had represented other students in disputes with universities.

For her part, Wagner says, "We knew she had the right case to test the law." The "right case" meant, first, that the perpetrators and victim didn't know each other. "Getting court sympathy when they do know each other is difficult," Wagner says. Second, statements made by Morrison could reflect "gender animus." Third, Brzonkala had already gone public. "If you're going to change policy," Wagner explains, "it's much better to have a real live person," rather than a Jane Doe. And finally, VAWA requires that the perpetrators' behavior be felony level, which in this case it was.

Nevertheless, Brzonkala and Wagner hit a brick wall in federal court, with a majority of judges ruling that VAWA was unconstitutional. This outcome actually bolstered Wagner's initial predictions. "We knew that some people were concerned with the constitutionality of the law, so we thought from the beginning that this would go to the Supreme Court," she says.

Today Brzonkala is just where Wagner expected her to be—at the High Court, swinging for the fences on behalf of all women. But it isn't going to be easy. Throughout the 1990s, the Rehnquist Court has steadily curtailed federal power, and Brzonkala's case represents a direct challenge to this effort. Chief Justice Rehnquist has already tipped his hand, having previously singled out VAWA as an example of Congress intruding on the traditional power of the states to prosecute rape.

When Congress passed the law, it declared that "[all] persons within the United States shall have the right to be free from crimes of violence motivated by gender." Paradoxically, many states welcomed the new federal law. In fact, attorneys general from 36 states have signed briefs arguing that Brzonkala deserves the right to have her case reheard by the first judge who ruled VAWA unconstitutional.

AS THE NINE ROBED SUPREME COURT JUSTICES enter the courtroom, Brzonkala rises with a capacity crowd of 350 spectators. The justices will spend the next 90 minutes prying apart legal arguments that hinge on the question of whether victims of gender-based violence can sue their attackers for damages in federal court.

Seth Waxman, the U.S. Solicitor General, representing the U.S. government, and Julie Goldscheid, an attorney for the National Organization for Women (NOW) Legal Defense and Education Fund, representing Brzonkala, attempt to show the need for a "federal remedy" to the problem of states not giving women equal protection.

Goldscheid tells the Court, "The states agreed that they needed federal help." The Supreme Court now has an opportunity to "further the legacy of civil rights legislation" by recognizing that women "have a right to recover damages when their civil rights are damaged through gender-based violence." The justices grapple with the question of whether gender-based violence affects interstate commerce.

Legal experts speculate that four justices will vote to uphold VAWA and three will dissent. All eyes are on Justice Sandra Day O'Connor, one of the two crucial swing votes and the likely author of the Court's decision. As the Court weighs up a host of federal statutes, O'Connor, who has been a staunch defender of women's rights, now questions the wisdom of treading on the traditional right of the states to prosecute rape charges.

Ruth Bader Ginsburg, the only other woman on the Court, seems to like the law. Peering over her glasses, Ginsburg says Congress's goal was not to displace state authority but "to provide an alternate forum. Why can't Congress do that?"

"Because this is not commerce," replies Michael Rosman, representing the two football players on behalf of the Center for Individual Rights, a conservative Washington, D.C.-based

FOR BRZONKALA, THE LINK BETWEEN RAPE AND COMMERCE IS NOT AN ACADEMIC ONE.

legal think tank. "This is violence, interpersonal violence, the kind of thing states have had as their exclusive province ever since the start of our country."

For Brzonkala, the link between rape and commerce is not an academic one. She says that for her own safety, she was forced to drop out of college—a circumstance that will affect her ability to earn a decent wage—while the men she charges with rape were initially allowed to stay on campus and maintain their football scholarships. The alleged rape took place just three weeks after she'd entered the university to begin her freshman year. She hung in for the rest of that year, went home for summer vacation, and then never returned to Tech.

As the courtroom empties, she allows as how she could tell the Court a thing or two about intrusions—and not the feds intruding on the states. "It's called rape," she says, her heels clicking down the marble stairs. "Rape is the real quote-unquote 'intrusion.' "

The plaintiff strides down the sidewalk as a scrum of reporters catches up to her, wielding notepads and video cameras and poking microphones in her face. She addresses them briefly and then strolls around the corner for a post-argument reception sponsored by NOW. Senator Joseph Biden (D.-Del.), who sponsored the VAWA law, is on hand to thank Brzonkala "on behalf of my daughter, my granddaughter, and every other woman I love."

BRZONKALA, WHO HAD NURTURED DREAMS OF becoming a nutritionist, makes her living these days as an assistant manager at Madam's Organ, a blues club in the trendy Adams Morgan neighborhood of Washington, D.C. At the long pine bar, Brzonkala is having a few laughs with her best friends, who also happen to be her coworkers. "This bar is staffed by strong, independent women—people who kept me sane and allowed me to ease into independence," she says.

There is a stark contrast between the woman relaxing with friends and the pensive plaintiff listening to dry legal arguments. Deep down, she says, lies a desire to shield herself from pain. As evidence, she points to her willingness to tell new acquaintances her history: "They tend to treat me with kid gloves if I tell them. And that's how I like to be treated. Plus, if they know, they might be careful about how they use the word 'rape.' It's not a word to be taken lightly."

The biggest step in her recovery came, she says, when she moved into her own place downtown: "I needed to know that I could stand on my own two feet."

Brzonkala's first chance to stand on her own two feet came in the fall of 1994, when she left her suburban home on a quite little cul-de-sac in Fairfax, Virginia. Heading off to Virginia Tech, four hours south, she waved good-bye to her father, Kenneth, a civil servant with the Federal Emergency Management Agency and her mother, Mary Ellen, an optician. She was also leaving behind several touchstones of her past. In her bedroom were swimming, softball, and basketball trophies. On one wall was a collage of smiling classmates at her senior prom. On another, an aerial photo of the Tech campus.

If the trophies would remind her parents of where she had been, the picture of Tech's campus would tell them where she was going: to a safe rural university that would midwife their daughter's passage to adulthood.

"Everything was going fine," Brzonkala recalls about her first few weeks at school. "I loved my classes." She had already made friends and probably could have played basketball for Tech but decided to forgo athletics to concentrate on her studies.

One night several friends from the women's soccer team invited her to a party off-campus. They were there for "three, four, or five hours," she says, and during that time she had "three, four, or five beers. I was by no means loaded."

After the party, Brzonkala and her friend Hope Handley walked back to their dorm, Cochrane Hall. As they approached, two guys whistled at them from a third-floor window, inviting them up for a nightcap.

"So we just go up," says Brzonkala. "We're going up to Hope's room, which is on the same floor, and we decide to drop in on these guys, just to say hello, nothing more. We go down the hall and they say, 'Oh, I'm so-and-so and so-and-so, and we're football players.' I almost cracked up, because I was a jock in high school, so it did not impress me."

What began as small talk soon degenerated into blatant come-ons, at which point Handley left the room. Handley remembered that she'd said good-bye when she left, but Brzonkala says, "It was my impression that she had gone to the bathroom. After a few minutes, she didn't come back. I got up to go, and that's when it all happened."

Morrison, a six-foot-one-inch defensive linebacker, weighing over 200 pounds, barred her from leaving and asked her for sex. "I am not that kind of person. I said 'No.' No is no, and that's all you need to hear."

After she refused a second time, he stopped asking, a point upon which she and Morrison both later agreed, with one major distinction. He says that he asked twice and then they fell into each other's arms. She says he pushed her onto his bed, forcefully removed her clothes, pinned her arms and legs, and pushed himself into her.

As soon as Morrison finished, Brzonkala says, his friend Crawford raped her. For about 15 minutes, she says, it was Morrison, then Crawford, then Morrison again.

"I was in shock, and I blanked out. When Morrison got off me, Crawford came in. Then Crawford left, and Morrison did the same thing again. The only thing I remembered was [Morrison] saying, 'You better not have any fucking diseases.' "

"I'M NOT THAT KIND OF PERSON. I SAID 'NO.' NO IS NO, AND THAT'S ALL YOU NEED TO HEAR."

For those who have questioned her judgment in going to the dorm room of two big jocks in the wee hours of the morning, Brzonkala has an answer: "We never learned about rape in high school. They thought they were protecting us. Do you know what my senior quote in my yearbook was? It says, 'I will trust you until you do something to make me not trust you.' I was just so naive."

Afterwards, Brzonkala walked down the long hallway to the stairwell. She says Morrison followed her. "I just walked ahead of him," she recalls. "It was weird. He said, 'Oh, maybe I can call you sometime?' And I just remember feeling disgust. I went back to my suite and just sat in the tub for hours. I put it somewhere way in the back of my head. Of course the next day I knew what happened, but . . ." Her voice trails off.

BRZONKALA SANK INTO A PARALYZING DEPRESSION. She rarely left her room for fear of running into Morrison or Crawford. To keep from being recognized by her assailants, she cut her hair into a bob and wore baggy clothes. Even sunshine seemed sinister. She slept all day, skipping classes. Her failing grades seemed a trivial matter. "At that point, I sort of felt that I'd lost my college life. I was terrified of everything."

Uncharacteristically, she started smoking and drinking every day. Alcohol was the easiest way to blot it all out. "She had a tight-knit group of friends before," her roommate Charlotte Wachter recalls. "And then, she never really left the room after that."

Three weeks after the alleged rape, Brzonkala swallowed a vial of pills she'd been taking for a hypothyroid condition. "She was trying to keep me from getting anyone to help her," Wachter says. "But I woke up the girl in the room next to ours, and we tricked her so I could go get help."

Brzonkala was treated at Montgomery Regional Hospital in Blacksburg and released. The suicide attempt had been a cry for help, but Brzonkala's parents were never notified, and she didn't tell Wachter what had happened to her. As the Virginia Tech Hokies went on to win the Big East Championship, Brzonkala bottled up her rage. When she went home for Christmas break, her parents were still in the dark and mystified by her abysmal academic performance.

Says Brzonkala, "I know that I can never understand, because I'm not a parent, what it's like having to see your child go through something like that. So I didn't really want to talk to them about it."

With football season over, avoiding her attackers was getting harder. "I was seeing them coming out of the dining hall," Brzonkala says. "And that was starting to freak me out."

One March night, she was hanging out in her dorm room when Wachter, who worked in the dining hall downstairs, casually mentioned that she'd overheard some football players boasting about how they liked to "get girls drunk and fuck the shit out of them." Wachter told Brzonkala that she didn't appreciate the comment because she had a friend who always regretted not having pressed charges after she'd been raped.

It was this story that finally gave Brzonkala the courage to speak. "I was raped," she said softly, then started to cry.

Suddenly, Brzonkala's bizarre behavior made sense. The baggy clothes. The short haircut. The hapless suicide attempt.

Wachter says Brzonkala did not know the names of her alleged assailants, so Wachter returned to Cochrane Hall the next day with a Hokies media guide. When she opened the glossy brochure, there they were. "That's him," Brzonkala said. "That's Crawford, the cornerback. And that's Morrison, the defensive linebacker."

Brzonkala was finally out of the closet. At the suggestion of her resident assistant at Cochrane Hall, she sought help at the women's center. The modest white clapboard house on the edge of the Tech campus is carpeted and cozy, with framed photos of women basketball, soccer, and softball players lining the walls. After opening up to rape-crisis counselor Donna Lisker, Brzonkala says, "I stopped crying for the first time in months."

Later, Brzonkala's attorney Eileen Wagner would uncover a startling fact: a number of other campus rapes had been reported that fall. (Wagner and her client will probably never know if charges were brought because that information is confidential.) Brzonkala soon confided in a small circle of friends, including a few women soccer players who in turn met with Tech's sports psychologist on Brzonkala's behalf. They also arranged for Brzonkala to meet with Tech football coach Frank Beamer, who quickly punted the idea of punishing his players. "He said his job was to protect his boys," Brzonkala says.

Beamer had been hired eight years earlier to restore pride in a team tarnished by scandals. He was now on his way to the Sugar Bowl with a ragtag roster of players nobody else wanted. With his eye on a Top Ten finish, the last thing he needed was to lose Morrison, his highly recruited starting linebacker.

It was time, Brzonkala knew, to level with her parents. Fortified with a drink, she dialed their number. "Mom," she said, "I have something to tell you."

Mary Ellen Brzonkala says she dropped the receiver when she heard the news. Kenneth Brzonkala, wringing his large hands, says he "just wanted to kill the two bastards."

The next day Brzonkala and her parents met in Lisker's office. "We talked about the judicial options," says Lisker. "There was the criminal system, reporting it to the local police; there was the campus judicial system, which meant going to the office of the dean of students; and there was civil litigation."

Brzonkala opted to go to the dean of students because she would not have to face her attackers. The next day she filed a complaint with Tech's disciplinary panel for students.

LEGAL EAGLES

BRZONKALA V. *MORRISON* will profoundly affect the way violence against women is treated in the United States. *Ms.* reporter Amy Aronson asked feminist law experts to comment on the case.

MARTHA DAVIS, legal director of the NOW Legal Defense and Education Fund The Court is really deciding how far Congress can go in protecting civil rights. We thought this was resolved in the '60s, but the Court has gone so far to the right that the question is up for grabs. This is also an opportunity to educate the Court and the country about the fundamental impact that violence toward women has on the economy. We are hopeful that *Brzonkala* will prevail. Congress was so careful in drafting the statute. They sifted through tons of evidence from state courts about the economic impact of violence against women. For the Court to ignore the considered opinion of Congress would be shocking. One possibility is a narrow ruling, in which case we'd go back to Congress to reenact the law with slightly different provisions.

CATHARINE A. MACKINNON, Elizabeth A. Long Professor of Law at the University of Michigan and visiting professor at the University of Chicago Law School This case is women's Civil War—the war over women's rights in civil society and women's full citizenship in the federal union. Sex-based violence with impunity denies women equal protection under the law and sex equality in society. The Fourteenth Amendment authorizes federal equality legislation. The antiequality side, as they did with race, argues that federal civil rights legislation violates states' rights. But the states are overwhelmed by male violence against women. VAWA does not take away state power; it gives women a law to take into our own hands. It recognizes that violence against us because we are women violates our civil rights, and the Constitution backs us up. Concretely, women can sue their abusers, and hold them responsible, without having to involve police or beg prosecutors. It shifts the balance of power toward sex equality. If Christy Brzonkala does not prevail it will be a staggering setback for human rights and an affirmation of the systemic nature of male dominance.

MARI MATSUDA, professor of law at Georgetown University Law Center and coauthor of *We Won't Go Back: Making the Case for Affirmative Action* (Houghton Mifflin) The right has supported efforts to prosecute crime, and this Court has been aggressive in dismantling the Bill of Rights when it comes to protections for people accused of crimes. The fact that this Court has

been dismantling these protections at the same time that it has been making it harder to prosecute violence against women says something about who it does and does not care about. When the Republicans had the appointment power, they sought out antifeminist High Court judges and made antifeminist principles a litmus test. The Democrats have not been equally aggressive. This shows that judicial appointments should be a critical focus for feminist activism.

Representative ELEANOR HOLMES NORTON (D.-D.C.) VAWA gives women what blacks have had since the Civil War— civil protection. There is still plenty of racial violence in this country, but there is less because those laws are on the books and are invoked. I'm concerned because of the skepticism I heard from the justices. Justice O'Connor, who has tended to understand women's issues, said, in effect, 'Your approach would justify a federal remedy for child support and alimony cases.' Nonsense. We had great debate in the House and Senate that led to a very narrowly written statute. Under VAWA, a woman has to prove more than a crime itself. She has to show that words said or actions taken prove a special animus was directed toward her because she's a woman. That's a very high burden to meet.

JUDITH RESNIK, Arthur Liman Professor of Law at Yale Law School This statute is about how to enable women to be fully authorized economic actors, free from the threat of violence. VAWA continues a process started in the '60s when Congress enacted civil rights statutes, many of them through its commerce-clause powers. State attorneys general told Congress they wanted help in correcting patterns of discrimination in state criminal justice systems. I'm struck that when some people talk about VAWA, they describe it as intrusive of state power over families. The fact that violence against women is seen primarily through the lens of family life is the result of a long history of discrimination that did not protect women from violence in the home.

DEBORAH RHODE, professor of law and former director of the Institute for Research on Women and Gender at Stanford University I'm guardedly optimistic that *Brzonkala* will prevail. There is ample precedent. The facts in this case are as good as you get. This reminds me of the struggle over the Equal Rights Amendment. In that instance, too, people said "The states can handle this." I remember one feminist attorney saying, "Yes, but that's like fighting the battle against slavery plantation by plantation." If the Court goes the wrong way, we'll be back to fighting things out one at a time.

At the first judicial board hearing, Crawford was acquitted because he had an alibi. Teammate Cornell Brown claimed he was with Crawford elsewhere that night, although he later refused to make that claim to the grand jury. The board found Morrison guilty of "sexual assault," based on his offensive "diseases" remark. He was suspended for two semesters but appealed the ruling, claiming that his "due process rights" were denied, and that the suspension was "unduly harsh and arbitrary." According to a May 22 letter to Brzonkala from Dean of Students Cathryn Goree, Morrison's appeal was denied.

He then retained attorney David Paxton, a big gun from nearby Roanoke. Paxton combed the facts and discovered an eye-popping glitch. Tech, it seems, had made a printing error. The word "rape" had been omitted from a description of sexual violence in the original printing of the 1994–95 student code of conduct contained in the university rule book.

The rule book was later reprinted with the missing word added. But by then it was too late because, Paxton argued, Morrison couldn't have known from reading the first printing that rape was included in Tech's sexual assault policy.

So on July 21 a second board hearing was held. Though he was on summer break, Morrison returned for the hearing. This time, he was found guilty of "abusive conduct," a lesser charge than sexual assault, again stemming from his "diseases" remark. The board confirmed his suspension.

Brzonkala received a letter from the board saying, "This action was taken because the preponderance of evidence provided during the hearing supports a finding of guilt."

The letter was dated August 4. Strangely, on August 3, Coach Beamer told reporters at a Big East Conference media day that Morrison would return for the fall football season.

Apparently, Beamer knew something that Brzonkala didn't. The decision to reinstate Morrison was made solely by the Tech provost, Peggy Meszaros. Meszaros had concurred with the "abusive conduct" finding, but in a letter to Morrison copied to Beamer, she reduced Morrison's punishment to a one-hour session with a Tech affirmative-action counselor. "While you were convicted of a serious charge," she wrote, "it is my determination that the sanction is excessive when compared with any other cases where there has been a finding of the Abusive Conduct Policy."

Brzonkala and her parents said they never received a letter informing them of Morrison's reinstatement. Brzonkala, who was home for the summer, read about it in the Washington *Post*. This development clinched her decision not to return for the fall semester. "Obviously," says Brzonkala, "they wanted to brush this under the rug."

"It was outrageous," her father says. "Had I sent my daughter back, without her ever knowing that Morrison was still there, she could have run into him in any dark stairwell. No one tried to call. Nobody wrote us a letter. If he were not on the football team, I guarantee he would have been gone. What was this, another printing error?"

In September, Kenneth Brzonkala confronted the dean of the university about Morrison's reinstatement and was told nothing could be done. At the beginning of November, Christy Brzonkala took her story to Terry Padalino, the editor in chief of the student newspaper, the *Collegiate Times*. Padalino says that when she heard it, she immediately sat down to tap out an editorial: "Something stinks in Blacksburg," she wrote. "For more than a year, a young woman, once a student at Virginia Tech, has been recovering from an assault she claims was made against her in the bedroom of a linebacker for Tech's 13th-ranked football team. . . . Her Tech college career is all but over. Morrison, on the other hand, is having a banner year as a member of the Big East Champion Hokies."

Padalino interviewed Beamer, but Meszaros did not return numerous phone calls. "She wouldn't see us," says Padalino, "even though we went to her office."

Nor could Padalino reach Morrison or Crawford, who also refused through their lawyers to talk to *Ms.* For two weeks,

Padalino sat on the editorial and a front-page story that was to accompany it: "It was a week before the final football game of the season. Because it was a big game, we decided to wait so that it wouldn't look as if the game was her motive in coming forward."

On November 28, 1995, the *Collegiate Times* hit the streets with a thud that reverberated all over campus. In her editorial, Padalino demanded that Meszaros be "severely disciplined for her heartless aiding and abetting of this malicious cover-up."

Soon after, an open forum was held for students, faculty, and townspeople in the student union building. About 250 members of the community, most of them angry, heard Meszaros read a 25-minute statement.

Brzonkala did not attend, but Leslei Syner, who had just formed a group on campus called Women Against Rape, was there to do the cross-examining of Meszaros. Syner said, "You do not have printed rules against murder, but does that mean you would condone killing?"

Many assumed that the university was coddling a star athlete. The Hokies were, after all, a top-ranking team in 1995, with only one loss. But in the months following, the pig-skinners would also rack up an astounding 21 arrests, six convictions, and four dropped charges. The team was filling the dockets of the Blacksburg courthouse, with Morrison and Crawford in the lead. Morrison was arrested on charges of being drunk in public and petty larceny. Crawford was arrested twice, once for hitting a service-station attendant with his car and once for the rape and attempted sodomy of another Tech student. The latter was settled out of court. This litany of crimes prompted Washington *Post* columnist Tony Kornheiser to wonder if the Hokies were in training for "the Convict Bowl."

Crawford was expelled because of the latest rape charge, and Morrison, whose deferred suspension was never enforced, finished college in 1999.

Now Christy Brzonkala's case rests with the Supreme Court. If VAWA is upheld by the Court, Brzonkala wins the right to have her case reheard by the first judge who ruled VAWA unconstitutional. The suit seeks $4 million from Morrison and Crawford and $4.3 million from Virginia Tech. The combined punitive damages equals the amount the university received for its 1995 appearance in the Sugar Bowl. Brzonkala also sought damages from the university for violating Title IX, which bars sexual discrimination by universities that receive federal money. According to the Associated Press, in late February Virginia Tech settled that suit, paying Brzonkala $75,000.

Brzonkala may go back to college but never to Tech. She says she's tired of being a poster child. "I am so over the cause," she says. "But it will be easier to sleep at night knowing all this is behind me."

Patrick Tracey is a freelance writer based in Washington, D.C.

WHEN PREACHERS
PREY

A minister's wife speaks candidly about the currents
of sex and power that flow between the men in the pulpit
and the women in the pews and the dangerous liaisons they can spark

By Marcia L. Dyson

I REMEMBER HOW BAD I FELT LAST SUMMER when I first saw the news photos of Sister Deborah Lyons, the wife of the Reverend Henry J. Lyons, the leader of the nation's largest and most influential Black Church organization, the National Baptist Convention (NBC), U.S.A. Arrested, fingerprinted and charged with burglary and arson, Deborah Lyons was accused last July of breaking in and setting fire to a $700,000 Florida home her husband apparently co-owned with his business partner, the convention's corporate public-relations executive, Bernice V. Edwards.

I, too, am a minister's wife. My husband of seven years, Michael Eric Dyson, is not only ordained in the Baptist church but is also a prominent professor, author and media commentator. The fact that he is as handsome as he is charismatic is something that is rarely lost on the sisters who hear his sermons or attend his lectures. But it's not the threat of women who are perennially attracted to my husband that kept me on edge during the Lyons controversy.

What I was reminded of by the Lyons melodrama as it unfolded last summer was the many other similar scenarios I've witnessed over my decades in the church. They always seemed to me to be signs of the undeniable power that the men in our pulpits have over the women in the pews. And too many times I've seen preachers exploit this power and even take it for granted, as if it were an entitlement—sometimes preying on vulnerable and lonely women,

at other times seeking out accomplices in sexual misconduct who are quite willing or, at best, self-deceived.

The fact is, long before I ever met my husband, I found myself in the position of the preacher's prey. More than 20 years ago, I was in an unhappy first marriage to an abusive man. At the end of my rope in that relationship, though committed to my faith and still praying for God's wisdom to show me the way to heal and grow within my marriage, I sought counseling from my minister. As far as I knew, I had no reason not to trust this man. Yet he betrayed me by seizing this vulnerable moment in the life of a naive and distressed woman as an opportunity for a sexual come-on.

This minister showed up at my home—calculating the very time he would find me alone—and tried to seduce me. While I managed to get loose from his embrace and get him out of my house, I was stunned and hurt. I couldn't imagine what I had done to encourage his advances. Nor could I bring myself to return to worship in his congregation. I said nothing to anyone and just stopped going to services. Only two months after this incident, I learned from a friend in my old congregation that the offending minister had just been asked to leave the church by the executive board because his wife had caught him in an affair with another church member.

It took me two years to find another church home. By then I had gone through a painful divorce, and I was relieved to be able to spend more of my leisure hours at my new church as a healing distraction. Still emotionally vulnerable, though, I yielded to the seductive charms of a married minister who visited my new congregation. He pursued me, but instead of firmly turning him away, this time I let my need for male companionship compromise my relationship with God. I indulged in the same corrupt delusion I've since seen many of my sisters use to justify an illicit relationship–that God Himself had sent this man to me.

But it proved to be the Devil's work after all. Our tryst failed to fill the void I felt in my life and led instead to an abyss of guilt and shame. It was a romance I certainly couldn't share with the world. I felt I had to protect the minister's reputation, although I later learned that his philandering was well known. Of course, the rumors already circulating about him didn't stop other sisters from stepping up and filling in as new links in his chain of fools.

So it was that I became familiar with the distorted perspective of the preacher's woman, just as I now live with the challenges of being a preacher's wife. I know what it is to be innocent prey to a predatory man, but I also know what it is to be complicit in predatory behavior.

It is well acknowledged that Black women are the very foundation of the Black church. We make up more than 70 percent of the membership, according to documentation cited by C. Eric Lincoln and Lawrence H. Mamiya in their valuable reference *The Black Church in the African-American Experience.* Despite our being such a key church constituency, women "are generally excluded from the church's central station of power, the pulpit," as my husband has written in *Between God and Gangsta Rap.* He terms this state of affairs "ecclesiastical apartheid." So while male ministers give plenty of lip service to the

church's reliance on Black women, that recognition does not spur them to envision a church where justice for women prevails.

Yes, male clergy who abuse their power and engage in sexual misconduct are unfortunately as pervasive in our churches as they are in White churches or in mosques and temples. Indeed, many powerful men, in God's house or the White House, have been subjected to temptation *and* have succumbed to it. But what disturbs me more are those who consider it a way of life or their right. Anthony L. Mitchell–a 26-year-old Harvard medical student who's also working toward a degree in theology at Boston University–recounts how he was once exhorted by his minister to look into the

'For many women, getting attention from the man in the pulpit is like receiving it from God. We may even view the minister as we would a glamorous entertainer or professional sports star. I've seen sisters rush for those seats in the first three rows in the sanctuary—to be close to the preacher.'

choir stand, which was full of women. "Many sisters are waiting for a man like you," Mitchell recalls him saying. "Just take your pick, boy. That's why they're there." Mitchell later understood that he was being initiated into the power dynamics between pulpit and pew, between male and female.

"The power one has in the pulpit is extraordinary," notes the Reverend Dr. Prathia Hall, a Princeton Theological Seminary–trained religious scholar and pastor of Philadelphia's Mount Sharon Baptist Church. (She was also recently cited by *Ebony* magazine as one of the nation's most distinguished women preachers.) "Men can believe that the power is their own, that it is a sign of God's favor.... There-

fore they believe that nothing they desire can be denied. And many women are attracted to this power."

For many women, getting attention from the man in the pulpit is roughly equivalent to receiving it from God. "It is difficult for women to separate this voice of authority, this messenger of God, who prays for you, who soothes you," says Dr. Evelyn Brooks Higginbotham, Harvard professor and author of *Righteous Discontent,* the groundbreaking religious history of Black Baptist women. "He has magnetism that a woman can never have. For women, the pastor can become a husband figure, a lover figure, not necessarily acted out but desired."

We may even view the minister as we would a glamorous entertainer or celebrated professional sports star. I have witnessed sisters who rush for those seats in the first three rows in the sanctuary–to be close to the preacher. We become sanctuary cheerleaders, rooting the minister on. Later we swell the reception line, wanting our Sunday best acknowledged by a hug from the man of God. "You're sure lookin' good there, sistah" is the admiring refrain many of us look for from the minister. Often women press notes into his palm: "Call me tonight, please. I can only confide in you."

The troubles we may take to the pastor have probably already been shared with a mother, a sister or an aunt. But while we may easily confide in other women, many of us still maintain a fairy-tale vision of a Black knight in shining armor who will deliver us and project that fantasy onto the minister. That's certainly an ironic setup for a downfall, because our most acute heartaches are often male-related. And we never seem to notice the other women who are engaging in the same wistful self-deception.

I am often reminded of my own moral failing when I see women who are attracted to my husband. Some of them are more brazen than I could ever be. "You know how blessed you are, girl, to have this man?" a woman once asked me while adjusting her cleavage to make certain that her ample bosom caught my husband's eye. "You better keep an eye on him and me."

But scores of others simply make long-distance phone calls to Michael for his advice–their pastors aren't as "sensitive" as he is, they tell him. They send him long letters, photos of themselves and gifts that have nothing to do with seeking spiritual guidance. Michael and I have had many conversations on how we deal with these women. Although it is very difficult, we have found it best to ignore them. I have to admit, though, I do get angry; then I often pray for these sisters because I see the ghost of my former self in them–haunted by the demons of loneliness and need. But my knowing their problems can't justify their actions, any more than it can excuse my own poor judgment in the past.

When Michael and I first met nine years ago, I talked with him frankly about my past experiences with so-called men of God. He also felt it was important in our relationship that I know and love him simply as a man with human failings like any other. When we decided to marry, we also decided I would always travel with him, as we foresaw that his very active preaching and teaching schedule would mean a lot of time on the road. It is now well known on his circuit that if you want to have Dyson as your guest preacher or speaker, you have to be prepared to send *two* tickets–the second one for his wife, Marcia. People often applaud the way we travel together, apparently taking pleasure in the sight of a Black couple obviously united in love and respect. But others, even some among the clergy, sometimes ridicule our keeping such close company with each other. One minister even had the nerve to warn Michael that he might "miss some good opportunities" by always having his wife by his side.

Let's face it: The bravado and machismo of many male ministers link them to their secular brethen. "You know all she needs is a good f–" echoes not just on the streets, around the watercooler or in the army barracks–it's heard even in the pastor's study. And a bigoted clergy also painfully interferes with God's healing for lesbian sisters. "In my late teens I struggled with my sexuality and confided in my minister," recalls Carrietta Jackson, a lesbian student at Union Theological Seminary. "The minister did not pray with me or console me as a child of God," she says. Instead, he told her she needed "straightening out" and said, "I'm the man to do it." Jackson recalls, "I was in shock. He was offering himself as a 'sacrificial lamb' to right the wrong [that he felt was] in my body."

Black women are so often called upon to appear strong, independent and self-confident. Church is the one place we feel safe enough to wear our vulnerability on the sleeves of our designer dresses. We feel secure in stitching our neediness into the hems of our softly tailored suits. When we share our tears and fears with our male ministers, we forge one of the most intimate relationships possible between two human beings. If we're the least bit careless about our principles and prayers, it becomes easy to confuse spiritual and emotional needs with erotic desires and to act on them inappropriately.

Most women who have been ensnared in such dangerous liaisons never speak up about their spiritual warfare, and they are wary of exposing themselves for a couple of reasons. First, they don't want to be shamed. Second, they don't want to be demonized as the woman who brings a brother down. Some sisters go to extraordinary lengths to defend the clergymen who become their lovers. "He has integrity," says a woman I'll call Kelly, who maintains a relationship with a married minister. "Our church grew substantially while he was pastor. He knows he can trust me. I wouldn't do anything to make people think badly of him."

Of course, imperfect men and women sometimes stumble, but when they earnestly repent sinful behavior and seek God's forgiveness, they should also find reconciliation in the Christian community. Still, we should never fail to censure ministers who employ their powerful positions to exploit, abuse or corrupt naive or vulnerable women. No less accountable are ministers who may presume to use their clerical authority to violate their own marriage vows with not-so-innocent partners. Such scandals don't simply hurt individual congregations. They distort the meaning and message of our Black faith to the wider community.

The status of Rev. Henry J. Lyons as a religious leader certainly did not exempt him from critical scrutiny, but it did seem at first to protect him from the complete public humiliation his wife endured. When allegations of questionable financial dealings on his part as well as the appearance of unseemly irregularities in his personal life prompted a small but distinguished group in the NBC to call for Lyons's resignation, Deborah Lyons tried to assume the full responsibility for her husband's problems. She made a public statement before the entire convention during its annual meeting in September, confessing that she was a recovering alcoholic, that her problems had added to her husband's burdens, that she had been mistaken about her husband's having an affair and had caused a good man unnecessary pain and embarrassment. She claimed the fire was an accident, though she subsequently pleaded guilty to arson.

Meanwhile, amid revelations of Edward's previous record of embezzlement in another organization and her own hand in NBC financial improprieties, the suspected "other woman" was fired from the NBC corporate public-relations position for which Lyons had originally hired her. She dropped from sight until she was arrested in Milwaukee a few months ago on Florida state charges connected with her alleged NBC financial schemes. Lyons was also arrested in February on theft and racketeering charges. But it looked as if he would be the only one given a break in this sad story. At last year's annual meeting, the convention delegation voted to let him keep his leadership role; so far, even his arrest seems to have changed nothing.

Black churches will suffer as long as a double standard prevails for males and females. For instance, in our loving churches teenage girls are condemned for out-of-wedlock pregnancies. They are often required to confess their sins and ask for forgiveness in front of the entire congregation, and they may be expelled from the choir or kept from participating in other public church functions. But the (usually older) men who impregnate them are overlooked and hence implicitly excused. Sometimes the father of the child sits on the deacons' row or in the pulpit. Then, too, Black men's lives are often given a higher premium than women's. "I was once told that one man standing up for God is greater than ten women standing up for God," says Anthony Mitchell, the Harvard medical and Boston University divinity student.

This point came home to me with thunderous clarity at a church baptism of year-old twins, a boy and a girl. The female was sprinkled with holy water. Few words were spoken over her tiny head. By contrast, the male was given a *Roots*-like baptism. His small body was held high near the cross. Charges of masculine protection were pronounced. Hands were laid on his head.

"There is neither male nor female: for you are one in Christ Jesus," writes the apostle Paul in the book of Galatians. We can no longer embrace a theology that reflects and reinforces our nation's sexism, patriarchy and misogyny. Ministers must look to

Christ's example of "feed[ing] my sheep" rather than aping disobedient biblical icons like David and Solomon, polygamous patriarchs of old.

I encourage sisters to face their needs honestly within the church, but also outside it. "It will take a conscientious coalition to openly discuss the particular needs of women in our houses of worship," says the Reverend Dr. Cheryl Townsend Gilkes, a Colby College professor and ordained Baptist minister. As much as we refer to an independent incorruptible moral will among women, we're human, too, and it takes a united spiritual community to keep us making the right choices and sticking with them.

How can imperfect humans avoid dangerous liaisons and unholy alliances? First, over the years I've learned to trust the wisdom and direction of sisters for my personal and spiritual needs. Sensitive male ministers should help direct sisters to strong women ministries, even if outside their own congregations. Of course, we must encourage each congregation to develop a thriving female ministry within its own walls.

Second, women must stop playing house in God's House, transferring real longings for a husband or lover onto the married minister. If Sunday church service is the one chance in the week you have to seek male attention, make sure you direct your attention to a man who is more appropriate and available. Or find an available partner in the world and bring him to church with you. Flirting on Sunday morning may feel like fun and look harmless, but it's never your prerogative to violate borders of sanctity and trust. As Reverend Carmen Lattimore, copastor of Victory Church International in Fort Washington, Maryland, says, "Love and re-

spect for one another, oneself and especially for God are key."

Third, churches must establish reasonable guidelines to address sexual misconduct by pastors and other members. The challenge will be to acknowledge unseemly behavior and deal with it quickly without encouraging sexual suspicion and repression. We must also take care to ensure the psychological well-being of our ministers. Some pastors are suffering from unknown hurts, unacknowledged pain and unresolved sexual conflicts. Often we expect them to function as superhumans without need for rest or repair. Such misplaced expectations only reinforce some ministers' resorting to sexual sin and abusive power. We must provide ministers with outlets–both spiritual and therapeutic–to vent their anger, cleanse their hearts and heal their hurts.

In many ways, ministers are cocooned inside a punishing, sanctified silence. As the New Living Translation of a Galatian passage reminds us: "Dear Friends, if a Christian is overcome by some sin, you who are godly should gently and humbly help that person back onto the right path. And be careful not to fall into the same temptation yourself."

Finally, those of us who claim to be Christians should, as the powerful words from the Old Testament book of Micah direct us, "do justice, love mercy and walk humbly with our God."

Marcia L. Dyson has published personal essays on spiritual growth and personal relationships among African-Americans. Most recently, her work has been anthologized in Men We Cherish: African American Women Praise the Men in Their Lives, *edited by Brooke Stephens (Doubleday). She and her husband live in New York City.*

Of Professors and Pedophiles

Barbara Lerner

AMONG THE subjects thrust to the forefront of consciousness in our sex-drenched age is child molestation. As recently as twenty years ago, Americans were far less concerned about this vile phenomenon, or at any rate were not exposed to it so relentlessly. But then came a string of sensational and highly publicized cases, some of which turned out to be other than what they at first seemed.

During the 80's, the most notorious such cases involved accusations of mass abuse at several nursery schools across the country. The proprietors of the McMartin Preschool in suburban Los Angeles were said to have raped their young wards and terrorized them with satanic rituals. The Amirault family of Malden, Massachusetts, was charged with sexually torturing dozens of children between the ages of three and six at their Fells Acres Day School. And a twenty-three-year-old teacher, Margaret Kelly Michaels, was accused of sodomizing the tots in her care at a New Jersey nursery school.

It gradually emerged that, as Dorothy Rabinowitz of the *Wall Street Journal* was the first to show in a series of trailblazing articles, most if not all of these nursery-school cases had less to do with

---

BARBARA LERNER, *a psychologist and attorney, runs a consulting firm in Chicago. She has written for* COMMENTARY, National Review, *and other periodicals.*

child molestation than with prosecutorial excesses and parental hysteria. Exposure of the deeply manipulative way in which testimony was elicited from the young "victims" eventually led judges and juries to acquit almost every one of the defendants or to overturn their convictions. But that hardly meant that real molestation was not taking place elsewhere. Indeed, as the 80's merged into the 1990's, a spate of sex-related murders of young girls soon seized the place in public attention formerly held by the nursery-school scandals.

There was, for instance, twelve-year-old Polly Klaas, abducted from her Petaluma, California, home in October 1993. A year later came Megan Kanka, a seven-year-old New Jersey girl whose death at the hands of a released sex offender prompted the passage of various "Megan's Laws" requiring the registration of such predators. In 1996, the body of JonBenet Ramsey of Boulder, Colorado, a six-year-old "beauty queen," was discovered in the basement of her own home. And in May 1997, seven-year-old Sherrice Iverson was molested and strangled by a California teenager who had lured her into a toilet stall at a Nevada casino.

Is child molestation really on the rise, or are we overreacting to a small number of sensational episodes? And if the latter, why have parents and others been so easily led to conclude the worst? As it hap-

pens, sorting through these troubling issues has already become something of an academic subspecialty, and a fashionable one at that. Two recent entries in the field are *Moral Panic: Changing Concepts of the Child Molester in Modern America** by Philip Jenkins, a professor of history and religious studies at Pennsylvania State University, and *Erotic Innocence: The Culture of Child Molesting*† by James R. Kincaid, a professor of English at the University of Southern California. Though the books differ in approach—Jenkins favors the post-modern historical mode, Kincaid prefers old-fashioned mass psychoanalysis—both authors agree on one fundamental matter: the recent burst of concern about child molestation has nothing to do with any actual danger posed to our children.

ACCORDING TO Philip Jenkins, the true incidence of child molestation in America has changed very little over the course of the 20th century. What has changed—radically and often—is our *perception*, the way we "construct the phenomenon." In some periods we are willing to see child molesters as immature individuals unlikely to cause serious harm. At other times—during our periodic "moral panics"—we exaggerate both the prevalence of the crime and

---

* Yale University Press, 320 pp., $30.00.
† Duke University Press, 368 pp., $24.95.

its destructive effects, "demonizing" molesters as violent serial predators.

The source of these moral panics, Jenkins maintains, is anxiety about sexual experimentation, especially among juveniles. Thus, the "great panic of 1935–57"—what Jenkins calls the "Age of the Sex Psychopath"—was sparked in his view by the permissive legacy of the free-wheeling 1920's and, later, by the weakening of parental supervision caused by the disruptions of World War II.

Wartime America in particular was marked, Jenkins writes, by "a greater occurrence of extramarital and premarital sexual contacts as well as new opportunities for both genders to discover or express homosexual impulses." Young people—most scandalously, young women—took advantage of the new dispensation. In the words of a contemporary observer quoted by Jenkins, "The great ports of embarkation crawled with giggling semi-pros in bobby sox; Manhattan's Central Park, San Francisco's notorious Turk Street, Chicago's Michigan Avenue, all reeked of precocious sex."

It was inevitable that this increasingly open sexuality would be met by what Jenkins calls "prurient horror" and a repressive backlash, which partly took the form of a sudden "discovery" that American society was being overrun by sex killers and pedophiles. So, too, with today's obsession with child molestation—just one more turn, Jenkins asserts, in the cycle of moral panic. Having suffered the liberating gales of the sexual revolution of the 1960's, the forces of reaction have again set out on a witch-hunt in an effort to tame unruly eros.

JAMES KINCAID, for his part, sees something rather different at work. The current "popularity" of the child-molestation issue, he suggests, has nothing to do with the unspoken fears that Philip Jenkins discerns. To the contrary, tales of child sex abuse are so ubiquitous today because they give us *pleasure*, erotic satisfaction. At heart, we are all pedophiles.

Nor, according to Kincaid, is this a new development. Adults in the modern West, at least since the Victorian era, have enjoyed lustful feelings and fantasies about children, a proposition Kincaid supports with scores of examples from literature and popular culture. Though the Victorians were not the first to eroticize children—he instances the (to him) highly suggestive Christian iconography of the infant Jesus—he locates the root of our own problem in the Victorians' inability to acknowledge their passion. Even Freud, he writes, the most liberated of late Victorians and a thinker of "ironic sophistication," failed to come to terms with the fact that we are sexually attracted to prepubescent children and they are sexually attracted to us.

As a result of this unhealthy repression and denial, Kincaid argues, we are forced to express our sexual feelings toward children in hostile and devious ways. Above all, we project those feelings onto pedophiles, hiding behind a cloak of self-righteous condemnation in order to dwell in loving, lingering detail on tiny bodies and the terrible things that perverts do to them.

What then to do? Needless to say, Kincaid does not recommend that we simply allow adults to rape and sodomize small children. But he urges us to settle upon some happy middle ground between muzzling our pedophilic lusts and letting them run wild. We must "find it in our hearts," he writes, "to be easier on ourselves and, consequently, easier on our children"—a prescription whose details he leaves to the reader's imagination.

PERHAPS THE first thing to say about all this is that, whatever the changing fads of academic discourse, shocking the bourgeoisie never goes out of style. Indeed, so commonplace has the urge to scandalize become that it is difficult to greet even two such egregiously amoral books as these with much more than a resigned shrug. Still, despite (or because of) their overweening obtuseness, Jenkins and Kincaid do in fact help us to see how we have reached our present sexual pass.

To Philip Jenkins, the idea of moral panic supplies the key to understanding the wild swings in our attitudes toward child molestation. What we are now experiencing, he avers, is just a replay of the fear-mongering that served to repress the fast and loose sexuality of American youth at mid-century, and is as little based in fact.

It is but a moment's work to point up the ludicrousness of this contention. Comparing the 1940's or 1950's with the 1990's, we see a steep rise in every measure of sexual danger and dysfunction: more unwed mothers, more broken families, more unwanted and aborted children, and a plague of sexually-transmitted diseases from AIDS to new drug-resistant forms of syphilis and gonorrhea. As for the incidence of child molestation itself, the statistics are famously slippery, as they are for every kind of sexual crime—a fact that both Jenkins and Kincaid gladly exploit in their attempt to discredit the idea that abuse is now more common. But it is highly unlikely that while every other measure of social and sexual pathology shot dramatically upward over the decades since the 1950's, the rate of child molestation alone should have remained unchanged.

Nor is it true, as I can attest from personal experience, that the postwar years were suffused with sexual fear. For young people like myself and my friends, who came of age in a Chicago where the notorious Leopold and Loeb child-murder case of 1924 was still talked about, such phenomena were freakish occurrences, hardly seen as a constant background danger. Though we were occasionally warned to steer clear of strangers, the thought never entered our heads that we need be wary of our neighbors, teachers, or preachers, much less our fathers, for fear they might have impure intentions toward us.

Jenkins is no less ignorant, or gullible, when he comes to the mating games of girls in those days. Though there may well have been "giggling semi-pros" among us, just as there have always been, the way my friends and I got our thrills with the sailors we picked up on Michigan Avenue and took into Grant Park with us hardly "reeked" of "precocious sex." We strolled and ran and laughed with them, but our intimacies consisted of wearing their hats, holding their hands, and occasionally kissing them good-by before running off to catch our buses and get home in time for supper. They were, after all, boys from small towns in the West and Midwest—shy, lonely, eager teenagers just like us, and as excited by the little we did as we were.

People born decades later find it almost impossible to grasp how safe American young people felt in those days, and how assured our parents were of our safety. And the reason they find it hard to grasp is simple: the moral panic of recent years—the one that is unreal no less than the one that is real—has no precedent in our history.

If Jenkins is useless in understanding the transformation of childhood from a time of relative innocence to one of sexual menace,

James Kincaid is of greater service—or at least his errors are. Like many self-proclaimed Freudians, Kincaid misunderstands the master's ideas. On his reading, Freud was a prophet of the sexual revolution of the 1960's, the first thinker to recognize that, if only we lived as our natural instincts dictated, we could occupy a worldly paradise, free of the limits and constraints imposed by repressive society. As Kincaid himself summarizes this view, all our sexual problems ultimately derive from "the main bullies of our culture: faith, law, and submission to them."

Whatever else Freud was, however, he was no advocate of free love and no enemy of law. In fact, in the Freudian scheme, civilization itself—that which makes us human—depends crucially on our ability to repress our sexual impulses. And as necessary as such limits are in relations among adults, they are doubly so in the rearing of children. For Kincaid, Freud's resistance to sexualizing children is the one hypocritical flaw in an otherwise liberationist creed. But Freud entertained no illusions about sexuality: it was indeed a basic life force, one whose vast destructive potential needed to be properly tamed.

ONE HARDLY has to be an advocate of Freud or of Freudianism to under-

stand that Kincaid-like illusions about sex are the stuff of which both behavior and attitudes have been fashioned since the 1960's. It was under the banner of the sanctity of their erotic instincts that countless members of the baby-boom generation kicked aside the sexual limits that, exceptions duly noted, had been respected by their parents. In doing so, they ended by making the world a more perilous place both for themselves and for the children that would be born to them.

Surely one of the most extraordinary things about the nursery-school cases of the 1980's was the readiness of parents to believe that their children had been forced to participate in bizarre public orgies conducted by brazen pedophiles—pedophiles who resembled the *parents themselves* in being white, middle-class, mainstream Americans. Something in the common experience of the baby-boom generation rendered it unusually credulous when confronted by charges of child molestation, and unusually susceptible to moral panic. What these parents knew, even if they did not acknowledge it, was that the dream of sexual liberation had a nightmarish underside, and pedophilia, fantasized or acted upon, was its manifest content. They had met the enemy, and, just as Pogo warned, it was themselves.

Legislating Morality

By Frank Turek

As the culture wars rage on, one question keeps surfacing: Can morality be legislated?

It never fails. Whenever someone from the "conservative" side of the political arena takes a stand on a moral issue, someone from the "liberal" side will invariably protest, "You can't legislate morality!" You have, no doubt, heard that objection many times. But is it true?

Morality is about right and wrong, and that's what laws attempt to put into legal form. Can you think of one law which doesn't declare one behavior right and its opposite wrong? The truth is, all laws legislate morality (even speed limits imply a moral right to safety on the roads). And everyone in politics–conservatives, libertarians and liberals–is trying to legislate morality. The only question is *Whose morality should be legislated?*

You say, "But what about the separation of church and state?" Well, despite all the attention this idea gets, the First Amendment says nothing about it. (It says, "Congress shall make no law respecting an establishment of religion, or prohibiting the free exercise thereof . . . ") But even if it did mandate the separation of church and state, the First Amendment does not prohibit legislating morality. In fact, the First Amendment *itself* legislates morality: it clearly implies that it would be *wrong* for Congress to establish a religion or prohibit the free exercise of religion; it also implies that any congressional attempt to abridge freedom of speech, the press or assembly would be morally wrong.

When lobbying for moral legislation in the public square, Christians must learn to cite documented evidence and appeal to the common ground of reason. This is exactly the strategy employed by the apostle Paul on Mars Hill before the Greek Philosophers (Acts 17: 16–33). He did not quote Bible verses to them, because they did not believe in the Hebrew Scriptures. He reasoned with them. We must do the same in our own non-Christian public square. One such reasonable distinction we must draw is the distinction between religion and morality. While it is true that morality comes from God, *for purposes of legislation,* there's a big difference between religion and morality: Religion involves our duty to God, while morality is more concerned with our duty to one another. Laws against murder, child abuse, rape and theft are moral–not just religious–issues because they are needed to restrain evil and protect the innocent. We can and should avoid legislating religion, but we can't avoid legislating morality–that's what laws inevitably do! We don't want to make a law to tell people how to worship, where to worship or even if to worship; that would be legislating religion. But we can't avoid making laws that tell people how we should treat one another; that's legislating morality. In short, legislating religion is unconstitutional, but legislating morality is unavoidable. All laws legislate morality.

Opposing Values

Let's use one of the most divisive issues in America–abortion–to illustrate that morality is always legislated and imposed on others by both sides in the debate. It's widely believed that the "religious right" (read pro-life) are the ones who want to cram morals down the throats of everyone else, while the "pro-choice" (read pro-abortion) folks are the reasonable ones who don't want to impose on anyone. Nothing could be further from the truth. In reality, both sides in the abortion debate are actively seeking to impose moral standards on others.

Everyone realizes what pro-life people want to impose: they want to protect the baby and thus impose on the mother the duty to carry her baby to term. But what is so often missed in this debate is that pro-abortion activists want to impose *their* morals on others as well: they want to impose the morals of the mother on the baby and, in some cases, the father.

When abortion is chosen, the morals imposed on the baby come in the form of a knife, vacuum or scalding chemical. Such a "choice" also imposes on the father by depriving him of fatherhood and the right to protect his own baby. So while the pro-life side seeks to impose *continued pregnancy* on the mother, the pro-abortion side seeks to impose *death* on the baby whenever abortion is chosen. The important point is that liberals, like conservatives, want the government to legislate and impose certain moral positions on others!

Whose Morality?

So, that brings us back to the big question: Whose morality should be legislated? Thomas Jefferson had the answer when he wrote in the Declaration of Independence, "We hold these truths to be self-evident, that all men are created equal, that they are endowed by their Creator with certain unalienable Rights, that among these are Life, Liberty and the pursuit of Happiness." Notice that our *rights* come from the Creator, and *life* is the first one stated. In other words, true morality comes from God. The apostle Paul wrote that such morality was "written on [our] hearts" (Rom. 2:15).

Thus, it is God who bestows on His creatures certain moral rights and obligations.

In an imperfect, fallen world these rights will conflict at times. In such cases, the lower right must give way to the higher right. When life and liberty conflict as they do on the issue of abortion, liberty must give way to life because life is the ultimate right. The right to life is the right to all other rights—if you don't have life, you don't have anything.

You may be thinking: "If this Moral Law is indeed 'self-evident,' as Jefferson declared, then why doesn't everyone agree about abortion?" We all don't agree about abortion because some of us "suppress the truth" about right and wrong (Rom. 1:18). We know the truth about right and wrong (i.e., the Moral Law) by how we react to what's done to us rather than by what we do to others. In other words, our reactions help us discover right and wrong better than our actions. For example, you may not be conscious of the Moral Law when you lie to someone (your *action*); but when someone lies to you, the Moral Law becomes as bright as the sun, because being lied to upsets you immediately (your *reaction*). Likewise, a pro-abortion activist might not think abortion is wrong if she wants the freedom to have an abortion (her *action*), but if you could put her back in the womb, her opinion regarding abortion would change immediately (her *reaction*). As Ronald Reagan said, "I've noticed all those in favor of abortion are already born."

How to Engage the Opposition

A popular statement invoked by those opposing the legislation of morality is this: "Don't cram your morals down my throat!" If Christians are to be effective in politics, then we must be able to answer this objection. To begin, it's important that we communicate with those in our culture with whom we disagree in a gentle, gracious manner, with an ear toward understanding their side. Without this,

it's doubtful that we'll even earn an opportunity to debate the subject. Second, we should point out to them that all political positions are attempts at legislating morality. Once again, the question is not whether morality can be legislated but *whose* morality should be.

The answer is very simple. We shouldn't impose *my* morality or *your* morality; we should impose *our* morality—the one inherited by us all. So when someone protests, "Don't cram your morals down my throat," simply respond, "These are not my morals. I did not make them up. I didn't make up the fact that abortion is wrong, that murder is wrong, that stealing is wrong. In fact, if it were up to me, I might like it if some of those things were not morally wrong. Abortion might help me get out of trouble, and theft could solve my money problems. So I'm not imposing my "personal" morality on you any more than a math teacher is imposing her 'personal' math when she teaches her students that $2 + 2 = 4$. Morality, like math, is not based on subjective feelings; it is based on objective facts."

If they say, "Well, that's just your interpretation!" You might respond this way: "Of course, but that doesn't mean my interpretation is false. I also interpret that Mother Teresa was better than Hitler, and that interpretation is certainly true. Your position is also an interpretation. For example, when you say that the unborn are not human beings so abortion is OK, you are making an interpretation. Why should your interpretation be the law of the land? Why should your interpretation go unchallenged? The question is not about *who* is interpreting; the question is, 'Whose interpretation and conclusion best fits the facts?' While many in our society may *want* to suppress the medical facts which affirm the humanity of unborn children, those facts compel the conclusion that the morality which should be legislated is the pro-life morality. This is the morality inherited by all of us, but only accepted by some of us. It is our common morality."

Christians As Political Activists

Some Christians believe that we should not be involved in lawmaking. They believe that we should stay out of politics and concentrate only on evangelism. After all, laws can't change people, only a commitment to Christ can. I believe this thinking overlooks three very important facts which support Christian involvement in politics.

First, there is no good reason why evangelicals cannot both win souls *and* participate in politics. Indeed, we are *commanded* to do both! When Jesus instructed believers to be salt and light (Matt. 5:13–16), He did not qualify that command by excluding politics. Moreover, why would it be wise for Christians to stay out of politics? Would the nation be better off if only non-Christians were allowed to provide the government with moral leadership? We should all be thankful that our Christian founding fathers got involved in politics, otherwise this country probably wouldn't exist today.

Second, since may people believe that whatever is legal is moral and vice versa, the law is a great teacher. It helps teach people right from wrong. Paul wrote, "Indeed I would not have known what sin was except through the law" (Rom. 7:7, NIV).

Third, the law actually does help change attitudes and behaviors. Two major moral issues in our nation's history prove the powerful effect of the law on attitudes and behaviors. The first issue is slavery. One hundred and forty years ago, there was so much controversy over the question of slav-

ery that many people thought it better to divide the nation and kill their own relatives rather than agree on a legislative solution. Today, outside of the tiny fraction of racist extremists in this country, everybody believes that slavery is morally wrong. Did attitudes change overnight because we outlawed slavery? No. However, behavior changed immediately because slave owners did not want to go to jail, and the law did help alter proslavery attitudes over time. Before the Civil War, slave owners could rationalize the obvious immorality of slavery under the cover of "it is legal." Afterwards, the law did not provide that convenient excuse, and attitudes slowly changed.

The second issue, abortion, also demonstrates the power of law to change attitudes and behaviors. For nearly the first 200 years of our nation's history, abortion was outlawed in all cases unless the mothers' life was in danger. (In 1967, a few states such as New York began to include rape and incest as other legal exceptions, but abortion on demand remained illegal). So when the Supreme Court decided *Roe v. Wade* in 1973, they overturned 200 years of judicial and legislative precedent as well as the laws of every state—all 50—which prohibited abortion. In effect, seven unelected judges reversed the expressed will of the nation's majority by judicial fiat. And when all 50 states have outlawed something, the prevailing attitude of the country is not hard to figure out—in 1973 the vast majority of Americans believed that abortion was immoral.

But today the country is about evenly split. What happened? Why has there been such a change in attitude about abortion since 1973? Simple: the law was changed. In a situation such as the reverse of slavery, what was once considered illegal (and thus immoral) became sanctioned by the federal government. Couple the impact of the law change with the fact that abortion has since been deceptively promoted as a private "choice" that entails a "safe medical procedure" to "terminate a pregnancy," and we can understand why more people now believe that abortion is morally acceptable.

For these and other reasons, Christians should work to pass moral laws. If we do not get involved in politics, then those with a "morality" that contradicts the values of Christianity will continue to legislate troublesome laws that bring our country pain and suffering and even death. As Edmund Burke declared over 200 years ago, "All that is necessary for evil to triumph is for good men to do nothing."

Frank Turek, *a graduate of Southern Evangelical Seminary, is a professional speaker and author who conducts training programs for businesses and apologetics seminars for churches and para-church organizations. He is the coauthor, with Norman Geisler, of* Legislating Morality: Is it Wise? Is it Legal? Is it Possible?, *now available in paperback from Bethany House; call (800) 328-6109, or visit your local Christian bookstore.*

PREGNANT? YOU'RE FIRED!

DESPITE LAWS THAT ARE SUPPOSED TO PROTECT PREGNANT WOMEN, GROWING NUMBERS OF MOMS-TO-BE ARE FINDING THE WORKPLACE ANYTHING BUT FAMILY-FRIENDLY. HERE'S HOW TO MAKE SURE THIS DISCRIMINATION DOESN'T HAPPEN TO YOU

BY STEPHANIE B. GOLDBERG

In 1995, Janet Rau, now thirty-two, was a rising star at Applebee's restaurant in suburban Atlanta. She was promoted to general manager after just a year and a half on the job. "I was the first female to hold that position within the franchise," says Rau. "In many ways, I was an experiment for them."

That March, she informed her district manager that she and her husband planned to start a family. "I didn't want to spring it on him as a surprise," she says. At her performance review in September, Rau says the manager remarked: "That's when I knew you weren't one hundred percent committed to your job."

Later that month, Rau announced her pregnancy. Rather than congratulate her, the district manager

> Once women have children, "employers mistakenly have a sense that they aren't going to be as productive," says one expert

said glumly: "We'll just have to deal with it." Rau was upset, but figured her boss simply needed some time to get used to the idea. A few weeks later, she experienced uterine bleeding and took a week off. When she returned, things were never the same. In November, her boss demoted her to second assistant man-

ager—two levels down from her previous post—and transferred her to another location. "It was devastating," she says.

Rau's boss gave her an odd explanation for the demotion—her restaurant had not performed successfully during the Atlanta Olympics. While that was true, Rau says the real reason the establishment lost business was its location in Cobb County, which had been ruled out as an Olympic site because it had an anti-gay resolution.

"You're doing this because I'm pregnant," she told him.

He denied it. But Rau, angry, started looking for legal help. A friend referred her to Atlanta attorney Nancy Rafuse (who, coincidentally, was pregnant herself). The lawyer agreed to represent Rau and

From *Ladies' Home Journal*, July 2000, 78-81, 145-146. © 2000 by Stephanie B. Goldberg. Reprinted by permission.

filed a claim with the Equal Employment Opportunity Commission (EEOC) against the owner of the Applebee's franchise for discrimination. From that point on, "it was very clear that they were going to make her so miserable she would just leave the job," says Rafuse.

Rau was denied promotions and reprimanded for missing work to care for her sick husband. She says the last straw came when an employee she had fired for pushing and threatening her was rehired by the company a week later. "I was afraid for my safety—and for the safety of my unborn child," says Rau, who resigned in 1998.

In August 1999, a jury decided that Rau had been discriminated against and awarded her $1.8 million in damages. Because federal law limits the amount of damages to $300,000, the award was later reduced to that amount plus $34,000 in back pay.

Rau, who is now a marketing consultant, contends the suit was never about money. "I knew I had done a good job, but invariably, doubts start creeping in," she explains. "To have a jury listen to the facts and draw the same conclusion I did is wonderful."

WHEN THE LAW IS NOT ENOUGH

Surprisingly, what happened to Rau is not uncommon. According to the EEOC, from 1992 to 1999, pregnancy discrimination complaints increased by 23 percent. This is in spite of the Pregnancy Discrimination Act (PDA) of 1978, which makes it illegal for companies with fifteen or more employees to hire, fire or withhold promotions on the basis of pregnancy or related conditions such as miscarriage.

In addition, under the Family Medical Leave Act (FMLA), which went into effect in 1993, workers who have been employed for at least a year at companies with fifty or more employees are allowed to take up to twelve weeks of unpaid leave annually for family-related medical situations, such as the birth of a child. They must be reinstated when they return to work—or placed in comparable positions in terms of pay, status and benefits.

So why is pregnancy discrimination still happening? According to experts, employers can find ways around the laws by claiming that hiring, firing and promotion decisions were made for valid business reasons. "Discrimination has become more subtle," explains Sandhya Subramanian, policy counsel for the National Partnership for Women & Families, an advocacy group in Washington, D.C. She says the stories she hears today are on the order of: "I got pregnant and I felt pressure to leave my job. Then I was terminated, and I'm convinced it had something to do with my pregnancy."

Some employers view pregnancy as a problem because they assume that once women have children they won't work as hard as they used to. "They mistakenly have a sense that workers aren't going to be as useful or productive," says Subramanian. Often, it comes down to corporate culture, adds Marcia Bram Kropf, vice president of Catalyst, a New York City research and advisory group that promotes the advancement of women in business. "Many industries grew up around the assumption that husbands work, wives stay home with the children and workers should be free to travel or stay late without any advance notice," says Kropf. "And if you're not doing that, you're not going to be seen as committed to your work—

THE SMART WAY TO NEGOTIATE A MATERNITY LEAVE

- DO YOUR HOMEWORK. Before springing the news on your boss, find out how other women have been treated. "You're likely to have problems if performance is evaluated by the notion that you have to be physically present at work to be a productive employee," says Cynthia Thompson, Ph.D., associate professor of business at Baruch College, in New York City.
- GIVE AS MUCH NOTICE AS POSSIBLE. By law, you're required to give notice at least thirty days prior to your departure. However, the experts recommend going beyond that. "Our research shows that women who experienced the fewest problems with maternity leave were more likely to have given their employers sufficient notice," says Ellen Galinsky, president of the Families and Work Institute, in New York City.
- DEFINE YOUR GOALS. Before talking to your boss, decide how long you want to be away and how available you want to be to your co-workers.
- PUT YOURSELF IN YOUR EMPLOYER'S SHOES. At the same time you notify your employer of your pregnancy leave, outline a plan for handling your work while you're away, suggests Cindia Cameron of 9-to-5, The National Association of Working Women.
- GET ALL INFORMATION ABOUT YOUR LEAVE IN WRITING. This avoids misunderstandings and puts you on much sounder footing if you have to contemplate legal action in the future.
- STAY IN TOUCH WITH YOUR BOSS WHILE YOU'RE ON LEAVE. It will be better for your career, says Cameron, "and it reduces the shock of returning to the office."

For more information, call the 9-to-5 Hotline at 800-522-0925.

even if you're outproducing your co-workers."

Bonnie Kerzer, a thirty-six-year-old sportswear designer and mother of two in Brooklyn, New York, was a victim of that outdated thinking about motherhood. After she announced her pregnancy in 1992, the president of the manufacturing company where she had worked for two years became unfriendly to her, Kerzer recalls. Three days before she was due back at work from maternity leave, "he called to tell me my job had been eliminated," she says. "I couldn't believe it."

The company claimed her services were no longer needed, but Kerzer was suspicious—especially when they hired another person to perform duties similar to hers. A former colleague confided to her that the president of the company had once remarked that Kerzer's pregnancy "was a sign that she was lazy." Kerzer was outraged.

She began looking for an attorney. "I had to see about eight different lawyers before I could find one who would take my case on contingency," she says. "It's not easy to file suit. You need to be very persistent."

In 1998, she received a settlement from her employer, the terms of which are confidential. "It would have been so easy to give up," she says. "But I knew I had been wronged and that I had to continue to fight."

PUSHING THE LIMITS?

When it comes to accommodating pregnant workers, some companies say that they're forced to bear too heavy a burden. Take the case of the Chicago-area auto leasing company that fired Regina Sheehan, a purchasing agent, in 1994, when she was five months pregnant. Sheehan, now forty-three, was fired several months before she was to take her third maternity leave in three years.

According to Sheehan, the company made no secret of its hostility toward her pregnancies. During her third pregnancy she had to take a three-week disability leave because

she was at risk for a miscarriage. When she returned, she was told by her supervisor, "Gina, you're not coming back after this baby."

Although her performance reviews had been satisfactory, Sheehan was closely monitored by the company to see if she was meeting her performance goals. When she was terminated, a supervisor told her: "Hopefully, this will give you some time to spend at home with your children."

"I was hysterical," says Sheehan. "I was going through a difficult pregnancy, and we really needed my income." She contacted a lawyer and filed a claim with the EEOC.

Her case went to trial in 1997. A jury awarded her $30,000 in back pay and attorney's fees, but the matter wasn't concluded until more than a year later, when the verdict was upheld on appeal.

Anita Blair, a lawyer and president of the Independent Women's Forum, a conservative group headquartered in Arlington, Virginia, believes that women like Sheehan are expecting too much from their employers. "That person is gone three months of the year and is getting full-time benefits for part-time work," says Blair. "It's not simply a problem for management, but it also demoralizes the other employees who have to cover for her."

As difficult as it may be for companies to handle one employee's three maternity leaves in three years, the law is the law, other experts contend. "It's disruptive in the sense that [companies] are used to an individual's habits and now they have to break in another person," acknowledges Houston employment lawyer Beatrice Mladenka Fowler. "But legally, their responsibilities are clear."

"Society is still catching up with the law," adds Subramanian. "Many employers are ignorant of their obligations, and a lot of people are unsure of their rights or hesitant about taking advantage of them."

FIGHTING BACK

If you suspect that you are a victim of pregnancy discrimination, keep notes of conversations with managers and document any reduction of responsibilities. If you plan to discuss your situation with your human resources department, you may want to consult an attorney, since your remarks can have legal consequences later.

Then, contact the EEOC promptly. From the day you experience a discriminatory act, such as denial of pregnancy leave or termination, you have 180 to 300 days to file a claim with the regional office of the EEOC, depending on your state. If your state or municipality has its own civil rights agency (you can find this out by calling the NOW Legal Defense and Education Fund, in New York City, at 212-925-6635), you may want to file a charge with them first and then file a complaint with the EEOC.

The agency will investigate your complaint. More than half of all claims filed are dismissed—nearly 55 percent in 1999—for lack of evidence.

Regardless of the EEOC ruling, you can still get your day in court by requesting a right-to-sue letter from the agency. From a practical standpoint, however, a lack of EEOC certification "can hurt a lot," according to staff attorney Yolanda Wu of the NOW Legal Defense and Education Fund. "It might make it harder for you to get an attorney, and the defendant would certainly use the fact in court to try to prove you have a weak case."

The good news is that after overcoming so many hurdles, you're likely to prevail in court. Jury Verdict Research, a Horsham, Pennsylvania, company that maintains a database of jury awards, analyzed pregnancy discrimination verdicts and settlements from 1993 to April 2000, and found that 61 percent of the plaintiffs won, receiving median awards of $56,360.

An alternative to litigation is private mediation, in which a neutral party hears both sides and makes a decision. Because it's a private proceeding, it's quicker, cheaper, more informal than litigation and more conducive to preserving relationships (this is especially useful if you plan to return to work at the company). If you don't like the mediator's decision, you can disregard it and file a lawsuit.

Preparing yourself emotionally for litigation is important, too. Many lawyers discourage women from bringing suit because these cases are so difficult to win.

Kathleen Williamsen, a thirty-one-year-old art teacher and the mother of a sixteen-month-old daughter, was turned down by two attorneys before she found one who would represent her. Williamsen filed a claim last year with the EEOC over her treatment by the Sewanhaka Central High School District, in Elmont, New York. She says she received good performance ratings during 1997, her first year of teaching. But then she got pregnant. "The thinking is that you're not as accessible once you have children," says Williamsen. "That you won't stay as late or work as hard."

Within a week of her announcement in October 1998, Williamsen received her first unsatisfactory performance review. Several more followed. Matt Jacobs, the president of her local teachers' union, claims never to have seen such a blatant turn-around in performance evaluations. "Her performance was not just good—it had been outstanding," he says.

Williamsen transferred to another school for the fall 1999 semester. She was denied tenure and lost her job this past January. She is now suing the school district.

"I try not to be bitter," Williamsen says. "I have my dignity and the knowledge that I did the right thing."

THE **HIDDEN** health threat

THAT PUTS EVERY WOMAN AT RISK

CAN YOUR HOSPITAL DENY YOUR REQUEST FOR AN ABORTION OR TUBAL LIGATION—EVEN IF YOUR LIFE IS AT STAKE? THE TRUTH WILL SHOCK YOU.

By LESLIE LAURENCE

KATHLEEN HUTCHINS WAS 14 WEEKS pregnant and working the drive-thru window at Dunkin' Donuts in Manchester, NH, when she felt something wet in her underwear. "I went flying to the bathroom," says Hutchins, "and that was it." Her water had broken.

That was two years ago. Hutchins, then 35, and her fiancé, Jeff Prieskorn, 38, were devastated. They had already lost one baby at six-and-a-half months, and now a second one seemed in jeopardy. After an examination and an ultrasound, Wayne Goldner, M.D., Hutchins's ob/gyn, gave the painful news: Chances that she could carry this baby to term were minuscule. And even if she stayed in bed for the next six months and delivered the baby, it would only have a 2 percent chance of survival. Hutchins could wait to see if the miscarriage continued on its own, or she could check into the hospital for an emergency termination. The doctor advised her not to wait. "Dr. Goldner told me if the fetus died inside of me I could get an infection, and I might have to have a hysterectomy," Hutchins says. "There was also a chance the infection could poison me

and I could die. It wasn't even a matter of discussion. I wasn't going through with the pregnancy."

But Hutchins's ordeal was only just beginning. Elliot Hospital, where Goldner usually sent his patients, had recently merged with Catholic Medical Center, the only other hospital in Manchester. As a condition of the merger, Elliot Hospital had agreed to abide by the Catholic Church's teachings on reproduction—meaning, among other things, that no abortions, even in emergencies, would be performed at either hospital. "The hospital said, 'You can't do abortions here—you've got to send that patient somewhere else,'" recalls Goldner.

Hutchins was shocked. "Their attitude was, let her quit her job and stay off her feet for six more months. If the fetus dies inside her and she gets an infection, *then* we'll do something about it."

Goldner arranged for Hutchins to have the surgery elsewhere. But Dartmouth-Hitchcock Medical Center was 80 miles away, and Hutchins had no way to get there on her own. Goldner decided to defy his superiors and

From *Redbook*, July 2000, pp. 112-115, 136, 139. © 2000 by Leslie Laurence. Reprinted by permission.

schedule the abortion at Elliot. "That's when the administrators started bullying me around," he says. "They threatened to cancel my hospital privileges and said that anyone who assisted me would be fired." In the end, Goldner's practice paid $400 for a taxi to take Hutchins to Dartmouth-Hitchcock.

Chances are you've read up on what your health plan covers and which doctors and specialists you can see. But your hospital's business dealings may actually have a bigger impact on your health. In the last five years, a record 132 non-sectarian hospitals around the country have merged with Catholic institutions. Though the motives of secular hospitals are usually financial—to stay competitive by sharing costs and streamlining services—the result is often a raw deal for women.

Abortion isn't the only procedure banned by hospitals under Catholic control. Prescribing birth control (even to treat endometriosis and ovarian cysts), performing surgery to sterilize women and men who've completed their families, treating infertility with in vitro fertilization and artificial insemination—all these procedures can become off-limits. Medical schools affiliated with Catholic hospitals can't train students to perform abortions or do research on fetal tissue. Doctors treating patients who have refused "extraordinary measures" at the end of their lives can't withdraw feeding tubes.

When the nonprofit group Catholics for a Free Choice reviewed 36 of the 43 Catholic-secular mergers completed in 1998, they found that almost half of these joint health centers did away with some or all reproductive services. (The Catholic Health Association of the United States, which represents more than 2,000 Catholic providers, calls the findings "misleading" but says it does not have a comparable analysis.)

And don't assume you can tell by your hospital's name whether it will deny you certain kinds of care. CareAlliance Health Services in Charleston, SC, as well as Northridge

---

EMERGENCY CONTRACEPTION? DON'T COUNT ON IT

In Catholicism, right and wrong may be absolute, but the application of the Church's ethical guidelines is anything but. Consider emergency contraception: The Church allows it in cases of rape—sometimes. Ironically, it's only given in instances where tests indicate that the victim was not ovulating at the time of the rape—in other words, when she is unlikely to have become pregnant anyway.

Yet, even when emergency contraception is Church-approved, its distribution is ad hoc at best. The New York State affiliate of the National Abortion and Reproductive Rights Action League Foundation conducted a survey and found that hospital responses were inconsistent and uninformed. Some examples:

- **At St. Francis Hospital in Poughkeepsie,** an emergency room staffer said, "We are not allowed legally to give emergency contraception."
- **At Benedictine Hospital in Kingston:** "You're talking to a Catholic hospital, so that should answer your question."
- **And at Mercy Medical Center in Rockville Centre:** "The ob/gyn residents would make emergency contraception available, but not officially."

Hospital Medical Center in California and Seton Shoal Creek Hospital in Austin, TX, all have Catholic partners—although you'd never guess it.

"This is one of the most serious threats to women's reproductive health care today," says Lois Uttley, the director of MergerWatch, a group that monitors risks to reproductive health care due to mergers between religious and secular hospitals; the group also provides advice to community members on how to fight proposed mergers. "When American women find out they must travel an hour or more to a strange hospital, to a doctor they don't even know, to have an abortion or to have a tubal ligation, they are disbelieving and outraged."

"THEY WON'T TAKE CARE OF US"

Zina Campos knows these frustrations firsthand. Early last year, this part-time health-care worker from Gilroy, a farming town on California's central coast, became pregnant with her ninth child. Campos, 34, decided to have her tubes tied after the birth. Her ob/gyn, Taki N. Anagnoston, M.D., agreed with her

decision. "One more pregnancy would drastically increase the chance of life-threatening complications," he says.

But that fall, Catholic Healthcare West—a chain of 48 health centers, both Catholic and nonreligious—purchased Gilroy's only hospital, South Valley Community. Anagnoston had to tell Campos he couldn't tie her tubes if she delivered in town at the renamed St. Louise Regional Medical Center, though he could do the procedure at Hazel Hawkins Memorial Hospital, about 20 miles away in Hollister. But Campos's insurance didn't cover her there, and the nearest hospital in her health plan that would allow the procedure was more than twice as far away. Anagnoston was opposed to her making the trip; Campos's last baby had arrived so fast she barely made it to the maternity ward in time.

"I felt like I wasn't given the right to make my own choice," says Campos. "I'm not saying they [Catholic Healthcare West] should change their values and morals and beliefs. I'm saying that if they won't take care of us, they should make sure we have someplace that does."

OST:
YOUR ABORTION RIGHTS

The Church's directives don't permit abortion. It isn't allowed for genetic abnormalities, and prenatal tests are not even permitted if a woman says she would consider aborting a defective fetus. Some Catholic-sponsored hospitals, however, allow abortion when a pregnancy endangers a woman's life. The reasoning: A physician is allowed to direct treatment toward the mother; if the fetus dies as a result, it's considered an indirect consequence of treatment, not an abortion. But ob/gyns rarely get to make decisions about what constitutes a medically necessary abortion. At Baycare Health System in Florida, for instance, doctors bring cases to a special committee chaired by a nun.

Catholic health-care officials say abortion is a moot issue, since only 7 percent are performed in hospitals. But in most states, clinics are required by law to be affiliated with hospitals in case complications arise. When a hospital won't provide backup, it effectively precludes the clinic from performing abortions. As Susan Berke Fogel of the California Women's Law Center points out, "When abortions are done in hospitals it's because that's where they have to be. They're emergencies."

Denying a mother the right to have a tubal ligation immediately following delivery isn't just an inconvenience, it's bad medicine. Doctors say that performing the procedure post-partum is easier (the uterus and fallopian tubes sit higher in the abdomen just after delivery, making them simpler to reach), safer, and less costly than doing it later as a stand-alone surgery, which requires another trip to the operating room and another round of anesthesia, usually general. Most of

the 10.7 million women in this country who have had their tubes tied (it's the most popular method of contraception in the U.S.) have done so immediately after delivery.

On November 17, 1999, Campos gave birth at St. Louise Regional Medical Center and begged Anagnoston to perform the tubal ligation. He hated having to refuse. "If I do the surgery, they'll take away my privileges and I won't be able to practice in this hospital," Anagnoston told her. "Some doctors can't even go across town to *another* hospital to perform an abortion or sterilization without losing their admitting privileges at the first hospital," adds Uttley of Merger-Watch.

Catholic health-care executives argue that their policies are both legal and ethical and that criticizing them is just Catholic-bashing. "There's no law in this country that says all services must be provided in all hospitals," says Reverend Michael Place, president and CEO of the Catholic Health Association. "If that were the case, every hospital in the country would have to have an open-heart-surgery unit."

Counters Susan Berke Fogel, legal director of the California Women's Law Center, "We're talking about broad-based medically necessary health services—that every woman has a legal right to—being denied based on religious beliefs. And that's discrimination against women."

Anagnoston concurs: "Catholics do a lot of good things. They run good hospitals, but in this case health care and religious beliefs do not belong together."

MONEY FIRST, WOMEN SECOND

Why would a nonsectarian hospital agree to a merger with so many strings attached? The short answer: money.

Managed-care and Medicare payments to hospitals have plummeted over the last three years, and more treatment has moved out of hospitals—60 percent of surgeries now take place on an outpatient basis—leaving

entire wings empty and many hospitals on life support. Nonsectarian nonprofit hospitals feel these financial blows especially deeply, which is why they are typically the ones (as opposed to private, for-profit hospitals) to pursue these mergers.

Catholic hospitals are comparatively flush. It's not just because they're tax exempt and have access to low-interest taxpayer-funded bond financing (all nonprofit hospitals have that advantage). More important, they tend to be part of a large health-care system. A 1998 study found that 79 percent of the 683 Catholic hospitals in the U.S. were part of multi-hospital chains, versus only 38 percent of other nonprofits. Being part of a big organization gives Catholic hospitals greater access to capital, enabling them, for instance, to invest in improvements. Chains also have the clout to demand higher payments from managed-care companies. Five of the ten largest hospital chains in this country—Ascension Health, Catholic Health Initiatives, Catholic Healthcare West, Catholic Health East, and Providence Health System—are Catholic; the largest of these, Ascension Health, has annual revenues of $6.5 billion.

Given the stakes, nonsectarian hospitals tend to be extra careful not to do anything that might jeopardize a pending deal. Negotiations are often conducted behind closed doors with top management only (even when federal law forbids it). Doctors are often left in the dark about how their practices will be affected.

During Elliot Hospital's 1994 merger talks with Catholic Medical Center in New Hampshire, Robert Cervenka, M.D., head of Elliot's obstetrics department, pointedly asked the hospital's CEO whether or not the deal would affect abortion practices there. (Physicians at Elliot Hospital had been allowed to end pregnancies up to the second trimester in certain situations.) "Up to and even after the merger, Mr. [Philip] Ryan assured Dr. Cervenka and other physicians that the practice of medicine at Elliot would not be altered by the merger," says New Hampshire attorney general Philip T. McLaughlin.

In 1996, two years after the hospitals merged, a physician at Elliot scheduled a first-trimester abortion for a patient carrying a fetus with severe abnormalities. "Someone leaked it to the press," says Goldner, "and anti-choice groups came out picketing the hospital." Elliot trustees–who were wary of undoing the merger–responded by banning *all* abortions except those that would save the life of the mother. Goldner and his colleagues offered to create a nonprofit corporation for women's health care off hospital property, but according to Goldner, an Elliot Hospital administrator told him, "If you think we're going to blow this merger because of your department, think again."

Similar scenarios have played out all over the country. Sandy Oestreich, president of the Pinellas, FL, National Organization for Women (NOW) chapter, recalls picking up her local newspaper in 1997 and reading that Bayfront Medical Center, a public hospital in St. Petersburg, had plans to form an alliance with St. Anthony's. The hospital boards told the city council that any services banned based on religious grounds because of this merger would only affect St. Anthony's. Yet in mid-1999, NOW and Planned Parenthood learned that doctors were no longer allowed to perform most abortions at Bayfront. And though the hospital denies pulling birth control pills from its pharmacy, Oestreich says she called the Bayfront pharmacy twice at the end of last summer and the pharmacist freely admitted, "Oh, we haven't had any contraceptive pills on the shelf since the merger." (Indeed, when we called the Bayfront pharmacy about oral contraceptives, we were told, "We don't carry them at all.")

DO MERGERS LIVE UP TO THEIR PROMISES?

Cash-poor hospitals are willing to put women's health on the back burner largely because they feel that a merger is the only way to keep from going bankrupt and shutting down. A "Talking Points" paper prepared by the Catholic Health Association makes this case: "[If mergers] did not occur, it is likely that some financially troubled non-Catholic facilities would not survive. Children would go without flu shots, accident victims without access to emergency rooms, and elderly citizens without needed medicines and hip replacements."

Reverend Place of the Catholic Health Association argues that Catholic hospitals have a reputation for providing good, low-cost care, especially in poor communities–one of the reasons nonsectarian hospitals seek them out as partners.

But Uttley questions how much these mergers actually benefit the poor. Nationwide, hospitals spent 6 percent of their earnings on charity care in 1997 (the latest year for which statistics are available). That same year, Catholic Healthcare West in California spent less than 1 percent of its earnings on charity care, according to a study by a 600,000-member health-care workers' union. "The truth is," says Uttley, "many of these religious hospitals are no better at providing care for the poor, and in some cases do even *less* than nonsectarian hospitals."

What's more, recent studies cast doubt on whether mergers help financially troubled hospitals stay afloat. A 1999 report by the nonpartisan Employee Benefit Research Institute stated that "there is no clear evidence that consolidation has had any effect on health-care quality or resulted in significant cost savings." And an American Hospital Association study of 3,500 hospitals found that when those in highly competitive markets merged, they saved *less* money than hospitals that stayed independent.

SCARING DOCTORS SILENT

Judy Stone, M.D., an internist at Memorial Hospital in Cumberland, MD, is fighting plans by her hospital's new Catholic partner that could ultimately close her hospital down. It's a lonely battle, says Stone: "Doctors and nurses are afraid to say anything. They're afraid to go to public meetings. We feel like we've lost our rights to free speech."

David Mesches, M.D., knows all too well that speaking his mind carries consequences. In 1998, when he was chief of family medicine at nonsectarian Westchester Medical Center and Catholic-affiliated New York Medical College, both in New York, he leased space in his private offices to a clinic that planned to perform abortions. In an interview in the local Kingston paper, *The Daily Freeman,* he remarked that abortion was "the law of the land." Within two weeks, the medical school fired him.

Then there's William van Druten, M.D., a psychiatrist at the Duluth Clinic in Minnesota. The clinic was considering a merger with St. Mary's Medical Center, and not only was van Druten offended when asked to sign a pledge to "respect and abide by" the Catholic Health Facilities' Ethical and Religious Directives, he also wrote to the hospital president to complain about "the long-standing practice at St. Mary's of offering prayers over the loud speaker and of placing a rood [crucifix] on the wall of every room. . . . Thoughtful Catholics recognize that it is not hospitable or charitable to use the vulnerability of illness as an occasion to proselytize for a religious viewpoint."

Later that year, when these facilities merged, St. Mary's president Sister Kathleen Hofer wrote in reply: "Since you have not signed the Agreement, your application is incomplete. Based on this consideration, your medical staff membership and clinical privileges at St. Mary's Medical Center have now expired."

Despite the threat to their careers, many physicians–even those who pledge to abide by the Catholic directives–vow to get around the rules. "Until they put a nun next to me," says Gilroy, CA, ob/gyn Erik Cohen, M.D., "I will give a patient all of her medical options and allow her to make her own decision."

Stealth medicine has many drawbacks for patients, however. Ob/gyn

Goldner, of New Hampshire's Elliot Hospital, was on call the night a young woman was brought into the emergency room after having been drugged at a local bar, locked in a room, and raped multiple times. "The emergency doctor on call doesn't give out rape contraception," Goldner recalls. "The patient sat a while, and the next doctor who came in gave her a prescription for two doses, the required amount. She threw up the first dose. The next two doctors on call wouldn't give her another prescription." When Goldner arrived, he did. "We had three or four ER doctors who refused to even counsel people about post-rape contraception," says Goldner. (The hospital has since changed its policy.) At another hospital, a staffer told a caller that she could dispense morning-after pills only if the women met her in the parking lot in the next five minutes.

To cover their tracks, doctors may also feel compelled to perform one procedure but write it up as another. This can result in an inaccurate medical record, which could compromise a woman's care down the road. For instance, say an ob/gyn prescribes oral contraceptives but doesn't write anything down in the patient's medical chart. And say, on a different occasion, the patient's primary care doctor diagnoses her with hypertension. Oral contraceptives combined with hypertension can raise the patient's risk of stroke. But the primary care physician wouldn't necessarily know his patient was taking oral contraceptives and might not think to ask.

"This is covert practice," says Janet Benshoof of the Center for Reproductive Law and Policy in New York. "And covert practice leads to unsafe practice."

UNMAKING THE DEALS

In August of 1998, soft-spoken 66-year-old ob/gyn Ross Rumph, M.D., stood with 100 other people picketing Integris Bass Baptist Health Center in Enid, OK, his professional home for close to four decades. Beside him were nurses, doctors, stay-at-home moms, businessmen, grandmothers, and prochoice advocates carrying signs with such slogans as "Protect family decisions," "We trust our doctors: Why don't you?" "Don't close Bass O.B.," and "Respect ALL faiths."

Rumph, who does not perform abortions on moral grounds, acknowledged the irony. "I was in league with the people who are usually my opponents," he says.

He took to the picket line when Integris announced plans to affiliate with Catholic St. Mary's Mercy Hospital. Both hospitals planned to close their obstetrics departments and open a new, freestanding, state-of-the-art women's health clinic. The hitch: Tubal ligations would be banned.

Integris officials tried to appease women by offering to transport anyone who wanted her tubes tied to a nearby hospital the day after delivery. "But women shouldn't have to be driven across town to get services,"

What you can do

For information on how to fight hospital mergers that can restrict *your* reproductive rights, contact:

- MERGERWATCH, c/o Family Planning Advocates of New York State, 17 Elk St., Albany, NY 12207; phone: 518-436-8408; www.mergerwatch.org
- CATHOLICS FOR A FREE CHOICE, 1436 U St. NW, Suite 301, Washington, DC 20009-3997; phone: 202-986-6093; www.cath4choice.org
- NATIONAL WOMEN'S LAW CENTER, 11 Dupont Circle NW, Suite 800, Washington, DC 20036; phone: 202-588-5180; www.nwlc.org
- AMERICAN CIVIL LIBERTIES UNION, 125 Broad St., 18th Floor, New York, NY 10004; phone: 212-549-2500; www.aclu.org
- PLANNED PARENTHOOD FEDERATION OF AMERICA, Public Policy Litigation and Law Department, 810 7th Ave., New York, NY 10019; phone: 212-541-7800; www.plannedparenthood.org

argued Vivian Atchinson, 45, who, along with a group of concerned citizens, complained about the policy to the Oklahoma Department of Health. "It's also an invasion of privacy. If you're being transported across town the day after delivery, everyone knows you're getting a tubal ligation. There were also concerns about separating the mother from her baby, and there was still the issue of how to pay your doctor for two separate procedures."

On March 6, 1999, the Enid *News & Eagle* ran a front-page story: "Women's center won't be built." St. Mary's CEO Frank Lopez said the hospitals withdrew their plans due to economic concerns and lack of medical staff and community support.

"It was never our goal to stop the building of the facility," says Atchinson. "We just wanted to protect patient rights. It shows what you can do when people get together." Doctors are still performing tubal ligations at Integris. As for St. Mary's, last April its management approved plans to sell the hospital.

Elsewhere in the country, antimerger campaigns have met with varying degrees of success:

- In New Hampshire, where the state attorney general's office conducted an extensive investigation of Optima Healthcare and its involvement with Elliot Hospital and Catholic Medical Center (CMC), a report released on March 10, 1998, stated that Optima (the hospitals' parent company) "failed to honor its social contract to both the Manchester community and to the distinct communities served by CMC and Elliot." In early 1999, the hospitals severed their connection, and doctors at Elliot can once again perform medically necessary abortions.

- In Cape Girardeau, MO, Saint Francis Medical Center and Southeast Missouri Hospital hoped to complete their merger without community opposition in 1999, but residents complained to the Justice Department when they learned that reproductive health services would be restricted. The attorney general nixed the merger for antitrust reasons.

- Last year, Beaumont Medical Center and Surgical Hospital and Christus Health in Beaumont, TX, terminated merger negotiations because community members opposed limitations on reproductive health services, including tubal ligations.
- In St. Petersburg, FL, community groups learned that Bayfront Medical Center sits on city-owned land, which it rents for $10 a year, and that in its lease with the city, Bayfront agreed to provide health care regardless of "sex, race, color, or creed." Because Bayfront has not offered a full range

of reproductive and other health services, the city council is suing the hospital in federal court for violation of separation of church and state, according to NOW's Sandy Oestreich.

- In Gilroy, CA, community members are pressing for a state investigation of Catholic Healthcare West's dealings with South Valley Community Hospital. "How can our legislators in Washington and Sacramento justify tax-exempt status for a religious organization that is violating federal standards and guidelines?" asks ob/gyn Cohen, referring to the fact that federal law requires tax-exempt organizations to include the community in decision making and not to discriminate against any

group of physicians. "Any other organization would lose its license or ability to accept Medicare and Medicaid patients."

Like Erik Cohen, Ross Rumph, and Wayne Goldner, former Florida State senator Jeanne Malchon—who is involved in negotiations to try to terminate the Bayfront–St. Anthony's merger—is fighting because she knows that the war over women's reproductive health is only the tip of the iceberg. "We've become a more diverse society, so we must protect everybody's rights. Say a Jewish group got control of a hospital and insisted every baby boy be circumcised. How do you think that would go over? Once you open the door to that kind of thing, where does it end?"

SPECIAL REPORT

CRIMINAL INJUSTICE

PHILADELPHIA'S ELITE SEX-CRIMES UNIT BURIED HUNDREDS OF RAPE CASES TO IMPROVE CITY CRIME STATISTICS. NOW, THEY ARE BEING UNCOVERED, THANKS TO AN UNUSUAL COLLABORATION—WITH WOMEN. MICHAEL MATZA REPORTS

Philadelphia's sex-crimes unit began as an elite squad, with a pledge to improve police attitudes about rape. Created in 1981 amid feminist pressure, the unit came alive during a period of enlightened awareness. Yet a shocking series of articles that ran in the Philadelphia *Inquirer* last fall and winter—analyzing nearly two decades of police investigations—revealed that the promise was hollow from the start.

With pressure from the top to show results, too few investigators, and a huge caseload, the sex-crimes unit had routinely buried thousands of rape complaints—coding them as noncriminal offenses or sweeping them off the books entirely—to make the city look safer. Since its inception, the unit used the term "unfounded" (meaning the investigator believed that the women had fabricated their accounts) and "investigation of person" (another noncrime category) to classify between one third and one half of all sexual-assault complaints, including rape—bestowing on the city one of the highest rape-arrest rates in the nation. Police higher-ups tacitly condoned the practice, while victims who courageously came forward typically never knew that their cases had been dismissed and their rapist was still prowling the city streets.

The newspaper's report last October about a 1997 attack was a case in point. It had all the makings of a classic nightmare.

"She awoke to a male on top, [who] covered her face with shirt and fondled her breast," the terse police report reads. The victim, a twenty-eight-year-old artist living alone in downtown Philadelphia, said the stranger entered her first-floor apartment through a door or window around four o'clock on a brutally hot June morning.

She told police that the man pulled down his pants and underwear, lay on top of her naked body, touched her everywhere, told her she was beautiful, then fled without raping her because she was able to talk him out of it. At the station house where crimes are classified, police supervisors accurately coded the incident "attempted rape." Then the case was reclassified after it was handed off to the sex-crimes unit. Despite her detailed description of the attacker, sex-crimes investigators doubted her story because the eight-inch gap between burglar bars on her apartment window seemed too narrow to admit an intruder, as the investigator who mothballed her case wrote. The result: The woman's case was labeled "investigation of person"—a noncriminal category that police commonly used to keep major offenses out of the city's official crime count. The case was parked indefinitely in statistical limbo, and the investigation was closed.

One month later, a young woman in the same neighborhood was choked and stripped naked inside her ground-floor apartment. She awoke to find her night-

clothes in a pile; her neck swollen and raw. The whites of her eyes swam with broken blood vessels. Her case, too, was written off as "investigation of person" by the sex-crimes unit.

Then, last year, amid the high-profile hunt for a serial rapist who murdered a University of Pennsylvania graduate student, police belatedly acknowledged the truth in the artist's account. Hair evidence left inside both women's apartments matched the rapist-killer's DNA, and he is still at large. The artist was his first known victim.

Women's groups urged an exhuming of the buried cases and demanded public hearings after the newspaper publicized the flagrant power abuses and deliberate oversights of the sex-crimes unit. A daylong session of the Philadelphia City Council hard testimony from police brass and women's advocates. Police Commissioner John Timoney, who took command in 1998, pledged improvements. He ordered a review of more than 5,000 cases, dating back to 1995, the statute of limitations on rape. He also sent an additional forty-five detectives to the unit, demanding accurate crime statistics.

Now being hailed as a model for other cities, the unit is being opened up to unprecedented scrutiny: The commissioner has asked women's groups (including Women Organized Against Rape, the Women's Law Project, and the University

the first time, an outside monitor will be looking over our shoulder, sharing ideas and letting us know if we're doing things correctly," he said.

And so, from a tarnished unit has come a way of handling rape cases that is the first of its kind in the nation. "The idea of collaboration between women's groups and police is very important," says St. Joseph's University criminologist Claire Renzetti, editor of *Violence Against Women,* an international journal. "Rape is the most underreported violent crime. And there's a good reason: Women don't feel comfortable with police in these instances." Others agree: "It's a major step forward," said Carol E. Tracy, executive director of the Women's Law Project, a legal advocacy group that will participate in the monitoring. "I have a hard time believing that the downgrading of crime is unique to Philadelphia. Rape-crisis centers and women's advocacy groups everywhere need to ratchet up their advocacy."

Philadelphia's sex-crimes unit has transformed itself in just over six months from a department that routinely dismissed brutally violent rape cases, into one that takes responsibility for its actions and takes care of its victims. The numbers speak for themselves: Rape arrests in the first two months of 2000 are up nearly 80 percent compared to the same period last year; police have arrested more than twenty people from the review of buried cases; reported rapes have risen 44 percent in the past three years (from 650 in 1997 to 934 last year); and the percentage of so-called unfounded cases has dropped from 18 percent in 1998 to about 8 percent last year, putting it in line with national norms. The unit is confronting a lot of anger and hurt. For years, it distrusted victims. Now, the challenge will be to win back their confidence.

Saving face: Tikesha Farmer's attack was originally blown off by investigators and later reclassified as rape (above).

of Pennsylvania's Women's Center) to help police decide when to believe sex-crime complaints and how to classify them. In addition, all of the 105 rape cases reported in 1999 labeled by investigators as "unfounded" will be reviewed by the advocates. Thereafter, such cases will be spot-checked on a quarterly basis.

Timoney has promised that if the groups find fault with the handling of any case, he will personally review it and order further investigation if appropriate. "For

> Porn.con?

> Seth Warshavsky was one of the youngest, brashest entrepreneurs on the Web. Whatever he told the media and Wall Street about his empire of sleaze, they believed. But now the feds are asking if it was all a scam.

>

> By Evan Wright

BY THE TIME HE WAS TWENTY-THREE, SETH WARshavsky was regularly being hailed as a visionary. In May 1997, his portrait appeared on the front page of the *Wall Street Journal,* and reporters began flocking to Seattle to cover the extraordinary rise of a new Net prince. Warshavsky was the founder of Internet Entertainment Group, an online porn company that, according to the *Journal,* used "savvy tactics" and "innovative technology that others are too timid to embrace" to "rake in millions." A Seattle native, Warshavsky was likened by *Newsweek* to the city's most famous son, Bill Gates, and hometown papers dubbed him "the Bill Gates of porn." *Time* compared him to both P.T. Barnum and Larry Flynt. But Warshavsky told reporters that his fledgling porn empire was just a steppingstone. With an apparent technical lead—he claimed that his Web sites offered the most advanced streaming technology anywhere on the Web—his goal was to transform IEG into a mainstream entertainment giant, a "Viacom for the new media."

Later that year, Warshavsky's renown increased exponentially when he released Pam Anderson and Tommy Lee's X-rated honeymoon video on the Internet. Each time he spoke to a reporter, Warshavsky talked up an array of new ventures he was starting: an online bank; Web sites for gambling, extreme sports, golf-equipment sales, attorneys' services, psychics and surgeons; a broadband deal to premiere Hollywood movies on the Web; and possible partnerships with RealNetworks and Excite@Home. He was profiled on *48 Hours* and interviewed by Barbara Walters, and he even testified before the Senate, proposing legislation to protect children from Internet porn.

In 1999, *Time* placed him fortieth in its Digital Fifty—a list of the most influential people in high tech—putting Warshavsky among those who had helped to make the digital world "a practical, cool and fascinating place." *Time* also noted that the company's "highly respected infrastructure includes a fraud-control database." That same year, IEG was reported to have earned $35 million on revenues of $100 million. Warshavsky planned a public stock offering that had Wall Street analysts predicting a market value for IEG that might reach hundreds of millions of dollars. He carried up to three cell phones and was so obsessed with dealmaking, he was once banned from a Seattle sandwich shop for disturbing customers by loudly conducting negotiations on his cell phone.

But Warshavsky's rise to national prominence as an Internet whiz kid was far more remarkable than reporters had imagined. He liked to tell them that he had been a precocious computer nerd who grew up on Seattle's idyllic East Side, not far from Microsoft's campus

EVAN WRIGHT *wrote about anarchists in Eugene, Oregon, in RS 837.*

> "**Power** is the only thing Seth thinks about, from the time he wakes up in the morning until he goes to bed at night," says IEG's former general counsel.

headquarters; he liked to say that he had made his first fortune while still in high school, when he started a phone-sex company more or less as a lark, and that one thing had led to another and here he was, poised to become one of the top players on the Internet.

This spring, federal investigators began looking into allegations of wire fraud, money laundering and tax evasion going back to ventures that Warshavsky had started during his troubled teenage years, when he was living by his wits and on his own after moving out of his parents' house at age fourteen. Taking advantage of the dot-com fever of the late Nineties, Warshavsky was able to sweet-talk the nation's leading news organizations and financial analysts into believing he was the prince of a rising digital empire.

Today, as Internet shares continue their tumble on Wall Street, the story of Seth Warshavsky and his dubious ways of doing business stands as a cautionary tale of Internet hype run amok. Though he will probably never make *Time's* Digital Fifty list again, Warshavsky may rank as the first and greatest con artist of the digital era. My assessment of his greatness is biased: Even though I have always liked him, and I worked for him for nearly a year, after he sued me last October, I helped to expose his alleged criminal activities.

I FIRST MET WARSHAVSKY IN JANUARY 1998 at an adult-industry convention in Las Vegas. At the time, I worked for one of the industry's most flamboyant figures, Larry Flynt, as an editor at *Hustler* magazine. Warshavsky emerged from the pandemonium somber and businesslike in a charcoal overcoat, a white scarf around his neck. Against the raucous backdrop, Warshavsky, flanked by a pair of black-suited attorneys, displayed an almost preposterous air of dignity. He extended his hand and introduced himself. "I'm Seth Warshavsky, president of Internet Entertainment Group," he said. "I'm a

huge fan of *Hustler,* and I want you to work for me." He vanished into the crowd, leaving behind the aura of a young man rushing toward his destiny. Much later on, after I had begun working for him, I found out that Warshavsky always hurried through trade shows because he was afraid that somebody he owed money to was going to kick his ass.

I started my job at IEG in November 1998, as a Web editor in charge of all sites, adult and non-adult. Company headquarters were located on the tenth floor of a glass and steel office tower on First Avenue in Seattle. White walls, black leather couches and splashes of abstract art provided a fitting atmosphere for the high-tech powerhouse that was being written up by the press.

Around the office, Warshavsky dressed in casual, hip attire: pressed jeans, a gold Rolex, a V-neck sweater worn without a shirt beneath, to show off his deeply tanned chest. Though the *Wall Street Journal* had described him as an "apple cheeked" young man, the impression he gave sitting at his desk was that of a thirteen-year-old about to turn forty-five. He had prematurely graying hair and at times conveyed the weary, exasperated air of a man who was stranded on a planet of intellectual inferiors. Only when he laughed–his eyes squeezed shut as he giggled maniacally–did he become the irrepressible boy tycoon portrayed in the media.

Warshavsky's most striking feature was a nervous tic. Every few moments, he would toss his head back and loudly clear his nostrils. "It's like a trumpet call or something," says

Brian Cartmell, a childhood friend of Warshavsky's who served briefly as IEG's president. "It's not one of those 'follow me' kind of noises. If you hear it, you should go away."

At times the snort came on like an explosive nasal seizure, causing his entire body to shake. Yet, in a strange way, the snort was a source of Warshavsky's charisma. It made it impossible to ignore him. He would radiate boundless confidence and enthusiasm, then become utterly helpless in the throes of a snorting fit. As I got to know him better, the snort seemed to hint at powerful forces working beneath the surface, functioning like a relief valve blowing off some kind of ambient soul sickness.

Warshavsky arrived in the office each morning just before ten in a whirlwind of ringing cell phones, snorts, barked commands to his secretary. Some mornings he toured the "design pit," a cramped warren of back rooms where IEG's innumerable sites were being built by nearly a dozen programmers and designers. He interrogated the employees like a general inspecting the troops. "Do it now!" was his signature command. Once, when a designer balked at some seemingly impossible order, Warshavsky pushed him away from the computer. After typing a few lines of code, Warshavsky triumphantly pointed to the screen, making sure everyone knew that he had bested one of his top designers.

"He's a formidable presence," recalls Patrick May, a reporter with the San Jose *Mercury News* who spent two days following Warshavsky. "It exhausted me being around him. He's in overdrive all the time."

Warshavsky often went off on tirades that were aimed at certain employees for no apparent reason. Epithets like "You fucking moron" regularly flew from his mouth. One employee, a middle-aged Chinese man, became, in Warshavsky's lexicon, "the fucking slant-eyed baboon." (Warshavsky denies ever saying this.)

"Power is the only thing Seth thinks about, from the time he wakes up in the morning until he goes to bed at night," says Derek Newman, who served as IEG's general counsel for nearly three years. You could see this need to dominate even in Warshavsky's ostensibly lighthearted moments, when a zany but somewhat cruel, clownlike side would emerge. After a box of frozen crab legs on dry ice arrived—a gift to somebody in the office—Seth commandeered it, put on a plastic bib, grabbed the wooden mallet that was in the package and started smashing open crab legs atop his secretary's desk. With shards of crab shell and gobs of cocktail sauce flying around the office, he handed out pieces of crab flesh to his employees, waving the mallet like an overgrown infant with a rattle.

At its peak, IEG had approximately 100 employees in its headquarters and at a crosstown facility known as the Arcade, which housed the sets for live performers as well as the customer-service and tech-support departments. Fairly or unfairly, a handful of employees were known as Warshavsky's "paid friends." Aaron Seravo was director of advertising. He worked in an isolated office on the eleventh floor, where he had been moved after a co-worker complained of harassment. His sole companion there was his assistant, Cole Peterson, a buddy from a rock band who appeared to do little but play computer chess all day; Peterson became known as "the paid friend to the paid friend."

Soon after I started at IEG, Warshavsky's drive for power began to apply to his own body. He developed an obsessive weight-training regimen and supplemented his hours in the gym with a rigid diet of high-protein foods; muscle-mass enhancers, such as a legal form of GHB that he got at a natural-foods store; and a precursor to human growth hormone.

Warshavsky was assisted in his quest by a three-woman secretarial team. Their job was to procure protein and yogurt dishes specially prepared by chefs from various Seattle restaurants. The team delivered these meals every two hours, whether Warshavsky was in the office or meeting his attorneys across town or at home. They also found nurses to do in-office blood tests to monitor his hormone levels, picked up refills for his tooth-whitening system, arranged for massages, scheduled the tanning sessions and booked his last-minute trips to Las Vegas, Los Angeles and Cabo San Lucas, Mexico. When needed, they also flew in a hormone specialist from California, who would arrive at the office dramatically attired in surgical togs, as if he'd just stepped out of the operating room.

Perhaps the oddest visitor to the IEG offices was a character named Cort St. George, who was one of Warshavsky's most valued paid friends, since he seemed to do pretty much whatever Warshavsky wanted him to. A former golf instructor and man about town in circles that he described as "Hollywood's sleazy underground," St. George had the blond good looks of a soap-opera star. He dressed in a California preppy style—loafers, khakis, polo shirts worn with a white sweater tied over his shoulders—and would sometimes interrupt a business conversation to ask things like, "Dude, does my hair look all right?"

St. George, who left IEG in 1999 to start a celebrity-scandal Web site, now expresses a mixture of awe and regret regarding his former employer. "When I first met Seth, I immediately saw his charisma," St. George says. "But I equate working with him as mental hell. I felt like I was Seth's hostage."

WARSHAVSKY SEEMED TO THRIVE on chaos. He relished confrontations, rising to these occasions and showing off his greatest talent, a gift that perhaps bordered on genius: an ability to make people believe just about anything. I saw this most vividly when a man showed up at the office offering to sell what he claimed were videotapes of a former heavyweight boxing champion having sex with a string of prostitutes. The seller, a heavy-set black man in a threadbare gold suit and diamond earrings, carried a half-dozen tapes in a tattered gym bag. He called himself Earl and spoke in a strained whisper, as if a block of ice were stuck in his throat. Earl wanted a million dollars for the tapes. Over the next twenty-four hours, Warshavsky, in a bravura feat of negotiation, bargained him down to $20,000.

When Warshavsky insisted on paying Earl with a check, Earl repeatedly demanded cash and threatened to get violent. Warshavsky was unfazed. "Earl," he said, "you can't fly out of here with $20,000 on you. It's a federal crime to carry more than $10,000 in an airport." He opened his wallet and produced a twenty-dollar bill, one with the new design just released that fall. Warshavsky held the bill up to the light and tore at the fringes. "See, there's metal threads in it," he said. "If I give you cash, you'll set off the metal detectors at the airport if you carry more than $10,000. You see what I'm saying, Earl? I'm writing a check for your protection."

Earl took the check.

Around that time, Warshavsky flew to New York to appear on *The View,* the morning chat show co-hosted by Barbara Walters. Walters began the show on the offensive, but Seth was ready. He won the audience over with a rousing speech about protecting children from pornography on the Internet. Despite Warshavsky's claims about the elaborate measures that IEG had taken to protect children, his company was host to a site called HardcoreCarnival.com. Its free splash page, accessible to people of all ages, presented a photo of a woman with a fist up her rear end.

DESPITE THE CIRCUS ATMOSphere, IEG managed to attract employees with impressive credentials. Warshavsky hired designers away from organizations like Microsoft and Intel, and retained prestigious headhunting firms like the Dallas-based Snelling Personnel to recruit executives. (In a typical postscript, IEG refused to pay the company for its services and was in turn sued by Snelling's Seattle office. That suit was settled, but Snelling still has personal claims pending against Warshavsky for misrepresentation and fraud.)

Nothing ever seemed to get done. During my ten months at IEG, the company lost two general counsels, three chief financial officers, a vice president of development, two network administrators, its entire marketing department, a chief technology officer and three of its four staff accountants, as well as half of the design department and a dozen tech-support staffers. Some mornings there was no telephone service. Employee paychecks bounced. The company was engaged in more than a dozen lawsuits with creditors seeking to collect unpaid debts. One day a photographer came in demanding $1,100 and claiming that Warshavsky had called him a "cocksucker" on the phone. He chased Warshavsky down the hall, shouting, "Give me my money, you little prick!"

IEG relied on its infamy as a purveyor of celebrity-scandal materials like the Pam and Tommy video to attract headlines and customers. But most of what it offered on its flagship Web site, Clublove.com, consisted of put-ons like "a dramatic re-enactment" of an alleged Kelsey Grammer sex video, using a model dressed as the TV star. The adult-content areas of the site included nude-picture galleries, the "101 Fuck Videos"–clips from XXX tapes–and supposedly "live" feeds of nude performers (these were often taped). Few of the picture galleries were ever updated, since vendors wouldn't supply new content. The video streams were often down, because IEG's infrastructure was falling apart. Disgruntled employees sabotaged vital software and sometimes made up for outstanding back pay by walking off with whatever computer gear they could grab.

Warshavsky's non-adult ventures fared poorly. The online bank went bust. The gambling sites ran into regulatory opposition. One site, OnlineSurgery.com, which was Cort St. George's brainchild, sold real-time streams of medical procedures. One early Webcast showed St. George's mother getting a facelift. From there it moved on to gory live streams showing brain surgeries and breast augmentations.

Warshavsky would storm around the office berating employees for failing to complete projects for which there were no resources. An online store run by Clublove.com regularly took orders for items like dildos and rubber vaginas, charging credit cards but seldom actually shipping anything. As it turned out, IEG often didn't have any such products to ship.

All the company had was a Web page to take the orders.

WITH PRINT REPORTERS AND TV crews showing up nearly every week, IEG's facilities became a backdrop for the surrealist productions that Warshavsky put on for visitors. He would lead them through the First Street headquarters before trooping across town to the Arcade, where performers stripped and masturbated in front of video cameras that sent live streams onto IEG's Web sites. Warshavsky claimed that 1,400 adult-entertainment Webmasters purchased IEG's streams for their sites. The actual number, according to a sworn declaration by one of IEG's staff accountants, was no more than sixty. On most days, the live-performance booths at the Arcade were empty. A supervisor simply replayed old videotapes, making it appear that they were live by typing banter from the supposed performer for the customers in the chat rooms. The system worked well. On some of its adult sites, IEG charged more than a dollar a minute for these "live" performances.

Before the media arrived, Warshavsky would phone ahead to the Arcade supervisor. She would call performers and have them rush in to fill the booths so that Warshavsky could then show off what appeared to be a dynamo of pornographic activities.

Warshavsky titillated the reporters and investors whom he led on tours with fabricated visions of growth, profits, new frontiers to be conquered. *Worth* told its readers that IEG's Web sites had 700,000 paying members, and *Time* spoke of revenue of $100 million and profits of $35 million for 1999. That same *Time* article contained this quote from investment analyst Gail Bronson: "So far as whether [IEG's IPO] would be successful, you betcha. We're talking real revenue, real earnings, real product."

The reporters and analysts, at this point, had no way of knowing that

---

> Seth Warshavsky was a pornographer whom other pornographers considered too dirty to do business with. What kept him going was good mainstream press.

reality distortion was a key element of Warshavsky's business strategy. Not only were checks to vendors and employees bouncing during this period, but in sworn declarations two of the company's four senior staff accountants would say they saw normal daily-revenue figures of about $30,000 (about $11 million per year) and "falling memberships." The declarations indicate monthly memberships of 30,000 not the 700,000 that Warshavsky claimed.

Perhaps the greatest irony of Warshavsky's success was that he was a pornographer whom other pornographers considered too dirty to do business with. Partnerships and traffic deals, even between rivals, are essential to the success of online adult companies, but IEG was unable to participate. "Seth burned a lot of people in the adult business," explains the president of a competitor. "He can't buy traffic. He can't buy ads. So he goes direct and advertises in the media. They say the name of his Web site every time he gets in the news."

FOR THE ELEVEN MONTHS THAT I worked at IEG, rumors of fraud circulated around the office. These concerns were even voiced out loud during a department-head meeting in early 1999, when top employees openly speculated that customer credit cards were being suspiciously overbilled.

I quit in September, and a week later I got a call from the company's new general counsel, Eric Blank, who told me that Warshavsky had asked him to sue me on the company's behalf for violating a non-compete clause in my employment agreement and for tortious interference—inducing employees to leave. (I was in negotiations for a job at a start-up Internet company, and I had hastened the departures of several IEG employees by helping them to find other jobs. Adding to Warshavsky's fury, I had directed the employees who reported to me to file complaints with Washing-

> ## As a teen, Warshavsky spent time in the mental-health system, moved in and out of foster homes and lived on the streets. "I'm amazed Seth is alive," says a friend.

ton state's Department of Labor and Industry when their paychecks bounced.)

Soon after letting me know of Warshavsky's intention to sue, Blank also abandoned IEG. According to Blank, Warshavsky had told him to file the lawsuit in order to get me to sign a sweeping confidentiality agreement. But Blank refused, telling Warshavsky to "fuck off." "I started feeling like I was helping a scam artist," he later told me. Blank, 31, had taken the general-counsel position at IEG two months earlier. He came from one of Seattle's largest law firms, Graham and James, with the purpose of helping to position IEG for its IPO. At six four and 230 pounds, he was physically imposing, and for three years, between Georgetown and the University of Michigan's law school, he had worked as a cop in Washington, D.C. Shortly after Blank quit, Warshavsky hired another lawyer to sue me.

He also named Blank in the suit. Warshavsky had vowed to spend "a million dollars," Blank says, to have him disbarred for his disloyalty. Blank seemed elated by the prospect of a battle with Warshavsky. And given the kinds of battles he'd fought as a cop, Warshavsky hardly seemed an intimidating target. One night a few years earlier, Blank was approaching a car on foot when the driver shot him in the chest. A Kevlar vest saved his life, but the bullet pulverized his ribs. Knocked to the ground, he fired his Glock 17 at the car and killed the driver. "Nothing improves your aim like getting shot in the chest," he says.

"Your hand is steady because you can't breathe, and your motivation is pretty high because someone just tried to kill you."

Blank set about gathering from our former colleagues compelling evidence of Warshavsky's rumored scheme to bilk credit cards. In nearly four years of operation, IEG had collected hundreds of thousands of credit-card numbers in its database. The system was run by a network administrator who reported directly to Warshavsky, and in the previous six months two of them had quit suddenly. One, Ron Chao, agreed to speak to Blank. Chao explained in detail how Warshavsky had ordered him to "reactivate" accounts belonging to customers who had canceled and to charge current accounts multiple times for the same transaction in order to raise extra cash. Chao provided a sworn declaration that read in part, "Seth demanded that I cause the billing system to generate between $400,000 and $2 million on various occasions. Just to be clear, the revenues Seth was demanding that I generate were not to come from corrections of system or database error but from rebilling of credit-card customers for purchases (usually monthly memberships) for which they had already been charged."

John Zicari, a customer-service rep at IEG, volunteered a statement that said in part, "I and others in customer service have noticed thousands of accounts that have been reactivated and billed. In July 1999, almost every account I came across in Clublove.com was billed two or three times, and some were billed as many as a dozen times."

Zicari's and Chao's statements regarding fraudulent billing were supported by eight others. Two former senior staff accountants also detailed an incident in which Warshavsky had faked accounting records. Somebody else provided an internal IEG e-mail containing a list of more than 5,000 credit cards that had been intentionally overbilled. A tape recording of IEG employees discussing double billing also surfaced.

Sharon Waxman, a correspondent for the *Washington Post,* caught wind of the lawsuits and came to Seattle to cover the legal action. When Warshavsky found out, he furiously tried to quash the story. If I and one of my co-defendants would fax the *Post* a letter asking it to hold the story until he could provide documents that would contradict our evidence of overbilling, Warshavsky would drop all claims against us and pay our legal fees of $20,000. The note we sent read: "It has come to our attention that some of the information we provided to you may be incomplete and could be inaccurate." Warshavsky provided the *Post* with further information, but apparently the paper was not convinced: The story ran with our allegations of deliberate overbilling substantially unchanged, but it also included Warshavsky's denials.

The settlement that Warshavsky proposed also included a confidentiality provision, to be negotiated at a later date. No final agreement was ever reached. Warshavsky sent a check to cover his end of the settlement agreement. It bounced.

T HE MOST SURPRISING THING about Warshavsky, I realized at the conclusion of the lawsuit, was how little I knew about him and how much I had to learn about the twisted, unlikely and in many ways sad story of his life. When his parents, Harold and Joyce, moved to Seattle, it was not to an elegant East Side suburb but to Ballard, a tough, grimy, working-class neigh-

borhood twenty minutes north of downtown. Harold was a cable-TV installer; Joyce answered phones at an insurance company. They lived in a single-story clapboard home with their brilliant but troubled son, a chubby, hyperactive, attention-starved kid who, recalls Eric Ensign, a sixth-grade classmate, "used to taunt kids to get attention. He had a snort. It always started when he laughed."

Warshavsky got his first computer in 1985, when he was twelve. In the days before the Web, young Warshavsky set up a bulletin board—a primitive chat room—and started exploring the new world of cyberspace. Hackers he met on bulletin boards traded secrets about how to break into phone systems and get free long-distance services. Armed with this knowledge, Warshavsky blossomed into a tireless phone phreaker—a telephone hacker—and mastered the intricate and laborious processes needed to override switches in the telecommunications grid. According to childhood friend Brian Cartmell, Warshavsky would construct "telephone bridges"—elaborate, illegal teleconferences in which he might bring together as many as sixty people from around the world. Warshavsky admits to certain "instances" when he "used a teleconferencing service and didn't pay for it." Warshavsky also says that by his early teens he left home because his parents realized that "they didn't want the financial burden of raising a teenager."

What actually happened was that Warshavsky's parents sent him to a psychiatric facility after the phone company warned them that their son

was committing fraud over the phone lines from their home. According to Toni Ames, a former US West investigator who helped to build the case against the young Warshavsky, his indiscretions were wide-ranging, sophisticated and serious. Yet Ames, like many people who have known Warshavsky, still has a conflicting view of him. Despite the fact that she helped to bust him, she felt that his parents had "dumped" him and once thought of adopting him herself. "Seth was being set up by older kids, eighteen and nineteen," Ames says. She recalls visiting Warshavsky in a psychiatric facility. "He was this emaciated little kid who looked like he was ten," she says. "If you talked to him about his parents, he was in a shell. If you talked about computers, it was like he grew to six feet tall."

Warshavsky never returned to live at his parents' house after the age of fourteen. "Seth's parents never wanted a kid like Seth," says Cartmell. "I don't think anyone can imagine how annoying he was back then, with his attention-deficit disorder, his hyperactivity. But you don't just kick him out of the house and send him to a mental hospital." Warshavsky's parents, who still live in Ballard, will only say that these accounts of Seth's childhood are "inaccurate." "I always knew Seth would do great things," says Harold Warshavsky. "I've always been proud of him." When Ames visited Warshavsky in a psychiatric facility for kids with drug and alcohol problems, she told the director that Warshavsky needed to be treated for "phone addiction." She says, "The director looked at me like I was crazy."

> **A fraud investigator recalls the teenage Warshavsky: "He was this** emaciated little kid. **If you talked to him about computers, it was like he grew to six feet tall."**

> "We're still laughing at what that guy did to us," says a former partner. "A kid runs circles around two businessmen."

But, she adds, "he was kicked out a few days after for breaking into the facility's phone system and doing his phreaker stuff."

It is hard to follow what happened to Warshavsky during the next three years. He does not dispute that he spent time in the mental-health system or that he moved in and out of foster homes and, for a while, lived on the streets. But he also does not offer many details. Of this period in Warshavsky's life, Cartmell says, "I'm amazed Seth is alive."

At seventeen, Warshavsky was on his way to becoming a hard-core loser. He was a high school dropout, he rented a room in an apartment in a crack ghetto, he drove a government-surplus postal jeep, and he sold fish outside a touristy restaurant called the Crab Pot on Seattle's pier. The one bright spot in his life was his friendship with Aaron Seravo, a waiter at the restaurant. "Aaron was cool," says Jimmy Kim, a mutual friend. "He was kind of scary, but people liked to hang around him. He liked to torment people. He once fed a friend of ours a shit sandwich. He made it from dog shit.

"Aaron taught Seth how to talk to girls," says Kim. Sometimes they'd cruise First Avenue, and if they saw a car full of pretty girls, Seravo would get Warshavsky to yell something obnoxious out the window, like "Suck my dick!" If the two had money, they'd go into the Lusty Lady, First Avenue's premier live-girl peep-show theater, where Warshavsky would amuse himself by tormenting the dancers—usually until he got kicked

out of the club. "Seth became demented around Aaron," says Kim.

In 1990, Warshavsky took his first stab at running a business when he launched a custom-T-shirt venture, Urban Apparel, that by all accounts was wildly successful—he scored contracts to supply local boutiques as well as the Nordstrom department store. But even as he was making money legitimately, Warshavsky got involved in a white-collar scheme, the records of which are sealed in the King County, Washington, criminal courthouse. According to the sources, Warshavsky and an accomplice were arrested trying to cross the border into Canada to sell computer equipment they had purchased with bad checks. His accomplice drew a felony conviction and served time in prison. Warshavsky, still seventeen, got off with probation.

IN THE EARLY NINETIES, JUST BEFORE he turned eighteen, Warshavsky entered the phone-sex business. As with porn videos, the boom was closely tied to advances in technology. Thanks to a combination of digital telephone switches and cheap computers, phone-sex operators were able to efficiently handle large volumes of specialized calls. Audiotext, as it is known within the industry, is a business that also combined all of Warshavsky's obsessions: his love of phone phreaking, his bent for shady dealings and the delight he took in his peep-show adventures with Aaron Seravo.

All it took to get started was a credit-card link—a little box like the

ones used in restaurants and bars—along with a couple of girls willing to talk nasty from their apartments, a cell phone and a toll-free number, which was 800-GET-SOME. He advertised on flyers that he posted on pay phones and in booths at the Lusty Lady. Customers who called rang directly into his cell phone. He took their credit-card information and routed them to the girls. "I was getting fifty calls a day and charging $34.95 per fifteen-minute call," Warshavsky claims today.

Within a year of starting 800-GET-SOME, Warshavsky traded in his jeep for an Acura, moved into a studio apartment on First Avenue and began hanging out at Casa-U-Betcha, an upscale Mexican-themed nightspot on First Avenue owned by two local businessmen, Peter and Jeff Steichen. "Seth was kind of a local character," says Peter Steichen. "He walked around with a cell phone in his ear, wearing an Armani suit. And he has that snort thing. But he was endearing. He had this incredible enthusiasm and was very bright."

Demand for phone sex had far outstripped Warshavsky's capacity to provide it. He dreamed of opening a central call center where dozens of operators could handle the volume in shifts, and he talked the Steichen brothers into putting up $100,000 as participating lenders for a facility in Southern California. Their partnership, dubbed the Telecom Development Group, ran into trouble after a few months and ended badly when the Steichens realized that they were being taken. "Seth is a thief," Peter now says. "He cooks the books. We never saw a dime. A twenty-year-old kid comes along and runs circles around two pretty experienced, pretty savvy and pretty cynical businessmen. We're still laughing at what that asshole did to us."

After the Steichens quickly ended their partnership with Warshavsky, he became the sole owner of the phone-sex company. Warshavsky denies any wrongdoing. "They got all their money back," he says. "They made fifty percent in eight months." Meanwhile, he rented space for another of his audiotext entities in the IBM building in downtown Seattle and opened a call center in California that employed more than thirty operators. He was still just twenty years old.

Soon afterward, Warshavsky became close friends with Ian Eisenberg, a phone-sex player whom Seth would later characterize as his mentor. Three years older than Warshavsky, Eisenberg was set to one day inherit the massive audiotext fortune amassed by his father, Joel, a man known as the George Washington of phone sex.

Eisenberg and Warshavsky began their business relationship as collaborators. Together, they designed a software program to streamline the billing process. But they soon became embroiled in a lawsuit over who owned the software. International Audiotext vs. Seth Warshavsky was Warshavsky's first major civil suit. After the preliminary hearing, Judge Nancy Holman issued an oral opinion that offered an illuminating portrait of Warshavsky, then twenty-one. "And with all [his] talent and impressiveness, I am concerned about just how irrepressible, and maybe irresponsible, Mr. Warshavsky can be."

Eisenberg and Warshavsky reached a settlement, but the experience seemed to awaken an addiction in Warshavsky that would rival his dependency on phones. Warshavsky became a litigation junkie. He once sued a local internet-porn rival for spitting in his face and calling him a "little pussy" on a Web site. More recently, Warshavsky sued a young woman for allegedly stalking him and throwing eggs at his BMW. Though he did not pursue the case to trial, it perhaps brought him special satisfaction. The alleged egg thrower was an eighteen-year-old girl whom, he says, he'd "hung out with occasionally." She was Julie Eisenberg, the kid sister of his erstwhile mentor Ian.

Warshavsky's dealings with Eisenberg exposed him to a relatively sophisticated world of business, where vast sums were being made from intricate technological and financial setups. Which makes it all the more remarkable that during this period he hooked up with a young guy named Sean Sullivan who was burglarizing computers from area businesses.

Shortly after Sullivan's burglaries began, Warshavsky took out an ad in a local paper to sell a laptop computer that had been stolen by Sullivan. The cops busted him, and he pleaded guilty to two counts of possession of stolen property—but later changed that plea to not guilty. Sullivan went to prison. When I recently asked Warshavsky about this, he said, "I was a kid. I didn't know what I was doing."

That seems an odd excuse given the fact that only a few months after his arrest, when he was twenty-one, Warshavsky and two partners invested $1 million to form their own long-distance phone company. The company, dubbed WKP, was born out of Warshavsky's desire to bill consumers directly for audio-text purchases. The way the business worked then, when you called a phone-sex line, you had to punch in a credit card number. But once Warshavsky had created his own long-distance company, phone-sex charges showed up directly on his customers' phone bills.

Warshavsky and his partners signed agreements with the Baby Bell phone companies to operate their national long-distance service and began billing several million dollars a month. Most of their revenue came from selling phone sex, but they also ran a regular long-distance phone company called Starlink Communications. Just eight years earlier, Warshavsky had been confined in a mental hospital after stealing services from US West. Now he was the president of his own phone company, and it was grossing $60 million a year. It was a situation that so alarmed the government, the FCC issued an opinion saying it was illegal for audio-text companies to enter the long-distance market. WKP chose to liquidate.

Despite the government crackdown, Warshavsky bounced back with a slew of ever more sophisticated schemes. He established ties with the small South Pacific island of Vanuatu and evaded FCC regulations by routing phone-sex calls there. He opened a company in Aruba and even started an above-board company to transmit voice data to Hong Kong.

WITH THE NEW REGULATIONS making the phone-sex business less profitable, Warshavsky turned his attention to the Internet in the mid-1990s. At the time, companies like GI, Time Warner and Microsoft were beginning to sink millions into money-losing Web sites. But Warshavsky was confident he could turn a quick profit in the new medium by using the Net to distribute pornography. He launched his first site in 1996, naming it Candyland after the children's game sold by Hasbro. The toymaker sued. Warshavsky was forced to rename his adult site Clublove—but only after receiving valuable free publicity.

A year later, Clublove became infamous for releasing the Pam and Tommy video, and Warshavsky emerged as a star. "After that," says

> After the Pam and Tommy video, "everyone said, 'This is the guy who knows how to make money on the Web,'" says a former employee. "Seth could tell people anything."

Cort St. George, "Seth could tell people anything. Everyone said, "This is the guy who knows how to make money on the Web. He took advantage of people's ignorance."

The posting of the video became the most celebrated event in the early history of the Internet. Pamela Anderson Lee's name became one of the most-searched items on the Web. According to the *Wall Street Journal,* notoriety from the sex video turned Lee's name into a brand to "rival Coke or Pepsi."

"Money was rolling in," says a programmer who worked at IEG in the early days. "But the double billing started then. Seth has always liked to do things a little underhanded."

This past March, assistant U.S. attorney Mark Bartlett, serving as the foreman of a grand-jury investigation, subpoenaed the sealed records of the lawsuit that Warshavsky had filed against me and two other defendants in October 1999. Agents from the FBI, the IRS and the Treasury Department interviewed Eric Blank regarding a criminal investigation into Warshavsky, and soon afterward, I met with Bartlett and an FBI agent in the U.S. attorney's office in Seattle. Bartlett informed me that Warshavsky was suspected of wire fraud related to allegations of overbilling customers on IEG-operated Web sites and also of laundering money through foreign trusts in order to evade federal income taxes. Bartlett's questions appeared to be based on many of the allegations I had helped to raise during the lawsuit, as well as on information provided by others who had worked with Warshavsky in business ventures going back to the early 1990s. No indictments have been filed, but as of early June, investigators from the Seattle U.S. attorney's office were still interviewing possible witnesses. Warshavsky downplays the significance of the investigation. He claims that he runs a completely clean operation that is completely above board. "Allegations of wrongdoing were made to the *Washington Post,*" he says. "Of course the feds are going to investigate."

Despite all the hits that Warshavsky has taken in the past year, he still pushes on, still putting the best face on his business—even though IEG has recently flirted with bankruptcy. He sold off its crown-jewel assets, domain names like Pussy.com and Blowjobs.com, to raise cash to stay afloat; he also brought in new designers and management. IEG successfully launched a redesigned adult site and announced a partnership with Heidi Fleiss, the former Hollywood madam and a convicted felon. One new senior employee resigned, describing the atmosphere at the company as "hopeless" and Warshavsky as "impossible to work with." As for the Fleiss deal, that also seems doomed. "All our dealings with him have been bad," says Jesse Fleiss, Heidi's brother and business manager. "We haven't given him any content, not a single photo. His first check to us bounced."

Jimmy Kim once told me that Warshavsky knew how to push everyone's buttons. "But he's got a button, too," Kim had said. "Alienation. That's why he's always on the phone, surrounded by people. Seth never cuts people off. They cut him off. But not Seth. He can't stand alienation." Which, perhaps, is why Warshavsky asked to meet with me this spring. He said he wanted to show me the results of a "$500,000 audit" he had commissioned to prove that "there was no intentional double billing" at IEG.

When he pulled up in his Porsche, squeezing it into a rubble-strewn construction zone to avoid the five-dollar parking fee in a nearby public lot, he waved and smiled as if greeting an old friend—not an ex-employee he'd accused of theft and whose fraud allegations had brought on a federal investigation.

His physical transformation was astonishing. When he stepped out of the car, he looked as though his head had been grafted onto the body of a short, powerfully built, barrel-chested man. We went into a Thai restaurant—he recommended the shrimp, fielded a couple of phone calls and made some needling small talk. There was a strange disconnect, as if Warshavsky were unwilling to acknowledge the enmity between us. I attempted to bring up the issue of credit-card fraud. "You did a terrible thing to me," Warshavsky said. "The whole situation with the lawsuit was crazy." I mentioned the federal investigation. "It's probably just a fishing expedition," he said. "Don't you think?" Warshavsky looked wary. His eyes were bloodshot. His complexion, normally a tanned golden brown, was gray. Even the familiar snort sounded tired, almost like a sigh.

I asked him whether he'd brought along the audit that he had promised would absolve the company of any wrongdoing. But now he said he couldn't show it to me. He went into a familiar mode, inventing a string of excuses. I asked him who had prepared the alleged audit. "I won't tell you who did the audit," he said. "It was a major, major consulting firm." He started to go on, but I interrupted him and told him he had to be the biggest, most amazing bullshitter I had ever met.

Warshavsky considered what I'd said for a moment and smiled. "I think I'm just an optimist. Like if I say the check is in the mail. It's because I look at the bright side, and I really believe I intend to send it. I never think about why I am the way I am. Something just directs me from inside."

WILL CYBERSEX BE BETTER THAN REAL SEX?

That depends on what lights your diodes. But judging by the quality of today's "teledildonics," some things (hooray!) will never change

BY JOEL STEIN

There are two fields in which I'm anxious to see technology improve: medicine and hard-core pornography. And since I'm not sick yet, I'm pretty focused on the porn thing. Luckily I am not alone in my stunted vision of utopia. The desire for newer, better smut has long been a major impetus behind technological progress: VCRS, DVDS, Web development and I believe X-ray glasses were all spurred by prurient desires.

The holy grail of pornography, though, has always been a machine that delivers a virtual experience so real that it is indistinguishable from sex, other than the fact that it isn't at all disappointing. Though prototypes have appeared in films (the Pleasure Organ in *Barbarella,* the Orgasmatron in *Sleeper,* the fembots in *Austin Powers*), reality has remained painfully elusive. In his 1991 book *Virtual Reality,* Howard Rheingold devoted an entire chapter to "teledildonics," his not-so-clever name for devices that allow people to have sex without being in the same area code. Rheingold imagines putting on a "diaphanous bodysuit, something like a body stocking but with the kind of intimate snugness of a condom" and having a virtual-reality sexperience over the Net. "You run your hand over your partner's clavicle and, 6,000 miles away, an array of effectors are triggered, in just the right sequence, at just

the right frequency, to convey the touch exactly the way you wish it to be conveyed."

Other than his fetish for Chinese clavicle, Rheingold is able to provide little that's useful in the way of information or specs. And in the nine years since he published his personal fantasies, there has been surprisingly little progress. Vivid, the world's largest producer of adult entertainment, promised to deliver an interactive bodysuit last September but missed its deadline. Sure, it had a $200,000 black neoprene suit with 36 electrodes stuck to the chest, crotch and other special places, but the suit didn't look very appetizing. Nor did it do anything. Vivid says it's waiting for FCC approval (interaction with pacemakers seems to be a concern), but the real reason it is lying low on the sex suit is that Vivid is a proud company, and it's not going to continue trumpeting a technology that is at best a long way from happening.

But there are less proud pornographers. SafeSex-Plus.com sells teledildonic devices that, it turns out, look a lot like dildonic devices. The company promised that if I used these gizmos in conjunction with their *iFriends.net* website, I could have a sexual experience over the Net. I got SafeSexPlus to send me the equipment and figured I'd use it with my girlfriend—until I realized that was the dumbest idea I'd ever had. Thinking more clearly, I decided this might be my one chance to get a porn star to have sex with me.

Wicked Pictures, a major adult-entertainment company, set me up on a cyberdate with one of its actresses, Alexa Rae, star of *Porn-o-matic 2000* and *Say Aaah*. I had never seen Alexa's work, but I was assured she was a complete professional. SafeSexPlus.com sent both of us toys, and we made an e-date.

I cannot fully describe to you the absolute repulsiveness of the sexual aid I was given—both because this is a family magazine and because the English language is not equipped for the task. It was supposed to be a disembodied part of a woman, but it was more like part of a really expensive Halloween outfit to which someone had haphazardly taped a lock of Dweezil Zappa's hair. It felt like wet latex, smelled like wet latex and looked like something Sigmund Freud might have used to make a very twisted point. I figured it was designed for men without hands.

The device plugged into an electrical outlet and came with suction cups. This frightened me even more than the Zappa hair until the people from SafeSexPlus explained that I was supposed to stick the suction cups on my computer monitor once the "cyberdildonics box" popped up. This box could be made darker or lighter by Alexa's controlling the box on her screen and would make my latex gizmo vibrate at higher or lower frequencies depending on how much light she decided to give me. I don't know what sexual experience was supposed be replicated by a vibrating disembodied female body part, but I didn't want any part of it.

I was to have the same sort of control over Alexa's marital aid, which I assumed would be somewhat less terrifying.

I assumed wrong. "It's a little scary," Alexa confessed as we talked on the phone and I squinted at a live picture of her on a tiny, fuzzy box on my screen. I'm pretty sure she's pretty and possibly blond. "It looks like it might hurt me. And it's making these ramming noises. Like a jackhammer." I had never prided myself on being a gentle and considerate lover; "ramming noises" and "like a jackhammer," however, were not phrases I was used to hearing.

Alexa, ever the playful one, told me she'd take off her top if I could make her light box change colors, so I got one of the tech guys at work to help me. Soon I could see her yawning on my monitor. This, I thought, was getting to be more like the sexual experiences I was accustomed to.

After 20 minutes, I think I got the color to change and the scary jackhammer noise to increase. "I get turned on by anything sexual," Alexa purred as she took off her top and jeans. "But not this."

We talked some more, and she told me she'd named herself after Billy Joel's daughter, which I thought was in bad taste. Then I realized, looking down at the giant latex pudendum jumping around my desk, that I wasn't in a position to comment on matters of taste.

Still, in the name of science I concentrated on the image of Alexa on the screen and tried to act sexy. "You are driving me crazy," I told her.

"Really?" she responded.

"No."

"Damn."

This was the high point of our encounter—that and when I admitted I was incapable of having phone sex. "Having good phone sex is just saying how you feel," she told me.

"I feel silly," I confessed.

"Not like that."

Eventually we decided to stop. "It has nothing to do with you," she said as she pulled her jeans over her hips. "We're just asking each other technical questions, and it takes away the sexiness." Virtual sex was indeed eerily like real sex for me.

Even if the technology vastly improves and if Alexa and I can one day consummate our awkward phone conversation, I don't think teledildonics is the next generation of pornography. Perhaps it might replace 900 numbers, with men paying to control the toys of women they can see on their screens, but that's about it. Most people will still want to enjoy their sexual fantasies alone, because even a programmable robot is going to be just an annoying, unsuccessful intermediary—not to mention a very difficult thing to hide in an underwear drawer.

And as far as real sex goes, no high-tech device can ever replace a living, breathing person. Because even if a machine felt real and looked real, it could never reproduce the real thrill of sex: knowing that another being is freely giving herself to you and that at least for a few minutes, you're not alone.

Now, why couldn't I come up with something like that when I had Alexa on the phone?

Beyond Orgasmatron

NEW FINDINGS AND RADICAL CHANGES IN OUR UNDERSTANDING OF ORGASM SHOULD MAKE IT EASIER TO HAVE STELLAR SEX, AND REAP THE MOTHER LODE OF REWARDS WE NOW KNOW COME WITH IT.

BY BARBARA KEESLING, PH.D.

Steven and Beth are making love. They've been doing it two or three times a week for six months in much the same way: Beth lies on her back with her legs in the air. Steven kneels in front of her, inserts his penis and begins to thrust. Beth grinds her hips and moans slightly. Steven thrusts quickly for 30 seconds, moans, and having ejaculated, withdraws. They hug and lie together in the "spoon" position. Both feel mildly disappointed, but that's how they normally feel after sex. He rolls over and goes to sleep. She stays awake, feeling anxious and depressed.

Next door, Karen and Jason are making love for the first time. They spend lots of time on oral sex and both get very aroused. When Jason enters Karen, she is already so aroused that she has an orgasm immediately. Jason can feel the walls of her vagina pulsing around him. He slows down his thrusting. Now he can feel Karen's breathing change as she goes into a second orgasm, which causes her arms and legs to spasm and her heart to race. Now his breathing quickens and with an extremely loud moan he has an orgasm and ejaculation. His whole body spasms. Jason says, "Don't stop. If you keep moving, I can go again." And he does, having two more orgasms in five minutes. Afterward, Karen and Jason feel energized and give off a glow. They are no youngsters. They are in their late 30s.

These two anecdotes illustrate a number of things (other than the fact that I am unlikely to land a job writing erotica any time soon). First, sex is good for you. Because sexual arousal and orgasm involve an interplay of several body systems, it's well known that sex improves our breathing and circulation, resulting in bright eyes, a facial glow and shiny hair. Sex can also improve cardiovascular conditioning, strength, flexibility and muscle tone, and has been known to relieve the symptoms of specific medical conditions, such as menstrual problems, osteoporosis and arthritis.

Arousal and orgasm also benefit our mental health. Because they cause the release of pleasure-inducing endorphins in the brain, they can relieve anxiety and depression, increase vitality and boost the immune system. Sex also creates an emotional and physical bond that is essential for social support. With all the mental and physical benefits of sex, it's like we're walking around with a complete health care system inside our own body.

The second major point that the opening anecdotes illustrate is that orgasm is not the same for everyone. Men and women have different expectations about lovemaking and orgasms. Orgasms can vary greatly in their physical and psychological intensity, and both men and women may be capable of greater orgasmic responses than we previously thought possible.

If sex is good for your health, good sex is even better, and really great, mind-blowing multiorgasmic sex is even better than that! I believe that recent findings about male and female orgasm are changing our understanding of orgasm so radically that in the near future, we will find evidence that orgasm can have an even more profound effect on our physical and mental health. And the changing views will make it much easier for the average man and woman to reap these psychological and physical benefits.

Defining Orgasm

Kinsey, Masters and Johnson, and other sex researchers defined orgasm as a reflex that occurs when muscle tension and blood flow to the pelvis reach a peak and are dispersed, and when the pubococcygeal (PC) muscle group that supports the pelvic floor spasms rhythmically at 0.8 second intervals and the heart rate accelerates rapidly (often as high as 180 beats a minute) and then slows down. For men, orgasm usually includes ejaculation.

Orgasm can involve changes in blood pressure, heavy breathing, muscle spasms in the buttocks, tension in the arms, legs and neck, facial grimacing, sweating, the sex flush (reddening of the skin on the chest and neck), tingling of the fingers and toes, yawning, moaning, screaming and uncontrollable emotional outbursts such as weeping and laughing (or bursting into songs like "Ah, sweet mystery of life, at last I've found you!"). Some people report a feeling of undefined sadness after orgasm, called post coital tristesse, which I always thought would make a great name for a rock group.

From a psychological standpoint, orgasm can provide a measure of relief or release, and encompass feelings of loss of control or even a sense of an altered state of consciousness, probably due to the release of endorphins.

I describe orgasms on a continuum from a localized genital sensation that is mildly pleasurable to a full-body orgasm with intense psychological sensations and all the fireworks—the kind of orgasm one of my clients calls "the psychedelic jackpot that lights up the universe." With this kind of variation, it's no wonder some women don't notice them.

The Female Orgasm

A brief history of orgasm reveals the radical changes in perspective over time.

Reprinted with permission from *Psychology Today*, November/December 1999, pp. 58-62, 84-85. © 1999 by Sussex Publishers, Inc.

In her excellent recent book, *The Technology of Orgasm* (Johns Hopkins, 1999), Rachel Maines describes the double standard of female orgasm in the Victorian era. Orgasm was considered both the cause and cure for hysteria, the latter assumption leading to the development of the vibrator. Also in the Victorian era, Sigmund Freud differentiated between what he called a clitoral orgasm and a vaginal orgasm. Female infants and children could masturbate by stimulating the clitoris and experience orgasmic sensations, he posited. By contrast, adult women could experience a vaginal orgasm (described as a deeper sensation) during intercourse. Failure to achieve vaginal orgasm in adulthood, he said, signaled psychological immaturity due to fixation at the phallic stage of psychosexual development.

Alfred Kinsey, in his monumental work *Sexual Behavior in the Human Female,* also held that as a girl grew up, her clitoral orgasms somehow evolved into vaginal orgasms. "The vagina itself should be the center of sensory stimulation and this, as we have seen," he said, "is a physical and physiologic impossibility for nearly all females."

Taking cues from Kinsey, Masters and Johnson concluded that, regardless of the source of the stimulation, all orgasms happened because they somehow activated the clitoris, either directly or indirectly, and caused PC muscle spasms. The clitoris then became the gold standard of female orgasm. I remember countless magazine advice columns from this era urging men to find "the man in the boat."

A problem with Masters and Johnson is that their studies focused on such minute physical details of arousal and orgasm that a lot of people started missing the big picture. For example, they said the clitoris retracts before orgasm. I knew several women who thought they had a problem because they approached orgasm with their clitoris waving in the breeze. Just because most people in a sex laboratory experience phases of excitement, plateau, orgasm and resolution doesn't mean that's the best or only way to make love.

With the publication of *The G Spot* (Reinhart and Winston, 1982), Alice Ladas, John Perry and Beverly Whipple demonstrated that the vagina contains at least one area that is sensitive and can trigger orgasm in some women. They also demonstrated the existence of female ejaculation. (This phenomenon was already known to individual women, many of whom thought they had lost control during sex and peed on their partner.) Research continues on the exact nature of the fluid contained in these ejaculations, but, in a radical change from only 15 years ago, sex researchers now assume that all women ejaculate, but often in amounts too small to be noticed.

In my book *Discover Your Sensual Potential* (HarperCollins, 1999), I explained how to stimulate an area in the upper rear of the vagina known as the cul-de-sac, also called the fornix. I relied on Masters and Johnson for a phenomenon called "tenting," in which, when a woman becomes really aroused, the muscles and ligaments surrounding the uterus lift it up and allow penetration into this extra inch or so of space behind the cervix, resulting in some incredible orgasmic sensations.

I also relied on a little-known article from the *Journal of Sex Research* published in 1972. In "Types of Female Orgasm," researchers Singer and Singer described vulval, uterine and blended orgasms. A vulval orgasm resembles what we consider a clitoral orgasm, with spasms of the PC muscle. The uterine orgasm results from stimulation deep inside the vagina. A blended orgasm (although it sounds like a designer coffee drink) combines the two.

The publication of *The G Spot* led the way for a continued alphabet soup approach to female orgasm: The U spot is the sensitive opening to the urethra; Debbie Tideman, in *The X Spot Orgasm,* describes stimulation of the cervix; I find that stimulation of the PC muscle that surrounds the opening of the vagina is very successful in enhancing orgasm. And in *Are We Having Fun Yet?* (Hyperion, 1997), Marcia and Lisa Douglas claim that the female genitals form an "orgasmic crescent" composed of erectile tissue—including the clitoris, the part of the clitoris that extends into the body, the G spot and the area surrounding the urethra—which swells with arousal in a sort of female erection.

Today, female orgasm still suffers from a kind of double standard: On one hand, we have new and expanded information about orgasm triggers. On the other hand, many women are still not regularly orgasmic and feel cheated, left out, inferior or resigned, because their expectation of having an orgasm is so low.

Feminist thought suggests that this history amounts to a conspiracy to prevent women from experiencing sexual pleasure, or at the least, a series of value judgments about the female body. But the picture reveals no conspiracy. What we have here is researchers starting out literally "in the dark." Rather than rendering this history obsolete, I see us building on it to discover stronger and more frequent female orgasms.

The Male Orgasm

Male orgasm is not without controversy. The prevailing view only several years ago was that orgasm and ejaculation were one and the same, and that men were not capable of multiple orgasm except in rare cases.

Several years ago, when I trained to be a sexual surrogate partner, what struck me most was that the male surrogate partners I met had that ability. And as a surrogate partner, I found that men I treated for premature ejaculation would, as an unexpected "side effect" of learning ejaculation control, experience spontaneous multiple orgasms.

At the time, there wasn't much reading available on the topic. In the *Journal of Sex Research* in 1978, Mina Robbins and Gordon Jensen reported interviewing 13 multiorgasmic men, concluding that it is possible for men to have multiple orgasms by separating orgasm from ejaculation. Sex therapists and researchers William Hartman and Marilyn Fithian wrote *Any Man Can* (St. Martin's Press, 1984), that described some rudimentary techniques that men could use to become multiply orgasmic. In 1989, Marian Dunn and Jan Trost, writing in the *Archives of Sexual Behavior,* expanded the thinking following interviews with 21 multiorgasmic men. They found that there are different patterns of male orgasmic ability, that men don't always lose their erection after an orgasm or ejaculation, multiple orgasms could be learned, and that expectations can limit men's orgasmic response. Recently, Beverly Whipple and colleagues, reporting in the *Journal of Sex Education and Therapy,* studied a man who experienced six orgasms in 36 minutes with no erection loss and no attempt to control ejaculation.

In a book I wrote called *How To Make Love All Night* (HarperCollins, 1994), I identified three patterns of male multiple orgasm: one is a non-ejaculatory orgasm (NEO) in which a man has an orgasm but inhibits ejaculation using the PC muscle. After several orgasms he then "releases the hounds." In multi-ejaculation, a man has several orgasms in a row, all accompanied by full or partial ejaculation. In a third pattern, a man has an intense orgasm and ejaculation, followed by less intense orgasms, or "aftershocks." All of these patterns can occur without erection loss.

Men who experience multiple orgasms report feeling energized after orgasm rather than depleted; are able to understand and enjoy their partner's arousal better; feel closer to their partners; have more options during a sexual encounter with the same partner—which promotes monogamy; and find that their partners had positive reactions. The men find that their orgasms were actually stronger and more intense because they were full-body orgasms rather than localized genital sensations.

The Implications Of These Findings?

We need to study the impact of psychological variables such as thoughts, fantasies and dreams on orgasm and then on physical health. If enhancing orgasm does prove to promote physical health and help relieve pain—and promote mental health by relieving anxiety and depression and protecting against stress—this is clearly an alternative to drugs. As part of this approach, we need to study the quality rather than the quantity or frequency of sexual encounters. Let's get over "Am I normal?" and move toward "Why not be fabulous?"

I would like to propose a new "sexual hygiene" movement in which the emphasis is on the relationship of sex to physical health, vitality, wellness, well-being and even creativity.

I think a useful framework from which to view sex education is one that uses expectations—a central concept in many areas of psychology. Expectations can either limit or enhance our sexual experience. In a sense, the current expectation of what many women experience during orgasm is too high—it's unrealistic to expect fireworks when you have no knowledge of your own response and no orgasm history. On the other hand, our current expectations are too low in that we expect prefer-ence, not passion, and performance, not pleasure. Sex education should promote aspiration, not limitations, stressing that when you're in a long-term relationship there's always more to learn about your own response and your partner's response.

Exploring Orgasmic Potential

The future of sex is not cybersex or the Orgasmatron, Woody Allen's futuristic orgasm-producing home appliance in his 1973 movie *Sleeper.* It's still arousal and orgasm with a living, breathing partner. Expanding our orgasmic potential may help end some of the gender divisiveness that many of us have experienced, and allow us to use our bodies to create shared emotional peak experiences that I believe form the basis of adult relationships. It's good to be sexually fit and orgasmic, but the meaning is more important than the techniques used to get there.

We haven't even come close to exploring our orgasmic potential. I'm not naive enough to believe that orgasmic energy powers the universe, cures cancer, or prevents mass killings (though it does a pretty good job of keeping me off the streets). In addition to all of the physical and mental benefits we can get from sex, we can also experience more and greater benefits if we individually and mutually unleash our orgasmic potential.

Here's a question we should all look forward to pondering: If both partners are multiorgasmic, how do you know when you're through making love?

Barbara Keesling, Ph.D., is a lecturer on human sexuality at the California State University at Fullerton, and has written nine books, including Getting Close: A Lover's Guide to Embracing Fantasy and Heightening Sexual Connection *(HarperCollins, 1999).*

READ MORE ABOUT IT

Liberating Orgasm, Herbert Otto, Ph.D. (Liberating Creations Inc., 1999)
How To Make Love All Night, Barbara Keesling, Ph.D. (HarperCollins, 1994)

Once there were only two: male and female. Men, mostly, were the big ones, with deep voices and sturdy shoes, sitting with legs splayed. Women, mostly, were the smaller ones, with dainty high heels, legs crossed tightly at the ankle, and painted mouths. It was easy to tell them apart. These days, it's not so easy. Men wear makeup and women smoke cigars; male figure skaters are macho—but Dennis Rodman wears a dress. We can be one gender on the Internet and another in bed. Even science, bastion of the rational, can't prove valid the lines that used to separate and define us. Although researching the biology of gender has answered some old questions, it has also raised important new one. The consensus? Gender is more fluid than we ever thought. Queer theorists call gender a social construct, saying that when we engage in traditional behaviors and sexual practices, we are nothing but actors playing ancient, empty roles. Others suggest that gender is performance, a collection of masks we can take on and off at will. So are we witnessing the birth of thrilling new freedoms, or the disintegration of the values and behaviors that bind us together? Will we encounter new opportunities for self-realization, or hopeless confusion? Whatever the answers, agreeing that our destinies aren't preordained will launch a search that will profoundly affect society, and will eventually engage us all.   —*The Editors*

By Deborah Blum

The Gender Blur

where does biology end and society take over ?

I was raised in one of those university-based, liberal elite families that politicians like to ridicule. In my childhood, every human being—regardless of gender—was exactly alike under the skin, and I mean exactly, barring his or her different opportunities. My parents wasted no opportunity to bring this point home. One Christmas, I received a Barbie doll and a softball glove. Another brought a green enamel stove, which baked tiny cakes by the heat of a lightbulb, and also a set of steel-tipped darts and competition-quality dart-board. Did I mention the year of the chemistry set and the ballerina doll?

It wasn't until I became a parent—I should say, a parent of two boys—that I realized I had been fed a line and swallowed it like a sucker (barring the part about opportunities, which I still believe). This dawned on me during my older son's dinosaur phase, which began when he was about 2 ½. Oh, he loved dinosaurs, all right, but only the blood-swilling carnivores. Plant-eaters were wimps and losers, and he refused to wear a T-shirt marred by a picture of a stegosaur. I looked down at him one day, as he was snarling around my feet and doing his toddler best to gnaw off my right leg, and I thought: This goes a lot deeper then culture.

Raising children tends to bring on this kind of politically-incorrect reaction. Another friend came to the same conclusion watching a son determinedly bite his breakfast toast into the shape of a pistol he hoped would blow away—or at least terrify—his younger brother. Once you get past the guilt part—Did I do this? Should I have bought him that plastic allosaur with the oversized teeth?—such revelations can lead you to consider the far more interesting field of gender biology, where the questions take a different shape: Does love of carnage begin in culture or genetics, and which

drives which? Do the gender roles of our culture reflect an underlying biology, and, in turn, does the way we behave influence that biology?

The point I'm leading up to—through the example of my son's innocent love of predatory dinosaurs—is actually one of the most straightforward in this debate. One of the reasons we're so fascinated by childhood behaviors is that, as the old saying goes, the child becomes the man (or woman, of course.) Most girls don't spend their preschool years snarling around the house and pretending to chew off their companion's legs. And they—mostly—don't grow up to be as aggressive as men. Do the ways that we amplify those early differences in childhood shape the adults we become? Absolutely. But it's worth exploring the starting place—the faint signal that somehow gets amplified.

"There's plenty of room in society to influence sex differences," says Marc

From *Utne Reader*, September/October 1998, pp. 44-48. Reprinted by permission of International Creative Management, Inc. © 1998 by Deborah Blum.

Breedlove, a behavioral endocrinologist at the University of California at Berkeley and a pioneer in defining how hormones can help build sexually different nervous systems. "Yes, we're born with predispositions, but it's society that amplifies them, exaggerates them. I believe that—except for the sex differences in aggression. Those [differences] are too massive to be explained simply by society."

Aggression does allow a straightforward look at the issue. Consider the following statistics: Crime reports in both the United States and Europe record between 10 and 15 robberies committed by men for every one by a woman. At one point, people argued that this was explained by size difference. Women weren't big enough to intimidate, but that would change, they predicted, with the availability of compact weapons. But just as little girls don't routinely make weapons out of toast, women—even criminal ones—

sexual encounters, more offspring, more genetic future. For the female—especially in a species like ours, with time for just one successful pregnancy a year—what's the genetic advantage in brawling?

Thus the issue becomes not whether there is a biologically influenced sex difference in aggression—the answer being a solid, technical "You betcha"—but rather how rigid that difference is. The best science, in my opinion, tends to align with basic common sense. We all know that there are extraordinarily gentle men and murderous women. Sex differences are always generalizations: They refer to a behavior, with some evolutionary rationale behind it. They never define, entirely, an individual. And that fact alone should tell us that there's always—even in the most biologically dominated traits—some flexibility, an instinctive ability to respond, for better and worse, to the world around us.

mal matches. One is that even with this apparently precise system, there's nothing precise—or guaranteed—about the physical construction of male and female. The other point makes that possible. It appears that sex doesn't matter in the early states of embryonic development. We are unisex at the point of conception.

If you examine an embryo at about six weeks, you see that it has the ability to develop in either direction. The fledgling embryo has two sets of ducts—Wolffian for male, Muellerian for female—an either/or structure, held in readiness for further development. If testosterone and other androgens are released by hormone-producing cells, then the Wolffian ducts develop into the channel that connects penis to testes, and the female ducts wither away.

Without testosterone, the embryo takes on a female form; the male ducts vanish and the Muellerian ducts expand into oviducts, uterus, and vagina. In other words, in humans, anyway (the opposite is true in birds), the female is the default sex. Back in the 1950s, the famed biologist Alfred Jost showed that if you castrate a male rabbit fetus, choking off testosterone, you produce a completely feminized rabbit.

We don't do these experiments in humans—for obvious reasons—but there are naturally occurring instances that prove the same point. For instance: In the fetal testes are a group of cells, called Leydig cells, that make testosterone. In rare cases, the fetus doesn't make enough of these cells (a defect known as Leydig cell hypoplasia). In this circumstance we see the limited power of the XY chromosome. These boys have the right chromosomes and the right genes to be boys; they just don't grow a penis. Obstetricians and parents often think they see a baby girl, and these children are routinely raised as daughters. Usually, the "mistake" is caught about the time of puberty, when menstruation doesn't start. A doctor's examination shows the child to be internally male; there are usually small testes, often tucked within the abdomen. As the researchers put it, if the condition had been known from the beginning, "the sisters would have been born as brothers."

Just to emphasize how tricky all this body-building can get, there's a peculiar genetic defect that seems to be clustered by heredity in a small group of villages in the Dominican Republic. The result of the defect is a failure to produce an enzyme that concentrates testosterone, specifically for building

will that wonderful, unpredictable, flexible biology that we have been given allow a shift, so that one day, we will literally be far more alike?

don't seem drawn to weaponry in the same way that men are. Almost twice as many male thieves and robbers use guns as their female counterparts do.

Or you can look at more personal crimes: domestic partner murders. Three-fourths of men use guns in those killings; 50 percent of women do. Here's more from the domestic front: In conflicts in which a woman killed a man, he tended to be the one who had started the fight—in 51.8 percent of the cases, to be exact. When the man was the killer, he again was the likely first aggressor, and by an even more dramatic margin. In fights in which women died, they had started the argument only 12.5 percent of the time.

Enough. You can parade endless similar statistics but the point is this: Males are more aggressive, not just among humans but among almost all species on earth. Male chimpanzees, for instance, declare war on neighboring troops, and one of their strategies is a warning strike: They kill females and infants to terrorize and intimidate. In terms of simple, reproductive genetics, it's an advantage of males to be aggressive: You can muscle your way into dominance, winning more

This is true even with physical characteristics that we've often assumed are nailed down by genetics. Scientists now believe height, for instance, is only about 90 percent heritable. A person's genes might code for a six-foot-tall body, but malnutrition could literally cut that short. And there's also some evidence, in girls anyway, that children with stressful childhoods tend to become shorter adults. So while some factors are predetermined, there's evidence that the prototypical male/female body design can be readily altered.

It's a given that humans, like most other species—bananas, spiders, sharks, ducks, any rabbit you pull out of a hat—rely on two sexes for reproduction. So basic is that requirement that we have chromosomes whose primary purpose is to deliver the genes that order up a male or a female. All other chromosomes are numbered, but we label the sex chromosomes with the letters X and Y. We get one each from our mother and our father, and the basic combinations are these: XX makes female, XY makes male.

There are two important—and little known—points about these chromoso-

the genitals. One obscure little enzyme only, but here's what happens without it: You get a boy with undescended testes and a penis so short and stubby that is resembles an oversized clitoris.

In the mountain villages of this Caribbean nation, people are used to it. The children are usually raised as "conditional" girls. At puberty, the secondary tide of androgens rises and is apparently enough to finish the construction project. The scrotum suddenly descends, the phallus grows, and the child develops a distinctly male body—narrow hips, muscular build, and even slight beard growth. At that point, the family shifts the child over from daughter to son. The dresses are thrown out. He begins to wear male clothes and starts dating girls. People in the Dominican Republic are so familiar with this condition that there's a colloquial name for it: *guevedoces,* meaning "eggs (or testes) at 12."

stances, behave differently than if the individual was a female."

Do the ways that we amplify physical and behavioral differences in childhood shape who we become as adults? Absolutely. But to understand that, you have to understand the differences themselves—their beginning and the very real biochemistry that may lie behind them.

Here is a good place to focus on testosterone—a hormone that is both well-studied and generally underrated. First, however, I want to acknowledge that there are many other hormones and neurotransmitters that appear to influence behavior. Preliminary work shows that fetal boys are a little more active than fetal girls. It's pretty difficult to argue socialization at that point. There's a strong suspicion that testosterone may create the difference.

And there are a couple of relevant animal models to emphasize the point.

consensus seems to be that full-blown "I'm a girl" or "I'm a boy" instincts arrive between the ages of 2 and 3. Research shows that if a family operates in a very traditional, Beaver Cleaver kind of environment, filled with awareness of and association with "proper" gender behaviors, the "boys do trucks, girls do dolls" attitude seems to come very early. If a child grows up in a less traditional family, with an emphasis on partnership and sharing—"We all do the dishes, Joshua"—children maintain a more flexible sense of gender roles until about age 6.

In this period, too, relationships between boys and girls tend to fall into remarkably strict lines. Interviews with children find that 3-year-olds say that about half their friendships are with the opposite sex. By the age of 5, that drops to 20 percent. By 7, almost no boys or girls have, or will admit to having, best friends of the opposite sex. They still hang out on the same playground, play on the same soccer teams. They may be friendly, but the real friendships tend to be boy-to-boy or girl-to-girl.

do the ways that we amplify differences in childhood shape who we become as adults?

It's the comfort level with this slipslide of sexual identity that's so remarkable and, I imagine, so comforting to the children involved. I'm positive that the sexual transition of these children is less traumatic than the abrupt awareness of the "sisters who would have been brothers." There's a message of tolerance there, well worth repeating, and there are some other key lessons too.

These defects are rare and don't alter the basic male-female division of our species. They do emphasize how fragile those divisions can be. Biology allows flexibility, room to change, to vary and grow. With that comes room for error as well. That it's possible to live with these genetic defects, that they don't merely kill us off, is a reminder that we, male and female alike, exist on a continuum of biological possibilities that can overlap and sustain either sex.

Marc Breedlove points out that the most difficult task may be separating how the brain responds to hormones from how the brain responds to the *results* of hormones. Which brings us back, briefly, below the belt: In this context, the penis is just a result, the product of androgens at work before birth. "And after birth," says Breedlove, "virtually everyone who interacts with that individual will note that he has a penis, and will, in many in-

Back in the 1960s, Robert Goy, a psychologist at the University of Wisconsin at Madison, first documented that young male monkeys play much more roughly than young females. Goy went on to show that if you manipulate testosterone level—raising it in females, damping it down in males—you can reverse those effects, creating sweet little male monkeys and rowdy young females.

Is testosterone the only factor at work here? I don't think so. But clearly we can argue a strong influence, and, interestingly, studies have found that girls with congenital adrenal hypoplasia—who run high in testosterone—tend to be far more fascinated by trucks and toy weaponry than most little girls are. They lean toward rough-and-tumble play, too. As it turns out, the strongest influence on this "abnormal" behavior is not parental disapproval, but the company of other little girls, who tone them down and direct them toward more routine girl games.

And that reinforces an early point: If there is indeed a biology to sex differences, we amplify it. At some point—when it is still up for debate—we gain a sense of our gender, and with it a sense of "gender-appropriate" behavior.

Some scientists argue for some evidence of gender awareness in infancy, perhaps by the age of 12 months. The

There's some interesting science that suggests that the space between boys and girls is a normal part of development; there are periods during which children may thrive and learn from hanging out with peers of the same sex. Do we, as parents, as a culture at large, reinforce such separation? Is the pope Catholic? One of my favorite studies looked at little boys who asked for toys. If they asked for a heavily armed action figure, they got the soldier about 70 percent of the time. If they asked for a "girl" toy, like a baby doll or a Barbie, their parents purchased it maybe 40 percent of the time. Name a child who won't figure out how to work *that* system.

How does all this fit together—toys and testosterone, biology and behavior, the development of the child into the adult, the way that men and women relate to one another?

Let me make a cautious statement about testosterone: It not only has some body-building functions, it influences some behaviors as well. Let's make that a little less cautious: These behaviors include rowdy play, sex drive, competitiveness, and an in-your-face attitude. Males tend to have a higher baseline of testosterone than females—in our species, about seven to ten times as much—and therefore you would predict (correctly, I think) that all of those behaviors would be more generally found in men than in women.

But testosterone is also one of my favorite examples of how responsive biology is, how attuned it is to the way we live our lives. Testosterone, it turns out, rises in response to competition and threat. In the days of our ancestors, this might have been hand-to-hand combat or high-risk hunting endeavors. Today, scientists have measured testosterone rise in athletes preparing for a game, in chess players awaiting a match, in spectators following a soccer competition.

If a person—or even just a person's favored team—wins, testosterone continues to rise. It falls with a loss. (This also makes sense in an evolutionary perspective. If one was being clobbered with a club, it would be extremely unhelpful to have a hormone [under] one to battle on.) Testosterone also rises in the competitive world of dating, settles down with a stable and supportive relationship, climbs again if the relationship starts to falter.

It's been known for years that men in high-stress professions—say, police work or corporate law—have higher testosterone levels than men in the ministry. It turns out that women in the same kind of strong-attitude professions have higher testosterone than women who choose to stay home. What I like about this is the chicken-or-egg aspect. If you argue that testosterone influenced the behavior of those women, which came first? Did they have high testosterone and choose the law? Or did they choose the law, and the competitive environment ratcheted them up on the androgen scale? Or could both be at work?

And, returning to children for a moment, there's an ongoing study by Pennsylvania researchers, tracking that question in adolescent girls, who are being encouraged by their parents to engage in competitive activities that were once for boys only. As they do so, the researchers are monitoring, regularly, two hormones: testosterone and cortisol, a stress hormone. Will these hormones rise in response to this new, more traditionally male environment?

What if more girls choose the competitive path; more boys choose the other? Will female testosterone levels rise, male levels fall? Will that wonderful, unpredictable, flexible biology that we've been given allow a shift, so that one day, we will literally be far more alike?

We may not have answers to all those questions, but we can ask them, and we can expect that the answers will come someday, because science clearly shows us that such possibilities exist. In this most important sense, sex differences offer us a paradox. It is only through exploring and understanding what makes us different that we can begin to understand what binds us together.

Deborah Blum is a Pulitzer Prize-winning science writer, a professor of journalism at the University of Wisconsin-Madison, and author of Sex on the Brain: The Biological Differences Between Men and Women (*Penguin, 1997*).

CAN YOU LOVE GOD AND SEX?

Praise the Lord, yes! A roundtable of leading sisters of the spirit discuss how we can achieve the kind of moral vision and faith that affirm both spiritual nourishment and sexual fulfillment as Black women

Facilitated by Marcia L. Dyson

BLACK WOMEN, FOR GOOD OR ILL, are intimately tied in the popular mind to the two most powerful forces in human reality–spirit and sex. But we rarely think about the essential relationship between these two forces; instead we are usually preoccupied with trying to establish moral distance between them.

'We're all trying to become the virtuous woman in Proverbs 31:10, but we have this burning within our very human bodies.'

Stereotyped images of Black women often emphasize these extremes–hot, hoochie-mama music-video vamps versus asexual, long-suffering mothers of the Black church–and our true voices are rarely heard on sexuality and spirituality in our real lives.

How, then, do we Black women address these contradictions? What can the church or mosque do to reduce the religious hypocrisy that exploits female sexuality even as it disciplines and condemns it? How do we confront patriarchy's worst effects yet endeavor to share our lives with Black men? How do we validate our lesbian sisters' right to live fully despite homophobic religious narratives?

Eight spirit-filled, sexually confident sisters met at ESSENCE to dispel myths, crush lies, rebuke stereotypes and celebrate the wondrous and complex interaction between spirituality and sexuality. Here are excerpts from their groundbreaking exchange.

Are We Eve's Daughters?

REV. MARCIA L. DYSON: How do our religious institutions shape our attitudes toward our bodies? Why are women the ones considered responsible for sexual sin?

REV. LINDA H. HOLLIES: The Bible grew out of the oral tradition of people of color, so we have a collection of myths that have been passed down through the generations. And there is this story in which woman is the evil, dirty temptress who brings down the whole world. But as I look at chapter three of Genesis, where the first sin is described, I see that Eve is *not* evil. Eve is the person who does the negotiation with the spirit of evil. God said, "Don't eat from the tree [of knowledge]." But girlfriend said, "God said we can't touch it." Eve knew that if she touched it, she'd have to deal with temptation. She was thinking all the time, although she made a bad decision when she willfully disobeyed God. So it seems to me that it's more complicated than just putting all the blame on Eve.

DYSON: But what does that say to the women in the church who sit Sunday after Sunday hearing about the things that we should not do? Every Woman's Day we are quoted Proverbs 31:10–"Who can find a virtuous woman? for her price is far above rubies." We're all trying to become this virtuous woman, but we have this burning within our very human bodies.

PROF. KELLY BROWN-DOUGLAS: We have to get a clearer understanding of what we mean by sexuality—that it is not simply about genitals. Sexuality has to do with the essential part of who you are, that thing about us urging us into relationship, into communion, into creativity—with ourselves, with one another, even with God.

Sources of Our Sexual Shame

IYANLA VANZANT: There was a common message about sex from my Native American Christian grandmother and from those people who taught me African culture and tradition: Good girls don't do it. And if you *do* do it, lie about it. Native American women, African women and clearly African-American women all dealt with the same three things: stigma, fear and shame.

> 'In the land of the free and the home of the slave, Black women had to use sex to save our men and families.'

PROF. EMILIE M. TOWNES: For most of us who are African-American, our histories go back to the auction block. Our bodies were put on display and seen as objects, and then we received a Christianity that said that slavery was okay for Black people. I don't think we've adequately understood the real impact that the auction block—and later, the hangman's noose—had on the images we all internalized

about our bodies. The consequence is the amount of violence in our homes. It affects the ways we deal with one another—we don't respect our bodies and we don't respect the bodies of those around us.

HOLLIES: Since Black women were brought to the land of the free and the home of the slave, we have had to use our sexual selves to keep our babies around a little longer, to get food and to save our men and families. We have a collective memory and a collective way of acting that out.

PROF. DELORES WILLIAMS: But our attitudes about our bodies do go back to the Bible; most African-American preachers draw off a common exposure to the Christian tradition and its tendency to understand a woman's body only in terms of child-bearing, not in terms of her sexuality.

TOWNES: Look at the nativity story—how Jesus was born in a stable to the Virgin Mary, the wife of Joseph. I have yet to hear discussed in the church the way in which that birth is a very bodily experience. His birth doesn't get linked up with the birth stories I've heard from women who have delivered babies. You don't hear any of the pain and suffering that Mary went through. And so Jesus becomes for us a model of antiseptic faith. We don't have ways to link into our bodies because we've taken Jesus out of *his* body.

MINISTER AVA MUHAMMAD: It is the interpretation of Scripture by males who, in my humble opinion, are threatened in this particular era. I don't believe sexism is an old thing; it was not considered unusual at all in our history for a female to rule a nation. As we are taught in the Nation of Islam, a nation can rise no higher than its women—which, of course, is the reverse of how contemporary society deals with us.

VANZANT: Very often when we engage in any kind of sexual expression, we lie about it and hide it. Theology continues to perpetuate that because it's always, "God said that Mary should have the baby. God said it; she

did it." There was no discussion, there was no consent from Mary. Her womb was just taken.

Sex and Self-esteem

DYSON: We say we are sexual beings. How do we express our sexuality without the guilt and shame that is laid upon us by our church fathers—and church mothers?

BROWN-DOUGLAS: We know there is an unhealthy expression of sexuality in the Black community, in the Black church, among our Black youth and so on. This is why I like how Emilie has written about it: "We are sexually repressed while at the same time being sexually active, and this is a dangerous combination." We aren't helping our youths or one another express sexuality in life-affirming ways. And one reason that's not taking place is because we won't have the sexual discussion. The church—it's irrelevant.

VANZANT: It may be irrelevant, but that doesn't mean it has to stay irrelevant.

BROWN-DOUGLAS: We somehow need to be able to say to our kids "Look, you are sexual beings. And that's not a bad thing; that's a *good* thing."

DARLENE POWELL HOPSON: But, as we all know, it's difficult to do that if your mother wasn't comfortable with her sexuality—and encouraged you to repress yours. Whenever I'm doing sessions with young girls, they may tell me something like: "This guy's interested in me and I'm interested in him. I'm considering having sex with him." And then I'll say, "You know, you're wearing a beautiful gold chain, and you have a brand new stereo, don't you? Now, if that guy asked you could he have that gold chain or could he have that stereo, what would you say?" And they come back with, "He's not getting my gold chain. He's not getting my stereo." I point out, "Yet you're considering giving him your body. So you're telling me that you value that stereo and that gold chain *more* than you value your body." That's where the problem lies to me.

DYSON: Sisters, how do we get women to stop selling their bodies cheap at their spirit's expense?

BROWN-DOUGLAS: You start where Darlene started, with "How do you feel about yourself?" Because a healthy self-concept leads to healthy expressions of sexuality. And then we won't have to say "Don't have sex."

Rape, Sexual Abuse and Recovery

HOLLIES: But what you're saying, Kelly, is that we all start on level ground. We do *not* all start on level ground. I am the daughter of a Black pastor who raped me from the time I was 11 years old. And my mother acted as though this didn't happen.

Iyanla has said that God took Mary's stuff. I don't believe that. I believe God waited for Mary to say yes. But my daddy *took* my stuff. And my mama sanctified it. And my daddy told me, "If you tell your mama, it will probably kill her; she's already had one heart attack." And then he cited the story of Lot's daughters in Scripture, and he said, "This is of God." This is something that happens not just in pulpits, but in our homes. My compelling reason for being in the ministry is to save the lives of sisters. But I was 40 before I could talk about it, because the church would not allow it.

HOPSON: But it's so helpful, your telling that story of healing, in the church, for the young girls who are either experiencing abuse or don't feel good about their sexual aspect.

HOLLIES: Not just the young girls, the women, the mothers. Because one out of three of us in this room has been raped—not just by our dads, but by somebody close.

DYSON: Well, then, Linda, how do we—as you say in the title of your book take back those yesterdays? How do we understand the power that we have?

HOLLIES: First of all, I had to look at shamed women in Scripture, even in the genealogy of Jesus. Jesus came through the tribe of Judah. Every woman in the genealogy of Jesus is a ho—H-O—by one standard or another. I mean, you start with Tamar, Judah's daughter-in-law, who was a righteous woman. After her first and second husbands [both Judah's sons] died [and neither one had given her children], she was sent off by Judah to her dad's house instead of being married to Judah's third son, as was the custom. But Tamar disguised herself as a harlot, set Judah up and conceived *his* child. So one of the first women named in Jesus' genealogy was made a ho by her righteous father-in-law. We haven't dealt with that.

> 'Looking at shamed women in the Scripture, every woman in the genealogy of Jesus is a ho—H-O—by one standard or another.'

WILLIAMS: You're saying that the church has to reinterpret its sources, or it can do nothing. Perhaps women have to do it. And I don't know if you'll have a Christian church when you get through. But we have to reinterpret the doctrines of the church.

Finding Your Personal God

HOPSON: When we talk about self-esteem, we are really saying that we want our daughters to feel worth being loved—so if they are engaging in sex early, they know that behavior is not consistent with their goals of feeling like a worthwhile and lovable person.

VANZANT: Okay, but I was raped by an uncle at 9, so the ability to understand that I was worthwhile was taken from me. I was an orphan, and my aunt and uncle were raising me because my mother had died and my father was running the street. When my uncle raped me, I told my aunt immediately, the same day. She confronted him and he said it didn't happen, and she believed him. So what that said to me was that I didn't matter. I proceeded to develop ways to hide—not only from the world, but from God—until my stepmother said to me, crass as this may be: "How much pussy did he take from you? You can't measure it." She said, "Don't think that that's all you are. You are so much more. Find yourself. Take this to God. Everything that concerns you concerns God."

HOLLIES: And I had to find a different kind of God, because that God didn't save me from my daddy. I had to move to a place where I could discover a God who could look into me, see who I am and value me just the same. And it took me years to get there. I didn't ask my mother [if she was aware of the abuse] until two years before she died. And my mama said what a lot of mothers have said: "I didn't want to know. I needed him to love me." So I had to find a different kind of relationship with a God who could love me. Because a God who allows you to be stolen from is a hard God to serve.

VANZANT: And do you know how I think of God now? Yemoja—that Black feminine core of God in Yoruba, the Black Madonna. And I think of Oshun, the Goddess of the River. When my stepmother said to me, "Find yourself," I found me *in* Yemoja, *in* Oshun, *in* Oya, *in* Inle, and then I realized that *Oh, these are just different aspects of God!*

DYSON: There are so many other stories like yours, from other women and girls who feel trapped, isolated, alone and ashamed.

BROWN-DOUGLAS: One of the crucial steps is to create a safe space, a protected space—we hope that could be the church, where women could tell their stories.

Sharing Our Wisdom

VANZANT: If we look at our culture stretching all the way back to West Africa, we'll know that we have always gathered on a *regular* basis in a *safe* space, and we do tell our stories. We gather in those circles to *heal*. That's part of our culture, and the women, those age 40 and over, become the midwives who bring the young girls through.

HOPSON: That's why we need to have that now, where there's somebody with whom a child feels she has a safe space to tell her stories.

WILLIAMS: And the church is supposed to be the safe place. We know that it's not.

HOLLIES: How could it be the safe space? My daddy was the pastor!

VANZANT: The first thing we have to do—as women—is to say to the men "Y'all, this is a problem." We have to come together among ourselves to tell our own truth.

BROWN-DOUGLAS: We can't act like sex has never been an issue in our own lives. Otherwise we're perpetuating a lie and our girls are trying to live up to a standard that nobody could live up to 'cause we didn't even live up to it.

TOWNES: We have to find ways to have fearless Bible study in churches. We don't deal with those hard passages in Scripture. We spiritualize some of these stories: We say the Song of Solomon was just a very nice poem, when what was going on was really a hot and heavy affair.

BROWN-DOUGLAS: We also have to be unafraid to bring other [secular texts] into the church. What's wrong with bringing in some of the stuff that our youths are reading, singing, watching and talking about? We have to be unafraid of youth culture and hip-hop culture. We have to be unafraid and begin to address those issues and talk about that *and* the Bible. A lot of issues that we put to the Bible, the Bible doesn't even try to answer. We have to be clear that the Bible *isn't* clear about homosexuality and heterosexuality! We have to open the Bible up in a different way, in a more *honest* way, in our churches.

What Is Healthy Sex?

DYSON: In terms of the religious traditions represented here, do they all have negative views about lesbianism, about homosexuality?

TOWNES: You know, we also need to include bisexual and transgender people.

MUHAMMAD: From our perspective, the Bible and the Koran are clear that homosexuality is not favored by the Creator. That is not a condemnation of the person. But it is viewed as being contrary to nature since the Originator's primary force is life and the re-creation of life. I think the Holy Koran uses the phrase "God created everything in pairs" and says that one of the primary desires of the Creator was and is to create and to reproduce.

Sex—the physical act of touching, hugging, kissing, embracing and then the ultimate union—is exciting because it is an act of creation. It is one of the most powerful experiences a human being can have, because it's reflective of creation itself.

DYSON: Sister Muhammad, you're saying that the reason for the sexual union is procreation, but what about women who cannot give birth or men who are impotent? Even beyond procreation the sexual union is the greatest communion one can have with God because it brings you to a sense of ecstasy; it's a joining of one's self to something higher than even we can experience.

BROWN-DOUGLAS: It's important to understand that to be a spiritual being is to be a sexual being. The point is, we must begin to help one another—our children, each other—develop healthy concepts of who we are and how we *express* who we are, not only sexually, but in other ways.

WILLIAMS: What indicates healthy?

BROWN-DOUGLAS: That it's life-affirming.

DYSON: The rappers Lil' Kim and Foxy Brown would say "I have good self-esteem; in fact, I'll show my body. There isn't a man [pulling my strings]." But I think they're wrong: They don't produce themselves; they don't manage themselves; they don't style their own images. The young sisters who are on the videos behind the male rappers feel that they have a healthy self-esteem—

VANZANT: Who are we to say that they don't have healthy self-esteem? We get so puritanical about it. I learned from Native American women that "life-affirming" is anything that supports and honors the going on of life—even if it means sometimes sitting back and allowing people to wear their boobs out. I'm praying for Foxy Brown.

BROWN-DOUGLAS: The church tends to be so proscriptive, telling people what to do and what not to do: Don't have sex. Don't masturbate. Don't do this. Don't do that. We've got so many people engaged in what we now call unsafe sex—and not just our youths. It's not a simple matter of "Just say no; don't have sex." I want you to ask yourself, does having sex enhance your life possibilities at this moment? Good sex allows you to be all of who you are.

HOPSON: But for a teenage girl, that's an awful lot of latitude. Sex for a teenage girl is not life-enhancing.

VANZANT: When our young people have a good definition of themselves, they're going to understand, *I don't have to [have sex] at 14. It's not good for me at this time!*

BROWN-DOUGLAS: Exactly. I'm not ignoring the complexities of what it means to be human, but I do believe that if you feel good about yourself, then you aren't going to make certain choices.

Self-Affirmation, Celibacy and Healing Love

DYSON: So how might Black women honor that aspect of self that is sexual and integrate it with that whole self? If you're gay and you're afraid to come out and let the family know, you can't affirm who you are.

BROWN-DOUGLAS: You've got to find ways to feel good about who you are in all of your uniqueness.

VANZANT: To develop a healthy concept of self, you've got to find those self-affirming images. Even today at 46 years old, I still have moments and days where I struggle with *I'm not good enough.* I still do. Those are the days I'm looking in the mirror, saying, *Work with me, baby; come on, save yourself, breathe!* Because those wounds are in my soul. But I'm fortunate enough to be married to a man I *know.* And he knows me. He was with me when I was 13 and wore a wig because my hair had fallen out from stress after I was raped. He was with me when I was 16 and Black. He was with me when I was 19 in the Black Panthers. He was with me when I was 21 in the mosque. He was with me at 30 when I was getting into Yoruba. So, he's been here; he knows me. So I trust him. *Some* days! On the days when my wounds are raw, he honors me enough to leave me alone.

HOLLIES: Here's my plug for celibacy: Every time you have sex with a person, there is a covenant that is made. All that you have, you give to that person, and all that person has is given to you; and there are so many different types of people living within us—what we've each drawn from people across the ages. It's a shame that it took science and the news media to say "When you sleep with somebody, you sleep with everybody they've ever slept with." It should have been coming across the pulpit all the time.

For me, the best way I can honor myself is to stay empty until I can find my completion. And my completion does not come through somebody diddling me. Sex for me starts in the morning with the way my husband says, "Hi, honey." You know, I can tell you with the first words that morning whether there will be sex in the house *that* night. Because it's the way I'm treated the whole day long.

DYSON: Tell us about the sexual *healing* that had to take place as the result of being raped by your father.

HOLLIES: The way my dad had stolen from me made a very deep and lasting impression on the way I related to any man. It took two ex-hus-bands before I could find a person I could be honest with.

One day, as I was sitting up in the hospital in Michigan looking out at a gray sky, the Holy Spirit revealed to me, "This is the life your mother lived." She lived the life of grayness—never engaged in life. I was also a very staid person. I wore dark colors, trying to keep attention from me. But that day, when I noticed the flowers, trees and clouds, just being colorful and wonderful—I was born that day to understand that God loved me the way I am. Black, raped, short hair, wide nose, everything else. God loved me. I was born that day in a hospital chapel in ways I couldn't have imagined before, in ways that my mama couldn't teach me. It became my mission and it is still my mission in life to teach other women that God loves you regardless of who you are and what you've done.

VANZANT: And He knows that you're not a virgin.

HOLLIES: Yes, She does.

VANZANT: I had to really get to that because I kept trying to hide it, even from God. I will say that one of the things I learned in the Nation of Islam that helped with my healing—something I think women need was to develop nonsexual relationships with men. I didn't know that I didn't have to sleep with every man who winked at me or said he liked me. And I found a brother in the mosque and another brother in Philadelphia who loved me. And there was no sexual energy at all. For three and a half years, I lived celibately and I had marvelous nonsexual relationships with men. That's what helped me do the healing.

HOLLIES: For me, sexual healing comes when you can find a new family, because most of us have been taught some very negative information in our families of origin, especially in dysfunctional Black families. Probably 75 to 90 percent of us deal with the "elephant in the living room" syndrome—what happens in this house stays in this house and we don't talk about it to nobody. You have to broaden your image of what family is, that you can tell the truth and let that group affirm you or validate your issues.

What Our Fathers Can Teach Us About Intimacy

DYSON: We're so concerned about men's relationship with their sons; we need to talk about their relationships with their daughters.

TOWNES: There are at least three pictures up in my mother's house now of my father in tender and loving poses with me as a young child. But I hit puberty, and he did what a lot of men do then with their girls—he separated himself. And I think I probably separated myself, too.

VANZANT: It goes back to intimacy. My father died when I was 30. My father never kissed me. I'm talking about my *father*—my biological father. Never kissed me, never hugged me, never embraced me—never, never, never, never, never.

DYSON: We live in a society that doesn't teach men what to do with that energy. Here you are, budding, breasts are coming, the female scents are coming, and it probably frightened him.

VANZANT: It did. And I've since come to understand that my uncle heard the cry for love I was sending out, but the only way he knew how to express love was sexually.

TOWNES: It wasn't until two years ago that I realized my chief problem was I did not believe in my own worth. And so I had to be careful not to try and practice being in a relationship before I knew more about this sense of *I am worthy.* I started into a relationship that began, for the first time in my life, out of friendship. Not that I didn't think that person was fine—all the emotions, all the hormones were raging—but I took the time, put on the brakes and said, *Okay, I need a friendship first.*

WILLIAMS: And I think getting in touch with and owning the erotic is very important for intimacy. By erotic, I don't mean pornographic—I'd like to make a distinction between the two. I mean letting the creative power that's within you come out and really affirming it.

I have struggled with intimacy. So much of my life has been spent in civil-rights activities that it's very difficult for me even to think of spirituality without politics. That's both a plus and a minus. The plus is that it keeps me aware that the political is part of what we do every day. The minus is that in a potentially sexual relationship, it's like, "What kind of politics is going on with this guy?" It's second-guessing people, so that's still problematic with me.

Affirming the God Within Us

MUHAMMAD: We were talking earlier about being a whole person—a spiritual, an intellectual and a physical person. But you know, as Jesus said, "Peace be still." As Iyanla said, "God is within." But we've allowed the God in self to go to sleep—that self-accusing spirit that knows the difference between right and wrong. So often we get disappointed because we think physical intimacy with someone will lead to a lifelong relationship. But physical intimacy is not a cause, it's an effect of a good relationship.

As a single woman, I made a few mistakes of my own, confusing physical intimacy with love. Then I went through nine years of being alone, and that's when I had my realization that God loves me: *There is a God, and He brought me here and I'm beautiful to Him, I'm valuable to Him.* Even if I *never* had a mate, it was all right. When I believed that and accepted this in my heart, my husband came

into my life. And I can say this now that I'm happily married: I love my husband, but I know and he knows that if he'd never come into my life, I still would've found satisfaction. My husband has given me a further sense of security and protection and trust. You can be free sexually and make love with total abandon when you know this person loves you—scars, rolls, cellulite, bunions, whatever—and will still wake up in the morning next to you, saying, "Give me a hug, hold me, touch me." But all of that is an effect. It comes out of somewhere that you and that person, whoever they are, have connected in the realm of the unseen. Then you don't have to worry about sexual techniques and such, because it's going to work.

DYSON: How can we look back at our yesterdays, look at the best of our rich African-American culture and traditions; what has embraced us and given us the best examples of how to honor ourselves?

VANZANT: We look back at ourselves and African-American history, look at those women—the "she-roes" and how they behaved. Harriet Tubman talked about her *passionate* love! She was still passionate about her man and loved him, but she didn't stop her journey. She didn't stop her work. She had a plan and she stayed focused. So we don't have to make sexual identity our be-all, end-all, know-all, do-all, but we don't have to ignore it either.

You know, in truth and in honesty, one of the things that is so critical—and we all have said it in one way or another today: Women, don't have sex with *anyone* if your heart is

closed—meaning that if your heart is filled with your anger or other painful stuff. Don't do that, because it's a violation of the ancient parts of you.

HOPSON: If you can't be vulnerable and open with someone, the question is, Why would you want to be physically intimate?

VANZANT: Escapism! Physical gratification. And sometimes also for economic reasons.

HOPSON: But we know that's not healthy, that's not being holistic. One of the things that I share with my clients is an affirmation—I think I learned some of this from Iyanla—I have them say "Dear God, I love you and being your child. You made me a sexual being and I want to experience closeness and fulfillment with my partner. My soul yearns for the pleasure and satisfaction of being spiritually and physically intimate with my partner." And to my partner: "I want to bond with you. I feel safe, close and secure with you. I want to understand you and fulfill your needs and desires. I want to deepen our relationship, and each time we make love I want to feel more connected and understood." And I think the "understood" part is critical, because when we do come together, what we're really searching for, what we're looking for, is to be understood.

Marcia L. Dyson is an ESSENCE contributing writer, an ordained minister and the author of the forthcoming book God Sings Soprano: Discovering the Female Voice of God *(Free Press).*

Satori IN THE BEDROOM

TANTRA AND THE DILEMMA OF WESTERN SEXUALITY

by Katy Butler

Freud once said that four people—two mothers, two fathers—lie in bed with every couple making love. If only that were all. Hugh Hefner is under the covers with us, and Carl Djerassi, who invented the birth control pill, and Alex Comfort, who wrote *The Joy of Sex*. Shere Hite is there taking notes, and a doctor from the Centers for Disease Control, and Pope John Paul II and Kenneth Starr. Cindy Crawford's perfect body may float in space above us, or Long Dong Silver's, daring us to turn on the light and look at how we don't measure up.

■ When a man sleeps with a woman, he sleeps with her past as well, including her memories of pregnancy, date rape, abandonment or shame. When a woman sleeps with a man, she sleeps with the young boy caught reading his father's *Playboy* magazines and the teenager in the back seat, expected to know everything without being shown. Each of us in the industrialized West carries into the bedroom not only personal memo-

This article first appeared in *Family Therapy Networker,* March/April 1999, pp. 22-32, 52. © 1999 by The Family Therapy Network, Inc. Reprinted by permission.

ries, but collective ones: we are layered with exhortations, like sedimentary rock. Sex, the Victorians told our great-grandmothers, is dirty: Save it for the one you love. The mature female orgasm, said Freud, is the vaginal orgasm: That comes only to women who resolve their penis envy. Women's sexuality, said the marriage manuals of the 1950s, is problematic, like the delicate wiring of an old MG: Husbands must be master mechanics. Vaginal orgasm is a myth, said the feminist theorists of the 1980s. Find the clitoris. Now.

Sleeping around will ruin your reputation, we were told in the fifties: Why buy the cow when you can get the milk through the fence? Sleeping around will free you, we

For most of us, our first sexual act was also an act of secret rebellion against our parents. The memory of this defiant split lives on in our cells in the disembodied, suppressed yet obsessed way our culture approaches sex today. Few of our fathers talked to their sons about how to enhance a woman's pleasure or prolong their own; few of our mothers ever told their daughters about the delights or even the location of the clitoris. We found out anyway, and paid the price.

In the dark recesses of our mental closets lies a negative cultural dowry—the muu-muus that missionaries gave the naked Polynesians; the *penitentes'* cat-o'-nine-tails; the chastity belt; and the confessional—all the

joke sunglasses, the rejected girl crying in the rain. It didn't matter what the details were or the context in which they occurred. All that mattered was the telling of them. Opening the paper, some of us imagined how our own intimacies would read some morning, printed in black and white and dumped on our neighbors' doorsteps.

What we read in the papers that day reflected the impoverished language we bring to sex. In 1931, the English novelist Virginia Woolf wrote in *The Waves*, "I need a little language such as lovers speak, words of one syllable." But we can speak of lovemaking everywhere except the bedroom. For the delicate skin that touches our lover's most tender places, we have no words except the

When a woman lies down in bed with a man, a light show of images plays over her body without her knowing it. When a man lies down with a woman, she wonders how he will look as a hero.

were told in the sixties: Smash monogamy. Men and women are pretty much alike, we were told in the seventies. Men are from Mars, women are from Venus, we are told today.

Many of us enter the bedroom now as if we have been told we are about to play a high-stakes game. There is no rule book, or else it's been hidden. Everyone else, we think, knows how to play. We charge down the field. We pass the ball. A whistle blows. The rules have changed. The teams are being shuffled. We'll be playing with a shuttlecock now instead of a ball, and the goalposts have been moved to the other end of the field. We start running and the crowd roars, but we're not sure what we did right. Now we are on the bottom of a pile of bodies. We are given five different rule books and told to choose one that suits us. (We have no idea what book the other team is playing from.) Bleeding from the shin, we strap on our battered equipment again and once more run down the field.

We lie down with all of this, and more, when we lie down in bed with each other. We sleep with the war between men and women fueled by patriarchy and differences in physiology, and with the uneasy cease-fire in the erogenous zone that followed the feminist and sexual revolutions. We sleep with the legacy of the 1970s, when you could find, on many a middle-class night-stand, the dry, clinical bestsellers of William Masters and Virginia Johnson, the pioneers of behavioral sex therapy. The bright lights of their science were supposed to banish our fears and superstitions, like crucifixes held before a vampire. Yet the fear of pleasure, and of being discovered having pleasure, still runs beneath our bedroom floors like an underground river.

trappings of the Augustinian Catholic tradition that declared sex a dirty distraction on the path to God and the source of original sin. ("As the caterpillar chooses the fairest leaves to lay her eggs on," wrote the poet William Blake two centuries ago, "so the priest lays his curse on the fairest joys.") All of this we bring into the bedroom.

When we sleep with each other, we sleep with images we've absorbed and, without knowing it, those our lovers have absorbed as well. Like fast food, images of other people's orgasms, stripped of context and connection, are now available 24 hours a day and consumed alone and on the cheap. They demand of us a bravado we rarely feel. They lurk eternally on the Internet and in the phone-sex banks, at the corner video store and in the *Congressional Record*. Our bedrooms are colonized by them. When a woman lies down in bed with a man, a light show of images plays over her body without her knowing it: red-satin garter belts, perhaps, or beaver shots or Marilyn Chambers or Monica Lewinsky or the *Penthouse* Pet of the Month. When a man lies down with a woman, images of imaginary men play over his face without his knowing it—the hero of Tristan and Iseult, perhaps, or a Tammy Wynette song or a romance novel. No wonder we feel split within ourselves and from each other. We expect sexualized romantic love to carry a greater psychological burden than does any other culture on earth while we simultaneously denigrate the sexual. And so we reverberate between sexual obsession and sexual shame.

Last September, we found on our doorsteps newspapers full of the details of the president's intimacies with Monica Lewinsky—the thong underwear, the cigar, the

pornographic, the childlike and the scientific. We speak of vaginas, labiae, clitorises, cunts, hair pies and "down there." We call it a prick, a dick, a sledgehammer, a penis, a pee pee or Mr. Happy. Our worst insults are sexual: *cunt, slut, whore, dickhead, pussy-whipped, cocksucker.*

And so we lie in bed with each other, reaching for pleasure, tenderness and connection, with both too much and too little to guide us: *Hustler* on the newsstand, Dr. Ruth or Dr. Laura on the radio and *Debbie Does Dallas* on the VCR. "You do not have to be good," wrote the poet Mary Oliver. "You do not have to walk on your knees for a hundred miles through the desert, repenting. You only have to let the soft animal of your body love what it loves." But that's a big *only*. No wonder we are sure that someone, somewhere, is having better sex than we are. No wonder someone, somewhere is pretending to have better sex than we are. No wonder we fear we will never get it right.

YET SOMETIMES WE DO GET IT RIGHT—or it gets us right. Many of us have experienced something in bed that the languages of pornography, sex therapy, feminism and the double standard could not contain. It might have been the afternoon we washed our partner from head to toe in the shower, kneeling under the spray to scrub even the soles of her feet, until washing became a ritual of tenderness and awareness. It might have been a dawn when we woke from a dream experiencing what the radical psychoanalyst Wilhelm Reich called a "full-body orgasm," in which we were the wave and also a body drifting at the water's edge, pulsating to our fingertips as the wave broke on the shore. It might have been a night a man looked into our eyes and stroked our nipples for hours until we gave in to our own responses rather than following what we imagined to be his timetable. Or a night a woman looked into our eyes while we were coming and we felt safe, seen and known.

In these moments, lovemaking is sensed as healing, wholesome and holy. Our focus broadens out beyond orgasm. Our small selves are no longer in command, and we give ourselves over, little boats on a deep river. The fear of not performing well disappears, the ghosts are banished from the bedroom and the present moment absorbs us. The West's self-created divisions—between sacred and profane, heart and pelvis, male and female, victim and predator, body and

O R NOT. SOME OF US WILL EMBARK instead on a quest for a fuller experience of intimate sexuality. We will use whatever tools we can, depending on who we are and the decade in which we set out. We may enter Reichian therapy, wrap ourselves in Saran wrap, read Nancy Friday, follow The Rules, or repeat phrases from *Men Are From Mars, Women Are From Venus,* but we will not give up. We want to banish the bedroom's ghosts or at least replace them with more benign presences. Risking the humiliation our culture visits on those who speak of their own sex lives rather than other people's, we will try to decolonize the bedroom. We sense that this quest requires not "more of the same"— not more sexual perfectionism or ever-more-

ing sexuality and intimacy, and enhancing sexual pleasure for long-term couples. It's not the techniques that count so much as Tantra's enlargement of the context in which sex is held—as pleasurable, inclusive, healing, and holy. This widening of the lens was apparent as soon as modern Tantrism first registered on the American cultural radar in 1989, when a 450-page book called *The Art of Sexual Ecstasy: The Path of Sacred Sexuality for Western Lovers* tried to sweep the clutter of negative sexual images out of the Western bedroom. Written by Margo Anand, a writer and sex workshop leader who had studied psychology at the Sorbonne and meditation in India, it was like no sex manual the West had ever seen. She spent eight

W*e lie in bed with each other, reaching for pleasure, tenderness and connection with both too much and too little to guide us. Yet sometimes we do get it right.*

soul—are temporarily healed. We understand what Walt Whitman meant when he wrote, "If anything is sacred, the human body is sacred," and what the 16th-century Anglican marriage ceremony meant when it included among its vows, "With my body, I thee worship." Our bedroom is no longer hostage to the porn palace, the sex lab or the unfinished war between men and women. For a moment, the bedroom becomes a ritual space where we enter trance and forget time.

For most of us, such moments are rare and random, despite the mixed sexual blessings of the past three decades. The sexual revolution rightly told us that sex could be a domain of pleasure and self-expression. But its prescription—quantity over quality— did not free us. The feminist revolution challenged the practice of sex as a ritual of loving female submission and encouraged women to speak of their sexual desires and sexual violations. It lit up ancient chasms between the genders, but did not bridge them.

Modern sex therapy helped thousands with simple, effective behavioral techniques, usually focused narrowly on achieving erection, intercourse or orgasm. Yet few of us have much of a clue about continuing to create the more profound joys of sexuality—especially after the first six months to two years of a relationship, when hormones subside and desire fades. We may move from arousal to contentment or indifference or contempt. We may not know how to contend with softer, slower erections and other changes related to aging. A surprising number of stable couples stop making love much, or altogether. The ghosts return to the bedroom. We may lie down in resignation in the bed we've made together, or walk once more out the door.

exotic partners or positions—but a broader context, a change at the metalevel. If we embark on this quest today, we may buy a book, watch a video or go to a weekend workshop on Tantrism, which is now the West's most popular form of adult sex education.

Presaged by the popularity in the 1960s of the *Kama Sutra* of Vatsyayana, a 3rd-century Indian sex manual, Tantra has become a postmodern hybrid. On the most prosaic level, it is nothing more than a pastiche of positive sexual attitudes and techniques drawn from Western humanistic psychology, Chinese Taoist sexology and classical Indian Tantrism—a wild sexual and religious tradition that influenced both Buddhism and Hinduism and flourished in India about 500 A.D.

This esoteric system used breath, visualization and other yogas to arouse, channel and transform energy throughout the body. Its meditations often took the form of visualizing gods and goddesses in sexual union. In India, adherents of the tiny sect of "left-handed" Tantra took things a step further: in secret rituals, they broke all the rules of their caste-bound society, consuming taboo foods, such as alcohol and meat, sounding yogic *bijas* or sacred syllables and coupling with one partner after another. In contrast to monastic traditions that suppressed sexuality and avoided women, *Tantrikas* welcomed the energies of aggression and sexuality and transformed them. Men did not ejaculate, and the goal was to move arousal up the spine to the brain in an explosion of enlightenment and bliss. Sex was not a dirty detour from the path to God, it was the path.

Today, Tantra's esoteric practices are being pressed into the service of goals that are tamer, more domestic and less religious: unit-

pages alone describing how to prepare a bedroom as a "sacred place," Anand wrote. Vacuum the bedroom and take out the newspapers and coffee cups. Bring in plants, flowers and candles. Drape a scarf over the bedside lamp to create soft lighting. Walk three times around the room with your partner, misting the air with a plant sprayer of scented water while saying "As I purify this space, I purify my heart." This, Anand implied, was as much a part of sex as kissing.

The suggestions might seem impossibly precious. But ceremonially cleaning the bedroom and bringing in flowers and soft light contained a metamessage: You do not have to go somewhere else or become a sliver of yourself to have sex. You don't have to "do the nasty" while hiding in the dark from your disapproving parents. When you bring flowers into the bedroom, you bring in more of yourself as well, and that can make you realize how much you had previously left outside the bedroom door. And if the bedroom is already inhabited by ghosts, why not bring in flowers as well?

In the place of pornographic slang and Latin words, Anand suggested Taoist phrases that were free of negative Western sexual connotations. Try saying "jade stalk" or "wand of light" for penis, she suggested; for vagina, substitute "cinnabar cave" or "valley of bliss." Or call them "yonis" and "lingams," after the Sanskrit words used to describe the stone sculptures of sexual organs that are still bedecked with flowers and worshiped in rural temples in India. "Behold the Shiva Lingam, beautiful as molten gold, firm as the Himalaya Mountain," she quoted the "Linga Purana," a Hindu ode to the penis of the god Shiva, Lord of the Dance. "Tender as a folded leaf, life-giving like the solar orb;

behold the charm of his sparkling jewels!" It was heady stuff for a culture where "testosterone poisoning" is a running joke and the only goddess worshiped is a virgin mother. And it cleared the decks for something new.

Anand and other teachers of modern Tantra suggested that sex could involve all of us, including the warring inner parts we think we've transcended but have merely avoided: the lustful and soulful; the wounded and voracious; the slutpuppy in her Victoria's Secret lingerie and the good girl in her flannel nightie; the sensitive postfeminist man and the crude teenage boy.

Last October, at a five-day, $795-a-person workshop for couples at the Esalen Institute, yoga and Tantra teacher Charles Muir wove these warring inner and outer sexual worlds together. On the first night, he spoke about his own sexual upbringing to 23 couples sitting before him in a circle. His listeners ranged in age from 22 to 73. Among them were two Latin American academics, four lawyers, a black woman doctor, two construction managers, two women who worked in television, several massage therapists from the Esalen staff and an Irish farmer. Some sat as entwined with their partners as trailing vines, while others betrayed, in their gestures and body language, uneasiness with each other and an inequality of love or desire.

Muir, who is now separated from his wife and coteacher, Caroline (she wanted sexual fidelity; he didn't), runs the Source School of Tantra in Maui, Hawaii, and leads frequent workshops around the country. He was wearing a silk shirt and an amethyst pendant.

There were shocked laughs, a snigger. The men thought they were long past this. The women didn't want to think their men had ever thought this way.

But there was a method to his crudeness. Once Muir bonded with the part of the men that had eternally remained the teenage boy, he gently, without emasculating them, brought them into the sexual realm of context, emotion, feeling and intimacy traditionally defined as female. "In lovemaking, women lead with their hearts," he went on more softly. "Men lead with their second chakra [their groins]. We hurt each other."

Tantra, Muir said, could help them make love stay. "The average couple makes love 2.3 times a week for the first two years," he said. "After two years, the average couple makes love once a week—and making love can be a well of energy and healing.

"Chemistry is temporary. You're going to learn to base love not on chemistry—which lasts six months or two years, if you're lucky—but on alchemy. When the chemistry is no longer there, alchemy says you take what is there and you change it. Become a master alchemist."

EASIER SAID THAN DONE, GIVEN SOME OF the histories that the couples revealed in private conversations. One couple came to Esalen to put the "pizzazz" back in their marriage; later they acknowledged they'd hardly made love in the nine years since the birth of their son.

Paula, a Mexican American academic in her fifties who was there with Carlos, the professor with whom she lived, had not had an orgasm in the year since her hysterec-

ever since. "All I knew," Russ told me one day, "was that I was to get my penis in her vagina and that was it." He had lain back, expecting Liz to arouse and satisfy him.

She said nothing that night, and nothing for many nights to come. She had no language then, no woman had language then for what she felt or wanted. "When you were born in 1937," she says, "it wasn't your place to show him."

Since then, they had rarely taken more than 15 minutes to make love. She spoke frequently, in front of Russ, of "40 years of shit and disappointment in the bedroom." Russ didn't treat her like a woman, didn't measure up. "I would love a flower on the pillow or a note," she said one day. "But Russ cuts articles out of the newspaper that he thinks I would be interested in. And I am. But it's not the intimacy I long for."

Couples like these could have taken their "sexual dysfunctions" and marital issues into the private confines of a sex therapist's office. But they were seeking something that Western sex therapy, for all its strengths, does not provide. Sex therapy's pioneers, Masters and Johnson, had brought thermometers, charts and transparent vaginal probes mounted with tiny video cameras to the study of sex. Sexual problems, they argued, weren't usually rooted in intractable intrapsychic or interpersonal conflict; they could often be solved by learning new behaviors. They, and those who followed them, taught women to masturbate to orgasm and men to squeeze their penises just below the coronal ridge, before they reached the "point of no return," to resolve premature ejaculation. Their techniques often worked with

By *emphasizing energy and context, the workshop provided something usually missing from standard-issue sex—love, sensuous touching and intimacy.*

He was slim, in his early fifties, with brown hair, protuberant eyes and spatulate fingers that gave him the look of an elongated frog. His language was closer to New York street than Hindu temple.

He had come of age in the Bronx, he said, during "The Great Fuck Drought of the Fifties." Everything he knew about sex, he said, he had learned from Johnny Patanella, the leader of his childhood street gang: *Get it up, get it in, and get it off. Fuck 'em hard and fuck 'em deep.* Muir said that before he discovered Tantra, he was a yogi on the mat and a "sleazebucket" in bed. He said that men give nicknames to their penises because they want to be on a first-name basis with the one who makes all their important decisions.

tomy. She had been raised a Catholic and was date raped in college. She still couldn't shake off a notion her mother had given her—that only bad girls are good at giving men sexual pleasure; at night, she still put on her pajamas behind the bathroom door. Carlos was in his forties; he had been divorced twice and had been raped and tortured a decade earlier in a South American prison.

Russ Solomon, a retired San Diego real estate developer, had raised four children with his wife, Liz, during 40 years of marriage. They looked as comfortable together as old shoes and clearly liked and respected each other. But sex, they said, had been disappointing on their wedding night when they'd both been virgins and disappointing

amazing ease, and they drained sex of some of its shaming power by making things seem as brisk, practical and scientific as a good recipe for apple pie.

But they also drained sex of magic. If their governing metaphor was the bedroom-as-medical-lab and sexual practice an an antiseptic medical-behavioral prescription, Muir's guiding metaphor at Esalen was the bedroom as temple and sexual practice as worship. And if sex therapy was predicated on healing people so that they could have sex with each other, Muir suggested that sexual pleasure itself could be healing.

In the course of the week, Muir gasped, held his breath, bugged out his eyes to demonstrate how men could use yogic breathing, pauses in lovemaking and finger pressure on

THE EVOLUTION OF MODERN Sex Therapy

Twenty years after the sexual revolution, in the most sexually explicit culture in the world, a surprisingly large number of people continue to have difficulties with the sexual basics. *The Social Organization of Sexuality,* a statistically balanced 1994 survey of the sexual habits of 3,432 Americans, found that 24 percent of the women questioned had been unable to have an orgasm for at least several months of the previous year. Another 18.8 percent of the women (24 percent of those over 55) reported trouble lubricating; 14 percent had had physical pain during intercourse; and 11 percent were anxious about their sexual performance. Equally high proportions of men reported interlocking difficulties: 28 percent said they climaxed too quickly, 17 percent had performance anxiety and 10.4 percent (20 percent of those over 50) said they'd had trouble maintaining an erection.

Before the 1950s, people with these sorts of problems were given pejorative labels like "impotent" and "frigid." Psychoanalytic therapy had little to offer them beyond symbolic explorations of their upbringings and "Oedipal" conflicts. Things got slightly better in the 1950s, when Joseph Wolpe and other behaviorists taught people to reduce their fear by breathing deeply and relaxing while imagining sexual situations that had made them tense. This was of some help, but things only really changed in the 1970s, after gynecologist William Masters and his research associate Virginia Johnson began studying the physiology of human sexual response in the laboratory.

Modern sex therapy—a repertoire of precise physical techniques that teach the body new responses and habits, lower anxiety and increase focus on the here-and-now—builds on Masters and Johnson's work. Therapy consists mainly of counseling and "homework" in which new experiences are tried and new skills practiced. If clients are too tense or reluctant to try something new, systems approaches, couples therapy, drugs and psychodynamic therapy may be tried as well.

Modern sex therapy often begins with instruction in "sensate focus." The pressure to have an orgasm, keep a firm erection or prolong intercourse is taken away. Instead, individuals or partners are told to set aside time to caress themselves or each other in a relaxed environment, without trying to achieve any sexual goal. Once anxiety is lowered, sex therapy often proceeds successfully especially in treating the following common problems:

Vaginismus. Vaginismus is the spastic tightening of the vaginal muscles and can make intercourse impossibly painful. It can be so severe that not even a Q-tip can be inserted in the vagina, and some women with vaginismus have never, or rarely, completed sexual intercourse in the course of years of marriage. Often the result of physically painful experiences like childbirth, painful intercourse, rape or molestation, it is a learned fear response. Therapy involves teaching the woman to relax and breathe while gently inserting the first of a graduated series of lubricated rods, starting with one as small as is necessary for comfort. In ensuing weeks, the woman uses incrementally thicker rods and then inserts her partner's finger and finally his penis into her vagina. Nothing is forced, and insertion is always under the control of the woman.

Premature ejaculation in men. Treatment involves lowering anxiety and teaching the man to become aware of his arousal during lovemaking, until he recognizes the sensations that precede his "point of no return." Then he practices what sex therapist Barbara Keesling, author of *Sexual Healing,* calls "peaking"—pausing before the point of no return and relaxing, breathing and stopping movement until his arousal subsides. After a few minutes' rest, the man returns to movement, stimulation and arousal. The "peak and pause" routine is repeated five or six times per homework session. The exercise can be done by a man masturbating alone, while his partner is giving him oral sex or during intercourse. Men can squeeze their pubococcygeal or PC muscles during the pause to dampen arousal, or the man's partner can squeeze on the coronal ridge just below the head of the penis.

Erectile difficulties in men. A common problem among older men, erectile failure is often caused by an interaction of physical and psychological factors. Smoking, diabetes, blood pressure drugs, alcoholism, neurological injury and normal aging can all worsen erectile problems. Treatment has been revolutionized since the introduction of Viagra, which not only helps men with primarily physical problems, but can also jump-start those suffering primarily from anxiety.

Men who awaken with erections or have them while masturbating can probably blame anxiety if they have trouble during intercourse: muscular tightness and breath-holding can send blood out of the penis, causing it to wilt. Sex therapy requires slowly disarming anxiety and performance pressure, and learning to enjoy sex with and without an erection. Therapy often begins with declaring intercourse off-limits and encouraging the couple to enjoy each other orally and manually, without demanding that the penis perform.

In the next "stop-start" phase, the man's partner stimulates him to the point of erection, stops until his penis becomes totally soft and then stimulates him again, repeating the process up to three times if the erection returns. Other exercises include "stuffing," which allows the man to become familiar with the sensation of being in the vagina without having to perform sexually. The female partner gently folds his flaccid penis into her vagina, using her fingers as a splint while lying in a scissors position, at right angles to the man, with one of his thighs between her legs. The couple then lies together for 15 to 30 minutes without moving. In subsequent sessions, as anxiety lessens, the man practices moving slowly while breathing evenly and staying relaxed.

Orgasmic difficulties in women. Therapy with "pre-orgasmic" women was pioneered by psychologists Lonnie Barbach of San Francisco, author of *For Yourself: The Fulfillment of Female Sexuality,* and Joseph LoPiccolo, a coauthor, with Julia Heiman, of *Becoming Orgasmic.* It has extraordinarily high success rates with women once written off as frigid. In group and individual programs lasting 6 to 10 weeks, women are given basic information about female sexual response and are encouraged to spend one hour a day on self-pleasure "homework," familiarizing themselves with their own anatomies and sexual responses, examining their vulvas with a mirror and speculum, massaging themselves, perhaps reading Nancy Friday's collections of sexual fantasies and masturbating. Most of the women soon learn to give themselves orgasms, and then gradually transfer their new skills to lovemaking. First they masturbate to orgasm in front of their partners, then learn to come while touching themselves during intercourse, and then teach their partners to pleasure them to orgasm using their fingers or penis.

Most women successfully transfer their new responsiveness to partnered sex. The exceptions tend to be women who have learned to reach orgasm by squeezing their thighs tightly together—a position that makes it virtually impossible for them to have an orgasm with a penis inside them. In LoPiccolo's clinic at the University of Missouri in Columbia, such women relearn a more fluid orgasmic response by deconstructing their masturbation rituals step-by-step and gradually learning to have orgasms without clenching their thighs. They may begin by simply uncrossing their ankles while masturbating and then slowly change their patterns until they can have orgasms with their legs apart.

If a woman can reach orgasm with digital stimulation from her partner, LoPiccolo considers the therapeutic goals have been met. Women respond orgasmically to a wide variety of stimuli—some to dreams and fantasies; others to the rubbing of an earlobe or breast; others to digital caressing of the clitoris or G-spot; and still others to intercourse. All are considered normal human variations. At an American Association of Marriage and Family Therapy conference last year,

LoPiccolo said that when couples come to him saying they'd like the woman to have an orgasm during intercourse, he doesn't consider this a therapy goal so much as a growth goal, like learning to dance. "If you want to learn the tango," he said by way of analogy, "You get tango lessons, not therapy."

KATY BUTLER

their perineums to delay or forgo ejaculation. He and his coteacher, yoga practitioner Diane Greenberg showed women how to take a man's "soft-on" and "use it like a paintbrush" to stimulate their clitorises and outer lips, or stuff it softly into the vagina. And he extolled the sensual pleasures of the half-erect penis. Referring to the *Kama Sutra,* he talked of varying strokes, pressure and speed. "If we go straight down the fairway—deep deep deep—we'll only be stimulating one area, guys," he said one afternoon, stroking a Plexiglass wand inside an anatomically correct, purple velvet and pink-silk "yoni puppet" from San Francisco's House of Chicks. "Try shallow, shallow, shallow, deep! The more variety, the more information floods the brain, and the more you wake up."

A sex therapist, or in a more enlightened society, a sex educator, could have said the identical words, but the context—playful, normalized and semi-public—would not have been the same. A miniature culture, as transient and self-contained as a dewdrop, was being formed. For a handful of days, as the couples strolled the Esalen grounds above the Pacific, moving from cabin to hot tub to class, nobody was too busy or too tired to have sex. Nobody read anything about Kenneth Starr, or looked at the *Sports Illustrated* swimsuit issue or downloaded pornography from the Internet. Every night, in their TV-free, phone-free cabins, they looked at and touched each other's flesh-and-blood bodies rather than electronic images and paper dreams.

In class, Muir held out to them the possibility that sex could be more than a source of pleasure: it could be a source of intimate bonding as well. He taught them how to lie together spoon-fashion and breathe in unison. Sex, he said, could be more even than emotional intimacy: it could be an interplay of invisible energies that coursed through each lover's body and radiated beyond it. Every day, he led participants in yogic breathing and stretching, and then asked them whether they could feel an "energy hand" the size of an oven mitt growing beyond their flesh-and-blood hands. He had

them fluff and clean their "auras" by sweeping their hands in circles a few inches from the body.

He acted not only as sex educator and yoga teacher, but priest. He taught them to chant one-syllable Sanskrit mantras designed to activate each of the body's seven *chakras* or energy centers that are believed to ascend the body's core. And he formed them into slow Tantric circle dances in which the men and women stared into the eyes of partner after partner while visualizing sending love and healing to virtual strangers.

If the West has defined male sexuality as the norm and female sexuality as the problem, Tantra glorifies the female: a woman's orgasms are said to increase her capacity to act as a channel for the flow of *shakti,* the universal female energy that powers the universe. And by deemphasizing the moment of ejaculation and emphasizing energy and context, the workshop provided the women with more of what they often complain is missing from standard-issue sex—love, sensuous touching and intimacy.

Under Muir's tutelage, lovemaking was not, as some feminists put it, a recapitulation of the power inequalities of rape, but a worship of the female and a reenactment of the drama of Shiva and Shakti, the Hindu god and goddess whose lovemaking created the universe. Partners were to see in themselves the flow of divine fundamental energies; the act of love as reproducing the first stages of the creation of the world.

Women, Muir declared, could and should have multiple orgasms, while men were depleted by ejaculation and should sometimes try the "valley orgasm"—orgasm without ejaculation. And he transcended the no-win squabble Freud started over the virtues of clitoral versus vaginal orgasms by teaching effective techniques for vaginal stimulation of the G-spot; he declared that women, too, could ejaculate when sufficiently stimulated.

This is a tall order of a culture in which 24 percent of women surveyed say that they, like Paula, have not had an orgasm during the previous year. A complex history lies behind this statistic. If the sexual lives of many men begin with repeated sexual rejection and

shame, the sexual lives of many women begin in choicelessness: breasts stroked in a laundry room by a best friend's father; the struggle lost in a back seat; the unwanted kiss from uncle, teacher, boss or neighbor. When women sleep with men they sleep as well with their fear or memory of the peeper, the flasher, the child molester, the rapist, the Don Juan, the womanizer, the sexual predator, the horrible first husband and the just plain jerk. Women, too, have a double standard: we divide men not into virgins and whores, but into predators and marriage material. In a reverse of the fairy tale, we fear that while we lie in bed, our lovers will metamorphose from Beauty to the Beast.

Such memories and fears, Muir suggested, are embedded not only in the brain, but in the cells of the body. His cure was a sexual ceremony to be held in the privacy of each couple's bedroom on the third night of the workshop. In a men-only meeting beforehand, he showed videotapes and coached each man on how to do for his lover what no therapist or body worker could do—massage her "Sacred Spot," the G-spot inside her vagina.

The G-spot, Muir said, is a little known and widely misunderstood area of sexual sensitivity—a raised, furrowed area of tissue about the size of a quarter, an inch and a half inside the front wall of the vagina, against the pubic bone. When stroked, it can become erect, firm and responsive and can trigger vaginal orgasms and ejaculation of a clear liquid. But it is also the dark closet in which old sexual pain is stored. "Sacred Spot" massage, he said, might release ecstatic sexual pleasure. It might also release old memories: the women might complain of numbness or bruising, or explode in fear, sobbing or rage. "This is Tantra kindergarten," he said, coaching the men to simply be loving and to be there, no matter what. "You get an *A* just for showing up."

After supper, before the ceremony began, the men fanned out to their cabins all over Esalen to take on the traditionally female task of "preparing the space" for the ceremony. While Liz and the other women relaxed and giggled in the Esalen hot tubs,

Russ cleaned their cabin, combed his white hair and took a shower. In another cabin, one of the construction managers lit incense and paced his room. On the other side of the garden, one of the lawyers scattered rose petals on the sheets. Carlos, the Latin American academic, arranged a vase full of flowers he had cut from the Esalen garden, cued up a CD on his laptop, lit candles, put on a formal Mexican shirt called a *guayabera,* turned back the sheets and waited for Paula.

When the couples shared their experiences in the group the next day, it was almost as though the sexes had exchanged roles. "Carlos massaged me so gently so tenderly," Paula said. "The other times he had massaged me it was like, let's hurry up and get this over with." After an hour or so, she

THE NEXT EVENING CAME THE TURN-about. After supper, Muir took off his amethyst crystal pendant, blue silk shirt and oatmeal jeans. He lay on pillows on the floor in his boxer shorts, holding a clear black plastic wand from a magic store at his groin like a surrogate penis. One man pushed his girlfriend to the front of the crowd. "I don't want you to miss any of this," he said.

Diane Greenberg knelt between Muir's legs and showed the women an unbelievable range of ways to pleasure a man's penis. She was competent and sure. She twirled her fingers around the wand like a feathery screw. She squeezed in at both at the top and the bottom, explaining that this way the blood wouldn't be forced out. She slapped it and tapped it and pretended to use it like a mi-

jected. "Then he'll agree to anything.") Next, Greenberg said, the women were to insert one finger into their man's anus and stroke and stimulate the exquisitely sensitive "sweet little hollow" at the base of the prostate. This, she cautioned, was a delicate business. "Rather than me entering him, I'll have him sit on my finger," she explained.

Then Greenberg turned to the men. "You're going to be penetrated, guys" she said, "as we are penetrated."

As Greenberg pulled the women into new territory, Muir took the men into the unknown as well. "Every man has gone through a war of his own that has robbed him of his *yin* [female aspect]," he said. "Each young boy is taught that men don't cry, don't feel. The job of reclaiming your yin is sweet. You won't wake up the same guy in the morning. Tonight, you get to be the illogical one. You get to have feelings tonight. Ladies, I want you to show up big. He may test you, he may be irrational. He may become terrified.

"You give and you're strong and you fix things" he said, turning to the men. "You're gigantic. How much can you let yourself be small and feel? Allow yourself to be penetrable and vulnerable? Five million homosexuals can't be wrong. There must be something up there that's good."

When Carlos and Paula described their night's experience in the group the next morning, Carlos was in tears—deep, strong tears. During the ceremony, he had reexperienced being raped and tortured in a South American prison and had not "left his body," as he had when having flashbacks before. He had also experienced something beyond the personal as though a great wind were blowing through him and breathing his body for him. And Paula had faced something she'd once held at arms' length. "Being raised Mexican Catholic, women who do that are sluts," she said, referring to the way she'd stroked Carlos' penis and penetrated his anus. "I gave myself permission not just to touch it with my eyes closed, but to look at it and be there in all my glory, and I felt pure."

Through Tantra, lovemaking becomes a form of worship and partners see in themselves the flow of divine fundamental energies.

said, Carlos had turned her over and asked permission to stroke her "sacred spot" with his finger. Not long afterward, she had her first orgasm in a year. "I just had a whole strand of pearls full of climaxes," she said. "It kept going on and on, the pleasure."

One woman—whose husband had left her for another woman 14 months earlier—was floored by the tide of anger and fear the exercise released. It was, she said, "like a bad acid trip." Other women came close to bragging about having multiple orgasms and ejaculations (one woman had 22 over an hour and a half), while their men were quiet, tearful and open. The men had taken on the traditionally feminine role of focusing wholeheartedly on the pleasure of another, and it had changed them. The construction manager cried, describing how he'd waited nervously for his girlfriend, terrified that he wouldn't measure up. Another man told the group that whenever he'd made love before, his consciousness had zigzagged back and forth, first checking in on his own erection and then checking in on his partner. "Last night, my presence was so totally focused on Andrea that I didn't have to worry about myself at all," he said. "When she came, I was wailing with her like I was having the biggest orgasm of my life, and I was totally limp."

Here, in a context where differences between men and women were not only acknowledged but glorified and mythologized, and where men's performance fears were out in the open, women were getting what they wanted.

crophone. She clasped her fingers and encircled the wand, running her thumbs in circles up and down the frenulum as though winding a bobbin.

She was leading the women into the dangerous territory of the slut goddess. If some women's sexual lives begin in choicelessness, others begin with an inner war: lying on a blanket on a hill on a warm night, grabbing at the hands that give such pleasure and pulling them away, worrying what the owner of these hands will call her to his friends the next day—*slut, pig, whore.* There are years of this, and then the rings are exchanged, the rice is thrown, the church doors open and the woman is expected to become as sexy and free as the bad girl she struggled for years not to be. Fear of taking on the slut archetype can persist through years of financial independence and supposed liberation, narrowing the range of pleasure a woman dares to give a man in the bedroom. By way of antidote, Muir and Greenberg spoke of Uma, a Hindu female divinity who "wears her sexuality on the outside." They lauded Hindu temple dancers and sacred prostitutes, and urged the women to try on this aspect of the powerful divine feminine. They encouraged the couples to let loose with noise—Esalen had heard lots of it, they said, and if couples got too self-conscious, they could shout or wail into a pillow.

Then Greenberg coached the woman on the coming evening's ceremony. This time, the women would "honor" the men, first massaging their bodies and their penises. ("First get him hard, ladies," Muir inter-

ON THE LAST DAY OF THE WORKSHOP, Muir urged the couples to try a "10-day test drive"—to connect somehow sexually, physically and emotionally for at least 10 minutes every day. By the time the couples were packing their bags, few of the men displayed the sexual bravado they'd come in with—the bravado this culture trains them for. One man, a lawyer, had told the group the first night that he'd come to the workshop because he wanted to experience a 30-minute orgasm. He left muttering about "Tantra kindergarten."

His desires had become simpler and more ambitious: to only connect with his wife of 22 years. One busy day he left work, met his wife at their son's soccer game and drove with her to the far end of the field, where

Tantra AT HOME

Modern Tantric techniques to improve anyone's sex life

Heighten Awareness of All the Senses
William Masters and Virginia Johnson introduced to the West a technique called "sensate focus," in which the receiving partner focused on his or her own sensations while being slowly and nonsexually caressed.

Tantric versions are more playful and aesthetic: Tantric teacher Margo Anand of Mill Valley, California, for instance, recommends that the receiving partner sit blindfolded on the bed, while the nurturing partner wafts a variety of smells, such as peppermint, licorice, gardenia, or even Chanel No. 5, under his nose. Next he is treated to sounds—bells, gongs, even crackling paper. Then he is fed distinctive-tasting foods—almonds, grapes dipped in liqueur, whipped cream, fruit or bitter-sweet chocolate. Finally, the nurturing partner strokes the receiving partner's body with pleasant textures—silk scarves, fur mittens or feathers. The ritual closes gently and formally. "With utmost gentleness, as if you had never touched him before, let your hand rest on his heart," writes Anand. "Allow your hands to radiate warmth, tenderness, and love."

Create Intimacy Through Gentle Contact Modern Tantrism focuses strongly on the subtle physical harmony between partners. In *Tantra: the Art of Conscious Loving,* yoga teachers Charles and Caroline Muir of the Source School of Tantra in Maui, Hawaii, recommend spoon meditation:

Lovers lie together spoon-fashion on their left sides and gently synchronize their breathing. The outer person, the nurturer, rests his right hand on the heart of his partner. Placing his left hand on her forehead, he visualizes sending love and energy from his heart down his arm and into her heart on his out-breath. On the in-breath, he draws energy back from her forehead and into his body in an endless circle.

The Muirs also recommend that partners do yogic breathing in unison: inhaling, holding the breath for a few seconds, exhaling and holding the breath out for a few more seconds. While breathing out, one partner visualizes accepting energy while the other visualizes projecting it. Couples can also inhale and exhale in counterpoint, visualizing "shooting out" energy on the out-breath through heart, head or groin and receiving it on the in-breath.

Focus on Connection Rather Than Orgasm Much of conventional sex therapy has focused on orgasm. Many previously unsatisfied women were liberated in the process, but it also turned intercourse into a big project, made orgasm the be-all and end-all of being together sexually, and defined any other sexual interaction as "the failure to achieve orgasm." Tantrism extols the joys of brief sexual connections without orgasm. In *The Tao of Sexology,* for example, Taoist teacher Stephen Chang recommends that couples practice the "Morning and Evening Prayer" for at least 2 to 10 minutes, twice a day. Every morning and evening, partners are to lie together in the missionary position, lips touching, with arms and legs wrapped around each others' bodies and the man inside the woman. The couple breathes together in a peaceful, relaxed state, with the man moving only enough to maintain his erection. "The couple enjoys and shares the feelings derived from such closeness or stillness for as long as they desire," writes Chang, who notes that orgasm sometimes follows without any movement. "Man and woman melt together, laying aside their egos to exchange energies to heal each other."

Enhance Sexual Pleasure Ancient and modern Tantric and Taoist sex manuals are full of sophisticated physical techniques designed to enhance the pleasure of both partners, stimulate orgasm in the woman and delay orgasm in the man. Chang, for example, recommends a Taoist practice called "Sets of Nine." The man slowly penetrates the first inch or so of his lover's vagina with the head of his penis only. He repeats this shallow stroke slowly nine times, followed by one slow stroke deep into the vagina. The next "set" consists of eight shallow strokes and two deep strokes, followed by seven shallow strokes and three deep strokes and so on until a final set of one shallow stroke and nine deep strokes. The "sets" help men prolong intercourse by balancing intense and less intense forms of stimulation and arouse women by stimulating the G-spot and numerous nerve endings in the neck of the vagina.

Separate Orgasm From Ejaculation In its most signal departure from Western sex therapy, modern and ancient Tantrism recommend that men, especially older men, frequently enjoy what it calls a "valley orgasm"—orgasm without ejaculation. Chang recommends that as the man senses himself approaching the "point of no return," both partners stop all movement while the man clenches his pubococcygeal or PC muscle (the urination-stopping muscle known to many women from the Kegel exercises they were taught to strengthen uterine and bladder muscles after giving birth). The man also slows and deepens his breathing, looks into his partner's eyes, connects with her heart and channels energy upward from his groin toward his heart and the crown of the head. Orgasm without ejaculation often follows. Ejaculation can also be reserved, without stopping the experience of orgasm, by pressing on what Chang calls "The Million Dollar Point," in a small hollow between anus and scrotum.

Honor Sex, But Keep It in Perspective "When sex is good," Charles Muir said at a recent workshop, "It's 10 percent of the relationship. When it's bad, it's 90 percent."

—KATY BUTLER

---

they kissed and held each other for 10 minutes in the car.

Some couples—like the pair who told me brightly that they wanted to put the "pizzazz" back in their marriage—left with little. Others took away all the bells and whistles you'd expect from a sex workshop: sobbing, wailing, energy releases, multiple orgasms, female ejaculations. Others left with something perhaps more precious: the understanding that good sex—wholesome, healing and holy—is an accumulation of small mercies, beginning with whatever mercy you need right now. Like being able to take off all your clothes in front of your lover, and touch his penis in all your glory and feel pure.

They went home—to San Diego and Cleveland and Denver, to the impeachment hearings and football games and a larger culture reverberating, more publicly than usual, between sexual obsession and sexual shame. Ghosts inevitably reentered their bedrooms. Old marital squabbles reared their ugly heads again. But sometimes old disappointments were held in a new way.

If anyone had come to understand the meaning of small mercies, it was Liz and Russ. On the night that Russ had pleasured her, Liz had come to their cabin door and found him still in the shower. Something about that melted her heart. "I brought to last night 40 years of lack of trust and feeling I'm not seen as a woman," she had said in the group next day. "I've stayed in the relationship oftentimes with doubt."

"I was so touched Russ was washing his body for me, that he would even be late to do this," she said. "All the resentment and fear was gone. I felt like a woman. It was enough."

"He put on a Japanese robe," she told the group, turning to her husband. "You looked very manly in it. I wore a white silk Dior nightgown and felt like a bride. When we slipped it off, I loved the look of my body. If we had only done this on our honeymoon, what a difference it would have made."

"She could have said, 'This is your obligation,' " said Russ. "But she dismissed all that. We didn't shout and cover our faces with pillows, but it's nice to know that it's possible. We take away the hopes and stories we've been told. I pray that we will remember."

"It was enough," said Liz. "Russ was willing, after 40 years of marriage, to try something. That was enough."

When they returned home, they followed Muir's suggestions for the "10-day test drive." Every day, she and Russ lay down with each other in the morning and the evening, and snuggled and held each other. "It's been wonderful," Liz told me. "There's been no anxiety, no repulsion. It's not about making love. It's about breathing together, holding hands, the eye contact, touching the heart, the forehead. We are doing our homework. But I'm not sure we're doing it right."

In her last sentence, I heard the reverberations of our culture's sexual perfectionism. She and Russ had returned to a society with bigger work to do than any person or couple can do alone. Yet they had grasped the essence of classical Tantra as practiced in India nearly two thousand years ago, and that essence is not purely sexual. At its base, it involves welcoming and transforming all energetic and powerful states, even negative and difficult ones, by holding them in a different context.

That context involves knowing that Saint Augustine and all his intellectual and spiritual heirs, including our parents and Larry Flynt and Kenneth Starr, were wrong: Sex is neither a nasty secret pleasure nor a sin, but a part of the pattern of the universe. To put it one way, the desire to make love, connect, procreate and survive has been programmed, along with pleasure, into our genes and dreams. To put it another: Sex is sacred—intricate and dangerous and pleasurable and utterly ungraspable.

Networker *associate editor Katy Butler, a former reporter for* The San Francisco Chronicle, *has contributed to* The Los Angeles Times, The New Yorker, The New York Times Book Review *and* The Washington Post. *For more information on Charles Muir, write to P.O. Box 69, Paia, HI 96779. Correspondence to Katy Butler may be sent to the* Networker.

Abnormal: Anything considered not to be normal, i.e., not conforming to the subjective standards a social group has established as the norm.

Abortifacients: Substances that cause termination of pregnancy.

Acquaintance (date) rape: A sexual encounter forced by someone who is known to the victim.

Acquired dysfunction: A difficulty with sexual functioning that develops after some period of normal sexual functioning.

Acquired immunodeficiency syndrome (AIDS): Fatal disease caused by a virus that is transmitted through the exchange of bodily fluids, primarily in sexual activity and intravenous drug use.

Activating effect: The direct influence some hormones can have on activating or deactivating sexual behavior.

Acute urethral syndrome: Infection or irritation of the urethra.

Adolescence: Period of emotional, social, and physical transition from childhood to adulthood.

Adultery: Extramarital sex.

Affectional: Relating to feelings or emotions, such as romantic attachments.

Agenesis (absence) of the penis (ae-JEN-a-ses): A congenital condition in which the penis is undersized and nonfunctional.

AIDS: Acquired immunodeficiency syndrome.

Amniocentesis: A process whereby medical problems with a fetus can be determined while it is still in the womb; a needle is inserted into the amniotic sac, amniotic fluid is withdrawn, and fetal cells are examined.

Anal intercourse: Insertion of the penis into the rectum of a partner.

Androgen: A male hormone, such as testosterone, that affects physical development, sexual desire, and behavior.

Androgen insensitivity syndrome: A developmental condition in which cells do not respond to fetal androgen, so that chromosomally male (XY) fetuses develop external female genitals. There also is a feminization of later behavioral patterns.

Androgyny: The presence of high frequencies of both masculine and feminine behaviors and traits.

Anejaculation: Lack of ejaculation at the time of orgasm.

Anorchism: Rare birth defect in which both testes are lacking.

Aphrodisiacs (af-ro-DEE-si-aks): Foods or chemicals purported to foster sexual arousal; they are believed to be more myth than fact.

Apoptosis: Programmed cell death that occurs naturally in living tissues. HIV may induce abnormal apoptosis in immune cells.

Apotemnophilia: A rare condition characterized by the desire to function sexually after having a leg amputated.

Areola (a-REE-a-la): Darkened, circular area of skin surrounding the nipple of the breast.

Artificial embryonation: Process in which the developing embryo is flushed from the uterus of the donor woman five days after fertilization and placed in another woman's uterus.

Artificial insemination: Injection of the sperm cells of a male into a woman's vagina, with the intention of conceiving a child.

Asceticism (a-SET-a-siz-um): Usually characterized by celibacy, this philosophy emphasizes spiritual purity through self-denial and self-discipline.

Asexuality: A condition characterized by a low interest in sex.

Autoerotic asphyxiation: Accidental death from pressure placed around the neck during masturbatory behavior.

Autofellatio (fe-LAY-she-o): A male providing oral stimulation to his own penis, an act most males do not have the physical agility to perform.

Autogynephilia: The tendency of some males to become sexually aroused by the thought or image of themselves with female attributes.

Bartholin's glands (BAR-tha-lenz): Small glands located in the minor lips that produce some secretion during sexual arousal.

Behavior therapy: Therapy that uses techniques to change patterns of behavior; often employed in sex therapy.

Benign prostatic hyperplasia (BPH): Enlargement of the prostate gland that is not caused by malignancy.

Berdache (bare-DAHSH): Anthropological term for cross-dressing in other cultures.

Bestiality (beest-ee-AL-i-tee): A human being having sexual contact with an animal.

Biological essentialists: Those who believe that sexual orientation is an inborn trait, resulting from biological factors during development.

Biphobia: Prejudice, negative attitudes, and misconceptions relating to bisexual people and their lifestyles.

Bisexual: Refers to some degree of sexual activity with or attraction to members of both sexes.

Bond: The emotional link between parent and child created by cuddling, cooing, and physical and eye contact early in a newborn's life.

Bondage: Tying, restraining, or applying pressure to body parts as part of sexual arousal.

Brachioproctic activity (brake-ee-o-PRAHK-tik): Known in slang as "fisting"; a hand is inserted into the rectum of a partner.

Brothel: House of prostitution.

Bulbourethral glands: Also called Cowper's glands.

Call boys: Highly paid male prostitutes.

Call girls: Highly paid female prostitutes.

Case study: An in-depth analysis of a particular individual and how he or she might have been helped to solve a sexual or other problem.

Catharsis theory: A suggestion that viewing pornography will provide a release for sexual tension, thus preventing antisocial behavior.

Celibacy (SELL-a-ba-see): Choosing not to share sexual activity with others.

Cervical cap: A contraceptive device that is shaped like a large thimble and fits over the cervix and blocks sperm from entering the uterus.

Cervical intraepithelial neoplasia (CIN): Abnormal, precancerous cells sometimes identified in a Pap smear.

Cervix (SERV-ix): Lower "neck" of the uterus that extends into the back part of the vagina.

Cesarean section: A surgical method of childbirth in which delivery occurs through an incision in the abdominal wall and uterus.

Chancroid (SHAN-kroyd): An STD caused by the bacterium *Hemophilus ducreyi* and characterized by sores on the genitals, which, if left untreated, could result in pain and rupture of the sores.

Child molesting: Sexual abuse of a child by an adult.

Chlamydia (klu-MID-ee-uh): Now known to be a common STD, this organism is a major cause of urethritis in males; in females it often presents no symptoms.

Cilia: Microscopic, hairlike projections that help move the ovum through the fallopian tube.

Circumcision: Of the clitoris—surgical procedure that cuts the prepuce, exposing the clitoral shaft; in the male, surgical removal of the foreskin from the penis.

Climacteric: Mid-life period experienced by both men and women when there is greater emotional stress than usual and sometimes physical symptoms.

Climax: Another term for orgasm.

Clinical research: The study of the cause, treatment, or prevention of a disease or condition by testing large numbers of people.

Clitoridectomy: Surgical removal of the clitoris; practiced routinely in some cultures.

Clitoris (KLIT-a-rus): Sexually sensitive organ found in the female vulva; it becomes engorged with blood during arousal.

Clone: The genetic-duplicate organism produced by the cloning process.

Cloning: A process involving the transfer of a full complement of chromosomes from a body cell of an organism into an ovum from which the chromosomal material has been removed; if allowed to develop into a new organism, it is an exact genetic duplicate of the one from which the original body cell was taken; the process is not yet used for humans, but it has been performed in lower animal species.

Cohabitation: Living together and sharing sex without marrying.

Coitus (ko-EET-us or KO-ut-us): Heterosexual, penis-in-vagina intercourse.

Coitus interruptus: A method of birth control in which the penis is withdrawn from the vagina prior to ejaculation.

Combining of chromosomes: The process by which a sperm unites with an egg, normally joining 23 pairs of chromosomes to establish the genetic "blueprint" for a new individual. The sex chromosomes establish its sex: XX for female and XY for male.

Coming out: To acknowledge to oneself and others that one is a lesbian, a gay male, or bisexual.

Computerized sperm selection: Use of computer scanning to identify the most viable sperm, which are then extracted to be used for fertilization of an ovum in the laboratory.

Conception: The process by which a sperm unites with an egg, normally joining 23 pairs of chromosomes to establish the genetic "blueprint" for a new individual. The sex chromosomes establish its sex: XX for female and XY for male.

Condom: A sheath worn over the penis during intercourse to collect semen and prevent conception or venereal disease.

Consensual adultery: Permission given to at least one partner within the marital relationship to participate in extramarital sexual activity.

Controlled experiment: Research in which the investigator examines what is happening to one variable while all other variables are kept constant.

Coprophilia: Sexual arousal connected with feces.

219

Core gender identity: A child's early inner sense of its maleness, femaleness, or ambivalence, established prior to puberty.

Corona: The ridge around the penile glans.

Corpus luteum: Cell cluster of the follicle that remains after the ovum is released, secreting hormones that help regulate the menstrual cycle.

Cowper's glands: Two small glands in the male that secrete an alkaline fluid into the urethra during sexual arousal.

Cross-genderists: Transgenderists.

Cryptorchidism (krip-TOR-ka-diz-um): Condition in which the testes have not descended into the scrotum prior to birth.

Cunnilingus (kun-a-LEAN-gus): Oral stimulation of the clitoris, vaginal opening, or other parts of the vulva.

Cystitis (sis-TITE-us): A nonsexually transmitted infection of the urinary bladder.

Deoxyribonucleic acid (DNA): The chemical in each cell that carries the genetic code.

Depo-Provera: An injectable form of progestin that can prevent pregnancy for 3 months; it was approved for use in the United States in 1992.

Desire phase: Sex researcher and therapist Helen Singer Kaplan's term for the psychological interest in sex that precedes a physiological, sexual arousal.

Deviation: Term applied to behaviors or orientations that do not conform to a society's accepted norms; it often has negative connotations.

DHT-deficiency syndrome: A condition in which chromosomally male fetuses have underdeveloped male genitals and may be identified as girls at birth. However, at puberty they begin to develop masculine secondary sex characteristics and seem to maintain masculine patterns of behavior.

Diaphragm (DY-a-fram): A latex rubber cup, filled with spermicide, that is fitted to the cervix by a clinician; the woman must learn to insert it properly for full contraceptive effectiveness.

Diethylstilbestrol (DES): Synthetic estrogen compound once given to mothers whose pregnancies were at high risk of miscarrying.

Dilation: The gradual opening of the cervical opening of the uterus prior to and during labor.

Dilation and curettage (D & C): A method of induced abortion in the second trimester of pregnancy that involves a scraping of the uterine wall.

Dilation and evacuation (D & E): A method of induced abortion in the second trimester of pregnancy; it combines suction with a scraping of the inner wall of the uterus.

Direct sperm injection: A technique involving the injection of a single sperm cell directly into an ovum. It is useful in cases where the male has a low sperm count.

Discrimination: The process by which an individual extinguishes a response to one stimulus while preserving it for other stimuli.

Dysfunction: Condition in which the body does not function as expected or desired during sex.

Dysmenorrhea (dis-men-a-REE-a): Painful menstruation.

Dyspareunia: Recurrent or persistent genital pain related to sexual activity.

E. coli (Escherichia coli): Bacteria naturally living in the human colon, which often cause urinary tract infection.

Ectopic pregnancy (ek-TOP-ik): The implantation of a blastocyst somewhere other than in the uterus (usually in the fallopian tube).

Ejaculation: Muscular expulsion of semen from the penis.

Ejaculatory inevitability: The sensation in the male that ejaculation is imminent.

ELISA (enzyme-linked immunosorbent assay): The primary test used to determine the presence of HIV in humans.

Embryo (EM-bree-o): The term applied to the developing cells when, about a week after fertilization, the blastocyst implants itself in the uterine wall.

Endometrial hyperplasia (hy-per-PLAY-zhee-a): Excessive growth of the inner lining of the uterus (endometrium).

Endometriosis (en-doe-mee-tree-O-sus): Growth of the endometrium out of the uterus into surrounding organs.

Endometrium: Interior lining of the uterus, innermost of three layers.

Endorphins: A chemical produced by the brain in response to physical intimacy and sexual satisfaction.

Epidemiology (e-pe-dee-mee-A-la-jee): The branch of medical science that deals with the incidence, distribution, and control of disease in a population.

Epididymis (ep-a-DID-a-mus): Tubular structure on each testis in which sperm cells mature.

Epididymitis (ep-a-did-a-MITE-us): Inflammation of the epididymis of the testis.

Episiotomy (ee-piz-ee-OTT-a-mee): A surgical incision in the vaginal opening made by the clinician or obstetrician to prevent the baby from tearing the opening in the process of being born.

Epispadias (ep-a-SPADE-ee-as): Birth defect in which the urinary bladder empties through an abdominal opening and the urethra is malformed.

Erectile dysfunction: Difficulty achieving or maintaining penile erection (impotence).

Erection: Enlargement and stiffening of the penis as internal muscles relax and blood engorges the columns of spongy tissue.

Erogenous zone (a-RAJ-a-nus): Any area of the body that is sensitive to sexual arousal.

Erotica: Artistic representations of nudity or sexual activity.

Erotomania: A very rare form of mental illness characterized by a highly compulsive need for sex.

Erotophilia: Consistent positive responding to sexual cues.

Erotophobia: Consistent negative responding to sexual cues.

Estrogen (ES-tro-jen): Hormone produced abundantly by the ovaries; it plays an important role in the menstrual cycle.

Estrogen replacement therapy (ERT): Treatment of the physical changes of menopause by administering dosages of the hormone estrogen.

Ethnocentricity: The tendency of the members of one culture to assume that their values and norms of behavior are the "right" ones in comparison to other cultures.

Ethnography: The anthropological study of other cultures.

Ethnosexual: Referring to data concerning the sexual beliefs and customs of other cultures.

Excitement: The arousal phase of sex researchers William Masters and Virginia Johnson's four-phase model of the sexual response cycle.

Exhibitionism: Exposing the genitals to others for sexual pleasure.

External values: The belief systems available from one's society and culture.

Exocytosis: The release of genetic material by the sperm cell that permits fertilization to occur.

Fallopian tubes: Structures that are connected to the uterus and lead the ovum from an ovary to the inner cavity of the uterus.

Fellatio: Oral stimulation of the penis.

Female condom: A lubricated polyurethane pouch that is inserted into the vagina for intercourse to collect semen and to help prevent disease transmission and pregnancy.

Female sexual arousal disorder: Difficulty for a woman in achieving sexual arousal.

Fetal alcohol syndrome (FAS): A condition in a fetus characterized by abnormal growth, neurological damage, and facial distortion caused by the mother's heavy alcohol consumption.

Fetally androgenized females: A condition in which hormones administered during pregnancy caused chromosomally female (XX) fetuses to have masculinization of genitals and perhaps of later behavior patterns, even though they were raised as girls.

Fetishism (FET-a-shizm): Sexual arousal triggered by objects or materials not usually considered to be sexual.

Fetus: The term given to the embryo after 2 months of development in the womb.

Fibrous hymen: Condition in which the hymen is composed of unnaturally thick, tough tissue.

Follicles: Capsules of cells in which an ovum matures.

Follicle-stimulating hormone (FSH): Pituitary hormone that stimulates the ovaries or testes.

Foreplay: Sexual activities shared in early stages of sexual arousal, with the term implying that they are leading to a more intense, orgasm-oriented form of activity such as intercourse.

Foreskin: Fold of skin covering the penile glans; also called prepuce.

Frenulum (FREN-yu-lum): Thin, tightly-drawn fold of skin on the underside of the penile glans; it is highly sensitive.

Frotteurism: Gaining sexual gratification from anonymously pressing or rubbing one's genitals against others, usually in crowded settings.

G Spot: A vaginal area that some researchers feel is particularly sensitive to sexual stimulation.

Gamete intra-fallopian transfer (GIFT): Direct placement of ovum and concentrated sperm cells into the woman's fallopian tube to increase the chances of fertilization.

Gay: Refers to persons who have a predominantly same-gender sexual orientation and identity. More often applied to males.

Gender dysphoria (dis-FOR-ee-a): Some degree of discomfort with one's identity as male or female, and/or nonconformity to the norms considered appropriate for one's physical sex.

Gender identity: A person's inner experience of gender feelings of maleness, femaleness, or some ambivalent position between the two.

Gender identity disorder: The expression of gender identity in a way that is socially inconsistent with one's anatomical gender; may also be described as gender dysphoria.

Gene therapy: Treatment of genetically caused disorders by substitution of healthy genes.

General sexual dysfunction: Difficulty for a woman in achieving sexual arousal.

Generalization: Application of specific learned responses to other, similar situations or experiences.

Genetic engineering: The modification of the gene structure of cells to change cellular functioning.

Genital herpes (HER-peez): Viral STD characterized by painful sores on the sex organs.

Genital warts: Small lesions on genital skin caused by papilloma virus; this STD increases later risks of certain malignancies.

Gestational surrogacy: Implantation of an embryo created by the sperm and ovum of one set of parents into the uterus of another woman who agrees to gestate the fetus and give birth to the child, which is then given to the original parents.

Glans: Sensitive head of the female clitoris, visible between the upper folds of the minor lips; in the male, the sensitive head of the penis.

Gonadotropin-releasing hormone (GnRH) (go-nad-a-TRO-pen): Hormone from the hypothalamus that stimulates the release of FSH and LH by the pituitary.

Gonads: Sex and reproductive glands, either testes or ovaries, that produce hormones and reproductive cells (sperm or eggs).

Gonorrhea (gon-uh-REE-uh): Bacterial STD causing urethral pain and discharge in males; often no initial symptoms in females.

Granuloma inguinale (gran-ya-LOW-ma in-gwa-NAL-ee or NALE): STD characterized by ulcerations and granulations beginning in the groin and spreading to the buttocks and genitals.

Hard-core pornography: Pornography that makes use of highly explicit depictions of sexual activity or shows lengthy scenes of genitals.

Hedonists: People who believe that pleasure is the highest good.

Hemophiliac (hee-mo-FIL-ee-ak): Someone with the hereditary blood defect hemophilia, primarily affecting males and characterized by difficulty in clotting.

Hepatitis B: Liver infection caused by a sexually transmitted virus (HBV).

Heterosexism: The assumption that people are, or should be, attracted to members of the other gender.

Heterosexual: Attractions or activities between males and females.

HIV: Human immunodeficiency virus.

Homophobia (ho-mo-PHO-bee-a): Strongly held negative attitudes and irrational fears relating to gay men and/or lesbians and their life-styles.

Homosexual: The term that is traditionally applied to romantic and sexual attractions and activities between members of the same gender.

Hookers: Street name for female prostitutes.

Hormone implants: Contraceptive method in which tiny hormone-releasing containers are surgically inserted under the skin.

Hormone pumping: A fertility-enhancing technique involving the injection of progesterone into a woman's system.

Hormone replacement therapy (HRT): Treatment of the physical changes of menopause by administering dosages of the hormones estrogen and progesterone.

Hot flash: A flushed, sweaty feeling in the skin caused by dilated blood vessels, often associated with menopause.

Human chorionic gonadotropin (HCG): A hormone detectable in the urine of a pregnant woman. Most home pregnancy tests work by detecting its presence in woman's urine.

Human immunodeficiency virus: The virus that initially attacks the human immune system, eventually causing AIDS.

Hustlers: Male street prostitutes.

H-Y antigen: A biochemical produced in an embryo when the Y chromosome is present; it causes fetal gonads to develop into testes.

Hymen: Membranous tissue that can cover part of the vaginal opening.

Hyperfemininity: A tendency to exaggerate characteristics typically associated with femininity.

Hypermasculinity: A tendency on the part of someone to exaggerate manly behaviors, sometimes called machismo.

Hypersexuality: Unusually high level of interest in and drive for sex.

Hypoactive sexual desire disorder (HSDD): Loss of interest and pleasure in what were formerly arousing sexual stimuli.

Hyposexuality: An especially low level of sexual interest and drive.

Hypospadias (hye-pa-SPADE-ee-as): Birth defect caused by incomplete closure of the urethra during fetal development.

Hypoxphilia: Creating pressure around the neck during sexual activity to enhance sexual pleasure.

Imperforate hymen: Lack of any openings in the hymen.

Impotence (IM-pa-tens): Difficulty achieving or maintaining erection of the penis.

In vitro fertilization (IVF): A process whereby the union of the sperm and egg occurs outside the mother's body.

Incest (IN-sest): Sexual activity between closely related family members.

Incest taboo: Cultural prohibitions against incest, typical of most societies.

Induced abortion: A termination of pregnancy by artificial means.

Infertility: The inability to produce offspring.

Infibulation: Surgical procedure, performed in some cultures, that nearly seals the opening of the genitals.

Informed consent: The consent given by research subjects, indicating their willingness to participate in a study, after they are informed about the purpose of the study and how they will be asked to participate.

Inhibited sexual desire (ISD): Loss of interest and pleasure in formerly arousing sexual stimuli.

Internal values: Intrinsic values.

Intersexuality: A combination of female and male anatomical structures, so that the individual cannot be clearly defined as male or female.

Interstitial cystitis (IC): A chronic bladder inflammation that can cause debilitating discomfort and interfere with sexual enjoyment.

Interstitial-cell-stimulating hormone (ICSH): Pituitary hormone that stimulates the testes to secrete testosterone; known as luteinizing hormone (LH) in females.

Intracytoplasmic sperm injection (ICSI): A technique involving the injection of a single sperm cell directly into an ovum. It is useful in cases where the male has a low sperm count.

Intrauterine devices (IUDs): Birth control method involving the insertion of a small plastic device into the uterus.

Intrinsic values: The individualized beliefs and attitudes that a person develops by sorting through external values and personal needs.

Introitus (in-TROID-us): The outer opening of the vagina.

Kiddie porn: Term used to describe the distribution and sale of photographs and films of children or young teenagers engaging in some form of sexual activity.

Kleptomania: Extreme form of fetishism in which sexual arousal is generated by stealing.

Labor: Uterine contractions in a pregnant woman; an indication that the birth process is beginning.

Lactation: Production of milk by the milk glands of the breasts.

Lamaze method (la-MAHZ): A birthing process based on relaxation techniques practiced by the expectant mother; her partner coaches her throughout the birth.

Laparoscopy: Simpler procedure for tubal ligation, involving the insertion of a small fiber optic scope into the abdomen, through which the surgeon can see the fallopian tubes and close them off.

Laparotomy: Operation to perform a tubal ligation, or female sterilization, involving an abdominal incision.

Latency period: A stage in human development characterized, in Freud's theory, by little interest in or awareness of sexual feelings; recent research tends to suggest that latency does not exist.

Lesbian (LEZ-bee-un): Refers to females who have a predominantly same-gender sexual orientation and identity.

Libido (la-BEED-o or LIB-a-do): A term first used by Freud to define human sexual longing or sex drive.

Lumpectomy: Surgical removal of a breast lump, along with a small amount of surrounding tissue.

Luteinizing hormone (LH): Pituitary hormone that triggers ovulation in the ovaries and stimulates sperm production in the testes.

Lymphogranuloma venereum (LGV) (lim-foe-gran-yu-LOW-ma-va-NEAR-ee-um): Contagious STD caused by several strains of Chlamydia and marked by swelling and ulceration of lymph nodes in the groin.

Male condom: A sheath worn over the penis during intercourse that collects semen and helps prevent disease transmission and conception.

Male erectile disorder: Difficulty achieving or maintaining penile erection (impotence).

Mammography: Sensitive X-ray technique used to discover small breast tumors.

Marital rape: A woman being forced by her husband to have sex.

Masochist: The individual in a sadomasochistic sexual relationship who takes the submissive role.

Massage parlors: A business that provides massage treatment; places where women can be hired to perform sexual acts in addition to or in lieu of a massage.

Mastectomy: Surgical removal of all or part of a breast.

Ménage à trois (may-NAZH-ah-TRWAH): *See* Troilism.

Menarche (MEN-are-kee): Onset of menstruation at puberty.

Menopause (MEN-a-poz): Time in mid-life when menstruation ceases.

Menstrual cycle: The hormonal interactions that prepare a woman's body for possible pregnancy at roughly monthly intervals.

Menstruation (men-stru-AY-shun): Phase of menstrual cycle in which the inner uterine lining breaks down and sloughs off; the tissue, along with some blood, flows out through the vagina; also called the period.

Microscopic epididymal sperm aspiration (MESA): A procedure in which sperm are removed directly from the epididymis of the male testes.

Midwives: Medical professionals, both women and men, trained to assist with the birthing process.

Mifepristone (RU 486): A progesterone antagonist used as a postcoital contraceptive.

Minor lips: Two inner folds of skin that join above the clitoris and extend along the sides of the vaginal and urethral openings.

Miscarriage: A natural termination of pregnancy.

Modeling theory: Suggests that people will copy behavior they view in pornography.

Molluscum contagiosum (ma-LUS-kum kan-taje-ee-O-sum): A skin disease transmitted by direct bodily contact, not necessarily sexual, that is characterized by eruptions on the skin that appear similar to whiteheads, with a hard seed-like core.

Monogamous: Sharing sexual relations with only one person.

Monorchidism (ma-NOR-ka-dizm): Presence of only one testis in the scrotum.

Mons: Cushion of fatty tissue located over the female's pubic bone.

Moral values: Beliefs associated with ethical issues, or rights and wrongs; they are often a part of sexual decision making.

Morula (MOR-yuh-la): A spherical, solid mass of cells formed after 3 days of embryonic cell division.

Müllerian ducts (myul-EAR-ee-an): Embryonic structures that develop into female sexual and reproductive organs unless inhibited by male hormones.

Multiplier effect: When biological and socioenvironmental factors build on one another more and more in the process of human development.

National Birth Control League: An organization founded in 1914 by Margaret Sanger to promote use of contraceptives.

Natural childbirth: A birthing process that encourages the mother to take control, thus minimizing medical intervention.

Natural family planning/fertility awareness: A natural method of birth control that depends on an awareness of the woman's menstrual/fertility cycle.

Necrophilia (nek-ro-FILL-ee-a): Having sexual activity with a dead body.

Nongonococcal urethritis (NGU) (non-gon-uh-KOK-ul yur-i-THRYT-us): Urethral infection or irritation in the male urethra caused by bacteria or local irritants.

Nonspecific urethritis (NSU) (yur-i-THRYT-us): Infection or irritation in the male urethra caused by bacteria or local irritants.

Normal: A subjective term used to describe sexual behaviors and orientations. Standards of normalcy are determined by social, cultural, and historical standards.

Normal asexuality: An absence or low level of sexual desire, considered normal for a particular person.

Normalization: Integration of mentally retarded persons into the social mainstream as much as possible.

Norplant implants: Contraceptive method in which tiny hormone-releasing cylinders are surgically inserted under the skin.

Nymphomania (nim-fa-MANE-ee-a): A term sometimes used to describe erotomania in women.

Obscenity: Depiction of sexual activity in a repulsive or disgusting manner.

Onanism (O-na-niz-um): A term sometimes used to describe masturbation, it comes from the biblical story of Onan, who practiced coitus interruptus and "spilled his seed on the ground."

Opportunistic infection: A disease resulting from lowered resistance of a weakened immune system.

Organizing effect: Manner in which hormones control patterns of early development in the body.

Orgasm (OR-gaz-em): A rush of pleasurable physical sensations and series of contractions associated with the release of sexual tension; usually accompanied by ejaculation in men.

Orgasmic release: Reversal of the vasocongestion and muscular tension of sexual arousal, triggered by orgasm.

Orgy (OR-jee): Group sex.

Osteoporosis (ah-stee-o-po-ROW-sus): Disease caused by loss of calcium from the bones in postmenopausal women, leading to brittle bones and stooped posture.

Ova: Egg cells produced in the ovary. One cell is an ovum; in reproduction, it is fertilized by a sperm cell.

Ovaries: Pair of female gonads, located in the abdominal cavity, that produce ova and female hormones.

Ovulation: Release of a mature ovum through the wall of an ovary.

Ovum donation: Use of an egg from another woman for conception, with the fertilized ovum then being implanted in the uterus of the woman wanting to become pregnant.

Oxytocin: Pituitary hormone that plays a role in lactation and in uterine contractions; brain secretions that act as natural tranquilizers and pain relievers.

Pansexual: Lacking highly specific sexual orientations or preferences; open to a range of sexual activities.

Pap smear: Medical test that examines a smear of cervical cells to detect any cellular abnormalities.

Paraphilia (pair-a-FIL-ee-a): A newer term used to describe sexual orientations and behaviors that vary from the norm; it means "a love beside."

Paraphiliac: A person who is drawn to one or more of the paraphilias.

Partial zona dissection (PZD): A technique used to increase the chances of fertilization by making a microscopic incision in the zona pellucida of an ovum. This creates a passageway through which sperm may enter the egg more easily.

Pedophilia (peed-a-FIL-ee-a): Another term for child sexual abuse.

Pelvic inflammatory disease (PID): A chronic internal infection associated with certain types of IUDs.

Penile strain gauge: A device placed on the penis to measure even subtle changes in its size due to sexual arousal.

Penis: Male sexual organ that can become erect when stimulated; it leads urine and sperm to the outside of the body.

Perimetrium: Outer covering of the uterus.

Perinatal: A term used to describe things related to pregnancy, birth, or the period immediately following the birth.

Perineal area (pair-a-NEE-al): The sensitive skin between the genitals and the anus.

Peyronie's disease (pay-ra-NEEZ): Development of fibrous tissue in the spongy erectile columns within the penis.

Pheromones: Human chemicals, the scent of which may cause an attraction or behavioral change in other individuals.

Phimosis (fye-MOE-sus): A condition in which an abnormally long, tight foreskin on the penis does not retract easily.

Pimps: Men who have female prostitutes working for them.

Placenta (pla-SENT-a): The organ that unites the fetus to the mother by bringing their blood vessels closer together; it provides nourishment for and removes waste from the developing baby.

Plateau phase: The stable, leveled-off phase of sex researchers William Masters and Virginia Johnson's four-phase model of the sexual response cycle.

Plethysmograph: A laboratory measuring device that charts physiological changes over time. Attached to a penile strain gauge, it can chart changes in penis size. This is called penile plethysmography.

Polygamy: The practice, in some cultures, of being married to more than one spouse.

Pornography: Photographs, films, or literature intended to be sexually arousing through explicit depictions of sexual activity.

Premature birth: A birth that takes place prior to the 36th week of pregnancy.

Premature ejaculation: Difficulty that some men experience in controlling the ejaculatory reflex, which results in rapid ejaculation.

Premenstrual syndrome (PMS): Symptoms of physical discomfort, moodiness, and emotional tensions that occur in some women for a few days prior to menstruation.

Preorgasmic: A term often applied to women who have not yet been able to reach orgasm during sexual response.

Prepuce (PREE-peus): In the female, tissue of the upper vulva that covers the clitoral shaft.

Priapism (pry-AE-pizm): Continual, undesired, and painful erection of the penis.

Progesterone (pro-JES-ter-one): Ovarian hormone that causes the uterine lining to thicken.

Prolapse of the uterus: Weakening of the supportive ligaments of the uterus, causing it to protrude into the vagina.

Promiscuity (prah-mis-KIU-i-tee): Sharing casual sexual activity with many different partners.

Prostaglandin: Hormone-like chemical whose concentrations increase in a woman's body just prior to menstruation.

Prostaglandin- or saline-induced abortion: Used in the 16th–24th weeks of pregnancy, prostaglandins, salt solutions, or urea are injected into the amniotic sac, administered intravenously, or inserted into the vagina in suppository form to induce contractions and fetal delivery.

Prostate: Gland located beneath the urinary bladder in the male; it produces some of the secretions in semen.

Prostatitis (pras-tuh-TITE-us): Inflammation of the prostate gland.

Pseudohermaphrodite: A person who possesses either testes or ovaries in combination with some external genitals of the other sex.

Pseudonecrophilia: A fantasy about having sex with the dead.

Psychosexual development: Complex interaction of factors that form a person's sexual feelings, orientations, and patterns of behavior.

Psychosocial development: The cultural and social influences that help shape human sexual identity.

Puberty: Time of life when reproductive capacity develops and secondary sex characteristics appear.

Pubic lice: Small insects that can infect skin in the pubic area, causing a rash and severe itching.

Pubococcygeus (PC) muscle (pyub-o-kox-a-JEE-us): Part of the supporting musculature of the vagina that is involved in orgasmic response and over which a woman can exert some control.

Pyromania: Sexual arousal generated by setting fires.

Quid pro quo: Something gained from something given.

Random sample: A representative group of the larger population that is the focus of a scientific poll or study in which care is taken to select participants without a pattern that might sway research results.

Rape trauma syndrome: The predictable sequence of reactions that a victim experiences following a rape.

Recreational marriage: Recreational adultery.

Refractory period: Time following orgasm during which a man cannot be restimulated to orgasm.

Reinforcement: In conditioning theory, any influence that helps shape future behavior as a punishment or reward stimulus.

Resolution phase: The term for the return of a body to its unexcited state following orgasm.

Retarded ejaculation: A male who has never been able to reach an orgasm.

Retrograde ejaculation: Abnormal passage of semen into the urinary bladder at the time of ejaculation.

Retrovirus (RE-tro-vi-rus): A class of viruses that reproduces with the aid of the enzyme reverse transcriptase, which allows the virus to integrate its genetic code into that of the host cell, thus establishing permanent infection.

Rh factor: A blood-clotting protein agent whose presence or absence in the blood signals an Rh+ or Rh− person.

Rh incompatibility: Condition in which a blood protein of the infant is not the same as the mother's; antibodies formed in the mother can destroy red blood cells in the fetus.

RhoGAM: Medication administered to a mother to prevent formation of antibodies when the baby is Rh positive and its mother Rh negative.

Rhythm method: A natural method of birth control that depends on an awareness of the woman's menstrual/fertility cycle.

RU 486: A French abortion drug; a progesterone antagonist used as a postcoital contraceptive.

Rubber dam: Small square sheet of latex, such as that used in dental work, placed over the vulva, vagina, or anus to help prevent transmission of HIV during sexual activity.

Sadist: The individual in a sadomasochistic sexual relationship who takes the dominant role.

Sadomasochism (sade-o-MASS-o-kiz-um): Refers to sexual themes or activities involving bondage, pain, domination, or humiliation of one partner by the other.

Sample: A representative group of a population that is the focus of a scientific poll or study.

Satyriasis (sate-a-RYE-a-sus): A term sometimes used to describe erotomania in men.

Scabies (SKAY-beez): A skin disease caused by a mite that burrows under the skin to lay its eggs, causing redness and itching; transmitted by bodily contact that may or may not be sexual.

Scrotum (SKROTE-um): Pouch of skin in which the testes are contained.

Secondary dysfunction: A difficulty with sexual functioning that develops after some period of normal sexual functioning.

Selective reduction: The use of abortion techniques to reduce the number of fetuses when there are more than three in a preg-

nancy, thus increasing the chances of survival for the remaining fetuses.

Self-gratification: Giving oneself pleasure, as in masturbation; a term typically used today instead of more negative descriptors.

Self-pleasuring: Self-gratification; masturbation.

Semen (SEE-men): Mixture of fluids and sperm cells that is ejaculated through the penis.

Seminal vesicle (SEM-un-al): Gland at the end of each vas deferens that secretes a chemical that helps sperm to become mobile.

Seminiferous tubules (sem-a-NIF-a-rus): Tightly coiled tubules in the testes in which sperm cells are formed.

Sensate focus: Early phase of sex therapy treatment, in which the partners pleasure each other without employing direct stimulation of sex organs.

Sex addiction: Inability to regulate sexual behavior.

Sex therapist: Professional trained in the treatment of sexual dysfunctions.

Sexual aversion disorder: Avoidance of or exaggerated fears toward forms of sexual expression (sexual phobia).

Sexual differentiation: The developmental processes—biological, social, and psychological—that lead to different sexes or genders.

Sexual dysfunctions: Difficulties people have in achieving sexual arousal and in other stages of sexual response.

Sexual harassment: Unwanted sexual advances or coercion that can occur in the workplace or academic settings.

Sexual individuality: The unique set of sexual needs, orientations, fantasies, feelings, and activities that develops in each human being.

Sexual orientation: A person's erotic and emotional attraction toward and interest in members of one or both genders.

Sexual revolution: The changes in thinking about sexuality and sexual behavior in society that occurred in the 1960s and 1970s.

Sexual surrogates: Paid partners used during sex therapy with clients lacking their own partners; only rarely used today.

Sexually transmitted diseases (STDs): Various diseases transmitted by direct sexual contact.

Shaft: In the female, the longer body of the clitoris, containing erectile tissue; in the male, cylindrical base of penis that contains three columns of spongy tissue: two corpora cavernosa and a corpus spongiosum.

Shunga: Ancient scrolls used in Japan to instruct couples in sexual practices through the use of paintings.

Skene's glands: Secretory cells located inside the female urethra.

Smegma: Thick, oily substance that may accumulate under the prepuce of the clitoris or penis.

Social constructionists: Those who believe that same-gender sexual orientation is at least partly the result of social and environmental factors.

Social learning theory: Suggests that human learning is influenced by observation of and identification with other people.

Social scripts: A complex set of learned responses to a particular situation that is formed by social influences.

Sodomy laws: Laws that, in some states, prohibit a variety of sexual behaviors, often described as deviate sexual intercourse. These laws are often enforced discriminatorily against particular groups, such as gay males.

Sonograms: Ultrasonic rays used to project a picture of internal structures such as the fetus; often used in conjunction with amniocentesis or fetal surgery.

Spectatoring: Term used by sex researchers William Masters and Virginia Johnson to describe self-consciousness and self-observation during sex.

Sperm: Reproductive cells produced in the testes; in fertilization, one sperm unites with an ovum.

Sperm banks: Centers that store frozen sperm for the purpose of artificial insemination.

Spermatocytes (sper-MAT-o-sites): Cells lining the seminiferous tubules from which sperm cells are produced.

Spermicidal jelly (cream): Sperm-killing chemical in a gel base or cream, used with other contraceptives such as diaphragms.

Spermicides: Chemicals that kill sperm; available as foams, creams, jellies, or implants in sponges or suppositories.

Sponge: A thick polyurethane disk that holds a spermicide and fits over the cervix to prevent conception.

Spontaneous abortion: Another term for miscarriage.

Staphylococcus aureus (staf-a-low-KAK-us): The bacteria that can cause toxic shock syndrome.

Statutory rape: A legal term used to indicate sexual activity when one partner is under the age of consent; in most states that age is 18.

STDs: Sexually transmitted diseases.

Sterilization: Rendering a person permanently incapable of conceiving, usually by interrupting passage of the egg or sperm.

Straight: Slang term for heterosexual.

Streetwalkers: Female prostitutes who work on the streets.

Suppositories: Contraceptive devices designed to distribute their spermicide by melting or foaming in the vagina.

Syndrome (SIN-drome): A group of signs or symptoms that occur together and characterize a given condition.

Syphilis (SIF-uh-lus): Sexually transmitted disease (STD) characterized by four stages, beginning with the appearance of a chancre.

Systematic desensitization: Step-by-step approaches to unlearning tension-producing behaviors and developing new behavior patterns.

Testes (TEST-ees): Pair of male gonads that produce sperm and male hormones.

Testicular cancer: Malignancy in the testis that may be detected by testicular self-examination.

Testicular failure: Lack of sperm and/or hormone production by the testes.

Testosterone (tes-TAS-ter-one): Major male hormone produced by the testes; it helps to produce male secondary sex characteristics.

Testosterone replacement therapy: Administering testosterone injections to increase sexual interest or potency in older men; not considered safe for routine use.

Theoretical failure rate: A measure of how often a birth control method can be expected to fail when used without error or technical problems.

Thrush: A disease caused by a fungus and characterized by white patches in the oral cavity.

Toucherism: Gaining sexual gratification from the touching of an unknown person's body, such as on the buttocks or breasts.

Toxic shock syndrome (TSS): An acute disease characterized by fever and sore throat, and caused by normal bacteria in the vagina that are activated if tampons or contraceptive devices such as diaphragms or sponges are left in for long periods of time.

Transgenderists: People who live in clothing and roles considered appropriate for the opposite sex for sustained periods of time.

Transsexualism: A strong degree of discomfort with one's identity as male or female, characterized by feelings of being in the wrongly sexed body.

Transvestite: An individual who dresses in clothing and adopts mannerisms considered appropriate for the opposite sex.

Trichomoniasis (trik-uh-ma-NEE-uh-sis): A vaginal infection caused by the *Trichomonas* organism.

Troilism (TROY-i-lizm): Sexual activity shared by three people.

Tubal ligation: A surgical cutting and tying of the fallopian tubes to induce permanent female sterilization.

Umbilical cord: The tubelike tissues and blood vessels originating at the embryo's navel that connect it to the placenta.

Urethra (yu-REE-thrah): Tube that passes from the urinary bladder to the outside of the body.

Urophilia: Sexual arousal connected with urine or urination.

Uterus (YUTE-a-rus): Muscular organ of the female reproductive system; a fertilized egg implants itself within the uterus.

Vacuum curettage (kyur-a-TAZH): A method of induced abortion performed with a suction pump.

Vagina (vu-JI-na): Muscular canal in the female that is responsive to sexual arousal; it receives semen during heterosexual intercourse for reproduction.

Vaginal atresia (a-TREE-zha): Birth defect in which the vagina is absent or closed.

Vaginal atrophy: Shrinking and deterioration of vaginal lining, usually the result of low estrogen levels during aging.

Vaginal fistulae (FISH-cha-lee *or* -lie): Abnormal channels that can develop between the vagina and other internal organs.

Vaginismus (vaj-uh-NIZ-mus): Involuntary spasm of the outer vaginal musculature, making penetration of the vagina difficult or impossible.

Vaginitis (vaj-un-NITE-us): General term for inflammation of the vagina.

Values: System of beliefs with which people view life and make decisions, including their sexual decisions.

Variation: A less pejorative term to describe nonconformity to accepted norms.

Varicose veins: Overexpanded blood vessels; can occur in veins surrounding the vagina.

Vas deferens: Tube that leads sperm upward from each testis to the seminal vesicles.

Vasa efferentia: Larger tubes within the testes, into which sperm move after being produced in the seminiferous tubules.

Vasectomy (va-SEK-ta-mee *or* vay-ZEK-ta-mee): A surgical cutting and tying of the vas deferens to induce permanent male sterilization.

Villi: Fingerlike projections of the chorion; they form a major part of the placenta.

Viral hepatitis: Inflammation of the liver caused by a virus.

Voyeurism (VOYE-yu-rizm): Sexual gratification from viewing others who are nude or who are engaging in sexual activities.

Voluntary surgical contraception: Sterilization; rendering a person incapable of conceiving with surgical procedures that interrupt the passage of the egg or sperm.

Vulva: External sex organs of the female, including the mons, major and minor lips, clitoris, and opening of the vagina.

Vulvovaginitis: General term for inflammation of the vulva and/or vagina.

Western blot: The test used to verify the presence of HIV antibodies already detected by the ELISA.

Wolffian ducts (WOOL-fee-an): Embryonic structures that develop into male sexual and reproductive organs if male hormones are present.

Yeast infection: A type of vaginitis caused by an overgrowth of a fungus normally found in an inactive state in the vagina.

Zero population growth: The point at which the world's population would stabilize, and there would be no further increase in the number of people on Earth. Birthrate and death rate become essentially equal.

Zona pellucida (ZO-nah pe-LOO-sa-da): The transparent, outer membrane of an ovum.

Zoophilia (zoo-a-FILL-ee-a): Bestiality.

Zygote: An ovum that has been fertilized by a sperm.

SOURCES

Sexuality Today: The Human Perspective, Kelly, Gary F., Fifth Edition, 1995. Dushkin/McGraw-Hill, Guilford, CT.

Pregnancy, Childbirth, and Parenting (Wellness), 1992. Dushkin/McGraw-Hill, Guilford, CT.

Test Your Knowledge Form

We encourage you to photocopy and use this page as a tool to assess how the articles in **Annual Editions** expand on the information in your textbook. By reflecting on the articles you will gain enhanced text information. You can also access this useful form on a product's book support Web site at **http://www.dushkin.com/online/.**

NAME: DATE:

_____

TITLE AND NUMBER OF ARTICLE:

_____

BRIEFLY STATE THE MAIN IDEA OF THIS ARTICLE:

_____

LIST THREE IMPORTANT FACTS THAT THE AUTHOR USES TO SUPPORT THE MAIN IDEA:

_____

WHAT INFORMATION OR IDEAS DISCUSSED IN THIS ARTICLE ARE ALSO DISCUSSED IN YOUR TEXTBOOK OR OTHER READINGS THAT YOU HAVE DONE? LIST THE TEXTBOOK CHAPTERS AND PAGE NUMBERS:

_____

LIST ANY EXAMPLES OF BIAS OR FAULTY REASONING THAT YOU FOUND IN THE ARTICLE:

_____

LIST ANY NEW TERMS/CONCEPTS THAT WERE DISCUSSED IN THE ARTICLE, AND WRITE A SHORT DEFINITION:

_____

ANNUAL EDITIONS revisions depend on two major opinion sources: one is our Advisory Board, listed in the front of this volume, which works with us in scanning the thousands of articles published in the public press each year; the other is you—the person actually using the book. Please help us and the users of the next edition by completing the prepaid article rating form on this page and returning it to us. Thank you for your help!

ANNUAL EDITIONS: Human Sexuality 01/02

ARTICLE RATING FORM

Here is an opportunity for you to have direct input into the next revision of this volume. We would like you to rate each of the 47 articles listed below, using the following scale:

1. **Excellent: should definitely be retained**
2. **Above average: should probably be retained**
3. **Below average: should probably be deleted**
4. **Poor: should definitely be deleted**

Your ratings will play a vital part in the next revision. So please mail this prepaid form to us just as soon as you complete it. Thanks for your help!

We Want Your Advice

RATING

ARTICLE

1. Another Planet
2. Rwandan Sorrow
3. Little Hope, Less Help
4. Breaking the Silence
5. Amsterdamned
6. The World Made Flesh
7. The Male Box
8. Never Too Buff
9. "The Uniform for Today Is Belly Buttons"
10. The Second Sexual Revolution
11. Are You Man Enough?
12. Male Sexual Circuitry
13. The Science of Women & Sex
14. America: Awash in STDs
15. Prostate Dilemmas
16. Too Much of a Good Thing
17. What Made Troy Gay?
18. Out of the Fold?
19. The Five Sexes, Revisited
20. Why We Fall in Love
21. The New Flirting Game
22. What's Your Love Story?
23. Are You Connecting On the Five Levels of Sex?
24. Eight Sizzling Sex Secrets (Only Lovers in the Tropics Know)
25. Celibate Passion: The Hidden Rewards of Quitting Sex

RATING

ARTICLE

26. Protecting Against Unintended Pregnancy: A Guide to Contraceptive Choices
27. How Old Is Too Old to Have a Baby?
28. What Mother Nature Teaches Us About Motherhood
29. Pregnant Pleasures
30. Sexuality and Young Children
31. Sex in School? It's Required! Sex Education Comes to Taiwan
32. Sex Ed: How Do We Score?
33. Teaching Schools a Lesson
34. Married With Children
35. Christy's Crusade
36. When Preachers Prey
37. Of Professors and Pedophiles
38. Legislating Morality
39. Pregnant? You're Fired!
40. The Hidden Health Threat That Puts Every Woman at Risk
41. Criminal Injustice
42. Porn.con?
43. Will Cybersex Be Better Than Real Sex?
44. Beyond Orgasmatron
45. The Gender Blur
46. Can You Love God and Sex?
47. Satori in the Bedroom

(Continued on next page)

ABOUT YOU

Name _____ Date _____

Are you a teacher? ☐ A student? ☐
Your school's name _____

Department _____

Address _____ City _____ State ____ Zip ____

School telephone # _____

YOUR COMMENTS ARE IMPORTANT TO US!

Please fill in the following information:
For which course did you use this book?
_____

Did you use a text with this *ANNUAL EDITION*? ☐ yes ☐ no
What was the title of the text?
_____

What are your general reactions to the *Annual Editions* concept?
_____

Have you read any particular articles recently that you think should be included in the next edition?
_____

Are there any articles you feel should be replaced in the next edition? Why?
_____

Are there any World Wide Web sites you feel should be included in the next edition? Please annotate.
_____

May we contact you for editorial input? ☐ yes ☐ no
May we quote your comments? ☐ yes ☐ no
_____